CHIEF
OF STAFF

ALSO BY SHERWIN MARKMAN

The Election: A Novel

Lyndon Johnson Remembered:
An Intimate Portrait of a Presidency
(edited with Thomas Cowger)

CHIEF OF STAFF

LYNDON JOHNSON AND HIS PRESIDENCY

★

W. Marvin Watson with
Sherwin Markman

THOMAS DUNNE BOOKS · ST. MARTIN'S PRESS
NEW YORK

THOMAS DUNNE BOOKS.
An imprint of St. Martin's Press.

CHIEF OF STAFF. Copyright © 2004 by W. Marvin Watson. All rights reserved.
Printed in the United States of America. No part of this book may be used or repro-
duced in any manner whatsoever without written permission except in the case of
brief quotations embodied in critical articles or reviews. For information, address
St. Martin's Press, 175 Fifth Avenue, New York, N.Y. 10010.

www.stmartins.com

Design by Kathryn Parise

ISBN 0-312-28504-3
EAN 978-0312-28504-3

First Edition: September 2004

10 9 8 7 6 5 4 3 2 1

In memory of Lyndon Baines Johnson, America's thirty-sixth President, in appreciation for the opportunity he gave us to serve, learn, and grow; with gratitude for his guidance and leadership, which always stretched us to be better; and expressing the thanks of a nation for what he did to improve us all.

For all those dedicated men and women—the best White House staff ever assembled—who so willingly and ably served our country when Lyndon Johnson was President.

CONTENTS

ACKNOWLEDGMENTS

The authors wish to give special thanks to Lady Bird Johnson, whose encouragement made this book possible. In addition, we thank the staff of the Lyndon Baines Johnson Library, especially Harry Middleton, Tina Houston, and Linda Seelke, who unselfishly provided their help and cooperation for the essential research necessary to write this book. We especially thank Marion Watson, Winston Lee Watson, Kimberly W. Rathmann, and William M. Watson III, who took the time to read the manuscript and suggest excellent improvements. We also thank Peggy Markman, who not only read and commented on the manuscript but spent untold hours at the LBJ Library assisting her husband.

I have devoted my time on this earth to working toward the day when there would be no second-class citizenship in America, no second-quality opportunity, no secondhand justice at home, no second-place status in the world for our ideals and beliefs.

LYNDON BAINES JOHNSON

September 16, 1972

COMING ABOARD

★

The telephone rang. It was 4 P.M., December 31, 1964, New Year's Eve. Excusing myself from my family, I picked up the receiver. It was Lyndon Johnson, the President of the United States, his voice so familiar to me with its unmistakable Texas hill country drawl, forceful yet—always with me—infused with intimacy and kindness, the voice of a man so used to command that it compelled the listener to bend to his will.

"Marvin!" he said, without preliminary. "Bird and I want you and your lovely wife, Marion, to come on down to the ranch tonight. We need you to celebrate the New Year's Eve with us."

"I don't think we can do that, Mr. President," I said. "We thank you and we're honored, but we just can't. Not tonight."

"Why not?" the President demanded.

I looked around the living room of my home in the small Texas town of Daingerfield. All of my family was sitting there staring at me—my wife, her mother, my own mother and father, and my three children, Winston Lee, Kimberly, and my one-year-old son, William. Winston Lee, our older son, had flown home from New Mexico Military Institute to be with us. I explained this to the President, but he was having none of it.

"It's too late," he interrupted. "My airplane is already on its way to pick up you two. It should be landing at Longview airport within the hour. You and Marion should leave as soon as you can. We will all have dinner when you arrive."

I looked at Marion, who was frowning. As always, she understood exactly what was happening. But I could also see that she had resigned herself to the inevitable.

"Yes, sir," I told the President. "We'll be there."

"Good!" the President responded, then added, "By the way, bring some clothes. You two will be flying back to Washington with us tomorrow. There's a lot we need to talk about."

"All right," I said, feeling both helpless and excited as I hung up.

I turned to Marion and repeated the President's invitations. "I suppose you had no choice," she said. "Just make sure we have a hotel reservation before we leave."

"Absolutely!" I assured her. "Now please go pack enough clothes for several days because we need to get going."

Marion hurried to do so while I made sure that while we were away someone would look after William as well as Kimberly, our thirteen-year-old daughter, and would also make sure that eighteen-year-old Lee got back to New Mexico. Then, after hugging and kissing our family good-bye, Marion and I rushed off to Longview and the President's airplane.

Other than the crew, we were the only passengers on the sleek little air force jet that flew us the 360 miles from northeast Texas to the LBJ Ranch seventy miles southeast of Austin. A runway long enough to accommodate the Jet Star had been built at the ranch and, when we taxied to a stop, sitting there alone in his golf cart, his face wreathed in a welcoming smile, was the President of the United States, waiting to greet us.

Lyndon Johnson was a big man, towering over me by at least half a foot, and although I was far from slender even back then, he seriously outweighed me even during those times when he was dieting. In that respect, from month to month one never knew whether he would be in his "heavy" or "light" condition. He was so aware of his considerable fluctuations of weight that he maintained two separate wardrobes for himself so that properly fitting clothing was always instantly available to him.

Like every politician I have ever known (and most of the rest of us), Lyndon Johnson was vain about his appearance. He took pains always to be photographed on his left side because he believed he looked better from that angle. But his most attractive characteristic was his unreserved animation. Energy simply flowed from him and engulfed everyone in his presence. He was also quick with his laughter and he could tell a story as well as anyone, complete with devastatingly accurate mimicry. In person he was immensely compelling and likable, and one of the great tragedies of his life as a leader was that so much of his personal warmth seemed to disappear whenever he appeared on television.

Many have commented about the forceful manner in which Lyndon Johnson presented himself to others, the way he would come close invading your physical space, leaning over you, touching you, grabbing your elbow or arm—all creating the impression of a dominating presence even larger than his actual size. That was all true and it was his natural method of communicating his will and bending you to it.

Somehow, with me, although he was so obviously bigger, his manner always softened and often was accompanied by a smile that seemed to say, "You are my trusted friend, Marvin, and I love you." Which was precisely how I felt about him.

Now, on this New Year's Eve, he drove us directly to the ranch house and announced, "We want you to stay upstairs in one of our spare bedrooms." Then he led us inside where we joined Mrs. Johnson and a dozen others, all close friends of the Johnsons—and of ours.

"Now that the Watsons have finally arrived, let's share some dinner," the President stated. And indeed we did, followed by an evening of animated conversation among happy people celebrating a new year full of endless promise for the President and First Lady. He had, after all, just won a massive electoral victory—his 61.9 percent of the popular vote exceeded even Franklin Roosevelt's 60.8 percent to become the largest majority in American history—and carried with him into office an extraordinary majority of his political party in both houses of the incoming Congress.

The next afternoon, Marion and I joined the Johnsons on the short helicopter ride from the ranch to Bergstrom Air Force Base where Air Force One awaited him. As always—so radically different from commercial flying—the engines started as soon as the President was on board and seated, and we were on our way to Andrews Air Force Base just outside of Washington. There, another helicopter—this one called Marine One because it is operated by my own former service, the Marine Corps—was waiting to whisk us to the south lawn of the White House. As many times as I have made that journey—before and since—the thrill of flying on these aircraft never disappeared.

I should make it clear that on this New Year's Day, I was not an employee of the President or a member of his staff. I was a devoted volunteer—no more or less than that—who, since first meeting and campaigning for him in 1948, had become his trusted friend. I had a perfectly good job as Executive Assistant to the President of Lone Star Steel Company. I was not only happy with my work, but Marion and I were content with the life we had in Daingerfield and Dallas.

Of course, none of that deterred the President from asking me to come work for him. He had started making that offer when he was a Senator, and he had become increasingly insistent with each passing year. I had always declined. Now, however, he was President of the United States, and during that flight to Washington I knew that he had planned all this to at last bring me onto his staff.

During the flight to Andrews, the President left no room for doubt about his intentions. He called Marion aside and informed her that he would be keeping me busy for a few days. Then he smiled, and said, "I don't want you to get bored while I'm using Marvin, so I have arranged for a nice real estate lady to meet you and take you around Washington."

"That's really not necessary," Marion protested.

"Of course it is," the President answered. "She will show you some homes you might want to buy or rent. I told her not to waste your time looking at anything more than five to ten minutes away from the White House because I want Marvin to live close to me."

Surprised, because I had promised Marion that we would never need to leave Daingerfield, she asked the President, "Has Marvin agreed to come work for you?"

Still smiling, the President said, "Not yet, but I believe he will."

When Marion returned to our seats, she told me what the President was planning.

"I don't know," I said, but I knew as well as she did that the inevitable was closing in on us. To that end, it was symbolic to us that the Johnsons would not hear of us staying in a hotel on this trip to Washington. They insisted that we remain at the White House as their guests. At that moment, to paraphrase Abraham Lincoln, we felt that but for the honor of it, we would rather not. But, of course, we did. In the end, we knew we had made the right decision.

The next day, starting promptly at 8:30 in the morning and continuing for several days, Marion and the real estate agent visited houses within the President's prescribed perimeter. Each day, Marion returned in an advanced state of sticker shock. We knew the prices of East Texas homes, and we were not prepared for the inflated costs of living in Washington.

In the meantime, the President put me to work. He assigned me the White House office next to his and handed me a list of names and a stack of FBI reports. "These are the people the former Attorney General Bobby Kennedy and his deputy, Nick Katzenbach, recommend I nominate as federal judges," he explained. "As you can see, there are a lot of vacancies to be filled. Well, these are *their* suggestions. I think they may be Kennedy people. My guess is there's not a Johnson person in the whole bunch."

"I don't doubt it," I replied, having already experienced Robert Kennedy's ambition and penchant for intrigue.

"What I want you to do is check out each one of these people. Read their FBI files. Then call our friends, especially Senators, Congressmen, and Governors. Ask them about these names and ask them to suggest people who would be loyal to us and our program."

"Yes, sir," I replied.

"I don't intend to stack the courts with Kennedy people," the President added.

"What about Republican Senators?" I asked. "Should I talk to them?"

"Of course—when they are our friends. Especially Everett Dirksen. Never ignore him! He will *always* return the courtesy. When you finish, give me a list of people I can rely on."

I went right to work on a task that was not totally unfamiliar to me. While Johnson was Vice President, his agreement with President Kennedy was that all presidential appointments in and from Texas would be channeled through Johnson's patronage. President Kennedy had been meticulous in keeping his word—in many instances, I am certain, overriding the objections of others, including his volatile brother. In all those cases, the Vice President had asked me to clear each potential nominee for loyalty to him and his beliefs. After that, of course, the names would have to pass muster with Texas's U.S. Senators as well as the American Bar Association. My job now would be essentially the same, only the area covered was nationwide.

Also on my agenda during that stay at the White House was to assure that the Texas delegation to the President's inauguration was properly housed and included in all the festivities. The President wanted it to be no less than perfect. There were already a large number of the President's friends hard at work on the momentous event, but the President wanted me as the chairman of the Texas Democratic Party to coordinate all activities of the Texas delegation with the inauguration officials. So, as I had done for him in many previous instances, I accepted this additional project as well.

As soon as these assignments were completed, Marion and I returned to Daingerfield. Then, almost immediately, we were on our way back to Washington to attend the President's inauguration on January 20, 1965. It was a grand affair and we were proud to be a part of it. Apparently, however, the word had leaked out (probably by the President himself) that he was planning on bringing me to Washington to work for him. It seemed that almost everyone we knew, especially those from Texas, was congratulating me, telling me what an honor it was to be asked and what a great experience it would be to serve the President of the United States. I kept denying the "rumor," but quite obviously nobody believed me.

Early the next morning, the President asked me to come to his bedroom where he got right to the point. "You and I both know that the time has finally come for you to come work for me."

"I don't want to leave Texas," I told him, not for the first time.

"Marvin, this is your President talking to you! Your President needs you! You cannot refuse your President any more than you refused to serve your country when you joined the marines."

"Yes, sir," I said.

"Since Walter Jenkins left me, I haven't found anyone to take his place," he continued. "You are the person I want. I know I can't order you to come. I can't draft you. But what I am asking you is far more important to your country than that. Your President is asking you to serve your country. Now, all you have to do is say yes."

I told him I would think about it very carefully, talk to Marion, and that I would give him my answer very soon. The President did not press me further that morning because, I have no doubt, he knew what my answer would be.

I wanted to talk to someone who had worked for the President, so I immediately sought out Texas governor John Connally, a longtime friend of the President—and of mine. I thought the views of the Governor would be especially valuable since he had served as an aide to Johnson when he was a member of Congress. As soon as we returned to Texas, I met for dinner at the governor's mansion with Governor Connally and his wife, Nellie. I explained the President's offer and asked for their counsel.

"You know you won't be able to refuse him again," Connally said.

I realized that, and told him so.

As we discussed the options, we decided that I would not work for the President as anything less than his chief of staff, although we agreed that he did not want to give anyone that title.

"The title really doesn't mean a thing," Connally said. "What counts is that you *will be* his chief of staff because your actual duties and responsibilities will add up to that."

We concluded that I should insist on some symbols of authority that nobody else can duplicate, such as having the President agree that I could attend *any* meeting he may have—without exception and without prior authorization by him.

The Governor said, "I'm sure you won't abuse the privilege, and he will know that. But you will always have that right. Also, you should request the opportunity to give your opinion regarding any subject or person prior to the time he makes his decision. Next, and you probably already know this, make sure that your office is next to his and physically closer to him than anyone else except maybe his secretaries. If the President agrees to these things, then it makes no difference what your title may be. You will be his chief of staff."

I nodded my head.

The Governor continued, "Marvin, if he wants you as badly as I think he does, he will agree to all of it. I know he likes you. More importantly, he trusts you. You won't have any trouble."

For the next week, Marion and I agonized over the matter. I was not exaggerating when I told the President that neither of us wanted to leave Texas. Our roots there were deep. Finally, Marion said that she was willing, in spite of the fact that Washington was a strange, foreign place to her and she would be leaving many friends and family behind in Texas. Her eyes were filled with tears when she said to me, "Marvin, if you feel that we must move, I am going with you. I know we will have a wonderful, exciting, and learning time."

Thus, we had reached our conclusion by the time the President called me on January 29, a Friday. "Are you coming up here?" he demanded.

"Yes, sir," I said. "But may I ask if we can agree on a few things first?"

"Tell me what you want," he said, and I repeated the essence of the conclusions I had reached in my meeting with Governor Connally.

The Governor's prediction was accurate. Without hesitation, the President agreed to my requests, although he added, "Of course, you need to understand that along with a few others who work for me up here, you will have the title of Special Assistant to the President. But you and I understand that you will operate as my Chief of Staff." Then the President said, "I also know that neither of us will ever regret this decision."

"When do you want me to start?" I asked.

"Monday morning," the President stated. As usual, I was amazed by how swiftly the President could act once he had what he was after. "I want you to fly up here tomorrow. I've just buzzed George Reedy to come in here. I'm going to have him announce your appointment at his eleven o'clock press briefing." Clearly, the President had been ready for my answer.

"I imagine we'll be staying in a hotel until we find a place to live," I said.

"There's no need for that," the President said. "You bring Marion and your family up here tomorrow. I've arranged everything. I've spoken to Jimmy Roosevelt, President Roosevelt's eldest son. He's living in Los Angeles while he runs for mayor. He has this beautiful home across the river in McLean, Virginia. Nobody is living there while he's gone. It's completely furnished and he told me that you and your family are welcome to rent his house until you find your own place."

"It's all arranged," the President continued. "Roosevelt's secretary will meet your airplane after you let us know when you arrive. I will see you after you get here."

Even before I accepted the President's offer, I had anticipated that if he expected absolute confidentiality from me, then I in turn needed someone I could equally trust, and I had decided that Mary Jo Cook would be perfect for the job. I had spoken to her shortly after my return from the inauguration and asked if she and her family would be willing to come to Washington with me if I went to work in the White House. She and her husband, E. A., had been our next door neighbors and close friends in Daingerfield for years. Mary Jo had even helped teach Marion to be a better cook. Of greater importance right now was the fact that Mary Jo was a teacher whose specialty was shorthand and typing. Now, I called her again and she told me that E. A. was interested in finding new work anyway, as was she. So they were willing to come to Washington and could make the move as early as the following week. I was delighted.

Anyone moving his family to a distant place—and Washington was far from Daingerfield in every way—knows how much time and effort is involved in making the change. In addition, there is the emotional turmoil of leaving family, church, and friends behind. So here it was, a Friday morning, and we were expected—*required* is the more accurate word—to leave the very next day. We had a one-year-old baby and a teenage girl to organize. We had parents and friends to notify. Finally, not only did I need to resign my job, but I had a full load of responsibilities that I had to leave behind, not the least of which was my position as Chairman of the Texas Democratic Executive Committee. Thus, this Friday became the most rushed and traumatic day we would ever experience. Yet, somehow, we got through it, and late the next day, Marion and I, together with Kimberly and William, accompanied by our Daingerfield housekeeper and friend, Claudine Whitmore, arrived at the busy terminal of Washington's Dulles Airport.

As the President promised, James Roosevelt's secretary was there to meet us, along with a car we had leased. She led us to the Roosevelt home and, as we walked in the front door, we heard the loud ringing of a telephone—not the intermittent sound of a normal call, but a nonstop, not-to-be-ignored, insistent clamor, the hallmark of a White House telephone connected directly to the telephone of the President. Apparently, this particular telephone had been installed only a few minutes before our arrival, and obviously he was wasting no time before using it.

I picked up the receiver and immediately heard the President's voice, asking, "Are you all settled?"

"We just walked in, Mr. President."

"Good. Enjoy your new home. Now, tomorrow morning I want you and Marion to come over here so that we can all go to church together."

"Yes, sir," I said.

Our first exploration of the Roosevelt home left us breathless. We had never seen a house so interestingly furnished. Roosevelt memorabilia was everywhere—photographs, framed letters, family mementos of every kind. The house was a celebration of Franklin and Eleanor Roosevelt. And the den was filled with the furniture that Woodrow Wilson had taken with him to

France when he negotiated the Versailles Treaty after World War I, the same furniture Franklin Roosevelt had brought to the summit conference at Yalta during World War II. Marion and I were thrilled and grateful for this opportunity to share the memories of the Roosevelt family.

The only problem was our cost to lease the Roosevelt house. The rent was high—extraordinarily so by East Texas standards. That expense was but one part of the financial equation we now faced, living in a very costly city on a limited income. In addition, there would be the unanticipated expenses caused by the President's desire that Marion attend many White House social affairs and host gatherings at our home, especially where Senators and Congressmen would be our guests. However, we knew that somehow we would manage it.

All I could do about my financial deficit was go to my Texas bank and borrow enough money to tide us over until, at some uncertain future time, I would earn enough to cover my living expenses. Fortunately, when that time came, I was able to pay off my debts over a few years' time.

On our first Sunday in Washington, we drove to the White House where we joined the President and Mrs. Johnson to attend the Episcopalian church services across the river in Virginia. Our sense of excitement was heightened by the knowledge that the church to which the Johnsons took us—Christ Church in Alexandria, Virginia—had been attended by every American President since George Washington, with the sole exception of President Kennedy.

On the ride to the church, the President—showing, as always, that he seldom missed any detail—noticed that Marion was wearing a white coat. "It won't stay white very long here in Washington," he commented. "The dirty air here will turn it gray or black soon enough."

At the church, the President led us down the center aisle to near the front where, stepping back, he motioned for Marion and me to enter the pew ahead of him and Mrs. Johnson. As soon as we were seated, a woman behind Marion leaned over and whispered something that sounded to her like, "Psst, the plaque, the plaque." Marion turned around and the woman whispered it again. Marion had no idea what the woman meant until after the service when it was explained to us that Marion had been sitting on the silver plaque designating where George Washington had sat and worshipped. By long tradition, only Presidents sat on that hallowed spot. Marion was mortified and apologetic. She had no idea, of course, and both the Johnsons laughingly assured her that this was only her first lesson in Washington's complex and sometimes murky protocol.

After church, we returned to the White House for a private lunch with the Johnsons in the family dining room. Then we all walked across the driveway known as West Executive Avenue that separates the West Wing from the Executive Office Building. There, in the basement, is the presidential bowling alley—built there long before the Johnsons arrived—and the four of us enjoyed a pleasant afternoon bowling.

Later that afternoon, Mrs. Johnson accompanied Marion on a leisurely tour of the White House, including the rooms never shown to the public, such as the West and East Wings, as well as the mansion, which contains the living quarters of the First Family. Mrs. Johnson was gracious and full of information she shared with Marion, but it would not be too long before this historic site would become very familiar to Marion and me.

In the meantime, the President asked me to sit with him in the Yellow Room, a part of the living quarters on the second floor of the White House that opens onto the Truman Balcony and spectacularly overlooks the South Lawn, the Washington Monument, and the Jefferson Memorial. I was totally awed by the unobstructed view of these grand symbols of America. We sat there while the President explained all that he expected of me in my new job. There was a lot of detail, but I have never forgotten the essence of what he said.

"Whatever you do, I always want you to stop first and think, 'If this is on the front page of the *New York Times* tomorrow, will I be proud of what I did? Will it reflect well on the President? On me? On my family?' If the answer is no, then don't do it!

"I don't want you to be a yes-man. I want you always to feel free to talk to me about any disagreement you have. But *never* reveal our differences to anyone else!

"I expect you, along with every other member of my staff, to work closely with Congressmen and Senators. Become their friend, socially as well as politically. But if it ever comes to a showdown, *never* let the Congress beat us. If they ever do that, they will smell blood and will run us out of town.

"One other thing," he added. "If you are going to function as my chief of staff, I want you to make certain that the staff—counting everyone working for me whether they are paid by the White House or not—totals *fewer* people than worked for President Kennedy."

I had no problem with anything he said and I told him so. The President's entire lecture was given in a soft, kind voice, more like the friend he was rather than a boss. As it turned out, he never spoke to me in any other manner. He never yelled at me and he never used profanity when he spoke to me. He did to others in my presence, but never toward me. I never knew—and never asked him—why this was so. Perhaps it was because of our long friendship, or because he knew that I never asked for this job. More likely, it was because he was aware of my deep Christian faith and abhorrence of profanity.

He ended this meeting by saying, "I want you to know how much I want and need you at my side." I was deeply touched and gratified and told him that.

It was early evening before we left for home. I felt that I had been running at full speed for three days, and I was exhausted.

Promptly at six-thirty Monday morning, February 1, 1965, a White House car arrived at my house to drive me to my first day of work for the President. At the time, I thought that was an early start, but as it turned out six-thirty was by far the latest I ever left home throughout my tenure at the White House.

The President had asked me to come to his bedroom by seven o'clock. I was early, so when the black Buick Electra, driven by Army Sgt. Robert L. Dionne, dropped me off at the West Executive Avenue basement entrance to the West Wing, I walked up the one flight to my new office. As I had requested, it adjoined the Oval Office and the intimate study that the President used for his most private meetings. While I waited, I sat in my chair, my mind swirling with all that had happened to me during the past month: jetted to the home of the President of the United States on New Year's Eve; his guest at the White House; airplanes, helicopters, limousines; church with the Johnsons; intimate and trusting talks with him; and now here I sat about to begin work. How did this all happen? Would I be up to the job? So much might be expected of me. I was, after all, only a forty-year-old from an East Texas town being pulled into the very center of the cauldron of government and politics that is Washington, D.C.

BEGINNINGS

I am a fourth-generation Texan, born in the small east Texas town of Oakhurst on June 6, 1924. My childhood was happy, although because of my small size, my high school years were marred by my inability to play football—the dream of every Texas young man of my generation. I did, however, manage to gain some competency in baseball and tennis, although by losing to the young man who ultimately became state champion, I concluded that athletics was not in my future.

Music was a different story, and my talent with a saxophone was sufficient to earn me a full scholarship to Baylor University in Waco, Texas—funds badly needed by me if I was to acquire a college education. At Baylor, I played in both the university band and the orchestra. Ultimately, I decided that although I enjoyed music, I was not interested in it as a career.

I entered Baylor in 1941, and any career decision was rudely interrupted by the onset of World War II on December 7. I was only seventeen but like almost every other American boy—and certainly all of my Texas friends—I wanted to sign up and fight. In those days, in that war, we looked upon those who avoided military serve as un-American. But my age required parental consent, and my parents refused to give it to me. In June 1942, I turned eighteen and registered for the draft. I would have volunteered immediately, but this time my parents persuaded me to wait until I was called. I listened to them for a while, but in April 1943, before my sophomore year was complete, I could no longer delay. I approached the Marine recruiter on campus and signed up on the spot.

The Marines wanted to assign me to the Marine Corps band, but I would not agree (which was my last exercise of free will for the next few years). I was full of patriotism—like every eighteen-year-old in those days. I wanted to fight for my country, and so the Marines shipped me to San Diego and boot camp.

Marine boot camp is deliberately designed to be a harrowing time. To me, the purpose behind boot camp makes sense. The Corps prides itself on molding an elite group of fighting men, which begins with that extraordinarily difficult regimen. By the time we concluded our fourteen-plus weeks, we had learned to follow orders, instantly and without question. When the sergeant said, "Do X," you did "X" precisely; X-plus or X-minus was not tolerated. According to the Marines, either you did as you were told or you got out of the Corps. We learned to submerge our individuality into our units. We were trained to measure up to Marine tradition. All of us who finished boot camp became Marines in every sense of the word. I survived realizing that the spirit the Marine Corps instilled in me was something I would value for a lifetime.

Many Marines died during the Pacific campaign of World War II. Yet, none of us thought of dying. I was not at all unique in wanting to fight on the front lines with my friends and comrades. I volunteered to become a Marine infantryman and was ordered to Camp Lejeune, California, for advanced infantry training. As it happened, because of my small size, my dream was denied—which, considering the fate of so many others from this training unit of the Marines, probably saved my life.

I felt great guilt, but my involuntary transfer eventually did bring me to Iwo Jima and Okinawa during the final stages of the war. I was assigned as a member of an airplane crew in a squadron that was using an experimental technology of air-to-ground rocket fire.

Our objective was to destroy the Japanese ships desperately attempting to ferry their troops home from China and Korea in time to resist the American invasion they expected.

In mid-August 1945, all of us knew that the invasion of Japan was imminent. As we learned from the battles for Iwo Jima and Okinawa, the invasion would be bitterly contested with a massive loss of human life. Still, there was no doubt that we would go forward regardless of cost.

Then, one evening a naval officer appeared in our mess building, gathered us around, and ordered us to listen up.

"Tomorrow," he began, "we are going to bomb Japan with the most powerful weapon ever used. They are about to experience the most destructive force ever deployed in warfare."

The officer definitely had our attention.

"What we don't know is how they will react," he continued. "Will they try to retaliate? Will they begin using the nerve gas we know they have? I doubt that they will do nothing."

"What do you suggest we do?" our commander asked.

"Every one of you should dig out your gas masks and keep them with you at all times. Also, starting right now, you should begin digging the biggest, deepest foxholes you can. Tomorrow night, all of you should remain on alert. We don't know what they will try, but be ready for anything."

We followed his advice. The news was not long in coming. The United States had successfully exploded an atomic bomb over Hiroshima. Whatever elation we felt was tempered by our fear of Japanese retaliation, which, as everyone knows, never came.

A few days later, a second atomic bomb exploded over Nagasaki. To our amazement, the Japanese surrendered almost immediately. Through the years, others—especially some of those who were not there, who have not experienced the fanaticism of Japanese fighting, and whose own lives were not at risk—have questioned our use of atomic weapons. But the rest of us have no doubt that the bombs caused their capitulation and saved at least a million American casualties, not to speak of the lives of additional millions of Japanese. Along with every other Marine who was there, I have never doubted the necessity and the wisdom of what President Truman decided to do to end World War II.

When I got home in the spring of 1946, it was too late to reenter Baylor, so I worked with my father until the fall semester began. While I was away, he had acquired his own Chrysler-Plymouth agency, the Watson Motor Company, and I enjoyed working with him in Grapeland, Texas, until I could return to school in the fall of 1946.

Back at Baylor, I changed my major to economics and prelaw. I no longer used my music scholarship because the GI Bill of Rights now helped pay for my education. I did need spending money, however, and I earned that by selling automobiles to students.

Not long after my return to school, I met Marion V. Baugh, a strikingly beautiful blond girl who had started college while I was in service. Her family was well known in central Texas. Marion and I were introduced at a wedding where she and I were the only unmarried attendants. She must have seen something in me, and I was happy because we were soon in love and were married a few months later.

I did well academically at Baylor, where I first became actively involved in politics. Actually, my interest in politicians began when I was a boy. I always attended political rallies in Huntsville, earning extra money selling refreshments. What really fascinated me, however, was the different personalities and speaking styles of the candidates who campaigned in my hometown. After the war—and especially because of the war—my interest in public issues grew and I closely followed the debates on the issues of the day.

During 1948, I was a junior and senior at Baylor and an activist on campus. Harry Truman was running for President, and in the Texas Democratic primary Congressman Lyndon Johnson was running for the U.S. Senate against Coke Stevenson, the Governor of Texas.

In those days, there was only one successful political party in Texas: the Democrats. If a politician won the Democratic primary, his election was assured. The Republicans, although they fielded a few candidates in the general election, were a nonfactor. Where I was reared, I don't believe I ever met an admitted Republican before I left home.

The lack of effective Republican opposition did not mean that elections went uncontested. Quite the opposite, because Texas Democrats were separated into two hotly differing factions: "conservatives" and "liberals." The defining issue between most of them was mostly the so-called "right-to-work" law. Being in favor of it meant opposing the ability of unions to close out nonunion labor in a business or industry. That meant you were a "conservative." If you supported the union position, you were a "liberal."

In 1948, Lyndon Johnson favored the right-to-work law and Governor Coke Stevenson did not. However, Congressman Johnson—along with powerful Texas politicians like Speaker Sam Rayburn and Congressman Wright Patman—had supported President Roosevelt and the New Deal. All of them had taken positions such as supporting social security and federal regulation of the stock markets, which in those days cost them politically in their home districts. Based on all I had heard and read, Lyndon Johnson was the man I wanted to support for Senator. This led me to help form and lead the Johnson for Senate organization on the Baylor campus.

I first met Lyndon Johnson when he came to Waco during that 1948 primary campaign. He arrived in a helicopter—I believe a first in Texas politics. It was a novel and exciting way to come to town, and it definitely brought out a crowd. He always circled the town and, just before he landed, he tossed out his Stetson hat, an act that invariably caused a stampede of people to retrieve it. Of course, Johnson had instructed one of his aides to be certain to get it back, even if he had to pay for it. Once Johnson's helicopter landed, he would bound from it and jump onto the back of a flatbed truck, where I was invited to join him.

The strongly positive impression I formed of him that day would last for a lifetime. In those days, his height was emphasized by his wiry thinness. He radiated enormous energy, more so than I have observed in any other person before or since. He was able to function on four hours of sleep a night. He had obvious intelligence and his grasp of issues impressed me. It is true that his level of energy and need for sleep changed after his 1955 heart attack, but not all that much, and even after that, his energy was greater than most men. But in 1948 he was a dynamo who enveloped everyone around him, including me.

He had a prodigious memory and quickly absorbed whatever he read or was told.

Even then, Johnson had strongly held beliefs concerning the equality of all Americans and the need to fight ignorance and poverty. Those beliefs had been formed early in his life and had been solidified during his years teaching disadvantaged Mexican Americans in Cotulla, Texas, and through his years working and serving in Congress as a protégé of President Franklin Roosevelt. There was no falsity in his beliefs and he expressed them throughout his life with unflagging devotion.

Lyndon Johnson was not a great public orator, but he was an exciting speaker who was both knowledgeable and sincere. However, in smaller groups, he had an amazing, instinctive ability to empathize with those around him. He never lost his skill of communicating with people he could see in front of him, especially if he could reach out and touch them. Television was not important to politicians in 1948. Thus, in that year, he was an out-standingly effective campaigner. It was only later, when television became all consuming, that Lyndon Johnson was penalized because he could not, in person, see and be seen by his audience.

He returned to Waco several more times during the 1948 campaign, of-ten accompanied by his wife, Lady Bird Johnson, a lovely and soft-spoken woman to whom I was also instantly attracted. She was, quite obviously, as intelligent and politically knowledgeable as her husband. Since I was always invited to be on the platform while he spoke, I slowly came to know both of them.

Lyndon Johnson won the 1948 primary by eighty-seven votes and went on to an easy victory in the general election. His narrow primary victory, however, earned him the appellation of "Landslide Lyndon." From what I know, he won that primary fairly, if narrowly, and his victory in the primary and the general election was upheld first by the Texas Democratic Executive Committee, and later by the U.S. Senate.

It had been a far different story in 1941 when in his first try for the Sen-ate many believe success was stolen from him, a fact that he never forgot and vowed never to permit again. That year he ran a solid campaign against in-cumbent Texas governor "Pappy" Lee O'Daniel. When all the votes suppos-edly had been counted, the results showed that Congressman Johnson had won by more than three thousand votes. Confident of victory, Johnson left Texas to drive to Washington as the youngest person ever elected to serve in the U.S. Senate. However, between Little Rock, Arkansas, and Memphis, Tennessee, while listening to the car radio he heard that some sixteen hun-dred O'Daniel votes were found in west Texas. He stopped the car and tele-phoned his campaign manager, Roy Hofheinz, who was in Houston.

"They have just 'found' sixteen hundred more O'Daniel votes," Johnson stated.

"You don't have to worry," Hofheinz replied. "That's only half your lead."

"You are wrong," Johnson said. "It's only the beginning. They are stealing the election. Please hurry to Austin and check the facts."

"But they can't do that," Hofheinz protested.

"Believe me, they are doing it right now," Johnson said. "I'm turning around and coming home, but I don't think there's anything we can do to stop them."

Johnson was right. O'Daniel, with total control of the party machinery, produced just enough "found" votes to change the result. Johnson never doubted that the outcome was the result of fraud, but he chose not to challenge the outcome. Instead, he bided his time and waited until 1948.

In both 1941 and 1948, Johnson was taking on a sitting governor with control of the political machinery. In the earlier election, the Johnson forces were overpowered. In the latter, Johnson had learned his lesson and never let down his guard. One of the crucial differences between 1941 and 1948 was that in 1948 Johnson never trailed his opponent. Nonetheless, Coke Stevenson repeatedly challenged the result. Johnson was defended by his trusted old friend and Washington lawyer Abe Fortas, and Coke Stevenson never proved any charge of wrongdoing.

I was a volunteer for Johnson in the 1948 campaign. From that time until the end of his life I was never anything but a "Johnson man." I had made a choice that would last for a lifetime. Johnson always knew it, and so did I.

Although Lyndon Johnson was grateful for my help, and told me that I could always have a job in his Senate office, I chose to continue with my education. As a matter of fact, I did not see Johnson again until 1951.

I continued at Baylor for one more year, earning additional money by teaching economics to underclassmen and grading economics papers. I loved teaching and always tried to expose students to the close connection between the world they knew and the economic principles they were learning. I was the only nondoctoral person permitted to teach economics, and it was exciting work.

When I received my master's degree in 1950, Marion was pregnant with our daughter, Kimberly. With our son, Winston Lee, and now our second child, it meant that she could neither return to school nor continue at her job. It also meant that there would be no law school or a doctorate in economics for me.

With one child and another on the way, we needed money. Despite the urgings of my professors and the offer of an academic scholarship from Brown University and Louisiana State University, I needed to find other employment.

THE 1950S:
PUBLIC SERVICE, POLITICS,
AND LYNDON JOHNSON

In the summer of 1950, with my master's degree in my pocket, I led my young son and a very pregnant Marion from Waco to San Antonio, where I accepted a job selling hearing aids. It did not take me long to discover that whatever my talents might be, they did not include selling products to consumers. I did not do well, but I kept at it through the birth of our daughter, Kimberly, in October. All the while, I continued to search for something more suitable for me. I turned down an offer from Gulf Oil in Houston and from my father in Grapeland. Then a marvelous opportunity came to me. Lone Star Steel was building a large plant just outside of the East Texas town of Daingerfield. There, the town fathers had decided to expand their Chamber of Commerce and were searching for a manager. I was offered the job. I eagerly accepted, and on February, 18, 1951, my family and I moved to Daingerfield where we made our home until we moved to Washington fourteen years later.

Being the manager of Daingerfield's Chamber of Commerce turned out to be a catalyst for other opportunities. My job permitted me to meet and work with people not only in Daingerfield but in an expanding area of surrounding communities. I was exposed to the problems of our own town and my job enabled me to actively participate in their solutions. I loved my work and knew I had made the right career choice.

I held the job for five years. During that time I also became city secretary and city judge—a position I held without complaint, despite the fact that I was not a lawyer. Most important for our family were the wonderful friends that we made. We were a part of a working community that believed in and could and would help each other.

Soon after I arrived in Daingerfield, I was offered another opportunity that proved to be a significant challenge. For years, visionary people had wanted to build six dams on tributaries to the Red River. The reservoirs thus created would furnish water not only to East Texas, but to parts of Oklahoma, Arkansas, and Louisiana. But the dam in Texas on Cypress Creek and lake was not going to get built on its own. It needed authorization and financial support that could only come from the Texas legislature and the U.S. Congress. In April 1951, at an area-wide meeting, we discussed and agreed to form a water district to negotiate a contract for space in an authorized dam area reservoir on Cypress Creek in Northeast Texas. In 1951, I was elected secretary, and in 1953, I became president of the Northeast Texas Municipal Water District, an involvement that continued until I moved to Washington. Before I departed, the dam was constructed, Lake of the Pines was formed, and the then largest man-made municipal water supply was created.

My work with the Water District brought me out of Daingerfield and into the neighboring counties and states that would be benefited by the project. I also began traveling to Washington where I met and worked with key members of Congress. I already knew Senator Lyndon Johnson, and his senate office became my unofficial headquarters. I also knew my congressman, Wright Patman, who had shared a desk with Lyndon Johnson's father when they both served in the Texas legislature. Congressman Patman told me that I should immediately enlist the support of Lady Bird Johnson (whose father and brother would be affected by the district) because she might, in turn, influence her husband. I did so, and the Congressman's prediction proved totally accurate. Thereafter, both Senator Johnson and Congressman Patman strongly backed the project. Through them, I met Sam Rayburn, the powerful Speaker of the House of Representatives, whose support was also critical.

By the mid-1950s, I needed more money than the Daingerfield Chamber of Commerce could pay me. I began searching for something else, and I received an offer to head the Chamber of Commerce in Gainesville, Texas, a town north of Dallas. I accepted the job, resigned from my position with the Daingerfield Chamber of Commerce, and drove to Gainesville to begin work, although until we could sell our home, I left my family behind in Daingerfield. For two days I worked in Gainesville, but then Congressman Patman, E. B. Germany (the President of Lone Star Steel, Daingerfield's largest employer), and Pat Mayes (publisher of a chain of newspapers) convinced me to return to Daingerfield to work with the Red River Valley Association to secure financing for the other authorized but unfunded reservoirs in the Red River basin.

It was a difficult decision, but the Gainesville people were most supportive.

Returning to Daingerfield satisfied my family, which never wanted to move, and it ultimately proved to be the correct choice for me.

In 1956, again at Mr. Germany's urging, I left the Red River Association and went to work for Lone Star Steel. I started in their public relations department, but soon I became Mr. Germany's executive assistant, a position I held until my move to Washington in 1965.

Mr. Germany was a powerful figure in Texas business and a most conservative political leader, but he never objected to any political task I ever undertook.

Although I worked in Lone Star's corporate headquarters in Dallas, I did not move from Daingerfield. Thus, I commuted the 137 miles several times each week. I was able to spend two or three nights a week at home, and it is with fatherly pride I can say that I never missed any of my children's school games or programs.

My volunteer work in politics continued to expand. Soon after moving to Daingerfield, I became active in the local Democratic Party. My travels for the Water District also brought me into contact with people outside my town and county who were interested in politics and government. Often, we found ourselves meeting and discussing our mutual problems and how best they might be solved. Soon our meetings became more organized and regular. By 1952 and 1953, we thought of ourselves as a "fellowship" of like-minded citizens, and our group had expanded until it encompassed the ten counties of our Texas senatorial district. Our informal organization was no secret and attracted attention from local and state politicians who started asking if they could appear before us when we met. Congressman Patman supported us and in 1954, Senator Johnson suggested that I organize another twelve counties, bringing us to a total of twenty-two counties of northeast Texas.

Despite the fact that Lady Bird Johnson was a wonderful asset to Senator Johnson in East Texas because she and her family came from Karnack in our part of the state, Senator Johnson's strength there was never great. In addition, he habitually had problems with the regular Democratic Party. It was important for him to have a group dependably loyal to him. All of us fit that mold.

We were not part of the official Democratic Party organization, although as far as I know, the regular party officials never resented us. Our objective was to lead in writing the platform and have a voice in choosing the people who represented us. Because we were not "official," we were free to endorse candidates in the primaries, the only election that counted in those years. Not only did we regularly do so, but the word soon spread that our backing was critical if a candidate hoped to win. It was not long before anyone running for statewide office came through our kitchen at least once during his campaign.

My involvement in our "fellowship" did not prevent me from actively participating in the formal structure of the Democratic Party, both locally and, after a few years, statewide as well. In 1958, I ran for and was elected (in my own landslide victory of one-half a vote) to the Democratic State Executive Committee. I hasten to add, however, that my margin of victory increased in subsequent elections: I won reelection the first time with 70 percent of the vote, and my reelections after that were unanimous.

Throughout the 1950s, I seriously considered running for office myself. Specifically, I had my eye on the congressional seat of Wright Patman after he retired. I told him and his response was encouraging, although he said he had no immediate intention of retiring. As it happened, he remained in office until long after I left the government and had joined Occidental Petroleum in California. By then, my years in Washington had shown me enough about how things work there to have burned away even a lingering desire to run for office. But even in the 1950s, my boss, E. B. Germany, was advising that I should not run for Congress. "If you win," he told me, "you will be just one vote among four hundred and thirty five. But if you stay active on the outside, like I always have, you may influence several votes." He was undoubtedly right. Still, I held onto my ambition for many years.

My trips to Washington for the Water District brought me into increasing contact with Senator Johnson. Through him, I learned that the critical backing I needed in Congress must come through the leadership, including the chairmen of the relevant committees. I was fortunate because Senator Johnson was elected Minority Whip in 1951, Minority Leader in 1953, and majority leader in 1955. House Speaker Sam Rayburn was also from Texas, and my own congressman, Wright Patman, was chairman of the House Banking and Currency Committee. All of them supported the Water District project.

Soon after I began spending time in Washington, I learned a valuable lesson about how one dealt with Senator Johnson's office or, for that matter, the office of any senator or congressman. It happened when I received some important information that I believed should be passed on to Senator Johnson. I called his office and asked to speak to him.

"He's not available right now," the receptionist told me. "Would you like to speak to his chief assistant, Walter Jenkins?"

"No," I said. "I need to deliver this message personally to the Senator."

"Mr. Jenkins will do that for you," she replied.

"I will call again," I said, refusing her offer.

That evening, I received a call at home from Sam Houston Johnson, the Senator's brother. "What do you want to tell him?" he asked.

"I'm sorry, but I need to talk to him myself," I said.

"That's not the way things work around here," he said, and hung up.

At 7 A.M. the next morning, my telephone rang and this time it was Senator Johnson himself. "You have some information for me," he began. "You tell me what is so important that you can't tell it either to my most trusted assistant or to my brother."

At that moment, I did not need a road map to realize that my insistence had been a foolish mistake. It was one that I never repeated. Over the years, President Johnson periodically reminded me of the incident, and we often laughed recalling my naïveté.

By the time Senator Johnson ran for reelection in 1954, I was a regular fixture in his Washington office. The Senator and I would have dinner several times a year.

He asked me to travel with him through east Texas during his 1954 reelection campaign, and I did. By then, my "fellowship" group had become a respected political influence, and we helped him whenever he came to our part of the state. My main function was to organize his political appearances and, a habit that continued throughout my years in the White House, he always included me in his meetings, regardless of their sensitivity. We became very comfortable with one another, a feeling we never lost. That campaign served to reinforce my belief, formed in 1948, that I was supporting a great man. I have never changed that opinion.

During Johnson's successful 1954 Senate campaign, and regularly after that, Walter Jenkins speaking for Senator Johnson asked me to join the staff. I always declined his offer, firmly but politely. The Senator never took offense, but neither did he stop Walter from asking. My refusals had nothing to do with my relationship with Senator Johnson, which had grown close, but had everything to do with the fact that I did not want to lose the freedom I enjoyed as a volunteer—a freedom I knew I would lose if I ever came on his payroll.

Senator Johnson's heart attack on June 2, 1955, came as a shock to everyone but himself. He always knew that the men of the Johnson family did not enjoy longevity. Nonetheless, after he absorbed this massive blow to his health, he fought hard to regain his strength. He stopped smoking and adopted a healthier diet. He began breaking up his days by taking naps, or so he said. Actually, those "naps" usually consisted of little more than going to his bedroom, changing into pajamas, and spending his time making telephone calls. His changed habits also began his constant struggle against gaining considerable weight.

During his convalescence, I saw that the fundamentals of this remarkable man had not changed. He had retained his amazing ability at recall, both of facts and what had been said and by whom as long as thirty years ago. He remained able to focus on a problem, blocking out everything that was extraneous. He also retained his impatience with delays. He always felt that if he could do a job in five minutes then those around him should do it at least that fast.

Finally, whenever he asked a question, he insisted on a direct answer. Much later he would tell the story that if he asked what time it was, someone like George Reedy (his longtime Press Secretary) would start telling him that he was either late, early, rushed, or delayed; and someone like Jack Valenti would begin explaining the importance of timing to the matter at hand. "But my friend Marvin will always tell me what I want to know," President Johnson would say. "If it is six o'clock, Marvin will tell me that, and nothing more or less. That's why I always keep him so close to me."

After Senator Johnson returned to Washington following his heart attack, he suggested that it would be helpful if I would host dinners for his friends and supporters, especially those from Texas. It was my pleasure to begin doing as he requested. Senator and Mrs. Johnson made a point of always dropping by to say hello to the dinner guests. It was their way of keeping in touch with some of the Senator's key constituents. One false rumor in the local Austin newspaper and others was that the notorious convicted Texas criminal Billy Sol Estes helped finance these dinners. That story was not true. I have never met or spoken to Mr. Estes, and the dinners were at my expense only.

Before the Democratic National Convention in 1956, Joe Kennedy, whom Senator Johnson had known for years, asked him to run for President. "If you do that," the senior Kennedy told him, "I would like you to select my son Jack as your running mate." Senator Johnson declined the offer. Later, in 1956, when Adlai Stevenson was nominated for president and uniquely and unexpectedly threw the convention open to select a running mate without guidance from him, Joe Kennedy approached Senator Johnson again, this time asking him to nominate his son for Vice President. Once more, the Senator declined, but Joe Kennedy's intense interest in his son's political future demonstrated that the father had very big plans for his son. Senator Johnson also concluded that Joe Kennedy was actively orchestrating John Kennedy's future.

Adlai Stevenson was, to put it mildly, anathema to Texas, especially running against the revered President Eisenhower in 1952 and 1956. Stevenson's negative reception was reinforced by his opposition to drilling oil in the Gulf of Mexico waters offshore of Texas. The rights to that oil had been retained by Texas when it became a state, and the proceeds from the drilling were used to partially finance the Texas school system. Texans did not want those funds taken away from them.

Nonetheless, Senator Johnson, along with Sam Rayburn, remained loyal to the Democratic nominee. They asked me to assist Warren Woodward in the 1956 Stevenson presidential campaign in Texas. I accepted that unhappy job and, despite the odds against us, worked day and night throughout the campaign. As usual, Mr. Germany, whose opinion of Stevenson was extraordinarily negative, permitted me the time for that task. As a matter of fact, of the 106 people who worked in the corporate office of Lone Star Steel, I was only one of two persons who supported Governor Stevenson. The campaign was, of course, hopeless from the start and Eisenhower easily carried Texas.

FROM LEADER TO
VICE PRESIDENT

As it turned out, my work in the hopeless 1956 Texas presidential campaign for Adlai Stevenson did not harm my standing with the Texas Democratic Party or its powerful congressional delegation. Senator Johnson, Speaker Rayburn, and Congressman Patman appreciated my commitment to the Stevenson effort. Because I had taken this responsibility at their urging, and because they wanted to be seen as loyal to the national ticket, they were grateful.

After 1956, I spent increasing amounts of time in Washington, at least once for more than a month. I used my Washington connections to foster the interests of my employer, Lone Star Steel, whose business included not only cast-iron pipe but oil field tubular steel and other related products. Of course, E. B. Germany, Lone Star's chief executive, was the primary moving force of the company, and his wide-ranging connections and well-honed political skills, along with his remarkable political acumen, principally drove the company's success. The success of Lone Star Steel was important to East Texas, where it was the largest employer. Although I assisted, it was Mr. Germany and his team who created a company that during these years produced steel at the lowest prices in the United States.

Mr. Germany was like a father to me and encouraged everything I ever attempted. He permitted me the freedom to support those I wanted to support regardless of how he felt. He never begrudged me the time I spent on politics. He always encouraged me and took pleasure in whatever successes I achieved.

I continued living in Daingerfield, but I was commuting to Washington as well as Dallas. Still, I found time to spend with my growing children and, increasingly, with the First Baptist Church in Daingerfield. I became a Sunday school teacher, Sunday school superintendent, and a deacon. Those years were deeply satisfying to my family and me. At different times, each of us had accepted Jesus as our personal savior and Lord.

Throughout, I remained active in politics. One of the results of my 1956 political activity was that I became involved with Democrats throughout Texas—well beyond the twenty-two county base that we formed in East Texas. I made many new friends. One of the most impressive was John Connally, a Fort Worth attorney who by the late 1950s was universally acknowledged as a rising star in Texas.

John Connally was an amazing man. The son of a Texas sharecropper, he ultimately rose to become John Kennedy's Secretary of the Navy, Governor of Texas, and a member of President Nixon's cabinet. He had charisma and good looks, as did his wife, Nellie, and their children. They had met at the University of Texas where John was president of the student body and Nellie was a popular beauty queen. It was a fact—and remained so all of their lives—that when they entered a room, conversations would stop and all eyes would gravitate toward them. Their mere presence commanded attention. Beyond that, John was unusually intelligent, not only intellectually but in so-called "street smarts." His mind was much like that of Lyndon Johnson's. He possessed a prodigious memory. He was also a gifted public speaker. Until the end of his life when bad investments ultimately bankrupted him, he succeeded in everything he ever tried.

Connally was first sent to Washington in 1939. His law firm wanted him to work for Congressman Lyndon Johnson in order to learn the ways of Washington. Nellie Connally joined her husband and shared an office desk with Lady Bird Johnson in her husband's congressional office. Later, when Johnson was President, a Dallas law firm tried to replicate Connally's Washington initiation by arranging to send one of its bright young attorneys, Bill Blackburn, to work for Lyndon Johnson in the White House. Blackburn subsequently became a distinguished Dallas lawyer, city council member, and a productive citizen of his community.

Connally became a friend of Lyndon Johnson—a friendship that, although tempestuous at times, lasted a lifetime. Their friendship did not diminish even when John struck out on his own. Despite the fact that John increasingly became a political conservative, he never wavered in his personal support of his mentor. During all the years of Johnson's public service, whether as Congressman, Senator, Vice President, or President, John Connally was always available to give whatever help was needed, ranging from wise counsel to furnishing key members of Johnson's staff. These included George Christian, who became President Johnson's press secretary, and Larry Temple, who moved from executive assistant to Governor Connally to Special Assistant to President Johnson.

During 1958 and 1959, John and I had many conversations concerning whom we should support for president once President Eisenhower's term ended. We both felt that Adlai Stevenson, having lost twice, had failed his chances, and in addition he was still largely not trusted in Texas. We believed that John Kennedy was too young and that Hubert Humphrey was too liberal. To us, the choice was obvious: The most competent and experienced man was Lyndon Johnson, then the Democratic Majority Leader in the Senate.

Senator Johnson had received almost universal praise, not only for his astute leadership, but just as important, for the effective way he had worked with President Eisenhower. However, we knew it was late to begin a national campaign. Kennedy and Humphrey were both well organized and financed, and Johnson did not have strong national name recognition. Still, we believed the country needed Lyndon Johnson and we were determined to do whatever we could to achieve his nomination and election. Accordingly, in the latter part of 1959, I formed and John endorsed the first "Johnson for President" organization, consisting of the eleven counties of northeast Texas that constituted the First Congressional District.

Our first major problem was Johnson himself. He was not ready to run for President. He told us that his work in the Senate was too important and time consuming to permit him to campaign. In no uncertain terms, he refused to announce his candidacy or to publicly support our efforts on his behalf. Nonetheless, he did not instruct us to close down our efforts. Neither did he help us or hinder us, which left us free to go forward while Senator Johnson waited to see what developed.

Our efforts began in Texas, starting with my hometown of Daingerfield. We created Johnson for President organizations throughout the state, each

staffed by enthusiastic volunteers. We also knew we needed a national organization. Thus, in the spring of 1960 we opened a Johnson headquarters
in Washington, D.C. Our office was run almost entirely by Texans (including Lyndon Johnson's two young daughters, Lynda and Luci), but our goal
was to reach out to the country at large to raise money and persuade those
who would be delegates to the 1960 Democratic National Convention. We
had neither the time nor the money to conduct a full-scale public operation.
Nor did we have a candidate willing to campaign on his own behalf.

In the meantime, Kennedy and Humphrey were garnering all the public
attention as they flailed away at each other in bitter primary battles in states
such as Wisconsin and West Virginia. Still, we were not without hope. The
eventual nominee of the Party would be selected by delegates chosen by their
state party organizations rather than in primaries, a fact far truer in 1960
than in subsequent years. Almost all of those delegates were party activists.
Also, some 80 percent of the 1960 convention delegates would be the same
people who were delegates at the 1956 convention. Thus, we had a limited
and identifiable target. We thought we had the best candidate, a conclusion
we did our best to sell to the working politicians who would make up the
bulk of the voting delegates.

Our campaign remained viable despite the massive publicity received by
Kennedy and Humphrey. It was very much alive when we moved our operation to Los Angeles on July 4, where the convention would open one week
later. On July 5, Lyndon Johnson finally broke his silence and acknowledged
that he would accept his party's nomination should it be offered to him.

During that final week before the convention, an overriding fact became
apparent to us. John Kennedy did not have the nomination locked up. His
vote was close to a majority, but he was not yet over the top. More important, he had no votes in reserve. If he did not win the nomination on the
first ballot, he was going to lose votes on the second ballot. That meant his
entire effort was focused on a first-ballot victory. For him, it was either immediate victory or ultimate defeat. The obvious strategy for us was to use
every possible political and parliamentary device to deny him that first ballot majority.

In our efforts, we found ourselves closely aligned with the organization
supporting the nomination of Adlai Stevenson as well as those supporting
Missouri Senator Stuart Symington, another candidate for the office, and

any other favorite son nominees. The Stevenson people saw the situation as we did and were also doing everything possible to deny Kennedy a first-ballot victory. My colleague Sherwin Markman, although unknown to me at the time, was a delegate from Iowa working on the Stevenson staff who found himself at the center of that strategy.

Markman's task on behalf of Stevenson—which we believed would benefit us—was to withhold from Kennedy the votes of Markman's home state, Iowa, on the ground that the Iowa delegates were pledged by their state convention to vote on the first ballot for Iowa's governor and favorite son, Herschel Loveless. Kennedy's margin was so close that without Iowa's votes he would not have his majority.

Loveless had been promised the Vice Presidential nomination by one of the Kennedy brothers. In exchange, Loveless had agreed to throw his Iowa convention votes to Kennedy on the first ballot. Markman had heard that identical promises had been made by the Kennedys to several others, including Minnesota's governor, Orville Freeman. Markman's first—and naive—idea was to get Governor Loveless and Governor Freeman to meet and compare promises, thus exposing the duplicity of the Kennedys. Neither governor agreed to the suggestion because each had been told that the Kennedy "commitment" was confidential.

Markman's next effort was to seek a ruling from the convention parliamentarian that Iowa was legally bound to cast its first-ballot votes for Loveless. By that time, however, the Kennedys were in control of the convention machinery and Markman's requested ruling was denied. His subsequent appeal to the convention chairman was equally fruitless.

Markman's struggle created considerable personal enmity toward him. Governor Loveless was livid and berated Markman publicly, telling him in front of several reporters: "If you don't stop what you are doing, I am going to destroy you, you no good SOB." Markman was shocked, but labored on. Just as shocking to Markman was the reaction of Ted Kennedy. Apparently the Kennedys believed that anyone supporting Adlai Stevenson should have been working for John Kennedy, and their efforts for Stevenson amounted to a personal affront to Senator Kennedy. Upon seeing Markman and knowing of his efforts to block the Kennedy nomination, Ted Kennedy had to be restrained from physically attacking Markman.

Ted Kennedy also played a critical role in denying Johnson delegate votes pledged to him. In the months preceding the convention, the delegates from Alaska had volunteered their pledge to support Senator Johnson, who had been the champion of making Alaska the forty-ninth American state. Thus, when they arrived in Los Angeles, they were bound by their pledge to vote for Johnson on the first ballot. In that respect, our position was identical to Markman's: we believed the delegates from Alaska were legally bound to honor that instruction. John Kennedy's razor-thin margin drove his people to focus on an effort to break that pledge, even in a state as small as Alaska. They did this at a hastily called midnight meeting of the Alaska delegation where Ted Kennedy met alone with them. Whatever he told them, promised them, or gave them remains secret even now. But the result was dramatic. Before the Kennedy meeting, all eight of Alaska's delegates were going to vote for Lyndon Johnson. After the meeting, Johnson did not have a single vote; they were all voting for Kennedy. Unlike Markman's effort on behalf of Stevenson, we chose not to make a public issue of this seemingly inexplicable change of heart.

What these incidents demonstrate is the accuracy of our conclusion that without the votes from Iowa and Alaska, Kennedy would not have been nominated. They also brought home to us what Hubert Humphrey suffered through in West Virginia and elsewhere when his defeat was engineered as much by Joe Kennedy's contributions as any other factor.

In the final days before the convention voted, John Connally suggested a debate between Lyndon Johnson and John Kennedy to be held at a caucus of the Texas convention delegates. Connally believed that Johnson's superior knowledge and debating skills would trip up the momentum of the younger candidate. Surprisingly, Kennedy accepted the challenge and the debate was quickly scheduled.

On the day of the debate, Markman was assigned the job of escorting Eleanor Roosevelt, an open supporter of Stevenson, to meetings of undecided and wavering delegates. Just before the debate began, Mrs. Roosevelt asked Markman to find a private hotel room where she could watch the debate on television. Markman did so, and along with two of Mrs. Roosevelt's aides, they went to that room. Mrs. Roosevelt sat on the couch while Markman sat on the floor, literally at her feet. During the ensuing debate, Mrs. Roosevelt made no effort to hide her antipathy toward John Kennedy. "I do not like that young man," she told Markman. "I do not trust him. More than that, I neither like nor trust his father, and Jack is no more than his father's tool."

Although he agreed with Mrs. Roosevelt's assessment of Joe Kennedy's influence over his son, Lyndon Johnson did not fully share her negative opinion of the father. The two of them had been friends for years and, as I have stated, as early as 1956 Joe Kennedy sought to form an alliance between Senators Johnson and Kennedy. Thus, I have always believed that it was Joe Kennedy more than any other person who convinced John Kennedy of the wisdom—indeed the necessity—of selecting Lyndon Johnson as his vice-presidential running mate.

I believe that Kennedy's vice-presidential decision was also affected by what happened during the debate before the Texas delegation. Senator Kennedy clearly won that contest. John Connally was wrong that Kennedy would be shown up as inexperienced and shallow. Quite the opposite occurred. Kennedy's good looks, good humor, affability, and mastery of the issues easily carried the day. But Senator Johnson also did well. Most especially, his performance was mature and professional, and his disagreements with Kennedy never became personal. The two of them concluded the debate with mutual respect. If it had been otherwise, Kennedy might not have chosen Johnson, regardless of the political logic and the urgings of his father. It is also my opinion that in appearing with Johnson on Johnson's home turf, Kennedy was deftly laying a foundation for the offer he ultimately made.

Although Lyndon Johnson, once he committed to enter the presidential race, gave his full attention to that campaign, he always knew how slim his chances were. It was only his realization that Kennedy's nomination could be blocked that gave him hope. But he never truly believed he would succeed. Thus, his disappointment was slight; he fully accepted John Kennedy's victory and was preparing to leave Los Angeles. Then lightning struck.

Much has been written about the hows and whys of Kennedy's decision to ask Senator Johnson to be his running mate. Certainly, most of us close to Johnson did not believe that it would happen. As a matter of fact, I left Los Angeles the morning after the Kennedy victory and was on the way home to Texas when I heard the dramatic news.

I will not repeat all the speculation about what happened during the argument that swirled around Senator Kennedy as he pondered his decision.

Neither will I speculate about what was in the heart of Robert Kennedy during those hours. What I will reveal, however, is what Robert Kennedy actually *did* in an all-out effort to convince Johnson to accept his brother's offer.

The people closest to Lyndon Johnson at the time—especially John Connally—strongly opposed the Kennedy offer. They argued that Johnson was and would remain Majority Leader in the Senate, a powerful position in our system of government. They also argued that if Johnson became Vice President, he would have little or no power and that his reputation would sink into insignificance. His main duty would be bridesmaid-in-waiting in case a young and vigorous President might die. They reminded him of the infamous statement of his fellow Texan, John Nance "Cactus Jack" Garner, Franklin Roosevelt's Vice President: "The vice-presidency is not worth a pitcher of warm spit."

Senator Johnson respectfully listened to the strongly stated advice of his friends, but he did not commit himself. It was clear to those around him that his decision could go either way. The Kennedys knew that too. They not only had decided that Lyndon Johnson was their choice, but they knew that they desperately needed him if they were to win the general election. Thus it was that John Kennedy's closest advisor, his brother Robert, was dispatched to meet privately with Lyndon Johnson's closest mentor, Speaker Sam Rayburn.

Speaker Rayburn provided a statement to his lawyer, Roland Boyd of McKinney, Texas. Later, that statement was sent to me for safekeeping at the White House. Although other versions of these events have been published, that memorandum reflects the speaker's recollection of exactly what happened.

It was close to three o'clock in the morning following John Kennedy's nomination. Sam Rayburn was in his hotel room bed. He had just fallen asleep after hours of worrying over what Johnson should do if, as he suspected might happen, the vice-presidential nomination was offered to Johnson. A knock on his door awakened him. When he opened it, there stood Robert Kennedy wanting to talk to him.

Kennedy got right to the point. "We want Lyndon to run for Vice President and we want you to persuade him to accept." Kennedy then went on to state his case: Johnson would make a strong candidate, indeed the strongest candidate; his place on the ticket was essential, especially for carrying Texas; and of course Johnson was eminently qualified to succeed Kennedy as President.

Speaker Rayburn did not tell Kennedy that he had been thinking about his response for hours. He did not repeat his conclusion that although it was true that Johnson's position as Senate Majority Leader placed him in one of the three most important positions in government, that was only possible because the Democrats had a majority in both Houses of Congress and the Republicans controlled the White House. Rayburn believed that if the same party controlled both ends of Pennsylvania Avenue, the Senate Majority Leader would lose most of his influence, and that was a position he did not want Lyndon Johnson to occupy.

The Boyd memorandum went on to state that Speaker Rayburn assumed that Kennedy had come to him because of an earlier speech Rayburn had made at an affair honoring him. There, the Speaker had stated: "I hate it that Lyndon Johnson has not won the nomination, especially since I was one of the people who convinced him to run. Nonetheless, I must say that John Kennedy is a fine, courageous, and able person, and the nation would be fortunate to have him as our President." The Speaker had concluded his remarks by saying, "John Kennedy is now our leader and it is our duty to go home and get him elected."

Word of that speech must have reached the Kennedys, who concluded that the Speaker could be an influential ally in their quest to convince Johnson to accept their offer. But Speaker Rayburn held his cards close to his vest. After Kennedy finished making his pitch, the Speaker thought for a moment, then said, "Well, I don't know about that. I have several misgivings."

"Tell me what worries you," Kennedy said.

The Speaker replied, "I would not attempt to convince Senator Johnson to run unless your brother goes on nationwide television before the next session of the convention and says, 'I want Lyndon Baines Johnson to run for Vice President of the United States with me.'"

Without hesitation, Robert Kennedy said, "That's a sound request and I think Jack will agree to it."

"Good," Speaker Rayburn said. "But there is more. Ever since the Civil War, we in the South have had to fight prejudice against our section. That prejudice has made us play second fiddle to the rest of the nation in our national conventions. So I am not willing to prevail on Lyndon to run unless the chairman of a big delegation from north of the Mason and Dixon Line goes before the convention and tells the delegates, 'I think Lyndon Baines Johnson should be the next Vice President of the United States.' "

"I agree with that too," Kennedy replied. "Is there anything else?"

"Yes," Speaker Rayburn said. "Finally, Jack must agree that if he and Lyndon are elected, Jack will make Lyndon a working Vice President. He must give Lyndon major responsibilities and thereby use his talents."

"All right," Kennedy said. "I don't think that Jack will have any problem with anything you suggest."

With that, Kennedy left to consult with his brother. A short time later, Robert Kennedy telephoned Speaker Rayburn to say, "I have spoken to Jack. He agrees with all of your conditions. He will carry them out if Lyndon agrees to run."

"Very well," the Speaker said. "I will talk to Lyndon."

Sam Rayburn immediately contacted Senator Johnson and told him about his conversations with Robert Kennedy. Johnson told Rayburn that while Robert Kennedy had been meeting with Rayburn, John Kennedy had been in Johnson's suite personally urging him to accept the nomination.

"Under these conditions, and especially because Jack has accepted all of my suggestions, you cannot refuse to run," the Speaker stated. "It's your duty to the nation to run."

Johnson responded, "If I do, some of my staunchest supporters are going to be very upset with me." As I later discovered, Johnson was referring to John Connally, among others. These people did not like Senator Kennedy's politics and some were concerned because he was Catholic.

But Johnson expressed his own belief by saying, "When the whole situation is viewed, I don't think there is any other answer but yes."

Speaker Rayburn spent the rest of that day monitoring developments. Well before the convention convened, he saw John Kennedy come on national television and tell the nation that he wanted Lyndon Johnson to be his running mate. That satisfied the Speaker's first condition. Then, at the convention, Pennsylvania governor David Lawrence nominated Lyndon Johnson for Vice President. Henry "Scoop" Jackson, Senator from Washington, seconded the nomination, as did William Dawson, a black congressman from Illinois. The Speaker's second condition was now satisfied.

Meanwhile, false stories were circulating that Johnson and Rayburn had put pressure on John Kennedy to select Johnson. Especially harsh were statements by Senator Jackson's staff who were telling the press that without that pressure, Kennedy would have chosen Jackson rather than Johnson as his running mate. Rayburn was livid because he knew the truth was precisely the opposite. He immediately dispatched his people to correct the record, and for the most part the Jackson version is no longer accepted. What is still misunderstood, however, is the fact that Robert Kennedy not only accepted his brother's choice of Lyndon Johnson, but actively and decisively worked to make certain it happened.

As for the Speaker's third condition, during the years when Lyndon Johnson served as Vice President, Speaker Rayburn's lawyer occasionally would ask, "How is the President doing on number three?"

The Speaker would answer, "Just like he said he would," always adding, "Jack Kennedy is the most gracious man I have ever known."

Whether Speaker Rayburn's third condition was in fact carried out is a matter of dispute. But I have no doubt that President Kennedy never knowingly backed away from his commitment. To the degree that Vice President Johnson's role was diminished under John Kennedy's presidency, I feel certain—based on what I know about how Vice President Humphrey fared under President Johnson—that any failure lay in a combination of the nature of the job, the power of a presidential staff to limit the access and responsibilities of the Vice President, and, in Johnson's case, as I shall explain later, the particular antipathy of Robert Kennedy toward him.

Johnson's decision to accept John Kennedy's offer was also made with his historical perspective that to his knowledge, no one had ever refused to accept the nomination when it was truly offered. Still, Johnson was correct in thinking that John Connally and many others would be unhappy about his action. In fact, Johnson was surprised by the intensity of Connally's reaction, which was to angrily leave Los Angeles for his home in Fort Worth. It was not until the final days of the campaign that Connally and Johnson spoke again.

Senator Johnson took the initiative in patching up his relationship with Connally. Johnson had been distressed by his old friend's separation from him and his refusal to help in the close presidential campaign. On the final Thursday before the voting in November, Johnson spent the night in Fort Worth. After he made his last public appearance of the day, we drove to meet with Connally in a parking lot. There Connally joined Johnson and me in Johnson's car. That conversation lasted for an hour and a half. Both Johnson and Connally honestly expressed their opinions with the bark off. Connally told Johnson that he had made a terrible mistake, and Johnson told Connally how hurt he was by Connally's actions. Back in August, I had agreed with Connally that Texas already had a strong voice in Washington through Speaker Rayburn and Majority Leader Johnson; and that being Vice President would only diminish Lyndon Johnson's authority. In the end, that long and frank meeting in Johnson's car succeeded in clearing the air between the two men. Their schism was healed.

Unlike Connally, however, I understood and remained with Johnson throughout the 1960 campaign. I accepted Senator Johnson's offer to travel with him, a job that kept me at his side through as many as twelve stops a day from September until November. Horace Busby, Johnson's longtime aide, Bill Moyers, who was then Johnson's young assistant, and George Reedy, his press secretary, also traveled with him, while Walter Jenkins, his Chief of Staff, remained in Washington, as did Harry McPherson, who was primarily responsible for writing Johnson's position papers and some speeches. Also back in Washington—and of immense help during the campaign—were two long-time Johnson secretaries: Mary Margaret Wiley (who later married Jack Valenti) and Marie Fehmer (who stayed on through his full presidency and later joined the CIA).

My responsibility was to coordinate Johnson's campaign. Our decisions were made in close cooperation with John Kennedy's staff, chiefly Ken O'Donnell. We assigned Cliff Cater, Johnson's affable, hardworking, and smart old friend, the task of remaining in Washington to maintain close liaison with O'Donnell. I worked easily with O'Donnell as well as with Larry O'Brien, Kennedy's other political leader. I found O'Donnell to be tough minded, with excellent political sense. O'Brien was equally competent, but not nearly as tough as O'Donnell. As for John Kennedy, he was unfailingly courteous, affable, and very likable. He was very bright and quick, and his attractive public persona was greatly enhanced by the impressive talents of his speechwriters, whom I always considered to be among the best. John Kennedy never failed to treat Lyndon Johnson with kindness and respect. For his part, Johnson considered himself a full member of the Kennedy team. In that, he slowly discovered that many members of the Kennedy entourage did not return his loyalty, led by the always-puzzling antagonism of Robert Kennedy. Throughout all the ensuing years, Johnson remained surprised by the strength of the younger Kennedy's enmity.

Throughout the campaign, we understood the reality that John Kennedy would take the big meetings and we would take the rest. Of course, our schedule was in constant flux, which is normal. We accepted our secondary role.

For each Johnson campaign stop, there was at least one and usually two advance men. This was an enormous undertaking because of all the appearances that Senator Johnson made every day. The primary problem was finding enough reliable people. Most were totally inexperienced—and that included me—in advancing for a national candidate, and there was little time for training. The skills they had to master included planning a local schedule after Senator Johnson arrived, one that served the purposes of the Kennedy-Johnson ticket. They had to do it without antagonizing the local politicians who often had quite different agendas, skewed to their own interests. Their views had to be deflected without appearing to dictate to them. Advancing was as much a diplomatic problem as a planning effort. It also required some talent at developing clever ways to attract the largest possible crowd and convincing the local authorities to estimate the crowd size at the maximum semibelievable number.

The campaign, although lasting only three months, seemed endless at the time. I averaged three and four hours of sleep a night, and at that I was getting more rest than Lyndon Johnson. The train trip was the worst for me. There are many advantages to this old-fashioned manner of politicking: it permits the candidate to get to places close to and easily accessible by the people. The problem for me—which may seem trivial but definitely was not so at the time—was that there was no place for me to bathe or take a shower on the train. I finally figured out a solution: when I could, I booked a hotel room near a railroad station where we stopped. When the train halted, I immediately ran to the room, took my shower, and hurried back. The problem was that in all of those stops, the candidate would speak from the rear platform of the train, and the instant he finished, the train would move out whether I was on board or not. It was always a close call for me, and there were times when I did not make it and had to find a car or taxi to drive me to the next destination.

The only breaks in the campaign came after the final Saturday speech and all day on Sundays. Senator Johnson always wanted to plan his schedule so that he could spend his Sundays in the sun, which he loved. He preferred Arizona and wanted to end each week somewhere near there. He also loved his ranch and happily settled on being home if it was possible. Wherever we were, the first thing that he did was shed his clothes, don a bathing suit, and jump into a swimming pool. As for me, if we were in Texas or close to it, I would arrange some way to get home to Daingerfield. It did not happen often, but the times it did were precious to me.

For Lyndon Johnson, his worst experience of the campaign happened in Dallas. His appearances in the city had been advanced by Barefoot Sanders, a man who later served as head of the Civil Division of the Department of Justice, as a Special Assistant to President Johnson, and during the presidency of Jimmy Carter was appointed a Federal District Court Judge in Dallas.

On this day in Dallas, Senator Johnson was scheduled to speak at a luncheon in the Adolphus Hotel. He wanted to clean up before his speech and Sanders had obtained rooms for that purpose at the Baker Hotel across the street. When he stepped out of his car, he was suddenly confronted by an unruly crowd of unfriendly, screaming people, carrying Nixon placards and shouting obscenities and such phrases as, "You damned Catholic Yankee!" and "Traitor!" Senator and Mrs. Johnson, with me leading them and Sanders following, struggled to make their way to the Baker Hotel door. There was no visible security for the Johnson party and it seemed as if the Dallas police did nothing to control the crowd. Barefoot and I did our best to protect the Johnsons, but as we slowly edged our way toward the hotel lobby, the angry mob surged around us. Then I saw that the uncontrolled people were stabbing Senator Johnson with the points of the pins on their Nixon buttons.

When we finally reached the hotel room, Senator Johnson removed his torn shirt. His back and chest were bloody from all of the pinpricks. We urged him to cancel his speech, or at least to find a way to get across the street without walking through that mob again.

"It's a hell of a note when Texas's own senior Senator and his lady can not cross the street in Dallas," Johnson declared. "I will not allow them to drive me out of my own state."

So, with his body wiped clean of blood and wearing a fresh shirt, he and Mrs. Johnson went outside and, heads up, once more walked through the still screaming crowd, again escorted only by Barefoot and me. The Johnsons were heckled, a placard hit the senator, and Mrs. Johnson was spat upon.

Demonstrations against Johnson were not limited to Dallas. Throughout the South, he was confronted by angry people who considered him a traitor to their way of life. For years, he had supported civil rights legislation. Those laws were weak compared to what Lyndon Johnson finally accomplished after he became President. Still, his support of the feeble civil rights bills sent to the Congress by President Eisenhower in 1956 and 1960, as well as his endorsement of the strong 1960 Democratic civil rights platform, led to very real resentment in the South.

As it turned out, the outrageous conduct against Senator Johnson in Dallas also resulted in a backlash of sympathy for him not only nationally, but in Texas as well. On his very next trip following the Dallas outrage—which was an appearance in Corpus Christi—he attracted the largest and friendliest crowd of the campaign. After this speech, he told me that, because of the public's disgust with what had happened to him in Dallas, he knew that he and Kennedy would now carry Texas. He was right about that.

Johnson always believed that the Democratic ticket would win the general election. Moreover, he believed that his place on the ticket would contribute to that victory, and not only in Texas. I remember the morning when he first expressed that confidence. It was during his first train campaign stop out of Washington, D.C., in Culpepper, Virginia. Notwithstanding that Culpepper was part of the South, the crowd was enthusiastic and friendly. In addition, almost everybody who was anybody had driven down from Washington to add his support. Johnson was extremely gratified. At that brilliantly successful stop, his last question to the crowd was, "What did Nixon ever do for Culpepper?" That became the battle cry of our campaign.

We spent election night at the Driscoll Hotel in Austin. Along with John Connally and one or two others, I stayed with him through the night watching the slowly developing results of that extraordinarily close contest. At around four o'clock in the morning, with the election still undecided, we walked across the street to get some breakfast at an all-night café. We had heard that John Kennedy—like Truman before him—had gone to bed, and we marveled that he could sleep. None of us could. Back in the hotel, we remained glued to the television coverage until, finally, at around nine in the morning, we knew that the Kennedy-Johnson ticket had won. Johnson was ecstatic, as were the rest of us. He went to bed knowing that he was the next Vice President of the United States.

VICE PRESIDENT

TO PRESIDENT

(1961–1964)

During the years of Lyndon Johnson's service as Vice President, I did not change my pattern of commuting to Washington. Nor did I diminish my contacts with his office. I still called every time I visited the capital, always speaking with his chief assistant, Walter Jenkins. When possible, I talked and visited with the Vice President, and at times he asked me to join him at his Washington home, The Elms. On other occasions, he and Mrs. Johnson also invited me to their Texas ranch.

Throughout those years, he made it clear that there was an available desk for me on his staff, but I continued to decline his offer. Meanwhile, my involvement in local affairs in Daingerfield and in a growing area throughout Texas continued to increase. Before I finally departed Daingerfield in January 1965, I held many responsibilities in addition to my full-time job with Lone Star Steel and my work with the Water District.

TEXAS ELECTS A NEW GOVERNOR

In 1962, John Connally decided to run for governor of Texas. At the time, he was serving as Secretary of the Navy for President Kennedy, a job he held at the patronage of Vice President Johnson. Of course, Connally was extraordinarily able in his own right, but the understanding between Kennedy and Johnson was that all presidential appointments from Texas would be controlled by Johnson. Naturally, this arrangement was unhappy news to Texas's

Democratic Senator, Ralph Yarborough, but there was nothing he could do to make President Kennedy break his promise to Johnson. Ultimately, Yarborough accepted this reality, but when it came to Connally, Yarborough differed with him with a passion that never diminished. That difference was based not only on the fact that Connally represented the conservative wing of Texas politics, but more important, there was never less than total distrust of each of them toward the other. Thus, when Connally resigned his federal office and announced his candidacy for Governor, Yarborough was in the forefront of those who fought to defeat him.

Yarborough's candidate was Don Yarborough, who was no relation, but who was a well-known liberal Democrat in Texas. However, John Connally was faced with an even bigger challenge. He had to defeat the incumbent Democratic Governor, Price Daniel, who was considered to be a fellow member of the conservative wing of the party. This battle was fought in the 1962 Democratic primary, which in those days—because there was no known effective Republican Party in Texas—was tantamount to the general election.

The primary was a bloodbath between the various candidates. Price Daniel was well known and popular in Texas, and he was also my friend. He had an extraordinary political history. A native Texan, he was a hero in World War II. After the war, Daniel went on to serve as State Representative, and then as Speaker of the Texas House of Representatives, as the youngest attorney general in Texas history, as U.S. Senator, and since 1956, had been Governor of Texas. In the year that he had resigned from the Senate, he had famously stated: "I would rather be Governor of Texas than President of the United States." Now he was seeking his fourth two-year term as Governor, and John Connally, who had never run for public office, was challenging him.

At that time, my political group in East Texas was generally recognized as a critical source of influence in our part of the state. Before Connally and Daniel announced their candidacies for governor, each of them approached me and asked if I would be the person to bring messages from each to the other, and otherwise give them my assistance. That created a dilemma for me because I liked and respected both men. I frankly told each candidate that his opponent had come to me and that I had not decided what I would do. The surprising result was that *both* Daniel and Connally agreed that I should act in the dual—and conflicting—capacity of northeast Texas campaign coordinator for *each* of them in the primary. I agreed to do it and—at least as far as I was told by both of them—I performed fairly and satisfactorily. I worked to get out the primary vote; I distributed their literature; and I traveled with each of them when they came to East Texas. Neither of them ever complained. I imagine that from their points of view, my dual role in effect neutralized me and, in light of my affection for them, I did not mind that at all.

John Connally received more votes than Price Daniel in the primary. Daniel was defeated by the fact that Texas's first sales and use tax became law during his time as Governor. At the time, Texas government was expecting a deficit and additional revenue had to be found. The legislature enacted a sales and use tax and Daniel vetoed the bill three times. He tried to protect himself by allowing the legislation to become law without his signature, but of course that did not help him politically. From the moment the sales tax became effective, the phrase heard all over Texas whenever a sale occurred was: "A penny for Price." It was devastating.

John Connally took full advantage of Daniel's problems. Nonetheless, Connally's initial primary vote did not exceed 50 percent. Therefore, a runoff primary was required. Not so surprisingly, Price Daniel had run third in the voting and Connally's runoff opponent was Don Yarborough. What had happened, of course, was that Connally and Daniel had split the conservative vote while Yarborough received almost all of the votes of Democratic Party liberals. The final primary election was a close contest, and Connally defeated Yarborough by some three thousand-plus votes.

It is a tribute to Price Daniel's outstanding qualities as a public servant to note that after his defeat in the gubernatorial election, he went on to serve as a member of the Texas Supreme Court.

Connally won the general election by some eight thousand votes, a sure sign that Texas was about to become a two-party state. Even so, Connally's victory was a personal triumph, especially when one considers that he began his campaign with only 4 percent name recognition in Texas. By 1964, Connally's popularity had soared and he was reelected with about 80 percent of the vote. Of course, in addition to his good work as Governor, his victory was fueled by sympathy toward him because of the wounds he suffered during President Kennedy's assassination in November 1963. Nonetheless,

Connally was an effective and popular governor—and a close friend and advisor to President Johnson.

Lyndon Johnson did not become involved in the primary struggle between Connally and Daniel. He maintained his friendship with both candidates. After Johnson became President, he appointed Daniel to replace Buford Ellington (who departed to successfully run for Governor of Tennessee) to the important office of Director of the Office of Emergency Planning, the agency that coordinates all federal efforts during national and state emergencies such as hurricanes, fires, and floods.

Because of his conservative outlook and policies, Connally's years as Texas Governor served to hold the Texas Republican Party at bay. Nonetheless, throughout the 1960s, the strength of Texas Republicans steadily grew. After Lyndon Johnson resigned from the Senate in 1961, Republican John Tower was elected to replace him. Tower was Texas's first Republican Senator since the Reconstruction years, but far from its last. Yet as long as Connally remained Governor, the Democrats retained control of the state government. That did not last. Although Connally loyally supported Hubert Humphrey, Johnson's Vice President, when Humphrey ran for President against Nixon in 1968, by 1972, when Nixon ran for reelection against George McGovern, Connally accepted the position of national chairman of Democrats for Nixon. When Nixon began his second term in 1973, Connally became his Secretary of the Treasury. On the other hand, when Lyndon Johnson died in January 1973, he was still a talking, working Democrat— and his family continues his legacy.

LYNDON JOHNSON AS VICE PRESIDENT

I am confident that President Kennedy intended to keep Lyndon Johnson fully occupied as Vice President, but it never worked out that way. It was a frustrating job for a man who formerly exercised such great power in the Congress.

The worst blow for Lyndon Johnson (and one that also was a great loss for the Kennedys, whose legislative program languished) was the failure to make use of his great skills with the Congress and especially with the Senate. In matters pertaining to the Kennedy legislative program, Johnson was often bypassed and was not often asked to help. It was as if he had nothing to offer in their dealings with Congress. He complained about it, but there was little he could do but carry out the assignments given to him. He was unhappy, and deservedly so.

Johnson became a world traveler on behalf of the administration, dispensing goodwill—but he seldom contributed to policy. Although he was dissatisfied at the time, the foreign contacts he made and the knowledge he gained about the world at large ultimately served him well after he became President.

In two areas, however, Lyndon Johnson was given the opportunity to make a strong contribution. The first was in the then lagging space program where Johnson as Majority Leader had sponsored far-reaching space legislation. While he was Vice President, Johnson never hesitated to encourage the President to continue the American efforts in space, and the President allowed Johnson to take an active role. In that, Johnson was effective in creating, maintaining, and increasing the public support the President so dramatically embraced when he publicly committed the nation to the goal of reaching the moon during the 1960s.

The second major authority the Kennedys granted to Vice President Johnson was responsibility for the civil rights program. Although the Kennedy administration never consulted Lyndon Johnson about the content of its civil rights legislation, or worse yet, it failed to use Johnson's skills in pushing that legislation through Congress, he was made chairman of the Committee on Equal Employment Opportunity. The goal of that committee was to create equal access to job opportunities by blacks and other minorities. As always, Johnson attacked the problem with all the energy he possessed. However, the Kennedy government was at best a reluctant player in the civil rights struggles because of its fear of alienating their southern base. Thus, even in civil rights matters, Lyndon Johnson, although he did his best, was reigned in by the administration he loyally served.

As I have stated, the lack of use of Lyndon Johnson as Vice President was endemic to the office and not the fault of President Kennedy. The personal relationship between the two men was always good. I never heard Johnson utter a critical word about John Kennedy. Johnson accepted his role, sometimes unhappily, and he always carried out whatever duty was asked of him. He knew what his job was—and what it was not. More than anyone else, he realized that like an assistant CEO in a large corporation, his role was to help execute policies developed by others. The fact is that the President runs the government through his own staff and cabinet.

Yet President Kennedy treated Lyndon Johnson infinitely better than Franklin Roosevelt treated Harry Truman. Kennedy always saw to it that his Vice President was briefed regarding every important subject. No matter of importance was withheld from him. Kennedy believed that his Vice President should be prepared to assume the presidency. Kennedy knew only too well that when Truman became President he had not even been told about our development of the atomic bomb. Kennedy was determined not to make that same mistake with Johnson. The problem was that the briefings of Johnson were often partial—and always late. That failure was not Kennedy's intention, but was the natural result of an overworked staff that was always overloaded with more important matters demanding their attention. Much later, my own experience with Vice President Humphrey echoed this unavoidable truth.

Johnson was permitted to have a political voice—albeit a small one—through his selection of Cliff Carter to work as his liaison at the Democratic National Committee. Carter had limited influence, but his presence served as a conduit of information to Johnson, which is not without significance in Washington.

VIETNAM UNDER KENNEDY

In late 1962 or early 1963, I made a trip to Washington. As usual when I arrived, I telephoned Walter Jenkins and invited him to join me for dinner. Jenkins told me that tonight he was expected to attend what he described as "an extremely important meeting" of the top Kennedy staff. He asked me if I would come with him. When I said yes, he told me that he would obtain their permission.

That evening, Jenkins and I arrived together at the home of Richard McGuire, a close Kennedy friend whose main function was to raise political money for the President. But this meeting had nothing to do with money. When Walter and I walked in, we found ourselves among the small group of people comprising President Kennedy's senior staff. Among others, I recall the presence of Kenny O'Donnell, Larry O'Brien, and McGeorge Bundy,

Kennedy's chief foreign policy advisor. I have no idea why this meeting was not held in the White House, but it wasn't.

We adjourned to a room in McGuire's home where one entire wall had been covered by easels containing detailed maps of Southeast Asia. Bundy began the discussion—using a pointer for emphasis—with a prolonged and detailed exposition of what was going on in that part of the world. I vividly recall what he explained: The Communists were rapidly expanding their activity through constant and effective military incursions into Laos, Cambodia, and—most especially—South Vietnam. Their actions were also increasingly successful and, if nothing was soon done, the entire region would fall into their hands. He explained that the Communist military effort was led by the forces of North Vietnam and was supported by both the Soviet Union and China. He concluded by stating that the question for the President was obvious: Should America stand aside and let this all happen? Or should the power of the United States be used to save South Vietnam from Communist control? Could we? If we permitted the Communists to gain victory, what would happen in the rest of Southeast Asia? Finally, if we were to fight them, where and how should that fight be conducted?

The ensuing discussion among the Kennedy people showed that their views were unanimous: the United States could not let the Communists win. Everyone recalled President Kennedy's many public statements that America would not hesitate to resist Communist aggression wherever it occurred. There was also discussion of the SEATO Treaty (the Southeast Asia Treaty Organization) that had been ratified by two-thirds of the Senate. The SEATO Treaty obliged the United States to come to the assistance of any member nation that was subjected to military aggression. One of those nations was South Vietnam; it was being attacked, and if we were asked, then the SEATO Treaty required us to come to its defense.

At that meeting among President Kennedy's most influential advisors, the conclusions reached were unanimous. Everyone believed that the policy of the United States must be to resist Communist aggression in Southeast Asia, and there was no known alternative but to do so by taking military action. There was no disagreement about the recommendation that would be made to President Kennedy.

The remaining question concerned the most appropriate place for American intervention. The discussion centered on strategic possibilities and risks. Where could American troops most easily be landed, supplied, reinforced, and supported by air and sea power? Put that way, the question appeared to answer itself: Laos and Cambodia were quickly rejected. Vietnam, with its long, open east coast was the obvious logical alternative. It was the only place with easy access to the South China Sea, a body of water large enough to permit safe naval maneuvers, and also close to our main air and supply bases in the Philippines. The unanimous conclusion of the Kennedy men was that a military stand must be made in South Vietnam, and, unavoidably, America must supply the necessary military force, including ships, planes, and men. Walter Jenkins, when it was his turn to speak, stated his agreement with all these conclusions. I did not say anything, but I too agreed.

The evening ended with a statement by the Kennedy people that no time should be wasted; that they would deliver their recommendations to the President the following day. Before I left Washington, Walter told me that the staff conclusions had been promptly conveyed to the President, who had expressed his complete agreement with everything that had been reported to him.

The staff recommendations made to the President were totally consistent with all the advice President Kennedy was receiving from his chief foreign policy advisors. These men, all of whom were later retained by Lyndon Johnson and who never changed their advice to him until the final months of the Johnson presidency, included Secretary of State Dean Rusk and Secretary of Defense Robert McNamara. Secretary Rusk, for example, had served as a Far East expert since the presidency of Harry Truman. As Secretary Rusk has stated:

> When the Kennedy Administration took office, the SEATO Treaty was part of the law of the land. How we responded under the SEATO Treaty was strongly linked in our minds with the judgments that would be made in other capitals as to how and whether we would react under other security treaties such as the Rio Pact and NATO. . . . The reputation of the United States for fidelity to its security treaties was not an empty question of face or prestige but had a critical bearing upon the prospect for making peace.

Furthermore, as early as June 1956, then Sen. John Kennedy made a speech entitled "America's Stake in Vietnam." In it, he totally embraced the so-called "domino theory" that held if we permitted South Vietnam to fall, the remainder of Southeast Asia would soon follow. He said:

> Vietnam represents the cornerstone of the Free World in Southeast Asia, the keystone to the arch, the finger in the dike. Burma, Thailand, India, Japan, the Philippines and obviously Laos and Cambodia are among those whose security would be threatened if the red tide of Communism overflowed into Vietnam. . . . And if it falls victim to any of the perils that threatens its existence—Communism, political anarchy, poverty and the rest—then the United States, with some justification, will be held responsible; and our prestige in Asia will sink to a new low.

Much later, President Kennedy discussed South Vietnam at a news conference held on September 12, 1963, when he stated:

> We are for those things and those policies which help win the war there. That is why some 25,000 Americans have traveled 10,000 miles to participate in that struggle. . . . Any action . . . which may handicap the winning of the war is inconsistent with our policies and our objectives. . . . We want the war to be won, the Communists to be contained, and the Americans to go home. That is our policy. . . . But we are not there to see a war lost, and we will follow the policy which I have indicated today of advancing those causes and issues which help win the war.

This statement by President Kennedy was made only two months before his assassination.

President Kennedy's unambiguous commitment to the military defense of South Vietnam was enthusiastically shared by his brother Robert. Thus, on February 18, 1962, then Attorney General Robert Kennedy publicly stated that American troops would stay in South Vietnam until Communist aggression was defeated. He went on to declare:

> We are going to win in Vietnam. We will remain [there] until we do win. . . .
> The United States will do what is necessary to help a country that is trying to

repel aggression with its own blood, tears and sweat. . . . This is a new kind of war, but war it is in every sense of the word. . . .

It was only after his brother's assassination when his own political ambitions came forward that then Sen. Robert Kennedy began singing an entirely different tune as he worked to create a persona that was in tune with the protesting students and many of the so-called intellectuals of the day. He sought to become their spokesman. However, when his brother was in power and Robert Kennedy spoke on behalf of the government of the United States, all of his utterances supported the policies recommended by his brother's staff, foreign policy advisors, and cabinet. He ignored all of that personal history when he acted on his own behalf to further his personal goals.

THE ASSASSINATION OF PRESIDENT KENNEDY

I was not in Dallas on November 22, 1963, the day President Kennedy was murdered. At the moment of the shooting, I was riding in an automobile, rushing toward Austin. The night before, I had made a speech in East Texas and had planned early the next morning to fly to Austin, President Kennedy's final public stop of the day. However, the weather was bad and six of us, including my son Lee, were in the car. The President was scheduled to appear at a major fund-raising dinner that night in Austin, and because I was one of the principal organizers of the affair, I needed to be there early.

During the drive, I turned on the radio. The first words I heard were: "The President has been shot." We listened in shock as the initial sketchy reports became increasingly specific until finally we heard the announcement: "President Kennedy is dead."

I assumed that Dallas was in chaos and it would be useless for me to try contacting Lyndon Johnson. Also, there were hundreds of people waiting for the President in Austin. I thought that the best service I could perform was to continue on to Austin and do what I could to assist.

The Austin dinner had been planned at the suggestion of Governor Connally. He convinced everyone that only one major fund-raiser should be held in Texas and that the best place for that was Austin. It was to be held at the Austin Municipal Auditorium and was called the "Kennedy-Johnson

Texas Welcome Dinner." That dinner was to be followed a short while later by a similar dinner in Massachusetts. The point of both dinners was not only to raise money for the 1964 campaign, but to demonstrate that John Kennedy intended to retain Lyndon Johnson as his running mate. The final event planned for that day was for the President and Mrs. Kennedy to be the Johnsons' guests at their ranch. None of this ever happened, of course. The tragedy in Dallas changed everything.

By the day of the assassination, we had already received approximately $300,000 from dinner ticket sales, with much more yet to come. That was a great deal of money in those days and it was the best possible showing of the true strength of the President and Vice President in Texas. We later tried to return the money, but most people elected not to accept our offer and instead permitted the national and Texas Democratic Party to retain the funds.

Much later, after the Warren Commission completed its investigation of the Kennedy assassination, President Johnson confided to me his personal assessment of what happened that terrible day. The President refused to publicly criticize the Commission in any way because, as he often told me, the national interest was best served by total confidence in the Commission's work. He believed it was dangerous and disruptive for him to seek to do otherwise. Yet, privately President Johnson thought that the Commission's investigation had needed more time. He never accepted its conclusion that Lee Harvey Oswald acted on his own. President Johnson died believing that there was another shooter and that the assassination had been orchestrated by Fidel Castro in retaliation for the failed attempts at his own assassination by the CIA as orchestrated by the Kennedys.

President Johnson also believed that the Secret Service had received unjust criticism for allegedly not adequately protecting President Kennedy. He often pointed out to me that the Secret Service had begged President Kennedy to use the bulletproof bubble top on his convertible while he drove through Dallas. They urged its use in part because of the mob assault on Mr. and Mrs. Johnson in Dallas during the 1960 campaign, and more recently upon Adlai Stevenson when he visited Dallas earlier in 1963. But President Kennedy overruled the Secret Service and insisted that he ride in an open car. As Lyndon Johnson often said, anyone willing to sacrifice his own life could successfully murder anyone else, including a President of the United States.

One particularly outrageous fallout from the investigation of President

Kennedy's assassination came in the form of a so-called investigation by the New Orleans District Attorney, James Garrison. Garrison's personal probe, in which he attempted to convince the nation of his fantasy that the assassination was the result of a government-wide conspiracy among Lyndon Johnson, the CIA, and other federal agencies, was given unwarranted credence when maverick Hollywood director Oliver Stone, in his movie *JFK*, attempted to make Garrison (played by Kevin Costner) into a hero who was the only one speaking the truth.

The fact is that Garrison was certifiably crazy. As the FBI later reported to me, Garrison was discharged from the Army in October 1951 because of "severe and disabling psychoneurosis." The FBI reports regarding Garrison documented that his mental illness was of a type requiring long-term psychiatric care and that it had preexisted his military service. Furthermore, Garrison's illness "interfered with his social and professional adjustment to a marked degree." To me, making this man a hero, or giving undeserved credence to his outlandish theories, does a marked disservice to all of us who care to know the reality concerning the assassination of President Kennedy.

Another source of misinformation comes from a book entitled *Blood, Money & Power* (Hanover, 2003), written by Barr McClellan. The *New York Times* described McClellan, who is the father of the Press Secretary to President George W. Bush, as "one of President Johnson's personal lawyers." That statement is untrue. Of far greater importance is the total falsity of the book's central allegation that Lyndon Johnson, along with Richard Nixon and J. Edgar Hoover, met the night before the assassination and conspired to murder President Kennedy. No such meeting ever took place. Many people have publicly stated that each of these men were elsewhere and apart on that night. There was no conspiracy and there has never been any evidence to support such a bizarre fabrication. Former Republican President Gerald Ford (a member of the Warren Commission) has written that "there is not one scintilla of truth to that accusation." Former Democratic President Jimmy Carter has written that McClellan's statements are "despicable and baseless." Finally, Lady Bird Johnson has written that "Secret Service records, the Warren Commission Report, the multiple independent investigations conducted by the FBI, Dallas police, and independent researches and journalists—not one of these EVER accused Lyndon of any foreknowledge or involvement."

THE 1964 DEMOCRATIC NATIONAL CONVENTION AND ROBERT KENNEDY'S ATTEMPTED COUP

After Lyndon Johnson became President, I continued to serve as the Executive Assistant to E. B. Germany, the CEO of Lone Star Steel. As I have written, Mr. Germany never prevented me from responding to President Johnson's requests for my service. One of the most significant of those requests came in May 1964.

I had flown to Washington with Blake Gillen, a friend and fellow Texan and longtime supporter of the President. While we were attending a White House luncheon, the President requested that we stay behind for a visit.

The President began in his abrupt way. "You know that President Kennedy chose Atlantic City as the site of the Democratic National Convention in August. I have no problem with that, but I want it to go off without a hitch. I also want to tell you that I am worried that it will not."

"What can we do?" I asked.

"John Bailey is the Chairman of the Democratic National Committee. As you two know, he is a Kennedy man in every way. Always has been, always will be. I don't want to fire him, but at the same time I know that he is not a Johnson man. He is in charge of the convention. That may be fine, but how can I know that for sure? What I need is someone I can trust to be in control of everything that goes on in Atlantic City. I need you to go there. Will you do that for your President?"

"But the convention doesn't begin until August 24," I argued. "That's months away, Mr. President."

The President brushed that aside. "I want you to start right now. I want this convention to be the best one ever held. What I need is for you to take as much time as necessary to make certain of it."

"All right, sir," I agreed, and Gillen did not object.

"Good. I will give you all the authority you need. Marvin, you will be in charge."

My first act after receiving the President's authority was for Blake and me to meet with John Bailey and Cliff Carter. I informed Bailey that the President had asked that I coordinate the convention. I told him that he would retain his public identity of controlling the convention, but in actuality he would report to me and follow my directions. I asked him if he had any problem with this change. He told me that he would do whatever the President wanted him to do. His only concern was not to be publicly humiliated. I told him not to worry about that because the President and I would protect his reputation. He seemed satisfied, and the three of us flew to Atlantic City.

First thing the next morning, Bailey called a meeting of the eighty or so people who served on his convention staff. He introduced us and told them that I was President Johnson's representative and that from then on they were to assist me in any way I might request.

A major problem in Atlantic City appeared to be the city's failure to live up to its agreement to provide adequate hotel rooms for the expected delegates, representatives of the media, and visitors, as well as sufficient facilities for the upcoming convention. With the opening of the convention rapidly approaching, I learned that the authorities in Atlantic City—and the State of New Jersey—had arranged for hotels that were often second rate and with inadequate rooms. In addition, the meeting spaces were sparse. If this was to be the great convention that the President wanted, radical improvements had to be made.

After five days of chronicling the oncoming disaster, I flew back to Washington and reported to President Johnson and Walter Jenkins. The President listened, thanked me, and, believing that my job was finished—at least temporarily—I returned to Texas. That was on a Saturday. But early the following Monday morning, my telephone rang. It was the President.

"You get back on a plane to Atlantic City and make it right," he said. "You have the authority. Now use it."

Blake and I went back to Atlantic City the next day. As it turned out, our assignment ended up taking several months to complete. Between the President's initial call and the adjournment of the convention on August 28, we spent a total of fourteen weeks living in Atlantic City. My only consolation was that Marion and the children joined me for the final weeks.

When Blake Gillen and I returned to Atlantic City, I requested a meeting of the New Jersey Convention Committee and the Mayor of Atlantic City. They agreed to meet that same day. I told them that I was unhappy with the plans for the convention. I stated that they were not fulfilling their legal agreements with the Democratic National Committee. I described the second-rate hotels and facilities that were being offered, and I told them they would either solve our problems right now or the convention would move to another city and state. I was not bluffing and they knew it.

They quickly assigned one of New Jersey's most effective bankers to do the job of making everything right. They promised me that they could and would do whatever was necessary, and they did. Within days, the changes were evident. Suddenly, all the best hotels became available to us, as did large and sufficient meeting areas and other convention facilities.

I was satisfied that physically the convention plans were now on the right track, and I reported this to the President. However, by that time an even greater problem concerned me. I had become suspicious of Robert Kennedy and his plans for the convention. I told President Johnson that in my opinion, almost the entire convention staff that had been selected by John Bailey and that they were acting as if they were on a holiday. I also said their loyalty appeared to be to the Kennedys and not to Johnson. I believed that out of the almost eighty of them on the payroll, no more than a handful were loyal to him and willing to work to make this a great convention.

The President did not hesitate, and said, "Marvin, you must stay there and make sure that it is my convention."

I immediately began looking more closely not only at the convention personnel, but at what they were planning for the convention. What I discovered confirmed my worst fears. When I finally unraveled the whole picture, I was convinced that a carefully orchestrated scheme was afoot whose objective was to displace Lyndon Johnson and nominate Robert Kennedy, not as Johnson's running mate, but as the Democratic nominee for President.

As I have stated, my suspicions began with the distressing discovery of the loyalties of the convention staff. As I walked among them, I saw nothing but Kennedy signs and posters above their desks, and Kennedy pins on their shirts and blouses. These did not identify which Kennedy they supported, but of course John Kennedy was dead and Ted Kennedy was not a factor. Johnson signs were nonexistent.

Next, I looked into the hotel arrangements these people had made for the state delegations. What I found astounded me. Texas and other southern and southwestern states expected to be enthusiastic for President Johnson had been assigned to the poorest hotels and those most distant from the convention hall. The best hotels were allotted to New York, Massachusetts, and other northeastern states traditionally in the Kennedy camp.

Of far greater significance was the seating plan for the delegates on the convention floor. There, the same pattern had been followed: Texas and other Johnson states were seated at the rear of the hall while the Kennedy states were positioned in front, directly facing the speaker's platform. From past conventions, I knew the great importance of preferred seating during any kind of floor fight. Those in front could get the attention of the convention chairman and the television cameras with far greater ease. In an all-out battle, that advantage could be decisive.

Finally, I asked to examine the program that the convention staff had planned for the convention. What I saw was that a Kennedy gala, hosted by Rose and Jacqueline Kennedy and all the other Kennedy women, was the only event scheduled for the evening before the formal opening of the convention. Robert Kennedy was to be their principal guest. Then, immediately following the opening, the delegates would be shown a specially prepared movie honoring President Kennedy and his achievements. I had no doubt that the movie would be highly charged and was intended to arouse the emotions of the delegates. My belief became a certainty when I saw that the Kennedy movie was to be followed immediately by a convention appearance and major address by Robert Kennedy.

I had been around politics and politicians long enough to realize what was intended: The accommodations, the seating arrangements on the convention floor, the control of the convention machinery (by which I mean admission tickets, microphones, and loudspeakers), the reception, the movie, the climatic appearance by Robert Kennedy, and most of all, the initial chairmanship by the Kennedy man, John Bailey, could be for no other purpose but to create such an emotional outpouring among the delegates that Robert Kennedy, who thought of himself as his brother's political heir, could be inexorably swept to the Democratic nomination for President.

I did not doubt that this plan was approved and coordinated by Robert Kennedy himself. I had watched the Kennedys operate politically for far too long—especially in the events leading up to John Kennedy's nomination in 1960—and I believed that they were behind everything I had discovered.

Although my conclusions were firm, I wanted one more piece of evidence before I told the President. I needed to confront John Bailey with what I had learned, face to face, and alone. I summoned him to Atlantic City and the two of us met in my convention office. I did not show my anger with him. Instead, I calmly recited everything I had discovered. He listened silently, not objecting, until I finally asked him: "John, I want an honest answer from you. I want you to frankly tell me whether or not what is going on here is a plan by and for Robert Kennedy."

He stared at me for a long moment. Then, sighing deeply, he said, "Yes."

I pressed on. "Is his plan to stampede the convention into nominating him for President?"

He nodded his agreement.

"And you have made no move to stop him, have you?"

"No, sir."

"In fact, you are going along with him, aren't you?"

"I had no choice, Marvin," he answered, for the first time attempting to defend himself.

"Well, John, you should know that I intend to inform the President about everything that I know. I expect that he will tell me to do anything and everything that is necessary to stop this."

"What do you think he will do about me?" he asked.

"What do you think he should do?"

"It wasn't my idea," he said. "I just went along with them. I'm begging you to give me another chance. I swear to you that I can and will be loyal to the President. All I ask is that you allow me to stay on as Chairman of the Democratic National Committee and open the convention. Please don't humiliate me."

I sat there staring at the man. On the one hand, loyalty was something President Johnson always demanded from those around him. John Bailey had failed that test. On the other hand, the assassination of President Kennedy had happened just over six months ago and was still fresh in everyone's mind. It remained politically important for continuity to remain between the slain President and his successor who thus far had not won the office in his own right. I was sitting with the man who not only had been President Kennedy's choice for Party Chairman but who ran the Democratic Party in Connecticut with a famously iron fist.

"We will just have to see about that," was my noncommittal response as our meeting ended.

I wasted no time making things right. My first step was to dismiss all but six of the eighty people on Bailey's convention staff. I made a number of calls to Texas, other states, and Washington, asking known supporters of Lyndon Johnson to come to Atlantic City as volunteers to run the convention. I had no trouble finding enough people for the job—and they were far fewer than the number that had been dismissed.

Next, all the hotel and seating assignments were changed. I made certain that the state delegations that could be counted on to support the President had all the preferred hotels and seating on the floor of the convention. I also took personal control of the microphones, speakers, and (actually, of considerable importance at a convention) the band. Thus, all the proceedings at the convention would be under my influence and decision.

Finally, I completely changed the convention program. I neither canceled the Kennedy film nor the Robert Kennedy speech, which was to follow it. Instead, I scheduled both events at the end of the convention, to take place only after the President and Vice President had been nominated. Anyone who remembers watching that convention knows what happened during and after that film and speech. When Robert Kennedy appeared and delivered his address, the emotional reaction of the delegates was overwhelming. If that had happened at the beginning and not at the end of the convention, the Kennedy plan might have worked.

The fact that I had uncovered and thwarted Robert Kennedy's scheme to seek the presidency did not deter him from lobbying for an alternative plan to become Lyndon Johnson's running mate for Vice President. Whatever the President might have thought of this under other circumstances, there was no longer any doubt that Robert Kennedy now could never be accepted by him. However, public perceptions had to be considered and a rationale chosen that would effectively but peaceably deny the office to Kennedy.

The reason given—and, naturally, it fooled no one—was that President Johnson would not select any member of his cabinet because he did not want politics to interfere with their ability to govern the nation. Of course, Robert Kennedy was still Attorney General and, therefore, now he would be ineligible to be chosen as Vice President. Lyndon Johnson knew he could never be his own man if Robert Kennedy was Vice President.

Johnson's announcement eliminating cabinet members from vice-presidential consideration was made on July 28, 1964. The convention was to open on August 24. Amazingly, Robert Kennedy's ambitions remained alive. There was one final issue that, if it could be properly manipulated, might open an emotional door at the convention through which Kennedy might yet secure the Party's nomination for President. That issue was the Mississippi Freedom Democratic Party, known as the MFDP, which was seeking to be seated at the convention as the recognized delegates from Mississippi, displacing the delegates selected by Mississippi's regular (and totally segregated) Democratic Party.

Lyndon Johnson recognized the opportunity the MFDP problem created for Robert Kennedy, and he took steps to defuse the situation. All that Johnson wanted was a smooth, issue-free convention. All that Kennedy wanted was the opposite. Thus, Johnson believed that if a compromise could be reached that prevented the issue from reaching the floor of the convention, the emotional opportunity sought by Kennedy would be denied him.

Johnson did not know what that compromise should be, but he did know that whatever form it took, it had to satisfy several important constituencies. These included Joseph Rauh, the well-known liberal Washington lawyer and former New Dealer who represented the MFDP; Walter Reuther, the powerful President of the United Auto Workers and the recognized political voice of organized labor; and the many Governors, Senators, and Congressmen representing the established Democratic Party in the South. Johnson did not care about the regular Democratic Party in Mississippi. Their loss was an acceptable cost to him. He believed that in any event, they would end up supporting the Republicans. He believed that if the other elements of the Democratic Party could be satisfied, the Democrats from Mississippi would be isolated.

The convention's Credentials Committee would initially consider the issue. The committee consisted of two delegates from each state. Johnson's control of the committee came through its chairman and his good friend, Pennsylvania Governor David Lawrence, and its chief counsel, Tom Finney, the law partner of Johnson's longtime advisor (and future Secretary of Defense), Clark Clifford.

However, Johnson also wanted more immediate influence concerning resolution of the MFDP problem. He began searching for a few people who could be trusted to effectively work toward the compromise he sought. He selected Price Daniel, the former Texas Governor, as one of his agents. He telephoned his friend Iowa Governor Harold Hughes and asked Hughes to recommend one other person. Hughes suggested that Johnson use Hughes's campaign manager, Sherwin Markman, and Johnson accepted him. Finally, Johnson called Senator Hubert Humphrey and asked the Minnesota Senator to give him his best man. In talking to Humphrey, who was making no secret that he wanted to be named as Johnson's running mate, Johnson stated that one way for Humphrey to prove his mettle was to make sure that he and his man successfully contributed to a solution of the problem. Humphrey suggested Walter Mondale, then Minnesota's Attorney General (who later replaced Humphrey in the Senate and ultimately became Jimmy Carter's Vice President, after which he unsuccessfully ran for President against Ronald Reagan).

President Johnson, who used his chief assistant, Walter Jenkins, as his conduit in speaking to these men, made it clear to each of them that he did not care how the problem was resolved. His only objective was to solve it by reaching whatever compromise would avoid a convention floor fight that created an opportunity for Robert Kennedy. Practically speaking, that meant coming up with a plan that would satisfy Joe Rauh, Walter Reuther, and the Party's Southern establishment.

The Credentials Committee convened in Atlantic City a few days before the convention opened. The only significant issue before it was what to do about the demands of the MFDP, a problem that was highly charged and very public. The topic dominated press coverage of the convention. As the media put it (possibly inspired by the Kennedys), President Johnson's ability as a leader and his skill in building consensus was now being severely tested and would be judged by how, if at all, he managed to block a major revolt from erupting at the convention.

In the week before the convention opened, thousands of protestors descended on Atlantic City. They were mostly young, angry, and determined to force the convention to seat the MFDP. Their emotions were fueled by the fact that just weeks before, three young whites from New York were murdered in Mississippi while attempting to register black voters. The seating of the MFDP delegates was the visible symbol of their anger. Like protestors before and since, any method—legal or illegal—was considered proper.

They had even managed to distribute counterfeit tickets permitting their entry into the convention where they were planning to invade and overwhelm its sessions unless their demands were met. As the opening of the convention approached, their number rapidly grew.

In the meantime, the struggle to find an acceptable compromise continued. Many private meetings were held, but no progress was made. A few days before the convention opened, there would a public hearing, nationally televised, where the MFDP leaders would testify. They presented two witnesses: Fanny Lou Hamer, a soon-to-be-famous black activist, and Dr. Aaron Henry, a black dentist who later also achieved great acclaim. Before their appearance before the committee, Tom Finney (who was counsel to the Credentials Committee) asked Markman, who was an experienced trial lawyer, to conduct the cross-examination of Mrs. Hamer and Dr. Henry on behalf of the committee. Finney's instructions to Markman were explicit: under no circumstances become aggressive. If you antagonize them, you will lose the national audience. You must be sympathetic with them. Your only objective is to get them to agree to principles we might use later to somehow forge a compromise.

Markman did as he was told. He made no attempt to limit their testimony. They expressed their arguments as fully as they wished. The only point that Markman pursued with them—and he was dogged but not assertive about it—was obtaining their agreement that the problem they so eloquently expressed was not merely a problem for Mississippi, but one that must be dealt with by the entire nation. It took some time, but both witnesses finally, although reluctantly, agreed with Markman's premise. In the end, it was precisely this point that ultimately formed the core of the compromise reached.

Getting that agreement was not easy. The full Credentials Committee was too unwieldy to negotiate. Instead, a subcommittee of five was appointed to deal with the problem and come up with a solution. Walter Mondale was named chairman. The other members were Price Daniel and Markman, both agents of the President, Irving Kaler, a delegate from Georgia, and Charles Diggs, a black congressman from Detroit.

At the first meeting of the subcommittee, Markman argued that any compromise should make maximum use of the testimony of Mrs. Hamer and Dr. Henry.

"How can that be done?" he was asked.

"They have agreed that the problem of their exclusion from the convention is not merely a Mississippi issue," Markman answered. "They have testified that it should be a matter of concern for the entire nation."

"And therefore?"

"Therefore, I suggest that we recommend that the convention create a number of extra delegates at large and then give those seats to representatives of the MFDP," Markman continued. "If the problem is nationwide, then all of the states should participate in making it right by creating room for them out of the entire flag and not just from Mississippi."

"How can the convention do that?"

"As I understand the law, the convention is free to make its own rules any way it sees fit," Markman said. "No court will interfere. If the convention wants to create delegates at large, it can do so."

No one on the subcommittee agreed with Markman that first day. For the time being, he was alone in his thinking.

There then ensued a series of protracted meetings between Mondale, representing the Credentials Subcommittee, and Rauh, Reuther, and Governors Connally and Sanders. Senator Humphrey, knowing his own political future was at stake, also joined the discussions. However, the negotiations foundered and no agreement was in sight after several days of talking. Mondale kept his subcommittee in almost continuous session as everyone struggled to find a way out of the dispute. Finally, the convention opened and one of the first scheduled events was to be the Credentials Committee report regarding who should be seated. But no such report was yet ready. Desperately, Mondale called one last meeting of his subcommittee. This time, he reintroduced Markman's original suggestion, and this time it was accepted by the other four members.

Armed with this authority, Mondale again sat down with Rauh, Reuther, Connally, and Sanders. To his surprise, they accepted the compromise and agreed to a plan that would seat two delegates from the MFDP as delegates at large at the convention. As for the regular delegation from Mississippi, they would only be seated if they agreed to take a loyalty oath to support the Party's nominee.

With this agreement in hand, Mondale and his subcommittee wasted no time reporting to Governor Lawrence, who immediately convened the entire

Credentials Committee. A motion was made to accept the compromise and forthwith recommend it to the convention. It was then that Joe Rauh lost his nerve. From the moment the compromise became public, Rauh's client (the MFDP) and its supporters were in an uproar. They believed that he had betrayed them and they were loudly demanding his resignation. Rauh, who was sitting with the Credentials Committee, felt he had no choice but to ask for a recess so that he could either persuade his client or renege on his agreement to the compromise.

Governor Lawrence and Mondale were initially inclined to grant the recess Rauh demanded. However, Markman knew that any such recess would probably doom the compromise. He forcefully objected to any recess. In doing so, Markman believed he was carrying out the wishes of the President as relayed to him through Walter Jenkins. The argument about Rauh's request for a recess was short but bitter. In the end, Lawrence and Mondale—and the rest of the committee—were convinced by Markman, and the recess was denied. The compromise was quickly approved and immediately delivered to the convention's chairman, Rhode Island Senator John Pastore. Governor Lawrence moved its adoption, Senator Pastore called for a voice vote, and despite a chorus of no's, declared that the report was adopted. It all happened so quickly that a floor fight failed to develop. Thus, the issue was resolved. As it turned out, only three members of the regular Mississippi delegation were seated because, as expected, the rest of them refused to take the required loyalty oath.

I should add that I learned of the forged convention credentials in the hands of supporters of the MFPD in sufficient time to thwart their plan to pack and disrupt the convention.

So ended Robert Kennedy's multifaceted struggle to become part of the 1964 Democratic Party national ticket. On August 25, the second day of the convention, he took his only remaining political option and announced his candidacy for Senator from New York. On August 26, Lyndon Johnson was nominated by acclamation, and he in turn chose Hubert Humphrey as his running mate for Vice President. On August 27, the day before his fifty-sixth birthday, Lyndon Johnson stood before the convention and proudly accepted his party's nomination for President. It had not been easy, but in the end, the 1964 Democratic National Convention ran as smoothly and successfully as President Johnson had wanted.

CAMPAIGNING FOR PRESIDENT

The convention ended the last week of August 1964, but for me, there would be no rest. Almost immediately, Lyndon Johnson asked me to be the coordinator of his campaign for President. To make matters even more difficult for me, earlier at the Democratic State Convention, Governor Connally asked me to serve as Chairman of the Texas Democratic Party Executive Committee. When I reminded President Johnson of my Texas responsibilities to organize his campaign, his response was, "All right, you take two weeks to go organize Texas. Then you come back and organize my campaign travels. If you can do both jobs, fine. If not, just remember that your President has to come first."

In the end—mostly because in those days I possessed a great deal of energy—I managed both responsibilities reasonably well.

I soon discovered that a campaign on behalf of a sitting President was far different—and in many ways far easier—than when your candidate is an outsider trying to get in. In our 1960 campaign for Vice President, we had to organize everything for ourselves, and of course we had to constantly adjust to the needs and suggestions of the presidential candidate. Now we had amazing resources available, none of which we had before—and none of which were available to our opponent, Arizona Senator Barry Goldwater.

These resources included Air Force One, the beautiful blue-and-white jet in which the president flew and that served as an indelible symbol of the power of the United States. Although the Democratic Party had to bear its expenses on all political trips, it was well worth the price. The airplane not only provided transportation, but by itself attracted crowds wherever we landed. It also contained unmatchable tools for communication and information. In that regard, the President's ability to reach out to anyone anywhere was provided by the White House Communications Agency (WHCA), a military detachment specifically assigned to serve the President. Finally, there was the Secret Service, which not only protected the President's security, but saw to it that his transportation on the ground was always available and safe. And of course it was now Lyndon Johnson who was running for President and Hubert Humphrey who responded to us.

For the greater part of the campaign, I traveled with the President as he crisscrossed the nation. When he wasn't traveling, he invited me to stay at the White House. My responsibilities did not differ all that much from what they were in 1960. The President's campaign was now directed in close consultation with the President, Walter Jenkins, and the campaign reelection committee.

Despite the presidential perquisites, it remained my responsibility to make certain that everything went right wherever Johnson stopped. For that, the advance men were essential. This time around, however, there was a cadre of experienced people, and because it was the campaign of a sitting President, I always had more than enough volunteers. In the end, President Johnson told me that he was pleased with the campaign.

It was a happy campaign. President Johnson was the beneficiary of an immense outpouring of public sympathy because of John Kennedy's assassination. However, he had also earned great respect because of the way he had assumed the presidency, calmed and reassured the nation, retained the slain President's Cabinet, and worked tirelessly to promote and ultimately enact into law so much of the previously stalled Kennedy legislative agenda. Wherever he went, large and enthusiastically supportive crowds greeted him.

The Johnson campaign was helped enormously by the perceived nature of his Republican opponent, Barry Goldwater. It was not that Senator Goldwater was a bad man, or even a dangerous man. In fact, he was a longtime personal friend of Lyndon Johnson. Goldwater was unabashedly conservative, which was not necessarily a disadvantage. What destroyed him was that he expressed his conservatism in such a manner that outside of his hardcore Republican base, he sounded so radical that people were frightened.

It was a fact of presidential politics in 1964 that although the hard-core members of each political party selected the nominees, their respective votes were about evenly split during the general election, accounting for approximately 70 percent of the total vote. That left 30 percent of the vote to be contested. Whichever candidate won that battle would win the election. By and large, those voters were moderate and independent. Radical ideas and practices were generally counterproductive in any effort to persuade them. That meant that a hard swing to the left or right by the candidate was a road to disaster.

Doubts about Goldwater were first fed by his odd choice as his vice-presidential running mate. He ignored all the known Republican governors and senators. Instead, he chose an obscure congressman from upstate New

York, William E. Miller. Throughout the campaign, Congressman Miller was totally ignored not only by President Johnson but also by the far more familiar and trustworthy Hubert Humphrey.

Of far greater significance, in his acceptance speech at the Republican national convention, Senator Goldwater managed to forever brand himself as an extremist when he spoke the following words: "Extremism in the defense of liberty is no vice. . . . Moderation in the pursuit of justice is no virtue."

The national press proceeded to crucify Goldwater for those two sentences, continuously "reporting" that they "proved" that he was a dangerous man.

It was Lyndon Johnson's opinion that Barry Goldwater lost the presidency by mounting a campaign that never backed away from those devastating sentences, which his campaign continued to emphasize by constantly reiterating the phrase, "In your heart you know he's right." From that moment, Lyndon Johnson had his theme from which he never lost his focus: he was a President who was experienced; he had good judgment; and, above all else, he could be trusted. Goldwater, on the other hand, was mercurial, untested, and beyond all else, he was a man who could never be trusted with his finger on the nuclear trigger.

The most infamous expression of Johnson's principal campaign theme was a television commercial showing a small girl picking daisies. As she did so, she softly counted, "Ten . . . nine . . . eight . . ." down to "one," at which point her image dissolved into the dreaded mushroom cloud of a nuclear explosion. Simultaneously, President Johnson, in a voice-over, was heard to state: "These are the stakes—to make a world in which all of God's children can live, or go into the dark. We must love each other, or we must die."

This television advertisement was brought to the President by his aide Bill Moyers. Johnson—and all of the rest of us around him—were appalled by the commercial. Johnson summarily rejected it, stating it went too far and airing it would bring nothing but a storm of negative publicity.

Moyers later admitted, "The use of the television commercial to destroy Goldwater was one of my mistakes. . . . It was the product of immaturity. . . . Was it right? No, I don't think so. It wasn't right, and it wasn't necessary." In any event, someone slipped up, and the commercial did run, although only once. The President was incensed when he learned of it and ordered that it be immediately withdrawn. However, as he knew would happen, the damage was done and the White House was flooded with the protests he had predicted. That was considered by many to be a serious mistake in the campaign.

WALTER JENKINS

In mid-October, President Johnson traveled to New York at the specific request of Robert Kennedy. The polls showed that Johnson had a healthy lead over Goldwater. However, Kennedy was being portrayed as a "non–New Yorker" attempting to "carpetbag" his way by dislodging a popular incumbent, Senator Kenneth Keating. Keating in turn recognized the downward pressure on his campaign caused by the successful effort to radicalize Barry Goldwater. Keating publicly disassociated himself from Goldwater as well as Goldwater's running mate, New York's own upstate congressman, William Miller.

Johnson agreed to Kennedy's request, and he and Kennedy spent a long and successful day traveling the state together. I joined them and, surprisingly, I saw no tension between them. I especially noticed how well Lady Bird Johnson and Ethel Kennedy got along. Actually, these two strong women always remained friendly.

That day ended in New York City where President Johnson and Senator Goldwater were scheduled to appear together at the Al Smith Dinner, a traditional nonpartisan affair where, for that one evening, the contending candidates forgot the bitterness of their struggle and treated each other and the audience to a show of good spirits and humor.

We were in the Johnsons' suite in the Waldorf Towers. The President was dressing to go out when George Reedy came in and nervously said, "Mr. President, there is a terrible rumor circulating among the press corps."

"What is it?" Johnson demanded.

"They are saying that Walter Jenkins was caught in some compromising homosexual activity," Reedy stated. "I tried to reach Walter, but I can't find him anywhere."

The shock in the room was palpable. "That's impossible!" the President exclaimed.

Lady Bird Johnson paled and whispered, "It just can't be true. We've known Walter and his family for years. I don't believe it!"

And neither did Jack Valenti or Bill Moyers, who were also present. Nor did I. Walter Jenkins was my dear friend, a man I had liked and trusted for almost as long as I had known Lyndon Johnson. He had worked with the President since his days in Congress. No man was closer to President Johnson, and no man was more loyal. He was the most powerful member of Johnson's staff, and he and his wife and children were like family to the Johnsons. As far as I knew, Walter never made a mistake, never caused trouble, and—most important right now—had never been in trouble. All of us who knew him so well could hardly comprehend what George Reedy was telling us.

"All right," Johnson said, breaking the stunned silence. "I need Abe Fortas. Marvin, you talk to him and tell him to find out exactly what happened and call me back as soon as possible. Now, Lady Bird and I are going to make a courtesy call on Jackie Kennedy."

Fortas had been one of President Johnson's lawyers for years and a man in whom Johnson had the greatest confidence. However, when the President and Mrs. Johnson returned from their visit with Mrs. Kennedy, Fortas had not yet reported.

The Johnsons then went to the Al Smith Dinner while I waited in their suite. It was not until they came back that Fortas finally telephoned.

"I haven't been able to meet with Walter, but I did talk to him," Fortas said. "Apparently, a week ago last Wednesday night, Walter went to a *Newsweek* cocktail party. He says he doesn't remember anything after he left the party until he found himself in custody at the police station. The police claim that he was caught in the men's room at the YMCA down the street from the White House. They have been staking out that place for a long time because it's a well-known homosexual hangout. Now they have charged Walter with solicitation of homosexual acts."

"The police have leaked the story," Fortas continued. "I don't think we can stop it from being in the newspapers tomorrow morning."

"Just keep working on it," the President said. "We'll be back in the White House tomorrow."

"I don't think that you should sit on this, Mr. President," Fortas said. "You've got to do something right away."

"What do you suggest?" Johnson asked.

"You must get Walter's resignation immediately," Fortas said. "You can't let his problem rub off on you. The election is only three weeks off."

"I don't believe any of it," Mrs. Johnson said. "I'm simply heartbroken. Can't we wait? Do you think he was drugged or trapped or something like that? Isn't there a presumption of innocence?"

The President nodded his agreement with his wife's theory.

"Maybe somebody is trying get at you through Walter," she said to her husband.

"If he's innocent, you do not accept the resignation," Fortas said. "Right now, I strongly urge you to separate him from the White House. Please don't waste any time doing it."

The President pondered Fortas's advice for a long moment. Then, his always-expressive face showing his sadness, he said in a surprisingly soft voice. "I would not want to do that." There was another long pause before he added, "All right, Abe. You get his resignation tonight."

"Please tell him that I will find work for him," Mrs. Johnson said. "He's given his life to us and I refuse to just drop him."

"That should help," Fortas said.

The President turned to me. "Call Deke DeLoach at the FBI. Have him quietly get them into this. I want to know everything that happened."

Walter resigned that same night, October 14. Fortas arranged for him to be hospitalized while the investigation continued. The Johnsons—and I—continued to believe that somehow Walter had been drugged at the *Newsweek* party he attended before he went to the YMCA. I still think that this is a possible explanation, although it did not look good when it came out later that this was the second time Walter was arrested for the same kind of activity.

Until his death many years later, Walter always claimed to have no memory of what happened that night between the party and finding himself in police custody. As for the FBI investigation, it never produced any further facts concerning the tragic incident.

To my knowledge, Lyndon Johnson while he was President never spoke to Walter again. Mrs. Johnson, however, did assist Walter in his work in television cable franchises in various Texas communities. Of course, she could not—and would not—have done that without the full knowledge and con-currence of her husband.

The Jenkins tragedy led to one other result. As I remember, the President asked Deke DeLoach to have the FBI conduct a full field investigation of me—despite the fact that I had not yet agreed to come work at the White House. The reason was that I was working in close proximity to the President, and I was bound to become even closer without Walter Jenkins. I learned about the investigation almost immediately when I began getting calls from friends and neighbors in Daingerfield who were shocked that FBI agents had suddenly appeared in town asking questions about me. Many of these people soon contacted me, asking, "Are you in trouble?" "Have you done something wrong?" I tried to reassure everyone, explaining that it was just the way the government does things when someone is closely associated with the President.

Thereafter, each member of the White House staff and each Presidential appointee was subject to a full FBI investigation. In addition, anyone sched-uled to meet with the President was subjected to "name checks" by which the FBI computers would discover if they had been charged or convicted of any crime anywhere, or had problems with the Internal Revenue Service. Before this system was put into effect, no prior investigation was made of any member of the President's staff.

VICTORY

Exactly as he had done in 1960, President Johnson invited me to join him and his family at the Driscoll Hotel in Austin while he awaited the election returns. This time, however, there was no tension in the room. In 1960, none of us knew how the election would turn out. Now, we confidently awaited official confirmation of the victory we never doubted would be ours. Our belief was confirmed from the moment we received the first returns. From the beginning, it looked like it was going to be a landslide. And it was.

When the final vote was tallied, Lyndon Johnson had won with 61 per-cent of the popular vote, the largest margin of victory of any President in

American history. The President was overjoyed, of course, but he was also humbled. He was surprisingly subdued as he received the concession of Senator Goldwater and then was flooded with congratulations by friends and supporters from Texas, the nation, and the world.

The election results from New York were of particular interest to us. They showed that Robert Kennedy had been right in seeking the visible support of the President. In New York, Lyndon Johnson overwhelmed Senator Goldwater, winning with 69.7 percent of the vote. Senator Keating, Kennedy's opponent, received 860,000 votes more than Goldwater. Nevertheless, he was defeated by Kennedy. However, Kennedy's margin of victory was 720,000 votes, almost two million votes less than President Johnson's margin of 2.7 million votes. It was clear that President Johnson had helped Kennedy and it was Johnson's "coattails" that had been critical to Kennedy's election. Kennedy should have been endlessly grateful. However, as we were to soon learn, Kennedy's gratitude—if he ever had any—did not last long, and his struggle to topple Lyndon Johnson continued. From then on, however, Kennedy would have the status and platform of the U.S. Senate from which to launch his attacks.

But Robert Kennedy and his plans were far from Lyndon Johnson's thoughts during that marvelous night of triumph. Johnson was at last now President in his own right, the legitimacy of his presidency validated by the overwhelming voice of the American people. Beyond that, his landslide had carried with it large majorities in both houses of Congress. With these majorities would come a historic opportunity to realize his dream of a "Great Society" for the country that he loved.

I returned to Daingerfield after the election, exhausted but pleased to be home with my family. I had missed all of them while I had been away. It was high time that I showed my wife and three children, including my year-old son William, that they really did have a husband and father.

A few weeks later, as Thanksgiving approached, friends of mine in East Texas decided that they wanted to host an "appreciation" banquet for me. I tried to dissuade them, but they were determined to go forward with a dinner at the small Alps Hotel in the nearby town of Mount Pleasant. The afternoon of the dinner, I received a call from Jack Valenti, who was with the President at his ranch.

"Marvin," Jack began. "You are going to be greatly honored tonight."

"I know," I said. "Some friends of mine are giving me a dinner."

"That's what I'm calling about," Jack said. "The President is coming too."

"Tonight?" I said, amazed.

"It's all set up. He will see you there."

That evening, when Marion and I arrived at the Alps Hotel, we found that that without our knowledge, the dinner had been moved to the Mount Pleasant Armory. The people in charge had concluded—quite correctly as it turned out—that the appearance of the President would bring out a crowd far larger than the hotel dining room could accommodate. It would be the first time that a President had ever visited Mount Pleasant.

We rushed to the armory and arrived just before the President, who had flown in on the Governor's DC-3, the largest airplane that could land at Mount Pleasant's airport. The President, along with Mrs. Johnson, Texas Governor and Nellie Connally, Congressman Wright Patman, and many of my friends and neighbors filled the hall. For one of the few times in my life, I was so emotionally touched that I was almost speechless. It was a wondrous night for me and my family. The pinnacle was reached when the President rose and spoke these words:

"Marvin is as wise as my father,
as gentle as my mother,
as loyal and dedicated and as close
to my side as Lady Bird."

1965

FIRST DAY

Monday, February 1, 1965, was my first day on the White House payroll. My official title was Special Assistant to the President, although I functioned as the President's Chief of Staff.

I met with the President on the previous Sunday evening. We discussed salaries, not only for me but for the rest of his staff. The Congress had already provided that no one in the Executive Branch (except the President, who was then paid $100,000 plus a $50,000 expense account, and of course was furnished his housing; the Vice President, who was paid $43,000, had a $10,000 expense account, and was not yet provided a home; and $35,000 salaries to Cabinet officers) should receive a salary in excess of that paid to Members of Congress, which was then set at $30,000. That night, with the President's agreement, I established the rule that no one working at the White House should earn more than $28,500. That would be my salary as well.

Before President Franklin Roosevelt, there was no such thing as a "White House Staff." Anyone working for the President—and it was usually no more than a secretary and an assistant or two—was borrowed from other departments of the government. Near the beginning of World War II, President Roosevelt stated that he needed help, and Colonel (later General) "Pa" Watson (no relation) was assigned as his military aide. As his presidency continued, his staff increased to about nine persons. When President Truman assumed office, he insisted that if the Congress agrees that the President needs a staff, then that cost should be included in an appropriation for the White House operation. By the time Lyndon Johnson became President, Congress had authorized fourteen slots for his "Special Assistants," plus other members of the President's staff.

When I joined the President, he told me that he insisted that his staff must always be fewer in number than that of any of his predecessors, especially President Kennedy. I saw to it that we never exceeded that goal. It was not until Richard Nixon became President that the White House staff began expanding, and that expansion has continued under every succeeding President. This exponential growth is dramatically illustrated by comparing the number of staff members listed in "The 1968 Congressional Staff Directory" (CQ Press) with those listed in the 2003 edition of the same publication. Thus, in 1968 there were twenty-four persons named as "key personnel of the Executive Office of the President." Compare this with the same publication's 2003 listing of seventy-five individuals in the same category—a threefold increase.

Two weeks before I came on board, there were nine "Special Assistants" whose duties the President described as follows:

1. Lawrence O'Brien—congressional relations
2. McGeorge Bundy—national security affairs
3. George Reedy—press secretary
4. Bill Moyers—legislative program
5. Jack Valenti—appointments secretary
6. Horace Busby—cabinet secretary
7. Richard Goodwin—urban affairs and conservation
8. Douglass Cater—education and international affairs
9. Lee White—special counsel

The President said, "There is no order or rank among them. All report directly to me. . . ." He also stated that Bundy, Moyers, Valenti, Busby, Goodwin, and Cater "from time to time help prepare messages and statements." Their actual duties were much broader. In reality, the President expected each member of his staff to be a generalist, willing and able to undertake any task he asked of them. Most of all, he wanted "can-do" people.

The President's list of Special Assistants did not include all of his staff at that time. Omitted were such important assistants as Mike Manatos, who headed congressional relations with the Senate; Henry Hall Wilson, who headed congressional relations with the House; Major General C. V. Clifton, the Military Aide at the time; Rear Admiral George Burkley, the President's physician; and William Hopkins, the Executive Clerk in charge of White House operations.

Long before it became fashionable to do so, the President was conscious of the fact that more women were needed in government. Thus, at the first annual presentation of the Eleanor Roosevelt Awards in March 1964, where he announced the appointment of ten women to high posts in the government, he stated, "I'm insisting that women play a larger role in this government's plans and progress." On his own staff, he appointed Esther Peterson, who had helped lead President Kennedy's Commission on the Status of Women, as Special Assistant for Consumer Affairs. When Ms. Peterson resigned, she was replaced in that position by Betty Furness, whom President Johnson described as "a plucky lady" who became "the symbol of consumer protection."

In addition, of course, there were the two chief assistants to Mrs. Johnson: Elizabeth Carpenter, her Press Secretary, and Bess Abell, her Social Secretary. Finally, Kenneth O'Donnell, who had been President Kennedy's Chief of Staff, remained on the White House payroll for almost another year despite my urgings that the President should seek his resignation because O'Donnell had no duties and did not work for President Johnson. Because of the situation's obvious sensitivity, the President never questioned O'Donnell's actions. Much later, on his own volition, O'Donnell finally quit.

This was the President's senior staff on February 1, 1965, the day I began my service. By the time I left the White House to become Postmaster General in April 1968, only Douglass Cater was still there. The rest had departed, most voluntarily, a subject I will deal with later.

As I briefly sat at my desk on my first morning, separated from the Oval Office by only one door, I began to realize the full extent of the job the President had given me and the various responsibilities that were now mine.

My first duty early that morning was to meet with the President in his bedroom. Thus, I wasted no time before quickly walking from the West Wing to the Mansion. The Secret Service agents on duty knew me from my previous visits to the White House and apparently had been briefed to expect me. In any event, I was not stopped as I took the elevator to the second floor of the Mansion. The President's bedroom door was slightly ajar. I knocked and entered. The President was sitting on the edge of the large, covered four-poster bed he shared with his wife, who was with him.

The President's bedroom was comfortable. It was not as large as Mrs. Johnson's adjoining private rooms, but it was big enough to accommodate his sizable bed as well as three television sets that he used to simultaneously monitor each of the networks. It also had a sitting area next to a working fireplace. There were two telephones in the room, one on a hook next to the President's side of the bed, and the other next to the fireplace—a telephone with which I become intimately familiar as I carried out his directions in the ensuing years. The bedroom windows, covered by bulletproof glass, provided a breathtaking view of the south lawn of the White House and just beyond, the Washington Monument. However, this morning—as was usually the case—the windows were covered by heavy drapes.

The President greeted me, thanking me for at last coming to work for him full time. Then, once again, he spelled out some of the responsibilities he intended that I undertake. As we had previously agreed, he acknowledged that I would function as his "Chief of Staff"; that I would have unfettered access to him and to any meetings he had with others; and that he would listen to my views or recommendations on any personnel or subject. He then proceeded to list some of the detailed authority he wanted me to have.

I listened carefully, all the while taking notes, as the President—who obviously had given careful thought to what he was telling me—listed what he described as "part but not all of my job description," which my notes summarize as follows:

1. Presidential appointments:
   a. Handling all hour-to-hour appointments;
   b. Joint (with the President) handling of future appointments;
   c. Handling teleprompter, necessary backup, briefing papers, etc., for all appointments; and
   d. Handling actual physical setup when a ceremony is involved—recording, security, advancing (when necessary).
2. Nominations/appointments to be made by President:
   a. Weekly meeting for review of possible nominations;

     b. Interviewing prospective nominees; and

     c. Coordinating placement on honorary appointments and advisory boards.

3. Federal-state relations.

4. Coordinating activities with Democratic National Committee (involves continuing contact with nationwide mailing list via letters, etc.).

5. White House security:

     a. Personnel—including review of all FBI reports and actions resulting therefrom;

     b. Authorizing all passes—temporary and permanent, White House and Executive Office Building (EOB); and

     c. Access to all FBI files and CIA cables.

6. Directing WHCA (White House Communications) activities.

7. Personnel:

     a. Reviewing all requests for personnel; and

     b. Security matters.

8. Congressional contacts.

9. Physical office locations:

     a. Allocating space in both White House and EOB; and

     b. Reviewing all proposed construction and furnishings.

10. Congressional Record (editorial inserts—selection of, writing leads for).

11. Liaison with White House Social Office.

12. Handling travel requests.

13. Daily mail:

     a. Presidential appointments;

     b. Presidential political matters; and

     c. Miscellaneous.

By the time the President finished his litany of my duties, Mrs. Johnson had excused herself and left the room.

I returned to my office. After lunch, the President walked in and said, "Let's take a walk."

With me following him, we entered the West Wing lobby, which in those days functioned as the lounge for the ever-present press corps. As always, the lobby was filled with loudly chattering newspeople who, when they saw us, suddenly became silent. Without a word to anyone, the President, still closely followed by me, walked through the lobby and out the door that opens onto the north lawn and driveway of the White House.

The driveway is semicircular, running from the northwest to northeast gates into the White House grounds. The President, with me striding beside him, rapidly walked from gate to gate, then circled back. We did that a total of three times, always followed by the reporters who were kept at a discreet distance by the Secret Service. The President continued chatting with me about my duties. When we came past the north entrance of the Mansion for the third time, the President stopped and told me he was returning to his bedroom and I might as well go to my office and get to work.

As the President left me, I was immediately surrounded by reporters loudly shouting questions about what the President and I discussed during our unusual walk. I was totally unprepared for this attention, and the answer I gave was, "We discussed the weather." Despite their unbelieving laughter, I neither changed nor elaborated on my statement to them. Of course, that did not endear me to them.

Later, when the President came back to the West Wing, he asked me about what I had told the press about our conversation. When he heard my answer, he laughed, and said, "Marvin, you did exactly right. Whatever you and I talk about is nobody's business but ours. Never tell anyone. You are free to disagree and even argue with me about anything. But always in private. As far as the rest of the world is concerned, you and I will always be of one mind about everything." That is precisely how I handled our relationship during the years I worked for him.

He never did tell me the purpose of his walk around the White House grounds with me, but I have always believed that it was his way of announcing that not only was I now working for him, but that the two of us had a close and special relationship.

Still later that same day, it became clear that the President meant what he said about me controlling access to him, and why he had stationed me directly next to the Oval Office door. There were three other entrances to that office. One led directly onto the West Wing hallway. A second opened upon the Rose Garden. However, whenever the President was present, both of these doors were always guarded by the Secret Service who were ordered never to permit anyone through those doors unless specifically authorized by the President or me.

The third entrance was the problem. That door led into the office occupied by the President's several secretaries headed by the redoubtable Juanita Roberts. Juanita had worked for President Johnson since 1953 when he was a Senator. She had remained in the army reserve, earning the rank of colonel. Now, because he was Commander-in-Chief, she was assigned to serve under him—another example of how staffing the White House functioned. Juanita was fiercely protective of her authority. She never let the other secretaries forget that she was the President's primary secretary, and her desk adjoined the door to his office. She fought hard to retain alternative authority to authorize access of people and documents to the President. Ultimately—but only with the active assistance of the President—I weaned her away from her attempts to get around me, but it was a struggle from beginning to end. Despite these differences, I always liked Juanita. In time, we developed a warm and trusting relationship. However, she was never a proficient secretary in any normal sense. She did not take good shorthand. Yet the President never replaced her. She returned his loyalty with dogged protectiveness that never wavered.

I learned how strongly the President felt about my controlling access to him when later that day John McCone, the CIA Director, walked past my desk, stating that he had to see the President. Then, unannounced, he entered the Oval Office. I followed him in, thinking that McCone was an important person who obviously should be able to see the President whenever he wished. I was wrong. The President did not say anything, but his scowling glare at me unmistakably conveyed his displeasure.

A short while later, McGeorge Bundy came through my office and walked straight into the Oval Office. This time, when I followed Bundy inside, the President angrily told him, "Don't ever do that again. Never come in here without first asking Marvin. No one is to get in here without first going through Marvin." Bundy, a proud man, was obviously unhappy with this new procedure, but he accepted it. From then on, that was the way it worked with everyone.

I learned one further lesson during my first week in the White House.

One of my first meetings in my office was with a lawyer from Texas who had been a big supporter of Lyndon Johnson. The lawyer had called me and insisted that I meet with him in the White House.

"What can I do for you?" I asked when he arrived.

"I am representing Jimmy Hoffa of the Teamsters Union," he said.

I was taken aback because I knew that Hoffa was then serving time in a federal prison. "There is nothing I can do for him," I said.

"I think that you can," the lawyer said. "His health is deteriorating and you can see to it that he is moved to a warmer climate."

"I can't do that," I said.

The lawyer was not deterred. "If you grant Mr. Hoffa's request, we will see to it that the entire debt of the Democratic National Committee is paid off."

"No," I said, as firmly as I could. "This is between you and the Justice Department, and I think that you should leave now."

The next morning, I told the President about this meeting. "You did exactly right," he told me, then added, "Don't you ever again meet with anyone like him unless you want to see it repeated on the front page of the *New York Times*."

And I never did.

OUR RELATIONSHIP

I quickly discovered that my relationship with the President and Mrs. Johnson did not change just because I was now on his staff. In every way, the Johnsons continued to treat me and my family with care and kindness. This was very evident by the efforts of Mrs. Johnson to ease Marion's entry into Washington life. It was not so difficult for me because I was kept busy all the time. I first went to work at the White House on a Monday morning. On the next three evenings, Marion was asked by Mrs. Johnson to help host the congressional wives while their husbands attended White House briefings.

We were invited to join the Johnsons for weekends at Camp David. The first time we were asked to spend a weekend there, I tried to decline, telling the President that we needed to stay with our daughter, Kimberly, and that our one-year old-son, William, would require a baby bed, which I was certain was not standard equipment at the presidential retreat.

" 'Don't fret about that," the President said. "Just bring them with you to the helicopter pad at the Pentagon. Lady Bird and I want all of you here with us."

As always, I did not argue, and at the appointed time the four of us appeared at the special helicopter landing area next to the Pentagon, and, I understand, the exact place where the terrorist-hijacked jet flew into the building and murdered so many good people on September 11, 2001. But on this Friday evening, the Pentagon was peaceful, and the presidential helicopter was waiting for us when we arrived.

As soon as we entered the main lodge at Camp David, William's eyes widened as he saw the bright red presidential hot line telephone. Before anyone could stop him, William grabbed the receiver and held it next to his ear. The President jumped up and yanked it away from William, while Marion and I quickly pulled him away. William was a hyperactive young boy and he squirmed out of our grip and ran back to the telephone, once more trying to talk into it. This time, the President wrapped his arms around William and picked him up. William, however, was having none of that. Somehow he managed to free himself from the President's grasp and, undeterred, had the telephone once more before anyone could stop him.

Finally, Marion and I managed to get William under our control while profusely apologizing to the President, but he did not show any anger, although I suspect he was unhappy with our younger son. Nonetheless, we (including William) were invited back to Camp David several times over the course of the following years.

Often we were not the only guests at Camp David. Joining us one weekend were Reverend Billy Graham and the author John Steinbeck and his wife. Reverend Graham is a polite and unfailingly outgoing and friendly man, and the President's favorite preacher—as he eventually was for us. Steinbeck, on the other hand, was a hard-talking, profane man who was as interesting as he was rough. Yet to our surprise, Billy Graham and John Steinbeck got along very well despite all their surface differences, and the Johnsons (and us) all enjoyed their lively company.

From time to time, we were also invited to join the Johnsons at their ranch in the Texas hill country west of Austin. There we stayed in their guesthouse. Both at the ranch and at Camp David, we were always treated like family.

Our weekends with the Johnsons were by no means all work. The President enjoyed swimming and bowling, and at the ranch he liked to drive himself around inspecting everything in sight. He always loved to hunt and would often take me with him. He was a surprisingly good marksman. Once during hunting season, while he was driving along a country road on his ranch, he spotted a deer several hundred yards away on the other side of a small stream. He picked up his rifle and his single bullet struck the animal, killing it cleanly by a shot through the neck. He drove across the bridge and the deer was loaded onto his car. Back at the house it was cleaned, butchered, and later eaten.

President Johnson loved to talk, especially about politics and politicians. He was a superb mimic and storyteller—perhaps the best since President Lincoln. Here are two examples:

This is a story he told to illustrate that he could laugh at himself: "When I had a generous introduction such as I have just received, I often said that I just wished two more people could be at the meeting, my mother and my father, because my father would have enjoyed it and my mother would have believed it."

This story was a sly dig at compromise: "He reminds me of many great men I have known, particularly the schoolteacher that came out to apply for a job during the Depression in my little town of Johnson City. The School Board was divided on whether the world was round or flat, and they asked him how he taught it. The poor fellow needed a job so much, he said, 'I can teach it either way.' "

The President never censored his remarks to me, and I was privileged to hear his frank views on whatever or whoever was on his mind. I was always equally forthright with him.

He knew I had what he described as "a passion for anonymity." Unlike so many others who surrounded him, I neither sought nor wanted publicity of any kind. Ultimately, my aversion to the press caused them to label me as "the mystery man of the White House." Unfortunately that led to a great deal of negative press stories about me, most of them untrue. I discovered that once a story has been written, that belief takes hold among a few reporters, and most of the rest merely follow along.

Periodically, the President asked me to meet with a reporter or columnist in order to stanch the flow of critical stories about me. I would do as he asked, and it usually resulted in a favorable article. However, that never lasted because at heart, the President did not want me to deal with the press. His true preference was that I avoid the press because he did not want me to talk to anyone about my work for him.

The President and Mrs. Johnson did visit us at our home in the Virginia suburbs of Washington. Sometimes their visits came with only a few minutes' advance notice. A typical instance occurred one Sunday afternoon after Marion and I returned from church. As I walked in the door, my White House telephone was ringing with the unique nonstop sound that indicated that the President was calling. When I picked up the receiver, he said, "Marvin, Bird and I are in the car. We're not too far away from your house and we've decided we'd like to share some of your Baptist lemonade."

Marion blanched when I told her we only had a few minutes to prepare for our honored but newly expected guests. Somehow we managed to straighten up the house, make the lemonade, and be ready to enjoy a lively afternoon entertaining the Johnsons.

When Lyndon Johnson became President, he invited all of President Kennedy's staff to stay on and help him. His offer was not well received, and within months most of the Kennedy staff departed. There were some exceptions: Lee White remained as Special Assistant; Pierre Salinger stayed on as press secretary until he quit to briefly become a candidate for the U.S. Senate; Mike Feldman continued as Deputy Counsel for a short while; for a time, Richard Goodwin kept on writing speeches; and McGeorge Bundy did not change his job as the President's National Security Advisor.

Larry O'Brien was the most conspicuous exception to the departing top staff of President Kennedy. O'Brien had been John Kennedy's campaign manger and then served in the White House as his chief liaison with the Congress. O'Brien was superb at his job and had developed close rapport with the congressional leadership as well as the membership in both Houses of Congress. In addition, O'Brien, working closely with the Democratic leadership in the Congress, could accurately count votes, a skill greatly admired by a President who considered that ability both essential and rare.

Although the President valued O'Brien's skills with the Congress, he always had some misgivings about his loyalty. Nonetheless, O'Brien stayed on with Johnson despite strong urgings from fellow former members of President Kennedy's staff. In time, their pressure on him to quit escalated to the point where, as he often told the President and me, they excoriated him as a traitor to the Kennedy legacy. O'Brien was deeply hurt by these attacks, but he never changed his opinion that he had a higher duty to serve the new President for as long as he was wanted and needed.

Shortly after I joined the President's staff, the President selected Larry O'Brien to be Postmaster General. Even so—and marking how much the President valued his lobbying skills—he did not relieve O'Brien from his responsibilities of assisting the White House congressional liaison staff. O'Brien remained in President Johnson's cabinet until March 31, 1968, when the President announced that he would not run for reelection. O'Brien then accepted Robert Kennedy's offer to become his campaign manager during his run for the presidency. Apparently, O'Brien had never lost his allegiance to the Kennedys, and they in turn forgave him for his years with President Johnson.

Johnson's efforts to retain President Kennedy's staff were matched by a similar desire to keep the members of his cabinet. In this regard, Johnson was somewhat more successful. It was my opinion—which I often expressed to the President—that he would be better served if his cabinet, like his staff, consisted of his own people. Johnson did not agree, and in many cases he was proved right. It certainly seemed that was true with Secretary of State Dean Rusk, Secretary of Defense Robert McNamara, and Secretary of Agriculture Orville Freeman. At the other extreme, there was Attorney General Robert Kennedy and Secretary of Interior Stewart Udall. Between these degrees of loyalty to Johnson were men with divided allegiance, such as Nicholas Katzenbach, Robert Kennedy's successor as Attorney General, and Labor Secretary Willard Wirtz.

Only four members of President Kennedy's cabinet remained with President Johnson until the end of his term: Dean Rusk, Stewart Udall, Willard Wirtz, and Orville Freeman. Ultimately, through attrition—not firings— President Johnson was able to appoint the remainder of the cabinet. All of them were persons of substance and considerable prior achievement. These included: Henry Fowler and then Joseph Barr replacing Douglas Dillon at Treasury; Larry O'Brien and then me replacing John Gronouski as Postmaster General; John Connor, Alexander Trowbridge, and C. R. Smith replacing Luther Hodges at Commerce; John Gardner and Wilbur Cohen replacing Anthony Celebrezze at Health, Education, and Welfare; Ramsey Clark replacing Katzenbach and Kennedy as Attorney General; and Clark Clifford replacing McNamara at Defense. In addition, two new departments were created during Lyndon Johnson's presidency: Housing and Urban Development, where Robert Weaver was Secretary until the final month of the Johnson administration, when he was replaced by Robert Wood; and Transportation, where Alan Boyd remained Secretary until January 20, 1969.

In my opinion, the White House staff that served President Johnson had no equal—before or since. I have identified many of them at various places in this book. And, of course, their wives and husbands, who not only paid the price of lost time with their spouses, but so often were also called upon to assist the President. Those—and all the others—should know how much the President valued their talents and devotion to our country and to him.

I have attached a photograph of the President with those on his staff who remained with him until January 20, 1969, the final day of his presidency. These are: Joseph Califano, Special Assistant for Domestic Affairs; Walter Rostow, National Security Advisor; Mike Manatos, Senate Liaison; Jim Jones, my assistant, who later assumed my duties as Appointments Secretary; Ernest Goldstein, Special Assistant; John Roche, who replaced Goldstein as Special Assistant; Barefoot Sanders, Special Assistant for Congressional Relations; Larry Temple, Special Assistant; De Vier Pierson, Deputy Special Counsel; Charles Murphy, Counselor to the President; Robert Hardesty, speech writer; Tom Johnson, Assistant Press Secretary; Harry Middleton, speech writer; Harry McPherson, Special Counsel; Larry Levinson, Assistant to Joe Califano; and William Hopkins, who was ultimately appointed as a Special Assistant (a title he did not want because it resulted in his loss of civil service protection when President Nixon took office).

I particularly want to mention Jim Jones who came on board as my principal assistant during my first week at the White House. Mrs. Johnson's Press Secretary, Liz Carpenter, had written me about a young army lieutenant who had assisted them on Mrs. Johnson's train trip during the 1964 campaign. I desperately needed help in my new job and I asked him to come in for an interview. I was so impressed that almost immediately I arranged to have the army transfer him to serve his Commander in Chief—and me—in the White House. I could not have made a better choice, and the years he spent working with me—and later assuming many of my duties when I became Postmaster General—were extraordinarily valuable to all of us.

There were, of course, many reasons why various members of the White House staff departed before that final day in office. Some were worn out or had other problems. Some left for better jobs or for financial reason. Some came with me when I became Postmaster General. A very few were asked to resign for various causes, which I will discuss later.

LONG DAYS AND NIGHTS

My early morning arrival on my first day working at the White House proved to be no aberration. It was the start of a never-ending schedule that saw my working day begin before seven each morning and not end before midnight, particularly on Mondays through Fridays. This was especially difficult on me because I have never been an early morning person. Nonetheless, my duties required me to adjust. It was painful, but I managed to do it for more than three years.

Saturdays often saw my working day end by midafternoon, although mornings remained very busy. I struggled to remain free for church and family on Sundays, but my efforts often failed. The President expected me at his side, even on weekends and when he traveled. Although he truly intended that I should relax with him; I nonetheless felt that I was always on duty—which, of course, was true.

My working days always began in the President's bedroom. A White House car would deliver me from my home to the West Wing of the White House. I would briefly stop at my desk where I would quickly examine the written material sent to the President that had accumulated through the previous night. These included FBI and CIA intelligence reports, and the *Congressional Record* (because he believed that what happened on Capitol Hill was as important as events anywhere in the world). Most of these documents had been previously delivered to someone I had designated to read and attach a one-page summary to each one. For a long time, that job was performed for me by Sherwin Markman, who was required to have the overnight reports and his summaries ready for me when I arrived in the morning. Unfortunately for him, he was required to begin work even earlier than I did, an unhappy task he gamely if not enthusiastically undertook. I would add those documents to whatever I had carried home the previous night and had summarized for the President. To the extent that I believed the President should see any of this material, I tucked it under my arm and carried it with me to his bedroom in the Mansion.

One of the continuing problems for President Johnson—as indeed must be the case for any conscientious President—is fitting the amount of material he is required to read into the amount of time he has to read it. Literally hundreds of people have legitimate access to the President. Most of them are committed, knowledgeable, and articulate. They have much to say to the President in the way of reports, suggestions, and opinions. They always believe that what they write is important and should be seen by the President. What they often do not recognize is that in the vastness of the President's responsibilities, their own memos are multiplied by the hundreds of other papers with just as much claim to his attention. The resulting mass of data, if not controlled, would soon overwhelm the President. President Johnson would read as much as possible between his heavy schedule of daytime meetings, and then there would be delivered to him back in the Mansion at night a foot-high stack of paper that he would read until well past midnight. His night reading was carefully numbered so that it could be instantly identified and recovered. There was never enough time for him to study more than a small percentage of what those around him wanted him to read.

Thus it was imperative that I do two things for him. First, I had to make a judgment on which documents he should see and which could be routed to others for action. Second, as I have stated, I had to read—or have read—the documents that I believed should be sent to him, and prepare and append a one-page summary of each of those documents. As for the first requirement, I was always sensitive to the fact that I must not make a mistake and send to others what he himself should see. As for the second, I always attached the full document to the summary so that the President, if he chose, could read the underlying memorandum. Still, the responsibility of getting the summary right was vital because he did not have time to go through each full document.

I arrived at his bedroom door on the second floor of the Mansion promptly at seven o'clock or earlier each morning. If his door was slightly ajar, I knew he was ready for me. If not, I waited. I never had to knock, nor was I ever kept waiting very long. As was true my first morning at work, Mrs. Johnson was normally still in bed with him. If she was sleeping—or trying to sleep—she had the bedcovers pulled over her head. Most often, she was sitting up next to the President, both of them reading. I believe that my presence neither deterred nor embarrassed her. He frequently would be finishing the stack of documents from the previous day. Often he would pass a document to her and ask her to read it and tell him what she thought.

Mrs. Johnson is an extraordinary woman and was a great helpmate to her husband. She was strong, vibrant, intelligent, articulate, politically savvy, and had a warm and caring heart. She was both knowledgeable and willing to state her frank opinions whenever she was asked, and sometimes when she was not, especially in the areas in which she had a particular interest, such as beautification, civil rights, conservation, and the President's programs to fight poverty. The President never discouraged her. He trusted her judgment.

Every morning when I arrived, I went through his "night reading" of the previous evening. Where a presidential decision was required, the document contained spaces at the bottom where he could check off "yes," "no," or "see me." Regarding those memos furnished him for his information and apparently not requiring any action by him, he would often talk to me about his views and request that I convey them to someone or ask the author to see him. If I had a different opinion on any subject, I was free to express myself— and I did. However, once he made a decision, I accepted and supported it.

The President never seemed to forget anything he had read or anyone he ever met. In going through his night reading, he often recalled not only a related memorandum he had read, even if it was days or weeks earlier, but he could cite the night reading number I had given to the previous document. I don't think he was ever wrong. However, because my memory, although reasonably good in those days, was nowhere as good as his, I took careful notes, because it was my duty to see to it that his directions were accurately delivered.

At times I did this by returning the memo to the sender with a note about what the President wanted. More often, I telephoned the person and orally passed on the President's remarks. This was especially true when the matter was extremely sensitive. It was the President's opinion—shared by me—that matters such as these should *not* be handled in written form. Sadly, that practice resulted in a stunted historical record, part of which I am attempting to fill through this book.

I also handed the President any new information that had come in through the night. We then worked our way through each of these in the same way.

Sometimes the President did not want any delay conveying his response. In those cases, either he or I would pick up one of his bedroom telephones, and (as the White House operators were famously and brilliantly capable of doing) quickly locate the person with whom he or I wanted to speak.

The entire process could consume as many as two hours each morning. When we finished, I returned to my office armed with all the paperwork and my notes. He expected me to see to it that his decisions were carried out precisely as he intended. I would immediately begin doing just that. The President, in turn, would shower and dress before arriving at the Oval Office sometime after ten o'clock. Of course, his arrival time was somewhat misleading to others who did not know that he had already been working for several hours.

I then continued my day at my desk adjoining the Oval Office. My "normal" working hours were spent carrying out his instructions through seemingly endless telephone calls and meetings. Almost always, the meetings were held in what was then called the "Fish Room" in the West Wing (which is now known as the "Roosevelt Room"), or in my office because the President wanted me to be instantly available to him and never out of touch. That meant that I did not leave the White House—and seldom left my desk—while the President was in the Oval Office. Usually my lunches were hurriedly eaten while I worked, although whenever possible I walked downstairs to the "White House Mess" in the West Wing basement where Filipino members of the U.S. Navy had since Harry Truman's presidency prepared and served delicious—and inexpensive—breakfasts and lunches for White House staffers. Sadly for me, because the President normally did not leave the Oval Office for lunch and his afternoon "nap" until after two o'clock—and he wanted me at my desk until then—all too often my opportunity of having my own lunch made me the last customer of the day.

His afternoon "nap" was another aspect of the President's day that led to some misconceptions regarding how much he worked. His habit, formed at the orders of his doctors following his 1955 heart attack, was to leave his office and return to the Mansion usually for a business lunch, after which he would go to his bedroom, undress, and don his pajamas. He was supposed to take a nap, but he almost never did. Instead, he spent several hours on the telephone persuading, cajoling, or simply gossiping with friends, acquaintances, and especially Senators and Congressmen, all because his restless mind would not let him relax during the day. Nonetheless, by the time he returned to the Oval Office around four or five o'clock he would be reinvigorated.

Unless there was a White House social affair that required his presence (which meant he had to leave his office by eight o'clock), his day did not usually end until nine or ten or eleven at night. Unfortunately, that did not end my day. He often asked me to return to the Mansion with him, sometimes to have dinner or supper with him. He would talk about the day just past and what lay ahead. When he retired to his bedroom—and I departed—he still had work to do, his "night reading." Thus, before he went to sleep he spent the necessary hours studying those documents and making the dozens of decisions required of him.

By the time I left for home, whatever the time, I also had more work to do. I carried with me whatever reading material I received late in the day and had been unable to study. My last task, done at home, was to read all of it, decide what he should see in the morning, and prepare the summaries. Then, at last I was able to go to bed. Throughout those years, my long and exhausting days robbed me of time with my wife and children, and that was painful for all of us. Yet it never ceased being exhilarating because I believed I had been granted a unique opportunity to make a small contribution to the President and to my country.

I have attached as Appendix 1 my daily diary for January 17, 1968, a typical day for me in the White House. It provides a snapshot of a day filled with telephone calls and meetings as I served the President.

A word about my social life during my White House years. Actually, it was almost nonexistent despite the countless invitations Marion and I received to receptions and dinners, especially at foreign embassies. I seldom had the time to attend any of them. Moreover, the President did not like people on his staff to become too socially active. He was leery of these affairs because he believed that the drinking and relaxed atmosphere only enhanced the risk that his people would gossip and reveal confidential information, all of which was anathema to him. Nonetheless, I did attend one embassy affair, a dinner at the Kuwaiti Embassy. I did this because Marion had become friends with the Ambassador's wife, who invited us—and about forty other guests—to the dinner. As innocent as this affair was, a story appeared in the next morning's *Washington Post* implying that my attendance indicated that I favored the Arabs over the Israelis—a totally false charge. Other exceptions occurred when the President asked me to attend an affair, almost always because he wanted me to fulfill a social or political obligation that he believed was necessary or desirable, and I considered all of them work, not play.

WHITE HOUSE OPERATIONS

From the beginning, the President was sensitive not only to the amount of money spent on the White House budget, but to the number of people who served on his staff. In both cases, less was decidedly better. As I have stated, his direction to me was to see to it that his budget and his staff never exceeded those of President Kennedy. To achieve his goal, I was required to become a very tough manager, eliminating unnecessary expenses which often did not endear me to some in the White House. I reviewed newspaper and other subscriptions arriving at the White House. I discovered much unnecessary duplication, eliminated it, and saved the taxpayers thousands of dollars a year, enough to pay the salaries of the President and me.

One other action I took was a study of the telephone system used at the White House that appeared to be unnecessarily costly. My purpose was to investigate the efficacy of the entire structure, including its security, its technology, and the extent to which telephones were being underused and thus could be removed. The telephones I ordered removed as a result of the survey saved the White House approximately six thousand dollars a month. As a part of that task, I ordered the White House operators to count all incoming and outgoing calls. In doing that, they logged who was calling whom, and that caused considerable dismay among some people on the staff while also reaping the unintended benefit of increasing my ability to identify some of the people in the White House who were talking to the media.

When I first visited the quarters of the White House operators, I discovered they were using a plug-in switchboard that had not been changed since 1926. There were a half dozen operators on duty at any one time and they had to manually connect all incoming and outgoing calls. One of the operators was exclusively assigned to the President's telephones, and another was a backup for the President and Mrs. Johnson. The remaining operators served the White House staff.

Not only was the system antiquated, it was also totally insecure. I was told that anyone within line of sight to the White House could, with the appropriate equipment, monitor any telephone calls to or from the White House or the Executive Office Building. All one had to do was look at the nearby Soviet Embassy and note how its roof bristled with listening devices to realize the immediacy of the risk. I asked if there was any defense available and was told that if all our trunk and office telephone lines were encased in lead, then they would be secure.

I immediately arranged: (1) that the entire telephone system be replaced with the most modern equipment available and (2) that all our telephone lines be encased with lead. I also ordered that the small presidential office adjoining the Oval Office be enclosed in lead, thus making the President's most intimate conversations immune from eavesdroppers. At approximately the same time, we also decided to make one of our embassies equally secure by constructing a lead-enclosed room within it. That was done at our embassy in Poland, and was the reason why that embassy was eventually used for the beginning peace negotiations regarding Vietnam.

Washington being what it is, a dark motive of attempted censorship was ascribed to me by disgruntled members of the President's staff who leaked the story to the White House press corps. The noted humorist Art Buchwald devoted an entire column to my actions where he "reported" that instead of telephones, I had engaged a Pony Express rider to facilitate communications between the East and West Wings of the White House; and that, because of my telephone logging operation, the White House was now referred to as "Stalag 1600."

Telephone usage was only a minor part of my quest to cut down unnecessary White House expenses. Another subject I tackled was abuse of the privilege of using White House cars. Those cars, all of which were driven by members of the military on assignment from the Pentagon, were supposedly limited to essential White House business. I requested the drivers to send me logs concerning each trip. I discovered, for example, that the cars were being used by a few wives to go to hairdressers and to shop. In addition, there were instances when a staffer, although having a legitimate need for using the car to attend a meeting, often would have the car and driver wait—sometimes for hours—until the staffer was ready to return to the White House. I considered that an expensive and unnecessary waste. I put an end to these practices and, at the same time, severely limited the number of people entitled to unrestricted access to these vehicles. None of this endeared me to the offenders, but the one person I served was happy.

I also took a close look at the number of persons working in each White House office. Not surprisingly, I discovered that the White House was not immune to the bureaucratic practice of "empire building," that is, a constantly expanding demand for more secretaries and assistants. All personnel requests had to be approved by me. I always took a hard look at each of them and had no hesitancy in rejecting anyone, or at times even requiring them to downsize their operation. No one was immune. I did not hesitate to suggest that each should limit their spending of taxpayer dollars to a minimum.

There was one member of the staff who turned out to be immune to any insistence that he must limit the number of his assistants. That was Yoichi Okamoto, the official White House photographer. Oki, as he was affectionately known by all of us, was given unlimited access to every presidential appearance and meeting. His only requirement was not to cause any disruption, a rule that he never violated. He was a superb talent and, subsequent to his tragic suicide after we left the White House, his work has been shown in museum exhibitions in New York as well as at the Kennedy Center in Washington.

When I first questioned Oki regarding the size of his staff, he asked me to accompany him to a warehouse he operated in Georgetown. I already knew that he was on the CIA payroll, but I was surprised when he told me that unlike others at the White House who were merely "on loan" from other agencies but worked full time for us, Oki actually continued doing work for the CIA.

When we arrived at his warehouse, Oki led me inside a large nondescript building where a half dozen men were hard at work at what I recognized as highly sophisticated photographic equipment. I had some knowledge of photo processing from a temporary assignment I had with the Marines at the end of World War II. What I saw in Oki's Georgetown quarters was far more advanced than anything I had ever known—and far greater than what Oki would ever need for his duties at the White House.

"Do you want to know what we are doing here?" Oki asked me.

"Do I need to know?" I asked.

Oki shook his head.

"Then don't tell me," I said. "Just continue doing whatever tasks you have been assigned."

Oki smiled and nodded. He never did explain, and I never needed to know.

Not long after I began working at the White House, I took a walking tour of the entire complex: Mansion, West Wing, and East Wing. The Mansion, of course, was the residence of the First Family, the primary locale for formal state dinners and televised press conferences, and was the part of the White House containing the lovely rooms seen by people on the daily public tours. The East Wing housed the First Lady and her staff as well as the White House social office and the offices of the Military Aides to the President. The West Wing contained the Oval Office, the Cabinet Room, and housed the Situation Room and the senior staff of the President. Of course, the "Executive Office of the President" was far too extensive to be contained within the White House. Thus, operations like the Bureau of the Budget, the Science Advisor, Office of Consumer Affairs, and so on, were located in the Executive Office Building just across West Executive Avenue from the West Wing, a marvelously baroque old building that housed the State and War Departments in the days before World War II.

On my tour, I insisted on seeing every part of the White House operations. I was eventually escorted to the then secret presidential bomb shelter that had been constructed deep under the White House basement when President Truman remodeled the entire structure in the 1950s. However, by the time Lyndon Johnson assumed the presidency, two facts were recognized by almost everyone: first, the White House would be a primary target of any nuclear attack upon the United States, and second, there was no way the White House bomb shelter could withstand the force of any nuclear blast occurring anywhere near it. In other words, the shelter undoubtedly would fail to protect the President. It was essentially useless. Nonetheless, when I first saw the facility, it was fully stocked and kept ready at all times.

When I descended into the basement shelter, I found sitting there Marine Major Haywood Smith.

"What do you do here?" I asked him.

"I stand ready," he replied.

"All day?"

"Yes, sir, until I am relieved by another officer. My orders are to maintain this facility for instant readiness in case we are attacked."

I shook my head in wonderment. I asked Major Smith to show me around. What I saw was a room about the size of the main foyer of the Mansion high above it. It was big enough to house the President, his family, and perhaps a few people on his staff, one of whom I later learned was to be me. The room was stocked with sufficient food and water to last a few days, and it contained some rudimentary communications equipment. It was, in short, not only unsafe, but also totally inadequate.

"Do you know how much warning the President will have?" I asked Major Smith.

"Assuming that we immediately learn of and can identify a Soviet missile launch, we calculate that he will have about twenty-two minutes before the missiles arrive here," Major Smith stated.

"And in that time, the President has to decide what is really happening," I said. "I mean, he must determine whether the attack is intended or is some kind of accident or mistake, who is responsible for it, and whether he should order us to retaliate."

"Yes, sir. That's what he must do," Major Smith said. "He won't have the luxury of time, that is for sure."

Previously, I had been present when the Pentagon officials briefed the President about America's long-standing policy of "Mutual Assured Destruction"—sometimes ironically referred to as "MAD"—which was meant to inform any potential aggressor that the United States, without question, would retaliate against any attack with its full nuclear arsenal. This American policy—first articulated by President Eisenhower's Secretary of State, John Foster Dulles—was intended to deter any enemy from launching a first strike against the United States because they would know beyond any doubt that we could not only survive any such attack, but would in turn and in every case respond with such force and vehemence as to destroy the civilization of whatever nation was insane enough to unsheathe their nuclear weapons against us. American policy was no bluff and every nation needed to unquestionably believe that we were not bluffing. That meant that it was essential that we would always—and with no hesitation—retaliate. In my opinion, that policy saved the world from nuclear holocaust.

Pentagon officials periodically would come to the White House and meet with the President to give him what some referred to as the "doomsday briefings." These men would sit with him and explain the brutal realities of the nuclear risks we faced and our ability to survive and retaliate. This is what they told us:

> The Russians are our greatest threat. That's because they have hydrogen bombs and missiles with sufficient range to reach anywhere in the United States. Of course, someday there will be other nations with those capabilities, but right now the danger from the Soviets is very real. Our policy is based on the assumption that they will attempt a first strike against us. If they do, we have no way of stopping their rockets. They probably will kill upwards of 100,000,000 Americans, and they will destroy much of our country. However, even so, we guarantee that we can absorb their attack and still launch retaliation that will inflict far greater casualties upon them. We can survive whatever they throw at us. On the other hand, our counterstrike will drive the Soviet Union back into the Stone Age. We know it. They know it. Therefore, on the assumption that their leaders are sane, we believe they will never launch an attack against us.

Because I was on Okinawa the day we dropped the bomb on Hiroshima, I vividly understood the risk of nuclear devastation that we faced. I would sit there, listening to these experts, and think, "This is no game. These are real men speaking about real weapons that can bring about a real world disaster." I knew, as did the President, that we must always be able and willing without question to retaliate, and of course we were. It gave us no comfort to also hear that the Soviet Union had precisely the same strategy as our own; that they too operated on the assumption that we would attack first (and, of course, such a preemptive strike was not an unheard of thought among some of our military men); and that they must be able to absorb that attack and retain the capability of destroying the United States. In those days, both superpowers were always armed to the teeth, and each of us had the existence of the other within the crosshairs of our respective gunsights.

It was a frightening time, made even more so because the President would have only twenty-two minutes (the estimated time from launch to impact) to analyze what was happening, who was responsible, why it was occurring, and whether or not to order the fatal counterstrike. Of course, whether the attack on us was intended or accidental made no difference to the humanity about to be incinerated. It was because of this all but nonexistent window of time that a military man carrying the codes that only the President could use to order a nuclear attack was always near the side of the President. These codes were inside a metal box only slightly larger than an ordinary briefcase. Their constant presence made it all very real to us.

Unfortunately, that assumed window of twenty-two minutes also assumed perfect intelligence, and that was almost certainly a fantasy. Thus, the actual time in which the President must act undoubtedly was probably far less—how much less I shudder to imagine.

The inadequate White House shelter was actually only the final option for the President, one he would use if there were no time for anything else. What else could be done to protect him in case of attack entirely depended on where he was.

One choice was a specially equipped Air Force plane that was always maintained at a location close to wherever the President might be. It was fully provisioned and had total communications capability as well as the ability to be refueled in flight. If the President could reach it, the airplane was available to him. Of course, there was also Air Force One, the regular Boeing 707 in which the President normally flew. However, it lacked the facilities and ability to fly indefinitely that was the hallmark of the special Air Force airplane.

The Navy provided another option. Two navy cruisers had been specially prepared for emergency use by the President in case of nuclear attack. One of these ships was fully ready to function as a presidential command post and was always stationed in the Atlantic close to the Maryland and Virginia shoreline. The ship offered sufficient space for the President, his immediate staff, and other top military and civilian leaders of the government. Of course, the ship could only be reached by the President if he was in or around Washington at the time he learned of an impending attack.

Although we never actually had a practice evacuation of the President to test his options, the President did spend one night aboard the cruiser USS

Northhampton, as she sailed north up the coast to Campobello Island—President Franklin Roosevelt's family retreat—where President Johnson and the Canadian Prime Minister held a summit conference. None of the other evacuation facilities were ever used by us.

The President's final—and preferred—option was the excavated mountain in West Virginia. There, several years earlier, at immense expense, a mountain had been hollowed to create an amazing facility to ensure the survival of the President and our government. A massive underground facility had been created to house and preserve the American government, or at least as many officials who could reach the mountain in time. There was sufficient space for selected Members of Congress, the Supreme Court, key members of the cabinet, the Joint Chiefs of Staff, other crucial military officials, and of course the President, his family, and his senior staff. The list of persons permitted entry was prepared by the Defense Department, submitted to me, and approved by the President. There was also a rudimentary plan to transport people to the mountain, but all of us knew that the chances of reaching its safety were theoretical at best.

Still, the facility was there and built sufficiently deep within the mountain to survive anything but a direct hit and thus might save those lucky enough to be inside when the blow was struck. Although we never rehearsed its use, I did inspect it. The shelter itself was impressive. It covered an area equal to at least four football fields. Inside, the area consisted of large rooms laid out as dormitories and conference rooms. The only private living space was for the President and his immediate family. It also contained banks of communications equipment, including television and radio broadcasting facilities through which the President could speak to the nation and the world. There was food and water in sufficient quantity to last for months. The entire shelter was enclosed, cocoonlike, within material intended to protect its occupants against radioactivity. Finally, a limited military contingent was always present, their assignment being to maintain the facility in constant readiness.

I was impressed by all that had been done to protect the President and the government. Despite the slim chance that he or any of us or our families would reach the shelter in time to save ourselves, I considered its carefully maintained existence to be essential to the credibility of the deterrent impact of MAD. Any enemy must always know that the United States had taken every possible step to protect itself against any eventuality.

Although we did nothing to alter the survival alternatives available to the President, we did away with the waste of a good Marine major who was assigned the task of guarding a useless bomb shelter under the White House. I recommended to the President—and he accepted—a plan that would solve two problems at once: usefully employing Major Smith and doing away with the Pentagon's wasteful system for transmitting military information to the President.

Major General Chester Clifton had served as Military Aide to President Kennedy, and was continuing in that capacity when I came to the White House. There was nothing wrong with General Clifton, but what made no sense was the procedure he employed to serve the President. General Clifton believed it essential to brief the President daily with all the other military aides present. It was a very impressive performance. However, not much new information was provided to the President. So after my first experience of this military briefing, I knew President Johnson would need a less formal presentation done less often.

I thought that this Pentagon-directed system was bureaucratic nonsense. If anyone over there had something the President ought to know, he could call him directly or, if necessary, come over and tell him face to face. That is why we had a Secretary of Defense and a Chairman of the Joint Chiefs of Staff, as well as other competent officials. But to filter all communications through one major general was make-work at best and, worse yet, risked misunderstandings while denying the President the opportunity to directly and immediately respond. I suggested that we do away with that Pentagon policy and President Johnson agreed. The Secretary of Defense was told that from then on, anything he or the military wanted the President to know should be conveyed to him in person or through the National Security Advisor.

Thereafter, General Clifton was transferred back to the Pentagon, and Air Force Colonel James Cross, who had flown the President since he was Vice President and was now the chief pilot on Air Force One, was directed to also serve as the President's Military Aide, thus creating one job out of two.

Colonel Cross turned out to be an excellent selection. He was a soft-spoken, efficient Texan, a can-do man the President liked. He served as the President's Military Aide until 1968 when, after serving a tour of duty in

Vietnam, he was promoted to brigadier general and made commandant at Bergstrom Air Force Base just outside of Austin.

As for Marine Major Haywood Smith, he was relieved of his duty guarding the basement bomb shelter, but he was not sent back to the Pentagon. I liked the man, and had been impressed by his frank statements to me concerning the ridiculously wasteful time he was spending maintaining an all-but-useless facility. Besides, being a former Marine myself (albeit a buck sergeant), I was conscious of the fact the Marine Corps had never received adequate recognition. When I served during the war, the Corps usually was given the lowest priority in receiving equipment and other supplies from the Navy, a source of endless complaints that were normally ignored by the senior service under which we nominally served. Thus, in Major Smith I saw an opportunity to give the Corps a modicum of recognition. I recommended that he should be appointed an Assistant Military Aide under Colonel Cross, the first Marine to serve in that capacity. The President agreed. It turned out that Major Smith not only fully justified our faith in him, but when Colonel Cross left the White House in April 1968, Major Smith was promoted to colonel and became the new Military Aide to the President. After his White House years, Colonel Smith also served in Vietnam.

In addition to Colonel Cross and Colonel Smith, the White House military aide's office also consisted of a representative from the Navy, Lt. Commander Worthington Hobbs, followed by Commander Sam Latimer, and Major Hugh Robinson from the Army—the first African American to ever serve as a Military Aide to a President. I also gladly mention Marine Sergeant Major William Gulley, who in truth was the glue of that office, the man who expedited every action required, and another can-do man I so admired and appreciated.

When I was delving into the subject of communications between the Pentagon and the Joint Chiefs of Staff, I noted that the membership of the Joint Chiefs consisted of the senior officers from the Army, Navy, and Air Force. No one from the Marine Corps sat as a full member of the Joint Chiefs. Traditionally, the corps was considered part of the Navy, which supposedly represented the Marine Corps. I approached the President with the problem, suggesting that in my opinion the Marine Corps had more than earned its right to sit as a full member of the Joint Chiefs. I believed he could rectify the wrong with his presidential backing of legislation expanding the membership of the Joint Chiefs. President Johnson agreed and with the help of Haywood Smith, the Congress was persuaded to enact the necessary legislation. With presidential backing, in January 1969, the Marine Corps became a full and equal member of the Joint Chiefs of Staff, a position it continues to hold.

In addition, I discovered that the corps was authorized to have only one four-star general. Each of the other services had many more officers of that rank. Thus, with the President's approval Haywood Smith and I again approached Congress, this time in the person of the House Armed Services Committee chairman, Mendel Rivers. It took a bit of persuading, but ultimately the Marine Corps received its second full general.

It was good to work again for the Corps.

LEAKS AND LEAKERS

Lyndon Johnson was not unique in despising press leaks of confidential information to the media, especially by those who worked for him in the White House or elsewhere in the government. As far as I am aware, his reactions merely echoed the feelings of every President who has ever served. I do not believe a President has many decisions to make that need public debate before he can make an intelligent determination. Unfortunately, some who worked for the President had their own agendas that were not necessarily those of the President.

These people soon learned that their personal road to fame ran through the Washington press corps and what has been described as the Georgetown cocktail circuit. They cultivated reporters by confiding inside information to them—off the record, of course. They became popular guests at embassy dinners and Washington cocktail parties because they became known as amusing and knowledgeable sources of gossip. Their propensity to reveal what they knew or suspected they knew was of course facilitated by the drinks they consumed. Thus, by revealing what the President thought and intended, they endeared themselves to what was called the "Eastern Establishment."

This Eastern Establishment included most of the nationally syndicated columnists and reporters, as well as representatives of major newspapers, magazines, networks, and publishers. Lyndon Johnson was admired by very few members of this group, most of whom had been captivated by President Kennedy and looked upon Lyndon Johnson as a rough, undereducated interloper. Their deeply imbedded cultural disdain for President Johnson was abetted by a few people on his staff who whispered so-called "secret" stories about him, thereby reinforcing the Establishment's already negative image of the President.

Those leaks and leakers enraged Lyndon Johnson, who rightly thought of them as disloyal not only to him but to everything he was trying to accomplish. Famously, there were times that his disgust resulted in his refusal to take an action, including making an appointment, that he had intended but that had been prematurely leaked to the press. Some might argue that he was only hurting himself, but my view is that because it became known that a premature leak might result in his refusal to take the leaked action that in itself became an incentive to stop those who otherwise were tempted to talk to the press.

One of the first jobs the President gave me was to uncover the names of the leakers and stop them. Other Presidents—before and since—have engaged in similar searches, but never with much success. What I can say about our efforts can be encapsulated by what was said to me around 1970 at Ford's Theatre by Dr. Henry Kissinger, who at the time was heading President Nixon's Office of National Security Affairs.

"How in the world did you ever stop leaks to the press?" Dr. Kissinger asked me.

"We never did stop them," I replied. "But we may have slowed them down."

"But how did you accomplish even that much?" Kissinger continued. "Every President has his leaks, but nobody else has ever been able to do anything about them. At least you had some success."

I smiled at the irony of being asked this question by the man I considered the most prolific leaker in the Nixon White House.

What I had done was this: in response to the President's need, I came up with several methods to unearth the names of White House leakers. By doing so, I created some unhappiness among the White House staff, who then proceeded to leak to the press what I was doing to uncover their identities. Their new leaks created some negative publicity directed against me, but that was preferable to criticism against the President.

The first step I took was to carefully read Washington-based stories and columns. My theory was that if a story or column contained information that apparently originated with someone in the White House, and soon a member of the President's staff was favorably mentioned by the same writer, then in all probability that person was the culprit who was being either rewarded or cultivated for future use. By no means was this proof, but it was a strong indicator, and was enough for me to begin a careful watch over the activities of the suspect, including what he knew and whether any of that ever became public.

Another method I employed was to carefully monitor all visits to members of the staff by representatives of the media. This listing was easily assembled with the assistance of the Secret Service and White House police, which kept careful track of every person who visited the working areas of the West and East Wings. The press had their own assigned area in the West Wing lobby, but every time they came through the door leading to anyone's office, their entry was noted along with the member of the staff they wished to see. The Secret Service also sent me lists of every instance when a member of the staff appeared in the press lobby and spoke to a reporter. Actually, this information was being assembled long before Lyndon Johnson became President.

Of course, Press Secretaries like George Reedy, Bill Moyers, and George Christian—as well as Liz Carpenter for Mrs. Johnson—were understandably in constant contact with the media. We did not have nor did we want a "spin office" that has become popular in recent presidencies. For the most part, the Press Secretary was the only authorized spokesperson for the President during our watch at the White House.

Nonetheless, there were a few times when a member of the staff was directed to meet with, and even leak information to, a reporter. For example, the President approved a Press Secretary's suggestion that Elizabeth Drew, a well-known reporter, spend an entire day with me, which she did by appearing at my home before seven in the morning and staying with me until I returned there close to midnight. The result was a favorable article about me that pleased the press office. Some suggested that it also helped the President.

However, as for others on the White House staff, it was disturbing and suspicious that some of them with no legitimate reason for doing so were often meeting at length with reporters.

Another clue for me was the frequency that a member of our staff would be a guest in the house of a reporter. As I have stated, the senior members of the staff were entitled the use of White House cars and drivers. Because the drivers were required to report each location where they took their passengers, I could know when they were dropped off at the homes of columnists like Joseph Alsop, who rarely wrote a kind word about the President.

It bothered the President when news stories began to appear that I was engaged in a search for leakers—stories that also detailed some of the methods I was using. These stories came from the very leakers I was attempting to uncover. Nonetheless, on balance, it suited the President's purpose that people on his staff knew about the activities. He wanted them to be concerned. He liked it when they repeated his own description of me as his "tough Marine sergeant." His idea was that although I might absorb all the negative publicity, everyone who worked for him would know that everything I did and every time I spoke or acted, it was on his behalf and likely with his approval. In that way, he figured, those with a propensity to leak would think twice before doing it. Furthermore, I did not hesitate to confront anyone I suspected of leaking information. I quietly would warn them. Thus, they would know that I was aware. Even if not totally successful, I believe that my work acted as an effective deterrent to White House leaks.

As I told Dr. Kissinger, I was not always successful. Nobody could be. The idea was to deter the leaking, and I think we succeeded more than we failed.

I have expressed my belief that those people who leaked to the press did so for a variety of reasons. One of the more understandable motives—although still unacceptable—would be their desired attempt to change a policy with which they disagreed by creating a public outcry against it. At least that person was acting out of conscience rather than seeking personal aggrandizement. Nonetheless, even that motive was in contravention of the understanding they had with the President. All of us who worked for the President had been told that we were free to disagree with him in private, especially before a presidential decision had been made, but once he had decided upon an action, we were bound to either follow his decision or resign.

Another motivation of those who leaked unauthorized information was their need to receive favorable publicity or recognition even though they had no disloyalty to the President or any desire to hurt him.

One final reason for leaking was that the leaker was seeking not only fame and favor but was either passively or actively disloyal to the President. In those cases, I believed that the guilty person should not remain on the White House staff.

McGeorge Bundy is an example. I believed that Bundy was a leaker in his area of responsibility and I confronted him. He reacted angrily and protested to the President, who politely heard him out. Bundy's leaking did not cease. It seemed he believed that his work was too important for him to be stopped. However, he misjudged the facts. In mid-1965, Bundy was gradually frozen out of the loop of knowledge and participation in critical foreign policy decisions. Nothing overt was said, but Bundy was smart and he knew that he was no longer fully used. Thus, in February 1966, Bundy resigned from the White House staff.

Another problem was presented by the actions of Richard Goodwin. I began focusing on Goodwin soon after I began tracking the identity of the White House leakers. He met all the criteria: he had an unusually large number of telephone calls and meetings with reporters, far more than I thought justified by his job as a speechwriter. He was known as a frequent attendee at Washington social affairs. In addition, news stories about him were invariably favorable. Of far greater significance was this: whenever he was with his friends or in public, he made no attempt to fully disguise his disdain for Lyndon Johnson. Despite the fact that Goodwin had been asked to continue on President Johnson's staff, reports I received—and there were many—consistently established Goodwin's lack of loyalty toward the President he now served. Apparently he was never able to embrace the reality that Lyndon Johnson was now his boss to whom he owed fidelity.

Yet Goodwin's talent as a speechwriter enabled him to remain on the White House staff for many months beyond when he should have been separated. Still, even while he remained in the White House, his work was increasingly scrutinized before it was used. In short, he was suspect.

By September 1965, Goodwin's conduct reached the point where he no longer could remain on the staff. On approximately September 19, I walked upstairs to Goodwin's office, located on the northwest corner of the West Wing's second floor, where I closed the door and stood before his desk. "You must leave the White House staff," I told him without preliminary.

Goodwin blanched in obvious shock. "Why?" he managed to ask.

"You lack loyalty to the President," I told him. "You leak inside information to your friends in the press and especially at the Washington parties you attend. Also, you have been removing White House documents from your office."

"I disagree," Goodwin said. "As for those documents, they are copies of my work, and I consider them mine."

"No," I said. "They are White House property."

"Are you telling me I can't go to parties?" he asked.

"Well, I understand that you are a single man and your social life is your business. But what you say at those affairs affects *our* business."

"Who is *our*?" he demanded.

"Never mind that," I said. "This is not negotiable."

"When am I supposed to leave?" he asked.

"Immediately," I said. "You can either resign or I will discharge you now. You choose."

Goodwin thought for a moment, then said, "If you give me until tomorrow, I'll resign."

I knew exactly what Goodwin intended. He wanted time to attempt to meet with the President and generate pressure on me to revoke the decision. But I knew that the decision was irrevocable, and that there was nothing he could do to change it. So I didn't argue, and gave him his extra time.

As expected, Goodwin tried to get in to see the President. He attempted backdoor entry through Juanita Roberts, the President's secretary, which did not work. He spoke to Bill Moyers and later to Jack Valenti. Both of them called me, but when I explained *why* Goodwin would be leaving, neither of them chose to pursue the matter. Thus, he resigned.

Despite the fact that Goodwin was no longer on the White House staff, I did learn that he was asked to help with a certain presidential speech, and that he did so. Nonetheless, his departure was followed by his increasing identification with those who opposed President Johnson and his policies.

Goodwin later married the noted historian Doris Kearns, who was a White House fellow in 1968 and later not only assisted President Johnson in writing his autobiography, *The Vantage Point,* but wrote her own biography of the president, *Lyndon Johnson: The American Dream.* Still, Goodwin has

always exemplified someone who for reasons of his own continued to serve
a President he neither liked nor admired.

THE FIRST YEAR OF THE 89TH CONGRESS:
A MAGICAL TIME

Lyndon Johnson has been rightfully depicted as a master in dealing with the
Congress. When he first came to Washington as a secretary to a Congressman, he dreamed that he would someday be a force in passing legislation.
Later, he served in that body, starting as an elected Congressman in 1937.
Johnson became a Senator in 1948, Senate Minority Leader in 1951, and
Majority Leader in 1953. As Democratic Leader of the Senate, he was
obliged to work closely with Dwight Eisenhower, the Republic President. He
did so with such grace and effectiveness that he and President Eisenhower
became lifelong friends.

Lyndon Johnson often told this story regarding the necessity of working
with his political adversaries: "I used to sit there across the aisle from Bob
Taft when he was the Majority Leader after President Eisenhower's '52 election, and Bill Knowland who succeeded him, and Everett Dirksen who succeeded him. Lots of times they said very irritating things and I was disposed
on the spur of the moment to tell them to go straight to hell, but I had already found out I couldn't make them go. And we had better think that
about other relations in this world. We just can't make them go."

What was most significant about Lyndon Johnson's years in the Congress
was that he developed close personal relationships with a wide range of
Members of both Houses, relationships that had nothing to do with party
affiliation. Although it was true that Sam Rayburn, Speaker of the House,
and Richard Russell, the highly respected Democratic Senator from Georgia, were Johnson's mentors, he never neglected the Republicans. They too
became his friends and confidants.

As President, Lyndon Johnson believed that relationships between the
White House and the Congress always should be cultivated. For example, he
knew that without the active support of Wilbur Mills, then the powerful
Chairman of the House Ways and Means Committee, Medicare could never
become law. Thus, the President saw to it that Mills was intimately involved

in every stage of development of that historic legislation. It was the same with Sen. John Sparkman, who controlled its destiny in the Senate.

Every member of President Johnson's staff was instructed to maintain close contacts with Senators and Congressmen regardless of party affiliation. He told us that our contacts with Congress should be constant and in no way limited to those instances when we needed their votes. Thus, he said:

> Become a good friend. Socialize with them. Have them over to your house for dinner. Let them know that you are their man in the White House. Be ready and willing to do favors for them; to help them get an answer for any problem they might have with any agency of the government; and to be there for them whenever they need you. Maybe you will never need to ask them anything in return, but they will always know that you are their friend, and, whether they realize it or not, they will feel beholden to you. When the time comes that you need their help, they will feel they should do what they can for you. Perhaps they can't give you their vote, because their constituency won't allow it, but they might be willing to forgo a filibuster or be absent from the floor of the Congress at a crucial time. Believe me, it works. You must never forget that.

Often the President used his unique storytelling ability as a means of communicating with and persuading his friends—and opponents—in Congress. For example, I have heard him use this anecdote:

> We had a little boy down in our country that ran out one day and said, "Mama, come here quick! I saw a big old lion in our back yard!" And Mother went out there and there was the old family dog Rover standing there. She said, "That's not a lion, that's Rover. Now, you told a story. You go up there in that room, stay an hour . . . and beg to the Lord to forgive you for telling a story." . . . In an hour, she came back, and she said, "Did you say your prayers?" "Yes." "Did you ask the Lord to forgive you?" "Yes." She said, "What did the Lord say?" He said, "Mama, the Lord said he thought it was a lion too." Now I don't know whether you see all these problems that face America, the priorities, the tinderboxes, the poverty and the filth and the [lack of] education and the disease, and the isolationism and the narrow nationalism and the protectionism. I don't know whether you see these lions or not. But I hope you do. And I hope the Lord thinks they're lions, too.

Notwithstanding the fact that there was a formally designated Congressional Relations Staff at the White House (directed by Larry O'Brien with Mike Manatos principally responsible for the Senate and Henry Hall Wilson for the House), no one in the White House, regardless of status, was excused from the responsibility of working closely with Members of Congress. We always returned their calls, intervened to solve their problems, met their families, had them to dinner, and did our best to become their friend, their "man" at the White House. Among all of us on the President's staff, we managed to cover the entire membership of the Congress, and it worked just as the President knew that it would.

President Johnson was always fully disciplined in the manner by which he oversaw the development and enactment of legislation he sought. It all began with his vision for a greater America. As Jack Valenti wrote in his essay "An Awesome Engine of a Man" in *Lyndon Johnson Remembered* (Rowman & Littlefield, 2003), on the night of President Kennedy's assassination, Lyndon Johnson, as he lay in his bed, said:

> I'm going to get Kennedy's tax cut out of the Senate Finance Committee, and we're going to get this economy humming again. Then I'm going to pass Kennedy's civil rights bill, which has been hung up too long in the Congress. And I'm going to pass it without changing a single comma or a word. After that we'll pass legislation that allows everyone anywhere in this country to vote, with all the barriers down. And that's not all. We're going to get a law that says every boy and girl in this country, no matter how poor, or the color of their skin, or the region they come from, is going to be able to get all the education they can take by loan, scholarship, or grant, right from the federal government. . . . And I aim to pass Harry Truman's medical insurance bill that got nowhere before.

That was his dream, but it was only the beginning of the process of bringing it to reality. When it came time to consider each specific piece of legislation, President Johnson started with a systematic campaign intended to enact his vision into law. His method was to begin with the appointment of a knowledgeable presidential committee of national business and professional leaders who were not in the government, persons who were powerfully influential and who would not be afraid to request as much funding as the legislation required. The president would assemble this group and force-fully give them his ideas.

At the same time, Johnson would meet with the relevant agencies of the government to inform them and to solicit their contributions to his ideas. He would not stop prodding them until proposed legislation was drafted.

The commission members would then present the proposal to the chair-men and ranking members of the appropriate congressional committees, asking them for their ideas and input. The congressional leadership of both parties was simultaneously consulted. It was only then that the legislative proposal was finalized. At that moment, it had the backing of significant national constituencies as well as powerful members of Congress.

However, the President did not stop there. Next he would invite key Senators and Congressmen who, together with outside experts, would meet in the White House for still further discussion. By this time, the full membership of all relevant committees had been involved in the process.

One result of this method was that opposition to the legislation was identified. Often, because the congressional leadership was behind the legislation, great pressure could be exerted on the dissenters who would know that by fighting their leaders they were risking congressional perquisites that would otherwise be theirs.

Of course, all of this did not end the process. The White House staff would now initiate a nonstop campaign of prodding the sponsors of the legislation to move the bills forward with all possible speed. On occasion, the President himself would make calls to the key Members, although he withheld his personal intervention until it was critical because he believed that his influence would be diluted by overuse.

Invitations to White House state dinners and parties always included Senators and Congressmen. He never neglected to bring Members with him when he flew Air Force One into their state. He made maximum use of the *Sequoia*, the presidential yacht, where he invited Members to join him for a leisurely evening of cruising on the Potomac River, or, in his absence, Marion and I and other members of his staff often hosted them.

Thus the President made certain that the Congress always knew what he wanted before he publicly presented it to them, realized the extent of his flexibility, and were never caught by surprise by any proposal he made. How dramatically different were his methods from the highly charged personal malice that all too often poisons relationships between the White House and the Congress, and especially the opposite political party in Congress. As far as I am aware, no President since Lyndon Johnson employed such a totally integrated and successful approach to developing, proposing, and enacting legislation into law.

The President often invited Members to meet with him privately in either the Oval Office, the Cabinet Room, or, with larger groups, the spacious East Room of the Mansion. In those meetings, he would exercise his marvelous talent for personal persuasion. I have never seen anyone better than Lyndon Johnson at communicating with people in small groups. His methods, which included humor, anecdotes, and nose-to-nose talking where he would not hesitate from invading anyone's "personal space" as he tightly grabbed onto their arms or shoulders, became well known as the "Johnson treatment." It definitely worked.

However, Johnson's marvelous ability to individually reach out to others could never be transferred to his appearances on television. We—and all the expert consultants that we consulted—tried endless variations attempting to structure a scenario where the true Lyndon Johnson could be seen by the nation. We never succeeded. He would simply tighten up and much of his magic disappeared. Perhaps it was because he felt that when he spoke to a national audience he had to appear "presidential." Whatever the reason, the richness of his personality disappeared whenever the television cameras turned on.

Of special significance in his dealings with Congress was President Johnson's old and close friendship with Senator Dirksen, the powerful Republican Leader of the Senate. Their relationship dated from the 1930s and transcended their political differences. For years, the Johnson and Dirksen families had known each other. They had socialized, eaten, visited, and gossiped together. Their mutual affection was genuine. Neither of them ever hesitated to speak frankly to one another, or to unabashedly use each other for whatever each of them might need.

None of this changed after Lyndon Johnson became President. Senator Dirksen frequently telephoned the White House and, if he did not wish to speak personally with the President, I was the person designated to deal with him. I always accepted his calls, or, if I was occupied, returned them as quickly as possible. In almost every instance, he had a request to make. Usually it was a suggestion regarding a presidential appointee being considered, or perhaps a project affecting Illinois, or a difficulty an important constituent was experiencing with some department of the government. He was invariably a gentleman with me. He never expressed his wish in the form of a demand, and he never raised his voice. In his deep, soft-spoken manner, he would quietly express himself. I knew the President wanted to accommodate whenever it was possible, and accordingly I always did what I could to satisfy him.

There were many instances when Senator Dirksen came to the White House at the end of his working day in the Senate. His visits were never publicized, but he was often there to have a chat with the President. It made no difference what the Senator had said or done on the Senate floor or in a speech denouncing the Johnson administration and its programs. Those actions and speeches were never personally directed at the President, which Johnson appreciated, and both men understood that what they did publicly was only "politics." It never affected their friendship.

When Senator Dirksen came to the White House, he and the President usually would meet in the President's small sitting room adjoining the Oval Office. There they would relax and regale each other with anecdotes and gossip, which they both enjoyed immensely. Eventually and unhurriedly, they arrived at the true purpose of their meeting. The President needed something from the Republicans and the cooperation of Senator Dirksen was essential to that goal. It was nothing as blatant as "this for that." They were far too wary and experienced for that. Instead, it often was an unspoken understanding by a friend of the requirements of the other.

The President, often with me present, would go through Dirksen's requests. The senator was always careful not to ask for much. If he wanted President Johnson to make an appointment, he was reasonably sure that the candidate would not be unacceptable to the President and could be put into office without ruffling too many feathers. If Dirksen wanted a federal project—usually but not always in Illinois—he tried to keep his request within budgetary limits. Sometimes the two men would bicker over items on the Dirksen list, but it was always in good humor. In the end, however, Senator Dirksen would be satisfied. That was crucially important.

What President Johnson needed from Senator Dirksen required far greater subtlety—and secrecy—from the senator. The programs of the Great

Society were philosophically unacceptable to the Republican Party in general and Senator Dirksen in particular. That meant that it was politically impossible for the Senator to actively support most of the President's legislative wish list. However, Johnson never asked Dirksen for public endorsements. He knew better. What he requested—and what Dirksen could do for him—was ensure a reasonable and civil debate, and where necessary, a kind of silent withdrawal that made it possible for legislation to be enacted into law. At times the President expected Dirksen to quietly arrange for just enough Republican Senators to be absent or to switch their votes to ensure passage of a particular bill. Sometimes, especially when the proposed Senate action was highly controversial, Dirksen quietly saw to it that there was not sufficient Republican support to enable a filibuster to succeed. Because of their long relationship—perhaps more than any other factor—President Johnson was able to achieve remarkable legislative victories.

Of course, President Johnson's legislative accomplishments did not begin in 1965. As he said to Jack Valenti immediately after the assassination of President Kennedy, Lyndon Johnson embarked on a determined course to enact into law as much of the Kennedy legislative program as possible. For reasons best known to President Kennedy's staff, Lyndon Johnson, despite his acknowledged genius as a legislator, had been excluded from any meaningful participation in promoting the Kennedy agenda with the Congress. Their failure to use Johnson is inexplicable to me, and was a terrible waste of Johnson's unique talents. Still, that is how they acted, and although sometimes ignored, Johnson absorbed the snub and was never anything but loyal to the President he served. The inevitable result of Johnson's disuse was this: at the time of John Kennedy's assassination—almost three years into his presidency—the bulk of his legislative agenda continued to languish in a Congress that stubbornly refused to respond to him.

Lyndon Johnson was determined to break the legislative logjam. Immediately after assuming office, he told the Congress and the public that as far as he was concerned, the most meaningful legacy to the fallen President was for Congress to enact the laws they had ignored. Thus, during 1964, President Johnson's declared mission was to turn Kennedy rhetoric into legislative reality.

I will not try to list all of the landmark legislation that Lyndon Johnson succeeded into making into law. That can be better seen in the Appendix 2: a listing prepared by President Johnson's Cabinet of the landmark laws enacted during each year of the Johnson presidency. It also must be said that all of that marvelous outpouring of legislation could not have been accomplished without the dedicated support of men such as Speaker John McCormack, Democratic Leader Carl Albert and Democratic Whip Hale Boggs in the House, as well as Democratic Leader Mike Mansfield and Democratic Whip Russell Long in the Senate.

These laws include much that remains relevant today, such as the creation of the John F. Kennedy Center for Performing Arts and, most important, passage of the Civil Rights Act of 1964. That law required that employment and all public facilities be equally available to blacks and whites alike.

The landslide election of 1964 changed everything for Lyndon Johnson. First and foremost, he was now President in his own right, and no longer only the spear-carrier for a fallen hero. He was free to lead with a program that was his own. As early as May 22, 1964, in his seminal speech at the University of Michigan, he had defined his dream for an America that would become "The Great Society." His landslide victory in the fall of 1964 not only gave him the largest margin of any presidential candidate in history, but he also carried with him into office a Congress with Democratic majorities not seen since the 1930s and Franklin Roosevelt.

The 89th Congress that came into being in January 1965 had a Senate consisting of 68 Democrats and 32 Republicans. The House of Representatives was even more lopsided: 294 Democrats and 140 Republicans (there was one vacancy). These vast majorities existed because of Lyndon Johnson's overwhelming electoral showing, and the Members of Congress knew it. Thus, the stage was set for greatest legislative outpouring in American history.

More than anyone else, President Johnson knew that 1965—the first year of the new Congress—was the time for action. To him, it was a fact of Washington politics that by 1966 the Members of both Houses would be focusing on their reelections and would become skittish and far less amenable to following his lead. During 1965, he applied constant and unyielding pressure on the Congress to pass the manifold laws that he proposed.

Appendix 2 lists the highlights of what was accomplished during that year, including the creation of Medicare. Amazingly enough, Medicare, which is now considered an untouchable program, was enacted despite the bitter opposition of 93 percent of the Republicans in the House of Representatives.

Among the other landmark legislation enacted during that year were Project Head Start for preschool children, Aid to Education, Aid to Higher Education, the Highway Beautification Act, formation of the Department of Housing and Urban Development, and the myriad laws that together encompassed the President's "War on Poverty." As Joe Califano has pointed out, "When LBJ took office, 22.2 percent of Americans were living in poverty. When he left, only 13 percent were living below the poverty line." At the core of the president's remarkable philosophy was his desire, as he often stated, to create "tax payers, not tax eaters" out of disadvantaged Americans. President Johnson believed that the federal government was the best available instrument to give people an equal start in life. After that, he expected them to work; to take full advantage of the opportunities that government actions provided for them. He never intended for people to be paid for doing nothing.

In 1964, the President led the Congress to enact the strongest civil rights law since the Civil War. On August 6, 1964, he signed into law the Voting Rights Act, for the first time ensuring the right to vote to *all* Americans, regardless of race or color. Nothing done since has had such an indelible effect on the American dream of total equality for all citizens. In so doing, Lyndon Johnson became, as the Pulitzer Prize–winning reporter Nick Kotz has written: "The greatest champion of civil rights since Lincoln and the president who accomplished the most to promote social justice for all Americans."

In bringing this legislation into law, President Johnson was expressing his deepest beliefs regarding this nation's obligation to its African American citizens. As he stated in his August 15, 1965, speech to a joint session of Congress:

> I speak tonight for the dignity of man and the destiny of democracy. . . . Our mission is at once the oldest the most basic of this country: to right wrong, to do justice, to serve man.
>
> The issue of equal rights for American Negroes is such an issue. And should we defeat every enemy, should we double our wealth and conquer the stars, and still be unequal to this issue, then we will have failed as a people and as a nation. . . . There is no Negro problem. There is no Southern problem. There is no Northern problem. There is only an American problem. And we meet here tonight as Americans to solve that problem.

The President further emphasized his principle when, on June 5, 1965, he told the students of Howard University in Washington, D.C.:

> As majority leader of the United States Senate, I helped to guide two of these bills through the Senate. As your President, I was proud to sign the third. And now very soon we will have the fourth—a new law guaranteeing every American the right to vote.
>
> No act of my entire administration will give me greater satisfaction than the day when my signature makes this bill too the law of this land.

Thus it was that in one historic stroke, the Voting Rights Act changed the political face of America. Truly—and at last—it totally enfranchised African Americans. Before its enactment, blacks living in most of the old Confederacy were, by one means or another, denied the right to vote. The whites held all political power in the South, as they had since the days of Reconstruction following the Civil War. They used that power to slam the door on vast numbers of Negroes who, if they were permitted to vote, might challenge and overturn white authority. In this vital respect, the issues supposedly settled by the Civil War remained unresolved.

Lyndon Johnson, although himself a Southerner, was single-minded in his determination to destroy the political racism that permeated so much of his region of the country. His commitment slowly but profoundly evolved as he matured. It began when as a young man he taught disadvantaged young Mexican Americans and became aware of the deprivations they suffered. Still, he was a Texan and, as he said in his autobiography, *The Vantage Point,* "Texas is a part of the South." He knew that "discrimination existed throughout the South . . . but we had deluded ourselves that the black people were happy and satisfied." Thus, he voted against six civil rights bills that came up on the House and Senate floors. Gradually, however, he recognized that he was living in "an America misled by a mask of submissiveness . . . that hid the deep despair inside the hearts of millions of black Americans."

In that respect, he often told the story of Gene Williams, his longtime black aide, Gene's wife, Helen, who was the Johnsons' maid, and Zephyr Wright, their cook. Once, when then Senator Johnson asked the three of them to drive the Johnsons' beagle from Washington to Texas, Gene refused. When the puzzled Senator asked why, Gene said, "Senator, you have no idea what it is like for us to drive through the South. When we are hungry, we cannot eat in a restaurant, so we buy some food and eat outside. When we are tired, we cannot sleep in a motel. We have to sleep in our car. When we have to go to the bathroom, we have to use the side of the road. What I'm saying is that a colored man's got enough trouble getting across the South on his own, without bringing a dog along."

This story as been retold many times. What has not been fully understood is that Gene's story made an indelible and powerful emotional impact on Lyndon Johnson. It can be fairly said to have created in him an unbreakable bond that forever cemented Lyndon Johnson the man and the politician to the great cause of civil rights.

President Johnson knew better than anyone that if he succeeded in granting blacks the right to vote, not only would they exercise their franchise, but they would undoubtedly vote many whites out of office—certainly the white supremacists—and most probably elect their own people to positions of power wherever they were in the majority.

President Johnson also knew that large numbers of southern whites—and not just those who were racists—would react negatively to this shift of political power. He foresaw the inevitable disappearance of the "solid South" where the Democratic Party was the unchallenged power base of an entire region. With the blacks now permitted to vote, southern politics would be changed forever. The South would no longer be "Democratic." In fact, he believed that it might become solidly Republican if the newly authorized voters failed to vote. Lyndon Johnson saw that the Democratic Party in the South would reform itself to include blacks and thus would become indistinguishable from the national Democratic Party. In other words, he knew that if he succeeded in enacting the Voting Rights Act, he would be—for a very long time—sounding the death knell of his own party's hold on power in the South. Of course, it all happened just as he knew it would.

Despite his certainty that the Voting Rights Act he so fervently pushed would destroy his party's power base in the South, Lyndon Johnson never hesitated. As he saw it, universal suffrage was the unarguable right of all Americans, the cornerstone of democracy. He believed with all his heart that it was his responsibility, his mission, his opportunity, and his privilege to seize the moment granted to him and take full advantage of the huge Democratic majorities.

Eighty-five percent of the House Republicans joined their southern Democratic colleagues in opposition to the Voting Rights Act. Nonetheless, the bill managed to pass the House and was sent to the Senate. There it faced implacable opposition from southern Democratic Senators who credibly threatened to endlessly filibuster until the legislation died. Although these Senators had failed to block the Civil Rights Act of 1964, the Voting Rights Act posed a far greater threat because it challenged their hold on power. Thus, their opposition was unmatched by anything that ever had preceded it. Led by their most respected elder statesman—and Lyndon Johnson's old mentor—Georgia Senator Richard Russell, they confidently prepared to crush the bill.

What they failed to reckon with was the power of the relationship between Lyndon Johnson and the House Republican leaders, Charles Halleck and Gerald Ford; and, most important, the close friendship between the President and the Senate Republican Leader, Everett Dirksen.

In the most meaningful meeting ever held between these two powerful friends, they once again sat down in the President's small private office. Except for the subject matter, it was no different from dozens of previous secret visits they had held. As always, Senator Dirksen knew what was about to be asked of him and, as always, he had come prepared with his "little list." The Senator was relaxed and cheerful as I led him into the Oval Office where the president greeted him like the old and trusted friend that he was. Then the two men disappeared into the President's private study, closed the door, and, with no one else present, talked for a long time.

I imagine that they may have had a drink and exchanged gossip before they got down to business. I know that when the Senator departed, a deal had been struck between them. The President told me he had Senator Dirksen's word that when the Voting Rights Act reached the floor of the Senate, Dirksen would see to it that just enough Republican Senators would fail to support a filibuster to ensure the bill could be voted upon by the full Senate. Thereafter, the Senate undoubtedly would pass the legislation.

That is precisely what happened. On August 6, 1965, Lyndon Johnson signed the Voting Rights Act into law, thus forever changing American politics. As he said at the time, "This is a victory for the freedom of the American Negro. But it is also a victory for the freedom of the American nation."

Although signing the Voting Rights Act was the most dramatic moment in President Johnson's fight to achieve meaningful equality for African Americans, his support for them never wavered throughout his presidency. He never ceased his efforts to do all that he could to improve their lot. That purpose lay at the heart of his poverty program, although he never failed to point out that there were many if not more poor whites everywhere and that the legislation was intended to meet the needs of all citizens regardless of race. Yet his primary focus was on American blacks. During the first years of his presidency, he appointed twenty African Americans to full-time executive positions, thirteen to judicial posts, and three as U.S. Marshals and Attorneys. In addition, he appointed thirty-two African Americans to presidentially appointed Advisory Committees. In total, he appointed the largest number of African Americans to full-time positions in the Executive Branch, not only in any Administration, but in all previous Administrations combined.

Many of his appointments were unprecedented. Thus, President Johnson also named:

- Robert Weaver, the first black Cabinet Officer
- Carl Rowan, the first black Director of USIA
- Samuel Nabrit, the first black Atomic Energy Commissioner
- Hobart Taylor, the first black Director of the Export-Import bank
- Patricia Harris, the first black Ambassador to Western Europe
- Hugh Smythe, the first black Ambassador to Asia
- Lietenant General Benjamin Davis, the first black Lieutenant General of the Army
- Thurgood Marshall, the first black Supreme Court Justice

One further example of an African American nomination that also illustrates President Johnson's shrewdly unique way of dealing with a powerful southern senator was his nomination of Andrew Brimmer as a Governor of the Federal Reserve Board. That nomination also required confirmation by the Senate, and in particular the approval of the powerful Chairman of the Senate Finance Committee, Louisiana Senator Russell Long. Since Brimmer was originally from Louisiana and his area of responsibility in the Federal

Reserve would include Louisiana, the approval of Senator Long was essential. However, Brimmer was black and Senator Long was an opponent of civil rights legislation. Furthermore, Senator Long did not know and had never heard of Andrew Brimmer.

President Johnson saw this latter fact as his opening to secure Senator Long's support of the Brimmer nomination.

President Johnson began by ordering the assembly of a voluminous dossier on the very well qualified Brimmer. Next, Johnson invited Long to meet with him at the White House. When Long arrived, Johnson first offered him a drink and the two of them chatted for a while. Then Johnson pulled out the Brimmer dossier and told Long that the notebook concerned the man Johnson intended to nominate to the Federal Reserve Board.

"I won't do it without your approval," Johnson said. "His name is Andrew Brimmer and he's from Louisiana. Do you know him?"

"No I don't," Long replied, acknowledging what Johnson already knew.

"He's an extraordinary man," Johnson said. "Let me read you a few things about him."

The President then proceeded to go through Brimmer's qualifications, pausing at each step to ask Long if he did not agree that Brimmer was exceptionally well qualified. At each step, Senator Long expressed his enthusiastic agreement with the President.

At the end, Johnson asked, "So will you support Brimmer?"

"Of course I will," Long replied. "I am proud that he hails from Louisiana."

The President then handed Long the Brimmer notebook, saying, "Here, you go through this and see for yourself."

Long slowly flipped through the pages. When he reached the final page, he saw a photograph of Brimmer and, for the first time, he realized that Brimmer was a very dark skinned black man.

Senator Long blanched, then laughed and said, "Mr. President, you got me there, but I will do just as I've promised. I'll support your nomination."

Thus, Andrew Brimmer's rapid confirmation by the entire Senate was assured. He became the first African American to serve on the Federal Reserve Board, a fact of great pride to President Johnson.

ROBERT KENNEDY

In sharp contrast with Lyndon Johnson's close friendship with Everett Dirksen, the Republican Leader, was his relationship with Senator Robert Kennedy, now the Junior Senator from New York and a fellow Democrat. As I have written, Robert Kennedy actively and decisively worked to secure Johnson's agreement to become his brother's Vice President, thereafter, he became embittered about the man who had taken his brother's place as President. After Kennedy won his campaign to become Senator from New York (with Lyndon Johnson's crucial support), he seemed always to be searching for ways to challenge—and hurt—the President. His efforts reached their climax in 1968, which I discuss later. For now, I want to describe an incident occurring in 1965 that upon looking back on it may be fairly judged as the first tentative stirrings in what eventually became Robert Kennedy's full-throated opposition to American policy in Vietnam.

As background, it should be recalled that while his brother was President, Robert Kennedy supported that policy and his views were expressed in fiercely anti-Communist rhetoric. Thus, in 1962, he stated, "This is a new kind of war, but war it is . . ." adding that American troops would stay in Vietnam until Communist aggression was defeated.

President Johnson, advised by the same men who had guided President Kennedy—Dean Rusk, Robert McNamara, and McGeorge and William Bundy—continued that same Vietnam policy after the assassination. Yet, for reasons personal and political, Robert Kennedy was unable to remain constant to his brother's legacy and, obviously hoping that the world would forget the words he previously had spoken, chose to reinvent his persona.

I first became aware of his change of stance in July 1965. It was early evening and I was at my White House desk when I received a telephone call from Sherwin Markman, the young lawyer from Iowa whom I had recruited to come to Washington.

"I was just handed an advance copy of a speech Senator Kennedy plans to give tomorrow," Markman told me. "In it, he attacks our Vietnam policy. As far as I know, he's never done that before, at least not publicly."

"How did you get hold of his speech?" I asked.

"A reporter I know called me and told me about it. He asked me if I would like to see it. I said I would and he messengered it to me."

"Stay where you are and I'll get back to you," I said.

The President was still in the Oval Office. I walked in and told him about Markman's call. "Do you think Markman can get Kennedy to back off?" the President asked.

"He can't say," I said.

"Tell him to try," the President said.

I called Markman and instructed him to go to Kennedy's Senate office and see what could be done about the Senator's proposed speech.

"Do you really want me to take that chance?" Markman asked. "What if Kennedy tells the press that the White House tried to pressure him? Won't we be putting ourselves into his hands if he decides to say that? Or, if he does change his speech, how is he going to explain himself without involving us?"

"See to it that we don't get blamed for anything," I said. "Just tell him not to mention us."

Markman agreed to try. Much later that night he reported to me what had happened.

Markman arrived at Senator Kennedy's office in the early evening. Kennedy was still there and met with Markman, along with Kennedy's two principal speechwriters, Peter Edelman and Adam Walinsky. Markman pointed out that Kennedy's proposed speech with its strong rhetoric opposing American policy in Vietnam would be given while David Bell, the Director of the U.S. Agency for International Development, was sitting on the platform.

"David was an old friend of President Kennedy," Markman said. "Your brother brought him into the office he now holds and his Agency is deeply involved in Vietnam."

"So what?" Walinsky shot back.

"I don't think the Senator wants to embarrass David Bell," Markman replied.

"Perhaps you have a point," Kennedy said to Markman. "Maybe I should soften what I say. What do you propose?"

At that point, the four of them began a careful reading of the advance text of Kennedy's speech, examining it line by line. Each time they reached a portion that was critical of American policy in Vietnam, Markman suggested that it should be dropped while Edelman and Walinsky vehemently argued for its retention. The Senator sat at his desk, quietly listening throughout the sometimes acrimonious discussion. Finally, looking at his watch, Kennedy announced that he was expected home for dinner because he had invited some guests. "The three of you stay here and keep working on my speech," he said. "It would be great if you reach some kind of agreement. In any event, I'll be back later and we will work it out." Turning to Edelman and Walinsky, he added, "You've got to give Markman enough so that I don't embarrass Dave Bell."

The two Kennedy aides were not happy with this last declaration, but it did seem to break the deadlock as the three of them continued their minute dissection of the Kennedy speech. It was close to midnight when the Senator returned, but by then the three exhausted young men had hammered out a compromise. For Edelman and Walinsky, the revised speech was barely acceptable, in that although it did not attack American Vietnam policy, neither did it endorse it. As they told Markman, they were merely postponing their assault until a more propitious time. But Markman was delighted with the result. To him, the new version of the Kennedy speech clearly accomplished his minimum goal of not eviscerating the President and his policies. As for the future, Markman harbored no doubts where Kennedy was heading.

Markman had a final request of the Senator. "The press already has the advance copy of the speech," he said. "It contains all that criticism of our Vietnam policy that we have just agreed to delete. They certainly will ask you about the discrepancies. What are you going to tell them?"

"That the advance text they received was merely a draft," Senator Kennedy replied. "It was delivered to them too early and by mistake. I had not cleared it. It is not what I intended to say and it is not what I said. The only words that count are the ones I say. Won't that do it?"

"Almost," Markman said. "But what if they specifically ask you if the changes were made at the insistence of the President or anyone on his behalf? What if they suggest that the White House pressured you? Or whether anyone on behalf of the President spoke with you?"

"Then I will lie," the Senator said, laughing. "Don't worry about it. I'll protect you."

Markman was satisfied, and when he reported to me on the telephone, I told him to make sure he attended the Senator's speech to make sure he kept his promises.

The next morning, Markman was present during the Kennedy speech. He told me that Kennedy delivered it exactly as had been agreed the previous night. Following the speech, Markman worked his way forward so that he could hear Kennedy as clamoring reporters surrounded him. The questions they shouted at the Senator were exactly those Markman had worriedly predicted, and he told me that he held his breath as he listened to Kennedy's answers.

"Why did you change your speech?" several yelled at the Senator.

"I didn't change a thing," the Senator calmly stated. "I said what I intended to say."

"We know that you changed it," they insisted. "We have your advance text."

"What you have is not my speech," the Senator said.

"Did the White House have anything to do with the changes you made?" someone demanded. "Did they talk to you about it?"

"No, they had nothing to do with it," the Senator said. "It's my speech and nobody outside of my office had anything to do with it."

Markman sounded immensely relieved when he reported to me. When I repeated the incident to the President, he was not impressed. "It's only temporary," he remarked. "Bobby intends to cause me as much trouble as he can. Count on that. Just you keep a careful eye on him."

Of course, the President was proven right. Within weeks, Robert Kennedy began to mount a ceaseless attack against our Vietnam policy. His criticisms continued unabated until his tragic assassination in June 1968. In all that he said, he totally ignored his past words, he acted as if his brother's policies had never existed, and he ceaselessly worked to forge his new identity as a Vietnam dove as well as a liberal—a new and improved Robert Kennedy.

HUBERT HUMPHREY

Hubert Humphrey was a joyously outgoing person. To be with him was always a pleasure. If my day was going badly but I was able to sneak downstairs to the White House staff mess for a quick lunch, and if I was fortunate to have the Vice President join me at the table, he would have me feeling better within moments. Quite simply, it was impossible not to be uplifted by his presence and the love of life he projected. I thoroughly liked the man.

President Johnson shared my feelings concerning Hubert Humphrey. Without question, the President liked his Vice President. They knew each other well and their friendship dated from the years they both served in the Senate.

Based on his frustrations when he was John Kennedy's Vice President, Johnson started his own full term as President with a sincere desire to fully involve Humphrey in every aspect of his administration. Yet despite President Johnson's best intentions, it did not happen that way.

I joined the Johnson White House only twelve days after Hubert Humphrey began his term as Vice President. One of my earliest directives from the President was that the Vice President should be kept fully informed and given duties and authority worthy of the office he held. Although President Johnson's direction to me changed, in the beginning I did my best to carry out his wishes.

I had the best of intentions. Bill Connell was Hubert Humphrey's Chief of Staff and the man I normally would contact to brief the Vice President. But whether through Connell or directly to Humphrey, keeping the Vice President totally up to date required me to brief one or the other of them several times each day. Simply put, I did not have the time to do that. Beginning with my long early morning hours with the President in his bedroom, the remainder of my days were overloaded with telephone calls and meetings required by the President. Almost no time remained for me to deal with the Vice President or his staff.

The inevitable result was that although I tried to carve out time for the Vice President, I failed far more often than I succeeded. Thus my briefings became increasingly sporadic when what was required was constant communication of an unending flow of information from the President to the Vice President. In short, because of my inability to keep Vice President Humphrey fully briefed despite my best intentions, I found myself treading the same water for the same reasons as had President Kennedy and his staff in dealing with Vice President Johnson. It certainly gave me a better understanding of at least one of the reasons Lyndon Johnson was never fully involved in the making or execution of the policies of the President he served.

Nevertheless, President Johnson tried to maintain close personal contact with his Vice President. First, the President made time to meet privately with Humphrey at least once each week, and throughout the Johnson presidency, Humphrey was invited to every meeting of the Johnson Cabinet.

However, the regular personal meetings between Johnson and his Vice President and my orders to keep Humphrey fully informed slowly changed—then disappeared—as the President became convinced that Humphrey was unable to remain silent about what he learned from the President. Humphrey seemed to have a compulsion to talk to the press. To Lyndon Johnson, that was a poisonous habit. The inevitable result was that except where it was unavoidable and proper, the President hesitated to confide in his own Vice President.

It was not that President Johnson did not share a similar vision with Hubert Humphrey. Quite the opposite was true. Both of them had a burning desire to help the less fortunate and a belief that the federal government was both obliged and able to lead that struggle. However, Humphrey had a naive faith in the press that was not shared by Johnson. Humphrey trusted reporters. He ceaselessly confided in them. He believed that if he was frank with them, then they would honor his confidences, understand his problems, and treat him well in their stories. He was an innately trusting man and he sincerely believed that in so doing he was serving the President.

But Lyndon Johnson did not share Humphrey's trust of the media. Johnson was incensed by premature revelations of his thoughts and intentions. To Johnson, if he trusted a man enough to share his ideas, he expected that man to never reveal what was said. Johnson believed that public disclosure only resulted in furthering someone else's agenda and was no more than an attempt to limit his own freedom to act in the manner and at the time he alone had the right to choose.

There was little doubt that Humphrey felt a compulsion to share information with his friends, including those in the media. Humphrey always surrounded himself with reporters. He liked them and they liked him. They accompanied him wherever he went, even on private lobbying excursions with Members of Congress on the presidential yacht, the *Sequoia*. He was always talking to reporters.

The President, of course, became livid about Humphrey's manner with the press. He was both angry and deeply disappointed. Yet throughout, Johnson never lost his affection for Humphrey.

President Johnson never directly confronted Humphrey for his actions. Instead, he dispatched me to meet with the Vice President and convince him to change his ways with the media. I met or spoke with Humphrey dozens of times attempting to do just that. I would patiently explain to him that the President did not agree with Humphrey's methods and that he felt hurt and betrayed by the leaked stories that invariably resulted. Humphrey always agreed with me and promised to change his ways. Of course, he never did, and in my opinion he never could. He was too outgoing, too trusting, and too needful to be universally loved to keep reporters at arm's length. He was never able to keep what he knew to himself.

Inevitably, President Johnson ceased his regular meetings with the Vice President and instructed me to strictly control what I told to him or his staff. Still, the President's affection for the Vice President did not diminish. He knew that Hubert Humphrey was loyal in his heart and was trying to help. He was our friend, not our enemy. However, Hubert Humphrey's way with the media was not that of Lyndon Johnson, and never could be. Thus, at times the counsel of Humphrey was lost to President Johnson, a result that neither man envisaged or intended.

Because I was the President's messenger, Vice President Humphrey and his staff always blamed me for not being fair to him. In truth, I was only doing what I believed and what also was the bidding of my boss, a fact none of them wanted to face.

THE PRESIDENT CONSIDERS RESIGNATION

On October 8, 1965, the President entered Bethesda Naval Hospital for a gall bladder operation. The medical procedure and its aftermath proved to be unexpectedly lengthy. He was not released from the hospital until October 20. During that time, he suffered great pain, although he continued trying to carry out the duties of his office. At times, I slept in the adjoining room of his hospital suite so that I could be available to him whenever I was needed.

During those days, he often spoke of the history of the Johnson men; how so many of them died in their fifties and that he was now fifty-seven.

He began talking to me about his doubts that he could continue carrying the burdens of the presidency. I argued that he should wait and not even think about that until he was out of the hospital and had regained his strength. He shook his head and asked me to get Abe Fortas, whom the President still thought of as his lawyer despite the fact that Fortas had been on the Supreme Court since that summer. The next morning, the president met with Fortas and asked him if a President was permitted to resign. When Fortas responded that he believed it might be constitutional, the President asked Fortas to draft an appropriate letter of resignation. Fortas did so, but thankfully, by the time the President received the draft his pain had subsided and he told me that he had changed his mind, that he would not resign. Nonetheless, from then on I always had a serious doubt whether the President would seek reelection. And in fact he never said that he would.

1966

A DEEPLY RELIGIOUS MAN

Although he was never obvious about it, President Johnson was a deeply religious man. He was a man of faith who believed in his Christianity and accepted Jesus as his Lord and Savior. Yet, as Jack Valenti has written, "Lyndon Johnson was the most tolerant man I have ever known about other men's religious beliefs." Thus, despite the fact that President Johnson was a member of the Christian Church and Mrs. Johnson was an Episcopalian, that never limited where they worshipped on Sundays. When I asked the President why he did not limit himself to a single church, he answered me, "They all worship God, and just maybe by my attendance at different denominations, I will encourage others to attend the church of their choice."

It is not generally known that the President had several specific passages from the King James version of the Bible that he not only strongly believed but often quoted—sometimes using the exact wording in his private conversations and public speeches. Perhaps the most familiar to followers of Lyndon Johnson are these words: "Come now, and let us reason together . . ."

The following are his favorite passages from the King James Version of the Old and New Testaments.

ISAIAH—OLD TESTAMENT

1:17 Learn to do well; seek judgment, relieve the oppressed, judge the fatherless, plead for the widow.

1:18 Come now, and let us reason together, saith the LORD: though your sins be as scarlet, they shall be as white as snow; though they be red like crimson, they shall be as wool.

1:19 If ye be willing and obedient, ye shall eat the good of the land.

ST. MATTHEW—NEW TESTAMENT

25:31 When the Son of man shall come in his glory, and all the holy angels with him, then shall he sit upon the throne of his glory:

25:32 And before him shall be gathered all nations: and he shall separate them one from another, as a shepherd divideth *his* sheep from the goats:

25:33 And he shall set the sheep on his right hand, but the goats on the left.

25:34 Then shall the King say unto them on his right hand, Come, ye blessed of my Father, inherit the kingdom prepared for you from the foundation of the world:

25:35 For I was an hungred, and ye gave me meat: I was thirsty, and ye gave me drink: I was a stranger, and ye took me in:

25:36 Naked, and ye clothed me: I was sick, and ye visited me: I was in prison, and ye came unto me.

25:37 Then shall the righteous answer him, saying, Lord, when saw we thee an hungred, and fed *thee?* Or thirsty, and gave *thee* drink?

25:38 When saw we thee a stranger, and took *thee* in? or naked, and clothed *thee?*

25:39 Or when saw we thee sick, or in prison, and came unto thee?

25:40 And the King shall answer and say unto them, Verily I say unto you, Inasmuch as ye have done *it* unto one of the least of these my brethren, ye have done *it* unto me.

25:41 Then shall he say also unto them on the left hand, Depart from me, ye cursed, into everlasting fire, prepared for the devil and his angels:

25:42 For I was an hungred, and ye gave me no meat: I was thirsty and ye gave me no drink:

25:43 I was a stranger, and ye took me not in: naked, and ye clothed me not: sick, and in prison, and ye visited me not.

25:44 Then shall they also answer him, saying, Lord, when saw we thee an hungred, or athirst, or a stranger, or naked, or sick, or in prison, and did not minister unto thee?

25:45 Then shall he answer them, saying, Verily I say unto you, Inasmuch as ye did *it* not to one of the least of these, ye did *it* not to me.

25:46 And these shall go away into everlasting punishment: but the righteous into life eternal.

GALATIANS—NEW TESTAMENT

6:9 And let us not be weary in well doing: for in due season we shall reap, if we faint not.

6:10 As we have therefore opportunity, let us do good unto all *men*, especially unto them who are of the household of faith.

EPHESIANS—NEW TESTAMENT

4:4 *There is* one body, and one Spirit, even as ye are called in one hope of your calling;

4:5 One Lord, one faith, one baptism,

4:6 One God and Father of all, who *is* above all, and through all, and in you all.

4:7 But unto every one of us is given grace according to the measure of the gift of Christ.

Attending church on Sundays was not a haphazard occurrence for the Johnsons. It was not done for political or public relations purposes. The President had deep religious convictions and felt a strong need to attend church services whenever he could. He would have preferred to do so without any publicity and with no press in attendance, but that was impossible because of the security requirements of the Secret Service that always resulted in a motorcade. In Washington, the President and Mrs. Johnson usually attended his own National City Christian Church and Mrs. Johnson's Episcopal church—and possibly another church—on different Sundays. The President's heartfelt faith was, for me, one of the most attractive characteristics of this complex man.

Following Luci Johnson's conversion to Catholicism on her eighteenth birthday, the President would sometimes take an evening to quietly accompany Mrs. Johnson and her to pray with the priests he called "my little monks" at St. Dominic's Cathedral where Luci worshiped.

The President believed in prayer, which always was for God's guidance in exercising the responsibilities of the burden he carried. He also believed that there was an unbreakable connection between his faith and his world duties. His faith echoed my own. As I once wrote, "What a different world it would be if we took God's spiritual and moral order equally seriously. Then there would be no hate, no discrimination, no abuse of power, no lying or deceit, no oppression, no persecution, no poverty, no crime, no war."

Lyndon Johnson always said that if you were called to be a preacher, teacher, or politician, and if you liked it and were good at it, you all had one thing in common: "You loved people." And if you loved people you were a part of God's plan to help others.

The President had several close spiritual advisors, including his own pastor, Dr. George Davis. In addition, Reverend Billy and Ruth Graham were often the President's guests at the White House and Reverend Graham was always available to counsel and give him moral support. Another was Reverend Calvin Theilman, an ordained Presbyterian preacher from North Carolina who was equally involved with ensuring the President's spiritual well-being. These ministers often read the Scriptures with the President and prayed with him whenever they were with him in the White House.

Lyndon Johnson was putty in the hands of preachers. However tough and profane he might be with others, that all disappeared whenever he was in the presence of a religious leader he respected.

Reverend Theilman was a longtime Johnson supporter as well as one of his spiritual mentors. Thus, he had served as Johnson's campaign manager in Lamar County, Texas, during his 1948 campaign for U.S. Senator—a county that Johnson carried with an eighty-seven-vote majority. During his presidency, Johnson attempted to broaden Reverend Theilman's contribution by sending him to Vietnam as an observer on several occasions. Each time, he returned with suggestions on how to improve America's actions in that beleaguered country. Unfortunately, the bureaucrats invariably shot down his ideas. For example, the Department of Defense rejected his suggestion that our armed forces chaplains be combined into a single corps for the reason that military chaplains had always separately served in each branch of the service. Likewise, civil servants in the Department of Health, Education, and Welfare rejected his view that our battle to win over the Vietnamese would benefit from input by Japanese experts who had excellent credentials in education. Nonetheless, Reverend Theilman remained a trusted spiritual advisor to the Johnsons, and thus he performed an invaluable service to them and to the nation.

RUNNING THE GOVERNMENT

One of the most difficult problems facing any President is how to impose his will upon the vast federal bureaucracy. In this case, the President's "will" means seeing to it that his programs and policies are faithfully executed. That, after all, is his constitutional duty and he is elected by the people to fulfill that role. Achieving a President's aims begins with his careful selection of the members of his Cabinet as well as their principal deputies. Next come the dozens of assistant secretaries who exercise great authority and who are also selected by the President. Finally, there are the thousands of hardworking people who make up the Senior Executive Service (also known as the "Supergrades"—the GS-16s,-17s, and-18s). These vitally important people have properly been described as the bridge between the top presidential appointees and the rest of the federal workforce.

In exercising control over the vast American government, the President must walk a fine line. The media are always searching for what they characterize as presidential or White House "interference" with the departments and agencies that are a part of the executive branch of the government, which after all are what the President has been elected to run. Nonetheless, all too many civil servants are likely to leak to the press any instance where the President or someone on his behalf attempts to interfere with their work. In my opinion, it is unfair for the President or his agents to be criticized for involving themselves in the execution of the President's policies. Still, the President and all of us working for him were aware of the firestorm of negative publicity that could follow any overt effort to reach out and suggest that any federal employee act one way or another.

Lyndon Johnson was sensitive to this problem and directed his staff always to reach out to the civil service only with the greatest care. To reinforce this policy, the President, at a meeting of his entire Cabinet, announced that they and not his staff would direct the operations of all government departments and agencies. Furthermore, if anyone at the White House violated his mandate, the Cabinet officer should immediately inform the President who would forthwith fire the offending staffer.

In truth, the President's announcement was not strictly followed. It was essential for him to oversee and give direction to the government he was elected to lead. For that, he needed his staff to convey his desires to those who actually made things happen. In the larger areas of policy, it sufficed for the President to work through his Cabinet. His directions usually were conveyed to them through me or another member of his staff. In every instance, the Cabinet officer had a perfect right to object and raise the matter directly with the President. That rarely happened, because everyone who worked in Lyndon Johnson's administration knew that although they were free to privately argue policy before the President made his decision, there came a time when they were expected to loyally follow that decision

It was even more difficult when dealing with the independent agencies of the government—although it could be done. For example, William McChesney Martin, then the Chairman of the Federal Reserve Board, insisted on a fiscally conservative policy that could unduly hamper the funding of Johnson's Great Society programs, the Chairman was made to understand that our money printing presses were not all that busy. After that, he softened his position and an accommodation was reached.

A different system was used on matters of lesser concern to the President. In those instances, there were two requirements imposed on the President's staff. The first was to locate in each agency and department a political appointee who had sufficient authority to see to it that a White House request was considered, and who knew without being specifically told that when a staffer made a request, it was made with the President's knowledge and authority. That person would see to it that the White House direction was considered without ever disclosing that it had been received from us. In this manner, we attempted to protect ourselves from any civil servants and their allies in the media.

President Johnson believed that faithful execution of his policies required loyalty to him. "Loyalty" meant a belief that he was leading the country in the proper direction. He knew that without such a belief in his presidency, his administration could not succeed. We spent a great deal of time and effort locating the right people for him to appoint to high positions in the government. In doing so, we installed a system of exploring whether prospective presidential appointees were and would remain loyal to the President.

John Macy was the official charged with the duty of making recommendations to the President regarding the hundreds of people he was required to appoint. Macy did an excellent job of investigating the technical qualifications of candidates for presidential appointments, and the lists he sent to the President always contained the names of competent people. However, Macy's lists never dealt with the question of support and loyalty to the President. For this, we needed someone who was totally committed to the President, completely trustworthy, politically shrewd, and, above all, discreet. In Douglas Nobles—an administrator, educator, and a friend of mine from East Texas who wanted to come to Washington and serve President Johnson—I found the perfect man for the job. Doug was smart, soft-spoken, and unthreatening by nature. However, beneath his gentle exterior he was tough as steel.

I quietly installed Doug in an office in the Executive Office Building. It was his task to keep a close watch over all of John Macy's recommendations. He investigated every one of them for loyalty to the President through his sources in the national and local Democratic Party and his contacts with Governors, Senators, and Congressmen. His presence and duties were no secret from Macy. Doug's insightful memos regarding the loyalty of suggested appointments were sent to me. As a result of Doug's reports, many of Macy's recommendations were rejected and returned to him for further action. In time, Doug's careful work resulted in the formation of an administration more closely attuned to the President who led it.

Our efforts did not stop with the presidential appointees. We also focused on the hundreds of persons holding the critical supergrade jobs in the government. Soon after I joined the President's staff, I began holding weekly meetings at the White House with those who had been promoted to supergrade status, foreign service officers, and judicial appointees. Before he resigned from the White House staff in late 1966, Jake Jacobsen (who had been a top aide to Texas Governor Price Daniel) often joined me in these meetings. My message to all presidential appointments was: put in more than a forty-hour week; set an example of work ethics; do not do any act if your decision would embarrass you or your family; never repeat the President's remarks to you; and do not write a book about the President. For lifetime appointments, I urged them to retire before their seventy-first birthday. All of them always agreed. However, although not too many books were written, on the other hand not many—if any—judges retired by age seventy-one.

Our objective in these meetings was to demonstrate that the President was aware of their importance and appreciative of their contributions to the execution of his policies. Our intention also was to instill in them a sense of inclusion with the presidency and thus build a degree of loyalty to the man who had been elected to lead them.

Unfortunately—but not unexpectedly—the fact that we were holding these meetings was leaked to the press. They in turn, treated our efforts as some kind of diabolical plan by the President to "control" federal employees. This kind of negative press is an excellent example of the unfair treatment to which Lyndon Johnson was subjected. I say this because as President, Lyndon Johnson had the right—actually the duty—to exercise leadership and influence over all federal officials, and in attempting to do so he was only executing the job for which he was elected. It was not only right for us to meet with federal officials, but we trusted that our meetings with them resulted in better government for all.

THE MEDIA

Unfair negative press coverage was a curse that President Johnson could never seem to shake. There are many examples, of which I will mention just a few.

Frank Comier, the Associated Press reporter covering a major presidential press conference, once seriously misquoted the President. When we asked him to review the transcript of the conference and then correct his mistake, he stubbornly refused. He told us that he was reporting "what he had heard" and that nothing, not even a tape recording, would cause him to change his story—and he never did.

A second instance of the power of the press related to our action in the Dominican Republic. The American Ambassador had phoned Washington from beneath his desk while rebels were shooting into the Embassy. He was desperate. He pleaded for American troops to prevent the slaughter of foreign nationals, including many Americans. President Johnson immediately responded and ordered the Marines to land and evacuate the threatened and frightened people. At the same time, the President went on television to inform the American people what was happening and why. The resulting operation was a total success. All foreign nationals who so wished were evacuated, and the only casualty was a broken ankle suffered when a Marine tripped while getting off his helicopter. Within a week, the polls showed that 86 percent supported the President's action.

However—totally ignoring the great American success—*The New York Times* began a drumbeat of criticism of the operation. In a few months, public support of the President's action dropped to below 40 percent.

A third instance was when, in early 1965, the President publicly predicted that his budget would be less than $100 million. Ignoring the President's consistent statements to that effect, the press almost uniformly "reported" that the budget would exceed $100 million. When in fact the President presented Congress with a budge of $98.5 million, the press, citing their own stories to the contrary, falsely accused the President of misleading the American public.

Another instance of the power of selective reporting—this time involving how television producers can edit in such a way that the true context and meaning of an interview is distorted—occurred shortly before Lyndon Johnson's death when Walter Cronkite filmed a lengthy conversation with the former President. When it was aired, the President believed that so much had been cut that his answers and statements had been changed beyond recognition. A serious protest was delivered to CBS, which upon reflection determined that the President should be permitted some redress. Thus the network decided to broadcast an unedited additional hour of a new Cronkite interview. Unfortunately, that hour was not shown until after President Johnson died.

Many historians have fallen victim to the fault that they often rely upon the prejudiced views of unreliable contemporary—and sometimes uncited—sources. Even when those views have been subsequently discredited, the later authors continue to refer to them. An egregious example was contained in the excerpts from author Robert Caro's projected three-volume work on Lyndon Johnson printed in the *Atlantic Monthly*. In an article published in the October 11, 1981, edition of the *Miami Herald*, Jack Valenti described Caro's Johnson project as follows: "In this era when the name of the game is to wound the leader, bleed him and bring him down, Robert Caro uncoiled a new savagery. . . . Caro reaches into the former President's grave to charge him with felonies worthy more of publication in a seedy scandal sheet. . . . It has no warranty, no names, confirmed by no witnesses, void of identity of those supposedly involved. All we have is Mr. Caro's brazen prose."

On April 19, 1990, over nine years later, in a C-SPAN interview of Caro conducted by Brian Lamb, Caro is read an Associated Press article that stated: "Former Johnson aide Jack Valenti accused Caro of being passionately bent on destroying the late President's reputation," to which Caro replied, "I don't think there's any truth in (the charge) . . . at all."

LEGISLATION

The year 1966 began the second and final session of a Congress controlled by the great Democratic majorities induced by President Johnson's 1964 landslide victory over Barry Goldwater. Yet, as the President knew better than anyone, the looming prospect of the fall midterm congressional elections, with the historical likelihood that the Democrats would suffer substantial losses, inevitably resulted in heightened fear of defeat by Democratic Senators and Congressmen, especially those from traditionally Republican states or districts. This need for self-preservation among Members caused increasing difficulties for a President with an undiminished hunger for historic legislative accomplishments.

President Johnson's philosophy of inclusion, whenever possible, of Republicans—and especially their leaders in Congress—in an unending effort to forge bipartisan consensus regarding proposed legislation was critical to his success with the Congress. His friendship with Senator Dirksen remained strong, as was his constant attention to Republican leaders in the House. And of course he urged each of us on his staff to intensify our efforts to maintain close personal contact with Senators and Congressmen so that among all of us serving the President, we covered the entire Congress regardless of political party.

Thus, the President continued his relentless effort to lead, cajole, persuade, and work the Congress. In the end, he compiled an incredible record of legislative accomplishments, even during the normally quiescent second session of the Congress. During 1966, the Congress enacted and the President signed into law legislation that including the following:

- Creation of the Department of Transportation
- The Freedom of Information Act
- The Truth in Packaging Act
- The Model Cities Program
- Creation of the Teachers' Corps
- The Child Safety Act
- Acts concerning traffic safety, highway safety, and mine safety
- Minimum wage increase

The President owed much of his legislative success to the tireless work of Bill Moyers and Joe Califano, Special Assistants who were largely responsible for successfully overseeing the progress from ideas to enactment of the President's domestic legislative program.

In addition, too much cannot be said concerning the brilliant contributions of Harry McPherson who, although only in his mid-30s, had served Lyndon Johnson since 1956. He was the Chief White House lawyer and the principle coordinator (and writer) of the President's speeches. As such, he was decisively involved in the development of legislation.

For all of the credit deservedly received by Moyers, McPherson, and Califano for their involvement in the President's legislative program, the man on our staff who has never received adequate credit is Douglass Cater, ably assisted by his deputy, Ervin Duggan. Cater, a true child of the South, had a quietly unassuming soft-spoken personality. Cater—who also worked as hard at his job as Moyers and Califano—always seemed to have time to listen to and absorb the opinions of others, especially those of Members of Congress.

Cater's responsibilities included the development of legislation that dealt with health and education, subjects he knew as thoroughly as anyone in the government. In doing so, Cater not only made the effort to become close friends with key committee people on the Hill, but, as a Southerner himself, he was able to communicate with them on a personal level. Beyond that, Cater took the time to include crucial Members of Congress in the initial development of ideas as well as in drafting the legislation and enacting the resulting Bills.

For example, where Moyers and Califano succeeded by the sheer force of their intelligence and willingness to work, Cater was equally effective using the techniques of being thought of as "one of us"; that is, comfortable with the conservative Southern barons who controlled the congressional committees with which he had to deal. This latter talent was all the more surprising when one realizes that Cater's views were as liberal as anyone on the White House staff. Among other things, Cater had been educated at Harvard, had taught at Princeton, and had been editor of *The Reporter,* a decidedly left-leaning magazine. But he was born and raised in Alabama, and he looked and sounded like the Southerner he was. He never ruffled the feathers of any Member of Congress, and they always trusted him. Thus he was extraordinarily effective with Congress, and President Johnson never felt less than total admiration for him.

As I have stated, all of us on the President's staff were imbued with the need to respect all Members of Congress, especially those who held key positions of power. An incident that illustrates how important this was to the President occurred when Sherwin Markman found himself in direct confrontation with Ohio's powerful Congressman Wayne Hayes.

By 1966, Hayes had achieved sufficient seniority and status in the House of Representatives to block or at least significantly delay legislation that the President considered critical. Thus, Hayes always had to be treated with great care despite the fact that everyone, especially his fellow Congressmen, disliked him and knew him to bully those unfortunate enough to work under him. Nonetheless, he had power and his brethren in the House deferred to him, as did the White House.

Much later, long after Lyndon Johnson left office, Hayes was caught red-handed in one of his sexual escapades, and he was eventually forced to leave Congress. But in 1966, his powers were undiminished, and although his colleagues privately knew his peccadilloes, his public persona remained unsoiled.

On the occasion in question, Markman had traveled to Paris. While attending a cocktail party given by the American Ambassador at his residence, Markman stood on the fringes of a group of Frenchmen being regaled by a very drunk Congressman Hayes.

Markman listened, aghast, as a slurring Hayes, unsteady on his feet, loudly excoriated the President. "All of you French need to know that Lyndon Johnson is a stupid jerk," Markman heard him say. "If you knew him like I do, you would know that he can't be trusted. He is a rotten President. Don't any of you ever forget that."

Markman could take no more, and before he fully realized what he was doing, he stepped forward and was standing face to face with the Congressman.

"I don't think you should be saying things like that, especially here in Paris," Markman said, trying to stay calm.

"Who in the hell are you?" Hayes demanded.

"I work for the President."

"Do you know who you are talking to too?"

"Yes, sir."

"So you think that gives you the right to try to censor what I say?"

"No, sir. All I am saying is that because you are an important Congressman and we are in a foreign country that you ought to be careful about what you say."

"Go to hell!" the congressman snapped and turned to walk away.

Markman could not stop himself from adding, "And you are very wrong about the President."

Hayes ignored him as he stomped off. Markman stood there feeling pleased with himself for having defended the President. Despite the fact that he had just publicly criticized a powerful Congressman, Markman believed he had done the right thing. He also thought that the incident was finished and that at the most, the very intoxicated man would forget about what just happened. Markman was wrong.

Markman was asleep in his hotel room when the telephone rang. It was almost three in the morning as he groggily picked up the receiver and heard the unmistakably angry voice of Congressman Hayes.

"So I finally found you," Hayes snapped.

"Yes, sir," Markman nervously said. "What can I do for you?"

"You've got that backwards," Hayes said. "It's what I'm going to do to you that you better worry about."

"What is that, Congressman?"

"I want you to know that the minute I get back to Washington, I'm calling the President and I'm getting you fired."

"For what I said at the Ambassador's party?" Markman asked, unnecessarily.

"You've got that right, sonny," Hayes stated. "Don't you think for a moment that your boss won't do what I ask. He needs me and he sure as hell doesn't need someone like you embarrassing me while I am in France."

Markman started to argue, but the Congressman hung up on him.

The day Markman returned to the White House, I called him and told him that the President wanted to see him right away. Together, the two of us walked into the Oval Office where the President was sitting behind his desk.

"What the hell did you do to Wayne Hayes?" the President demanded of Markman. "I just got off the phone with him. He wants you fired, and believe me he is dead serious about it."

"I was only standing up for you, sir," Markman said. "Congressman Hayes was very drunk and he was way out of line in the terrible things he was saying about you. I didn't think it was right for me to stand there and let him get away with tearing you up in front of a group of foreign nationals while we were in our own Embassy residence. I told him that I thought he should stop it."

President Johnson scowled and Markman's heart sank as he realized that he was not going to be praised for having defended the President. Instead, the President said to him, "Have you any idea how important Hayes is to us? He is chairman of the House Subcommittee on State Department Organization and Foreign Operations. I don't need him angry at anyone who works here. You have to make things right with him, and I want you to do it now."

Markman blanched. "How can I do that, Mr. President?" he asked.

For the first time, the President smiled. "Don't worry about losing your job. I'm not going to fire you. If I wanted to do that—and I don't—I wouldn't let Wayne Hayes or any other Congressman dictate who can and can't work for me. You know how I feel about never letting the Congress think that they can roll over me. If any of them ever get that bit in their teeth, there never will be an end to it."

"Yes, sir," Markman said, relieved.

"But you need to go to his office right now—and I mean this morning. You are going to apologize to him, and you are going to keep on apologizing to him until you make him happy. Do you think you can do that?"

"But he was wrong, sir," Markman said. "The things he said about you were awful."

"I don't give a damn," the President said. "All I care about is keeping him on board with my legislative program. I need him for that. Otherwise, I really don't care what he thinks about me."

"All right, sir, I will try," Markman said.

"No, you'll do better than that. I want you to say or do whatever you must to get him back on board with us. If you have to grovel in front of him, then that's what you will do. I know that he's a bully. So I also know that he's going to love to see you prostrate yourself in front of him. Now, you go to him and I don't want to hear from you until you've made things right."

Markman looked sick as we left the President's office. He ordered a White House car from my office and I tried to make him feel better. "Just think of what you are about to do as your daily sacrifice for your country," I told him, smiling. But Markman did not look happy as he left me to carry out the President's order.

Markman had once wanted to be an actor, and as he was driven up to Capitol Hill, he was thinking that his meager skills were about to be fully tested. When he arrived at Hayes's offices and identified himself to the receptionist, he was immediately ushered inside.

Congressman Hayes was seated behind a massive desk, scowling fiercely at Markman. "Did you come here to beg to get your job back?" Hayes began.

"No, sir. I came to apologize to you. What I did in Paris was wrong—very wrong. I should never have said the things I said to you. I had no right to embarrass you. What I did was stupid and I am very sorry."

John F. Kennedy, Speaker Sam Rayburn, and Senator Johnson. Rayburn helped persuade Johnson to accept the Democratic nomination for Vice President. 1960. *Texas Monthly.*

Senator Johnson and Lady Bird Johnson being mobbed by a hostile crowd in Dallas during the final days of the 1960 campaign. *Texas Monthly.*

Jack Valenti, President Johnson, and Watson, followed by Secret Service agents, walking on the Pennsylvania Avenue sidewalk in front of the Executive Office Building next to the White House. No date. *Marvin Watson.*

Watson being walked around the West Lawn of the White House with President Johnson on Watson's first day on the job. On the far right is Lem Johns, the head of the President's Secret Service detail. The others are reporters. February 1, 1964. *Marvin Watson.*

President Johnson and Watson at the President's desk in the Oval Office. No date. *Marvin Watson.*

The "Johnson Treatment":
Getting up close and personal
with Justice Abe Fortas. No date.
LBJ Library.

Landing by helicopter on New York City's East River Drive. Shown are Watson,
unidentified, Robert Kennedy, Markman, President Johnson, and unidentified.
October 12, 1966. *Sherwin Markman.*

White House Situation Room meeting during the Arab-Israeli Six-Day War.
Shown are Clark Clifford, Llewllyn Thompson, Under Secretary of State Katzenbach,
Secretary of State Rusk, Watson, President Johnson, National Security Advisor Bundy,
and Assistant National Security Advisor Rostow. June 8, 1967. *Marvin Watson.*

Thurgood Marshall calling his wife to tell her the President Johnson is about to
nominate him as the first African-American on the Supreme Court.
Watson is in background. June 13, 1967. *LBJ Library.*

President Johnson reciting a humorous anecdote to Soviet Premier Kosygin at the Glassboro Summit Conference. Shown, from left to right, are Watson, President Johnson, the American and Soviet translators, and Premier Kosygin. June 23, 1967. *Marvin Watson.*

Luncheon meeting at Hollybush during Glassboro summit. At this moment, Secretary McNamara, with great emotion, is describing to Premier Kosygin the potential horror of any nuclear exchange between the U.S. and the Soviet Union. Also seen are the Soviet translator and President Johnson. June 23, 1967. *LBJ Library.*

Getting the news first. President Johnson looking at one of the two wire service ticker tape machines he kept in the Oval Office, watching the news the instant it is printed. With Watson on the phone. July 13, 1967. *LBJ Library.*

A restrained President Johnson greeting Rev. Cotesworth Pinckney Lewis in Williamsburg immediately following church service, concerning which the Reverend had deliberately misled Markman and the Secret Service by assuring them that if the President attended church service Lewis would not attack the President in his sermon. Linda Johnson and Lady Bird Johnson are also seen. November 12, 1967. *LBJ Library.*

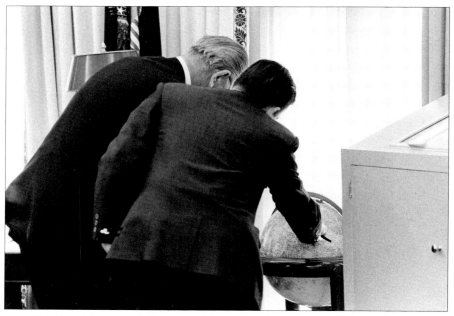

President Johnson and Watson studying globe, planning around-the-world trip.
December 1967. *Marvin Watson.*

A crucial White House luncheon regarding the Tet Offensive in Vietnam.
Seated starting to the left of President Johnson: Secretary of Defense McNamara, Clark
Clifford, General Wheeler, Press Secretary Christian, National Security Advisor Rostow,
Assistant Press Secretary Johnson, CIA Director Helms, and Secretary of State Rusk.
January 30, 1967. *LBJ Library.*

Lady Bird and President Johnson. No date. *LBJ Library.*

Keeping the Republican leadership briefed regarding the Tet Offensive.
House Leader Ford, Senate Leader Dirksen, and President Johnson in the White House.
January 30, 1968. *LBJ Library.*

President Johnson being guarded by Secret Service agent Clint Hill (who famously jumped over the back of President Kennedy's limousine at the time he was fatally shot). Watson is also shown. February 1, 1968. *Marvin Watson.*

A political meeting in the Cabinet Room shortly before President Johnson decided
not to run for reelection. Shown, from left to right, are James Rowe, Watson,
John Criswell, and President Johnson. February 7, 1968. *Marvin Watson.*

Lady Bird assisting President Johnson just before his March 31, 1968 speech,
which stated that he would not seek reelection. March 31, 1968. *LBJ Library.*

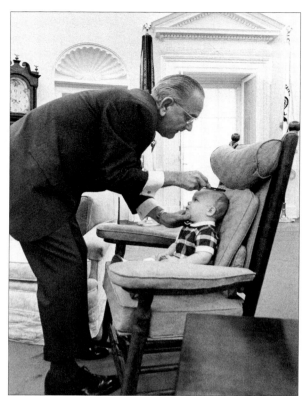

President Johnson with his grandson, Patrick Lyndon Nugent. April 3, 1968. *Marvin Watson.*

Crucial Oval Office meeting immediately following the assassination of Martin Luther King. Shown from left of President Johnson: Louis Martin, Speaker McCormack, Chief Justice Warrant, Judge Leon Higginbotham, Harry McPherson, Justice Thurgood Marshall, Clark Clifford, Walter Fauntroy, James Farmer, unidentified, unidentified, unidentified, and Roy Wilkins. April 5, 1968. *LBJ Library.*

Texas Republican Senator Tower testifying for Watson at his confirmation hearing for Postmaster General. April 1968. *Marvin Watson.*

Watson swearing in as Postmaster General in the Rose Garden. His son, William, has just untied the shoelaces of the President. Inscribed to William from the President. April 25, 1968. *Marvin Watson.*

To Bill Watson
from his friend
Lyndon B. Johnson

Meeting with President-elect Nixon in the second floor sitting room of the White House mansion: the Nixons' first time visit to the presidential living quarters despite his eight years as Vice President. Shown are Mrs. Nixon, Watson, Lady Bird Johnson, Nixon, and President Johnson. November 11, 1968. *Marvin Watson.*

Lady Bird Johnson and Watson dedicating "Beautification" stamp. Inscribed by Lady Bird Johnson. January 16, 1969. *Marvin Watson.*

The President's staff during the final weeks. Seated: Joe Califano and Walt Rostow.
Standing first row: Mike Manatos, James Jones, and Ernest Goldstein.
Standing second row: Barefoot Sanders, Larry Temple, President Johnson,
De Vier Pierson, and Charles Murphy. Standing third row: Robert Hardesty,
Tom Johnson, Harry Middleton, George Christian, Harry McPherson,
Lawrence Levinson, and William Hopkins. January 1969. *LBJ Library.*

LBJ departing Washington for Johnson
City, Texas. Marvin and Marion Watson
are shown to the right of the President,
along with many others from his staff.
January 20, 1969. *Marvin Watson.*

Formal portrait of Johnson and his Cabinet. From left to right: Secretary of Defense Clark Clifford, Secretary of Health Education and Welfare Wilbur Cohen, Secretary of Commerce C. R. Smith, Secretary of Agriculture Orville Freeman, Secretary of State Dean Rusk, Secretary of the Treasury Jospeh Barr, Secretary of the Interior Stewart Udall, Secretary of Transportation Alan Boyd, and Attorney General Ramsey Clark. Standing: Secretary of Labor Willard Wirtz, Vice President Hubert Humphrey, President Lyndon B. Johnson, Secretary of Housing and Urban Development Robert Wood, and Postmaster General Marvin Watson. *LBJ Library.*

Formal portrait of Lady Bird with Cabinet wives. From left to right: Mrs. Alan Boyd, Mrs. Stewart Udall, Mrs. Willard Wirtz, Mrs. Orville Freeman, Mrs. Dean Rusk, Mrs. Lyndon B. Johnson, Mrs. Hubert Humphrey, Mrs. Marvin Watson, Mrs. Clark Clifford, Mrs. Wilbur Cohen (standing), Mrs. Ramsey Clark, and Mrs. Henry Fowler. *LBJ Library.*

Hayes's manner instantly changed. Quite suddenly, he was smiling broadly. "Have you told the President what you just said to me?" Hayes asked.

"Yes, sir," Markman lied. "I told him I had thought about what happened all the way home from Paris, and that I realized how wrong I was. He said that if I understood that much, then I should be man enough to come up here and tell you to your face."

"Yes, I agree with him," said the beaming Congressman.

"That's why I'm asking you to give me another chance," Markman said, feeling the bile rise in his stomach, but somehow managing to keep his expression thoughtful and serious.

Markman's abject apology caused a remarkable change in Hayes's attitude. It was like a shade had suddenly lifted from his face as his expression instantly became welcoming and his manner friendly. To Markman, it was obvious that his words were highly gratifying to the Congressman because Markman was demonstrating to Hayes that, although Markman had not been fired, Hayes had sufficient influence to force the President to cause one of his assistants to humiliate himself. Hayes was ecstatic and what better way to demonstrate how big a man he was than to act magnanimous.

"You've done the right thing, son," he said to Markman. "I not only forgive you but I want to tell you that you are a brave young man to find the guts to come up here and admit your mistake."

"Thank you, sir," Markman said, forcing himself to return Hayes's broad smile.

"As far as I'm concerned, the matter is over," Hayes said.

Markman rose to leave, but Hayes waved him back to his chair. He was in no hurry for this meeting to end. For another hour, Hayes spoke to the presidential assistant, regaling him with congressional gossip and repeatedly stating how pleased he was to help the President carry forward with his programs. Markman did not say much, but he wasn't expected to talk, only listen to the exuberant Congressman. Hayes was thoroughly enjoying his moment of triumph over the President and it was not until an aide discreetly informed Hayes that he had another appointment waiting that he reluctantly walked Markman to the door of his office and said good-bye.

When Markman returned to the White House, I escorted him in to see the President. An obviously shaken Markman reported that he had done the

President's bidding and that apparently it had worked. "That was the most difficult thing I have ever had to do," Markman told the President. "That man may be crazy, and I had to sit there like I was enjoying every moment with him."

"You did the right thing," was the President's only comment. "Now you can go back to work."

Markman paused, and then said, "Believe it or not, Mr. President, but I left there with the impression that Congressman Hayes now thinks I'm his buddy."

"So much the better," the President said. "I want everyone on the Hill to think of you and Marvin and everyone else who works for me as their buddy. That's the way we get them to vote the right way."*

THE WORKINGS OF THE AMERICAN PRESIDENCY: VIETNAM THEN AND NOW AS RELEVANT HISTORY

To understand America's involvement in Vietnam, one must go back to World War I and its aftermath. Following that horrible conflagration, world leaders, including President Woodrow Wilson, concluded that international security could be achieved by an alliance of the civilized nations of the world. Thus they formed the League of Nations. That dream was denied when, largely because of America's historical sense of isolationism, we refused to join. As a result, the League largely remained toothless and ineffective.

Then came World War II, an almost planet-wide disaster that lasted from 1939 to 1945. Following our hard-won and enormously costly victory, the nations of the world, this time led by the United States, formed the United Nations in an effort to prevent a repetition of the previous failure to prevent horrific aggression.

It soon became apparent that the United Nations organization, although

*Some of the substance of the Wayne Hayes confrontation, as well as subsequent episodes concerning Glassboro, Williamsburg, Markman's ghetto trips, and Congresswoman Hansen (discussed later), are also recalled in Sherwin Markman's two essays in *Lyndon Johnson Remembered* (Rowman & Littlefield, 2003). They appear in this book with permission of the publisher.

valuable, was too cumbersome to be truly effective. Thus, the North Atlantic Treaty Organization (NATO) was established during the presidency of Harry Truman. NATO proved hugely effective in protecting Western Europe from the onslaught of the aggressive ambitions of the Soviet Union. Greatly impressed with NATO's success in combating Communism, we looked toward forming similar multinational organizations in other regions of the world.

Accordingly, in 1954, President Eisenhower fully backed by bipartisan support in Congress, led us into the Southeast Asia Treaty Organization (SEATO). That treaty was also signed by Australia, New Zealand, France, Pakistan, the Philippines, Thailand, and the United Kingdom. In the treaty's key provision, each party agreed that armed aggression in Southeast Asia against a treaty member would be resisted "at the invitation or with the consent of the government concerned." With the consent of all the signatories, South Vietnam was added as a protocol state fully protected by the treaty. Interestingly, such future "doves" regarding our entry into the Vietnam conflict as Senators Fulbright and Mansfield voted to ratify the SEATO Treaty.

In the late 1950s, North Vietnam began a large-scale campaign of military aggression against South Vietnam. In his response, President Eisenhower stated: "We reach the inescapable conclusion that our own national interests demand some help from us in sustaining in Vietnam the morale, the economic progress, and the military strength necessary to its continued existence in freedom."

President Eisenhower began sending American military forces into South Vietnam. In the beginning, they were called "advisors." In July 1959, the first of these American "advisors" was attacked and killed by the Viet Cong.

On the morning of January 20, 1961, as President Eisenhower and President-elect Kennedy stood in the foyer of the White House just before riding to the Capitol for John Kennedy's inauguration, President Eisenhower turned to Kennedy and stated (as he later told Lyndon Johnson): "The main problem I leave you is South Vietnam and its protection under SEATO."

Both Presidents Eisenhower and Kennedy believed—as did President Johnson until after the 1964 election—that North Vietnam would never directly attack American troops; that the killing that had already occurred was an aberration. As it turned out, they were wrong, but until it happened they continued to act as if the assumption was true. Accordingly, President

Kennedy escalated the number of American military forces in South Vietnam. By the time of President Kennedy's assassination, he (supported by all of his principal advisors) had committed more than twenty-five thousand American troops to that country.

The Kennedy administration orchestrated one further disaster in South Vietnam: the assassination of its leader, Ngo Dinh Diem, on November 1, 1963—just weeks before President Kennedy's own tragic death. The removal of Diem destabilized South Vietnam to a far greater degree than the American backed perpetrators envisioned.

This was the situation in Vietnam when Lyndon Johnson took office on November 22, 1963: the SEATO Treaty, backed by two previous American Presidents and the Congress, was in full force and effect. Under that treaty, the United States and the other signatories were obligated to defend South Vietnam when it was militarily attacked by North Vietnam. Furthermore, America was all too aware of the Communist doctrine of unending expansion. President Truman had fought it in Greece and Turkey, and NATO was poised to defend Europe against them. Now, we believed that capitulating to Communist aggression in South Vietnam would have a "domino" effect throughout all of Southeast Asia, making that entire region of the world vulnerable to Communist control.

When President Johnson assumed office, he knew that two American Presidents had approved SEATO's implementation in South Vietnam; sizable numbers of American troops were already in place there; and the newly leaderless government of South Vietnam was in total disarray.

To understand President Johnson's reaction to this situation, one must remember that he was a Texan where the principle that "my word is my bond" is both tangible and binding. Thus, he fervently believed that America's obligation under SEATO was "our contract, our commitment, our treaty" that the country he now led must honor.

Furthermore, every key aide to President Kennedy—all of whom now served Lyndon Johnson—unanimously agreed that America must stay the course in South Vietnam regardless of its cost in men and resources. These advisors included Secretary of State Dean Rusk, Secretary of Defense Robert McNamara, National Security Advisor McGeorge Bundy, and the Joint Chiefs of Staff, including General Maxwell Taylor.

President Johnson did not limit his advisors to members of his administration. He took care to include the congressional leaders of both political parties. He also sought out a group of men who came to be known as the "wise men" of American foreign policy. In *The Vantage Point,* President Johnson writes that they were composed of former Secretary of State Dean Acheson, Undersecretary of State George Ball, General Omar Bradley, McGeorge Bundy, Arthur Dean (who had negotiated the Korean War settlement), former Treasury Secretary Douglas Dillon, Ambassador Henry Cabot Lodge, retired diplomat Robert Murphy, General Mathew Ridgeway, Gen. Maxwell Taylor, and Deputy Secretary of Defense Cyrus Vance. Also consulted were former New York Governor Averell Harriman, former U.S. high commissioner in Germany John McCloy, and Clark Clifford, who had been a confidant of President Harry Truman. Added to this illustrious group were two former Presidents: Eisenhower and Truman, with whom President Johnson maintained a continuing close relationship. He saw to it that both Presidents were kept fully briefed. They were often consulted and both knew that they were free to express their opinions without constraint.

As for how a President makes vital national decisions, it is inaccurate for anyone to say that President Johnson ever did so unilaterally and without total input from the best experts he could find to advise him. I am certain that is equally the case with any other President. A President is not a monarch sitting on a throne making decisions and issuing decrees. Of course, he is the elected leader of the nation, and he is the Commander in Chief. But a President is always searching for the wisest advice he can get, and if it is possible, he is also searching for consensus among those advisors. Thereafter, his duty is to express that consensus and convince the American public that it is the correct policy for them to follow. A President has been given the highest honor that the people can grant to another: They have freely elected him as their leader, and they are the President's sole earthly judges. Thus, the President has but one question to answer during his time in office: Did I do all that I could to protect the people and our nation?

This was the case with President Johnson and the war in Vietnam. Although he ultimately failed to convince many of the American people, and most especially the American media, that our Vietnam policy was correct, he nonetheless never stopped trying. Not only was he following a national policy of Communist containment that had been consistent American doctrine since the first days of the Cold War, but in the years of his presidency he never failed to fully consult with every available expert.

As I have written, initially there was never less than unanimity among all of these advisors. On each and every occasion that these men were asked for their judgment, they told the President that the policy we were following in Vietnam was correct. Thus, despite increasing demonstrations against that war, the most knowledgeable people advising the President did not tell him that he was doing anything other than the right thing for America.

It must be the same for any President. His decisions as to whether to go to war, where to fight, how to mount our attacks, and every other aspect of American policy and the means to implement it are, I am certain, not made by him in isolation. His leadership undoubtedly reflects the informed opinions of the men and women around him whom he trusts and who are the wisest, most experienced people available to him.

President Johnson, however, took one additional—and probably unique—step. Despite the unanimity of the advice he was receiving, he was very aware of the increasing signs of dissent around the country. One day while I was sitting with him at a meeting of his key advisors, he abruptly broke into the discussion to ask, "Do any of you hear those demonstrators marching in front of the White House?"

Everyone nodded, and someone—I think it was Secretary Rusk—stated, "They are only kids, Mr. President. They don't understand anything about this problem."

"You're probably right," the President said, looking around the room. "But there are a lot of young folks out protesting these days. They probably include some of your own children."

No one sitting there wanted to admit to the truth of the President's remark, although McNamara (and Markman) later said that their own children were indeed among the marchers.

"I agree that they probably don't know what they're shouting about," the President continued. "But that doesn't mean I shouldn't listen to them. After all, I am their President too."

"I hope you aren't going to invite them into the White House," someone said.

"No, but what I am thinking is that I want to give them some kind of voice in this room," the President said.

Then President Johnson recessed the meeting in the Cabinet Room and asked George Ball to join him in the Oval Office. I went along and listened to their conversation.

"George, I know you support what we are doing in Vietnam," the President began.

"Yes, sir, I do," Ball stated.

"You are very articulate in how you express your opinions," he continued.

"Well, Mr. President, I am a lawyer, as you know," Ball said, smiling.

"A damned good one," the President said.

"Thank you, sir. I do my best for you."

The President paused. "That's exactly why I've decided to give you a very special task. From now on, I want you to argue the case for those demonstrators marching out there."

Ball looked shocked. "I'm afraid I don't understand," he said.

"What I mean is that from now on, every time there is a meeting like the one we just finished, I want you to present the arguments of those youngsters. I want you arguing their case as effectively as you can. The big difference between you and them is that you can present their arguments based on your access to every piece of information available to everyone else in the room—including whatever may be sensitive or classified. In that way, I and everyone advising me will have to deal with the best arguments that can be made against what we are doing."

"But why me, Mr. President?" Ball said. "You know that I agree with everything we are doing in Vietnam."

"I'm asking you because you are probably the best lawyer in the room. You know how to assemble the facts and express the best possible arguments. You've had a lifetime of experience doing that for clients even when you don't agree with them. You've made a very good living at that, George. Now your President is asking you to use those same skills for your country."

"Of course I will do as you wish," Ball said. "But may I ask one more question? Why do you want me to do this?"

"Because I have never trusted any situation where everyone I talk to gives me the same opinion. Maybe there is only one right answer regarding Vietnam, but I still want that advice to be tested and defended against the most effective arguments that can be mustered. That's the only way I'll feel comfortable with the advice I'm receiving."

"That makes sense," Ball said. "I will do my best."

"I know you will," the President said. "What I need is for you—always—to dissent as persuasively as you can every time you think of a good argument that can be made. I will never stop you."

From that moment on, in every private meeting among the President's principal advisors, George Ball became the articulate spokesman against American policy in Vietnam. The arguments he expressed—always calmly but forcibly stated—were, to say the least, annoying to the President's other advisors. Privately to the President, these men voiced their objections to Ball's vigorous arguments, and they were amazed that a President they always viewed as impatient and intolerant of dissent never took any action to suppress Ball.

In time, Ball's expressions of dissent were leaked to the press, which began treating him as a hero, a "man of peace" who was not afraid to courageously stand up to the President. But the media did not know that Ball was only doing the President's bidding. What they never appreciated was that President Johnson had deliberately created a situation where his advisors were forced to defend their opinions against the most effective, knowledgeable, and articulate adversary the President could pit against them.

I want to add a word about the Gulf of Tonkin Resolution adopted by the Congress on August 7, 1964, by a unanimous House and with only two dissenting votes in the Senate. That resolution authorized the President to "take all necessary measures to repel the armed attack against the forces of the United States and to prevent further aggression . . . (and) to assist any member or protocol state of the . . . (SEATO) Treaty requesting assistance in defense of its freedom." Much has been written about whether American ships in the Gulf of Tonkin were in fact attacked by North Vietnamese forces earlier that month—the main assumption behind the passage of that resolution. Although I was not yet in the White House at that time, I was told by the President that the only reliable reports he received consistently claimed that an attack on American ships had been launched by North Vietnam; that the attack had been renewed; and that our military leaders were insisting upon sufficient authority to protect our own forces. As I have stated, a President must rely on the accuracy of the informed opinions of his advisors. Subsequent doubts are for historians, not for a President who must act based on whatever he is told by the people he assumes know the facts.

In late 1964—contrary to all of the advisors' previous assumptions—American troops on the ground were attacked by the Viet Cong, who killed five, wounded fifty-six, and destroyed twenty-seven airplanes. When that occurred, the President believed that he had no choice but to order sufficient additional forces into South Vietnam to protect the troops already there. Our troop strength gradually increased throughout 1965. By the end of the year, American strength in South Vietnam had grown to approximately 184,000 troops, aided by additional forces from Australia, South Korea, and New Zealand, as well as 600,000 armed forces from South Vietnam. At that time, all of President Johnson's advisors believed that the dramatic increase in our combined forces in South Vietnam would ultimately break the will of North Vietnam to resist. In fact, the advisors were wrong, but none of us knew it at the time.

What the press and public also did not know was the extent to which the President agonized over what was happening in Vietnam, especially the casualties among the American troops he was ordering into battle. His "wise men" were continuously telling him that the war's "turning point" was "just around the corner"—a corner that was never reached. They were advising him that America had no choice but to continue the war to its conclusion. Despite the arguments of George Ball, the President remained convinced that our policy was both essential and just. Nonetheless, President Johnson suffered over the increasing loss of life among American troops in Vietnam. He could not get over the feeling that we were involved in an endless quagmire. Often, he could not sleep through the night, and the officers in the Situation Room would be surprised when a concerned President suddenly called or appeared and asked them to give him the latest information regarding what was happening in that far-off country.

Slowly and inexorably, American troop commitments in South Vietnam continued to grow. In each instance, those increases were requested by the military backed by the civilian leadership of the Department of Defense. Not once did President Johnson refuse their requests. Throughout, the President never ceased his search for a peaceful solution. He used every available diplomatic channel to communicate his willingness to massively assist North Vietnam to recover and grow—if only it would stop its aggression against

South Vietnam. But—backed by China and the Soviet Union, whose dreams of world domination had not diminished—North Vietnam never responded.

Then, in early 1968, the "wise men" and President Johnson's newly appointed Secretary of Defense, Clark Clifford, suddenly reversed their advice to him and, for the first time, said that the United States must seek peace and withdraw. It was only then that Lyndon Johnson determined that all requests for further escalation would be denied in an all-out effort to bring North Vietnam to the peace table.

Although there is no such thing as an exact historical parallel, the problems we currently face in the Near East have an eerie resonance to those dealt with by President Johnson in Vietnam. I would categorize these similarities into four areas: (1) the making of American policy; (2) the need to gain and retain the support of the American people; (3) the need to win the "hearts and minds" of the civilian population living in and near the nation we are trying to save, liberate, and rebuild; and (4) the necessity of placing political limits on the use of American power.

There is also more than a faint echo in the growing dissent of today and the increasingly disruptive protests and demonstrations that plagued us as the Vietnam War continued and success eluded us. When we started in Vietnam, the American people—and the Congress—supported our policy. We learned to our sorrow that their support was not deep and did not last. As time went on and casualties and costs increased, the crucial backing of our policy by the people began to erode. I well remember the day when Walter Cronkite, then the dean of television anchormen, read an editorial where he withdrew his backing of our policies. At that moment, President Johnson said, "If we have lost Cronkite, we may have lost the people."

Rightly or wrongly, an American President cannot effectively lead without the support of the American public. If that is lost, so is the President. We learned that lesson in the most painful way, and what was true then could be true again. As George Santayana famously said, "Those who cannot remember the past are condemned to repeat it."

Another striking similarity between the struggle in Vietnam and America's war against terrorists and dangerous aggressors is our effort to win the support of the people in and around the world as well as within the nations and regions where we are fighting. The phrase "winning the hearts and minds" of the people is surely being repeated regarding this twenty-first-century war.

Now as then, we face the almost impossible task of separating those who are friendly to us from those who despise us. In Vietnam, the Viet Cong could seamlessly blend into every village, and either through fear or support, the others in the village refused to identify them. Now we are faced with a Muslim population consisting of people believing in various interpretations of their religion and equally varying political philosophies. This has resulted in a population that at best tolerates us, and at worst despises us, but seldom feels love for us. Unless they choose to reveal themselves, we cannot distinguish among them. There is quite simply no way of separating our sworn enemies from those who are not. Worse yet, even those who abhor terrorism for the most part also oppose American policies in the Middle East, especially our support of Israel. We cannot ignore the screaming masses seen on the streets of the Islamic nations and the Palestinian areas in the Middle East. As we watch the violent demonstrations, we can have little doubt how difficult, if not impossible, is the task of persuading them that we are not their enemy.

My own experience does not permit me to be optimistic. I can only hope that the outrageous conduct of the Muslim fanatics ultimately will destroy their base of support among their populations. Yet quite obviously the fanatics have great support, and any President and his advisors—just like President Johnson and his—faces the daunting task of winning "the hearts and minds" of another society.

One final similarity between the war in Vietnam and the war against terrorism is America's self-imposed limits on the use of our military power. It is true that in Vietnam, America did not unleash its full military potential, either in the forces we deployed or in the targets we selected. It is also true that a good argument can be made that if we had used our total power in Vietnam, the ultimate military outcome might have been different. It is true that the fact that we did not do so was based on political judgments made by our elected leaders. I am sure that each President tries his best to make decisions that will protect our nation and its people. He must make the hard decisions because the easier ones can be and are made by others. The difficult choices a President makes are invariably based upon his own best judgment in close consultation with his most trusted advisors.

Regarding Vietnam, President Johnson and his advisors decided that although our objective was to defeat the Viet Cong and stop North Vietnam's invasion of South Vietnam, we must do so without escalating the struggle into a war between American and China, the Soviet Union, or both. What happened in Korea when American forces reached the Yalu River and drew the Chinese army into the war was a vivid memory to all of us. We did not want to repeat that mistake in Vietnam. Thus, we made sure that we did not bomb close to the Vietnam-China border. With equal care, we excluded targets such as the Haiphong Harbor where Soviet ships regularly resupplied the Vietnamese. Most important, we never used nuclear weapons.

As for the number of American troops deployed in Vietnam, until 1968 the President honored the military's requests and judgments. Invariably, they told him that the numbers they asked for—and received—would be sufficient to win the war. They were wrong, as their ever-increasing demands ultimately demonstrated. It was not until 1968 that President Johnson for the first time refused to approve any further escalation. By then, he and most of his trusted advisors—notably led by Clark Clifford, his newly appointed Secretary of Defense—concluded that the military was wrong and that the war in Vietnam could not be won except by taking risks the President would not take and at a price the country would not pay.

These were the judgments we made, and yes, they were political in nature. That is what leaders in a democracy do, and it is the philosophy behind America's long tradition of civilian control of the military. Thus, it was disingenuous for President Bush to have claimed that political considerations are not involved in our use of the military in the war against terrorism. Indeed, it is fair to say that political thinking *must control* how and where we exercise our military power.

It is true that the analogy between Vietnam and the war against terrorism is imperfect. As I have stated, there never is a perfect historic fit. But the similarities are striking and are ignored at our peril.

Two examples are illustrative. First, in Vietnam we did not use nuclear weapons and other weapons of mass destruction—and that includes tactical weapons to aid ground operations—even though we may have had those weapons in abundance. We withheld using that power because, if we did, their use would also eviscerate political support not only from friendly nations, but also from the rest of the world. That is a political judgment that limits use of our military power.

Another example is the fact that although President George W. Bush is convinced that nations in addition to Iraq harbor terrorists and are developing biological and nuclear weapons, we stay our hand against them because of our concern that if we broaden the countries we attack we will further fragment the world and weaken our own ability to control events. That too is a political judgment, which controls our military responses. Therefore, now as then, our elected leaders must make critical political decisions regarding prosecution of wars. It is wrong to claim otherwise.

TAPING

I do not know when the practice of secretly recording conversations at the White House began, but the system was in place before and during the time I worked for President Johnson. While I was there, it was operated under the supervision of the White House Communications Agency, an Army unit commanded by Colonel (later General) Jack Albright.

For President Johnson, the system came about for the simple reasons that Juanita Roberts, the President's principal secretary, could not take adequate shorthand. After an occasion when Attorney General Katzenbach unsuccessfully attempted to dictate a memorandum to her, the President decided that some kind of recording system should be inaugurated. Thus, Colonel Albright was directed to install and service an operation whereby the President could record all of his telephone conversations by merely pressing a button. When he pressed that button, he alerted one of his secretaries sitting in her office adjoining the Oval Office, and she turned on a recorder that contained only two twelve-minute tapes. Since the device was not located in the Oval Office, no one sitting with the President was aware that the telephone conversation was being recorded. The President had a similar system installed in his bedroom, at Camp David, and at the LBJ Ranch.

President Johnson considered the existence of the recording system a secret and he wanted it to remain secret. Almost none of these presidential conversations were transcribed while he was President, and when they were, care was sometimes taken to disguise them. For example, one of the rare transcriptions was a telephone conversation between the President and the rogue black congressman from Harlem, Adam Clayton Powell. Because Powell was in such disrepute (on March 1, 1967, the House of Representatives overwhelmingly voted to exclude him from the 90th Congress), the President wanted the transcript altered so that it appeared to be a conversation between Congressman Powell and one of the President's legislative assistants.

Harry Middleton, Director of the Johnson Library, authorized these recordings to be made public. They form the basis of the books written by the historian Michael Beschloss. I am aware that many people, including Mrs. Johnson, have approved this decision, and that they believe that the release of the taped conversations serves the memory of President Johnson by demonstrating his true character and humanity.

I am not among those who agree with that decision. My opinion is based on the fact that President Johnson unequivocally stated that he did not want any of his tapes released to the public until fifty years after his death. I believe that the President's clear directions should have been honored. In my opinion, President Johnson wanted his recorded conversations to be the final word regarding what he said and did. He knew that there would be a number of inaccurate reports by those with whom he dealt; he wanted to wait while those who would speak falsely did so; and then, after all were gone, he intended for the facts to be known through his own words.

While he was in office, I asked the President to permit me to record all of my telephone conversations. My reason was that I had learned most senior officials in Washington had a "second ear" on every phone call. They used someone's shorthand to record most conversations. McGeorge Bundy and Walt Rostow were two White House staffers who did this. I felt that I needed the recordings to protect myself from inaccuracies. As far as I am aware, I am the only person on his staff for whom this was done. In my case, Colonel Albright installed a recording system that I could neither activate nor turn off. Every one of my calls was recorded. I have sent these tapes to the Johnson Library.

Late in his presidency, President Johnson had one further recording system installed that was so secret that at first only the President, Colonel Albright's people, and I knew of it: they installed hidden microphones within the conference table in the Cabinet Room. Only the President could activate those microphones by pressing a button next to his chair. If they were turned on, all conversations in the room could be recorded. Eventually, the entire Cabinet was informed of the system. As far as I know, this facility was used only once at a Cabinet meeting, with all members forewarned of the record being made. I note that none of the tapes thus far released by the Library reflect nontelephonic conversations. Should these tapes still exist, I am informed that one day they will be transcribed and made public.

In January 1969, when President Johnson was leaving office, he ordered Colonel Albright to remove all of these recording systems. Colonel Albright did so, but as we all know from the Watergate hearings, President Nixon installed an even more sophisticated system of recording conversations, one that was not limited to telephones and one that was voice activated. Thus it could not be controlled by the President—a fact that I am sure President Nixon lived to regret.

Finally, our security people informed me that my house and telephones were not secure from prying electronic spying by others, including countries that were both friend and foe. I was instructed to assume that everything I said, except over the lead-enclosed telephone lines at the White House or in the President's small private office adjoining the Oval Office, was being monitored by others. I was told to always conduct myself accordingly. I did my best to do so.

LUCI'S WEDDING

In the summer of 1966, the serious work at the White House was happily interrupted by the wedding of the President's younger daughter, Luci. Always a vivacious young lady, Luci had converted to Catholicism in 1965 when she was eighteen. The President and Mrs. Johnson did not try to stop her. As a matter of fact, the President often included attending Catholic masses on Sunday mornings. At times, when the pressures of his office became extraordinarily intense, he would go with Luci—sometimes late at night—to pray with the priests at a Georgetown Catholic church.

Now, at nineteen years of age, Luci was to be married to Patrick Nugent. The wedding was planned for Saturday, August 6, 1966, at the National Shrine of the Immaculate Conception. A large crowd was expected to fill the church. The day before the wedding, the President was informed that the church was not air-conditioned, and that the weather for the wedding day would be typical for a Washington August—hot and humid. When the President realized that every guest at Luci's wedding would be forced to suffer in the oppressive heat at the church, he told me he had called Warren Woodward (a friend of the Johnson family and a man who reliably got things done) to ask him to get the church cooled down by the following day. As always, Woody completed his task—just in time.

The wedding went off perfectly and everyone remained comfortably "cool" throughout the ceremony. The only distraction occurred when Luci's older sister, Lynda, fainted. As it turned out, Lynda's spell was caused by nothing more serious than that she had stood with her knees stiffly locked. As I had learned years before while in the Marine Corps, that posture will cause even the strongest to lose consciousness.

But the wedding and the attendant celebrations were a happy respite for a President increasingly beset by problems.

THE DEMOCRATIC NATIONAL COMMITTEE

Historically, the Democratic National Committee (DNC) was given great prominence by President Franklin Roosevelt, or more specifically, by his most trusted political advisor, James Farley, who was then known as "Mr. Democrat." Farley, a well-seasoned politician from New York, was named Postmaster General after Roosevelt was elected president. They continued their close collaboration until 1940, when their relationship permanently foundered over Farley's strong belief that no President, including Roosevelt, should seek more than two terms in office.

The falling out between Roosevelt and Farley directly led to the diminished importance of the Democratic National Committee. Before 1940, the DNC was kept under Farley's firm control. After that, when it became apparent that Roosevelt was going to break his commitment to Farley that he would never run for a third term, Farley and Roosevelt's Vice President, John Nance Garner of Texas, joined together in an effort to stop Roosevelt. Their motives have been questioned by others (both of them had ambitions for higher office), but their not-too-secret alliance against Roosevelt ensured retribution by the President. Garner was dumped from the 1940 ticket and replace by Henry Wallace. As for Farley, Roosevelt insured that Farley's principal vehicle of power, the Democratic National Committee, thereafter was all but ignored.

Years later, John Kennedy needed the DNC and gained full control over it before and during his campaign for the presidency. After Kennedy's narrow defeat of Richard Nixon, he continued to use it as his permanent political vehicle. By then, the Committee's staff was totally dedicated to Kennedy. It was headed by Connecticut's loyal political boss, John Bailey, and by Richard Maguire, its treasurer. After my experience at the 1964 Democratic Convention, I was convinced that the DNC was still a Kennedy vehicle and not dependably loyal to President Johnson.

After I became a part of President Johnson's staff on February 1, 1965, he gave me the responsibility of controlling on his behalf all political activities. That included oversight over the Democratic National Committee. Because of the 1964 Convention experience, we decided that except for traditional functions such as get-out-the-vote campaigns, we would put strict limits on its activities, authority, and budget.

The President decided, consistent with his policy of retaining continuity with President Kennedy's people, to retain Bailey and Maguire as Chairman and Treasurer of the DNC. However, because they were not Johnson choices, actual power at the Committee was vested in three Johnson men: Cliff Carter, the Texas businessman who had been Johnson's liaison at the Committee since 1960; John Criswell, a young Johnson loyalist from Oklahoma, who despite an unassuming title actually functioned as the de facto chairman of the Committee; and Arthur Krim, a close New York friend of President Johnson and the head of United Artists, who became the chief fund-raiser for the President. All of these men reported to the President through me, although because he was such a good friend of the Johnsons (the Krims built a home near the LBJ Ranch in Texas), Krim spoke to the President whenever he chose. He was, however, meticulous about keeping me fully informed.

The President's 1964 election campaign was successful without significant assistance from the DNC. President Johnson believed that he was not beholden to it for his landslide victory. Thus we began a focused program to downsize its activities as well as its influence and authority. That did not mean that we ignored the immense debt the Committee had accumulated before and during John Kennedy's 1960 presidential campaign and (because of his heavy use of the Committee) during his thousand days in office. Not surprisingly, the Committee's staff and budget had grown enormously, and the debt was unpaid when Lyndon Johnson became President.

Once in office, President Johnson believed that he had the responsibility of seeing to it that the DNC's debt was eliminated. He never shirked from that duty even though the money he raised for that purpose was badly needed elsewhere, especially for the 1966 midterm congressional elections.

The President instructed me to oversee raising enough money to totally eliminate the Committee's debt. Arthur Krim was given principal responsibility over this project. He was magnificently successful, and before Vice President Humphrey began his own campaign for the presidency in 1968, the Committee's debt was paid off in its entirety.

The fact that the President honored his duty to repay past debts of the Committee did not prevent him from taking a hard look at the Committee's future, especially during the time of his presidency. He believed that the Committee's greatest value occurred when the Democratic Party was out of office. It was then that the Party needed an organization that could rally its supporters and give voice to its message. However, when the Democrats controlled both the presidency and the Congress, the Committee lost these roles and the justification for its existence became limited to prosaic political functions. Even in that regard, we found that the state parties did most of the work, including the Committee's most basic function of getting Democrats to register and vote. All of its other powers became centralized in the White House and in the congressional leadership. Thus, at the President's direction, I began a process of radically cutting the Committee's staff and budget.

In the latter respect, although Bailey and Maguire—who were John Kennedy's people—asked that they be permitted to retain their jobs, that did not prevent us from materially diminishing the organization they nominally headed. That effort is illustrated by the fact that in 1965 the Democratic National Committee spent $1.75 million, while for 1966, Chairman Bailey, seeing the writing on the wall, requested an annual budget of $1.1 million, a 40 percent decrease. After Arthur Krim and I met with Bailey regarding his budget request, we recommended that the Committee's operations could be curtailed even further. We suggested that a total of forty-three Committee employees could be eliminated in 1966. The President consented and agreed that the Committee's budget be cut to no more than $1 million.

An amazing change in the finances of political parties has taken place since we left office, one that far exceeds any inflationary factors. For example, in 2001, the Democratic National Committee received $128 million in federal and nonfederal funds (which was far below the over $231 million received by the Republican National Committee). This explosion of political money is both dramatic and disturbing.

Our efforts to limit the size and influence of the DNC were not without opposition, especially from Senator Robert Kennedy. For example, he tried to stop Krim from raising money because he believed the money was only used by the President. He was totally mistaken because all that money went to the Democratic National Committee. Krim used the "President's Club" for $1,000 or more political contributions from wealthy supporters of the President. In the fall of 1966, Senator Kennedy made it known to us—and to potential members of the President's Club—that he would keep track of these people and put their names in his "black book," whatever that was. Of course, Kennedy's threats did not stop or even slow contributions to the President's Club

Another objection to the President's Club came from Gerald Ford, then the Republican leader in the House of Representatives. Congressman Ford attempted to mount an investigation aimed at demonstrating that President's Club members received special treatment, especially regarding Department of Justice decisions. He never got his investigation off the ground, and even if he had, he could not have shown preferential treatment because it never happened.

To briefly jump ahead, I should mention that in the fall of 1967, when the President was actively considering whether or not he would run for reelection, he consulted with James Rowe, a man whose political experience dated from the days of President Roosevelt. These discussions revealed considerable disagreement regarding the role of the Committee in the President's possible 1968 campaign. Rowe strenuously argued that the Committee should be reinvigorated and widely used by the President, especially for contacting and persuading disaffected younger voters. The President carefully considered Rowe's suggestions, but his lack of faith in the Committee remained unchanged through March 31, 1968, when he withdrew as a candidate for reelection.

THE 1966 MIDTERM CONGRESSIONAL CAMPAIGN

The fact that the President had minimal use for the Democratic National Committee in no way diminished his intense interest in the congressional elections scheduled for November 1966. He was grateful for the unwavering support he had received from the 89th Congress and he wanted to do all that he could to preserve its large Democratic majorities. During the summer and early fall of 1966, the President traveled extensively throughout the United States in an all-out effort to assist Democratic candidates by energizing their congressional campaigns.

The President did not limit his assistance to speech making. He realized that political campaigns are expensive, and he was determined to see to it that the Democratic candidates received money. He did that through his appearances at fund-raising dinners. He also saw to it that Democratic congressional candidates for reelection received direct gifts of money given to them by Jake Jacobsen and me on his behalf.

An example of the latter occurred in early October 1966. Previously, the President had directed that an amount of cash should be raised and given to each congressional Democrat who was running for reelection to either the Senate or the House of Representatives. Several hundred thousand dollars were collected under the direction of the President's friend Arthur Krim. That cash was delivered to me in the White House where it was locked in my office safe. Once the cash was available, word was sent to every Democratic congressional candidate for reelection that I would like to meet with him.

I began the meetings with a short speech telling them how much the President appreciated their work and that he was committed to doing everything he could to assist them in their campaigns. Then, one by one, I invited each of them to meet privately with Jake Jacobsen and me in my office. There, with only the two of us and the candidate present, I delivered the envelope.

There was one variable in the amount of cash I delivered: If the candidate had an opponent, his envelope contained two thousand dollars; but if the candidate was unopposed, the amount was a thousand dollars. Several candidates in the latter category declined my offer. Though the amounts were small—even by 1966 standards—every Congressman and Senator was grateful for the gesture of support that was made on behalf of the President. Because the money was delivered to them in the White House, it was a symbolic demonstration of the President's appreciation and gratitude.

We were aware of the sensitivity of our deliveries of cash, and we went to considerable lengths to retain total secrecy concerning our actions. We thought that all the Senators and Congressmen clearly understood the necessity for secrecy, but as I learned, that necessity was not understood by all of them.

In one instance, a Democratic Congressman from California missed my White House meetings. A short time later, he had his office call my secretary, Mary Jo Cook, and ask her, "When can [he] come over and pick up [his] money?" She was aware of how concerned we were that the cash donations in the White House not be made public, so she sent me a memo describing her conversation with the Congressman's office. She informed me that she had instructed the Congressman to handle the matter via Arthur Krim or Larry O'Brien. Then she added: "Heavens! Top Secret! Hush! Hush!"

While the critical congressional campaign was in full swing, the President traveled to Asia to attend a vital meeting of the SEATO Treaty nations in Manila. I accompanied him and the trip turned out to be successful, but it was brutally difficult physically. We departed from Andrews Air Force Base on October 17 and flew respectively to Honolulu, Pago Pago, and New Zealand before landing in Australia. We arrived in Manila on October 23 for the three-day SEATO meeting among President Johnson and the heads of government of South Vietnam, Thailand, the Philippines, Australia, and New Zealand. Despite the fact that South Korea was not a signatory to the SEATO Treaty, its troops were bravely fighting in South Vietnam, and thus its President also attended.

President Johnson was pleased with the conference, but for him the high point occurred when he decided to fly to Cam Rahn Bay, the large American military base in Vietnam. Immediately after the conclusion of the SEATO meeting, with the greatest secrecy and security (and, this time, his plans were not leaked), we flew from Manila to Vietnam to meet with our troops and to confer with General Westmoreland and our other commanders in the field. It was a highly satisfying experience for him, and he was extraordinarily pleased by the enthusiasm with which was he was received by our troops. He spoke to them, shared lunch, and met with as many of them individually as possible. He left Vietnam feeling very good about the morale of the American military.

Unfortunately, while in South Korea, a stop on our return to the United States, the President created a problem that would hound our press office for months. In his enthusiasm during his speech to the troops stationed there, he mistakenly stated that his forbears had fought at the Alamo. Although it was true that the President's ancestors had participated in every American war, not one of them had been at the Alamo. The press immediately picked up on his mistake and lacerated him for it. The simple truth was that the President had been carried away by the emotions he felt while speaking to our servicemen. However, no excuse was acceptable to the media. They neither forgave him nor attempted to explain his mistake. Instead, they added his error to their litany of events they described as his "credibility gap," an unfortunate phrase that increasingly hounded him throughout 1966.

It was during this trip to Asia that as the President's chief security officer, I gained so much respect for the FBI, and why thereafter I trusted the accuracy of their information and intelligence. Following the President's return from Vietnam to the Philippines, he was scheduled to make stops in Thailand and Malaysia. In this instance, the Secret Service and the CIA assured us that the President would not be subject to anti-American protests in Malaysia. However, Deke DeLoach, the FBI representative, warned us that demonstrations against the President were planned and would take place when he visited that country. I accepted the FBI's advice and proper precautions were taken. As we landed in Malaysia, I asked the head of security for that country if there were any organized demonstrations. He said, "Not to worry," and so I was not concerned. I should have been. As we passed by a parklike setting, I saw a man lying underneath a white covering who had just been shot by the Malaysian security forces. Apparently the local police had allowed a group of demonstrators to gather and start their protests. They had been ordered to disperse and had refused. Their leader had then been killed with one bullet shot into his head. They were then again asked to disperse, and this time they did. Thus, DeLoach had been right in his warning to us, and the other security agencies—ours and theirs—had been wrong.

I should add that perhaps the most important reason for the higher accuracy of FBI information is the fact that the Bureau operates under a budget massively larger than the Secret Service, and even in excess of the CIA. Thus, the FBI was almost always able to put far greater numbers of people into the field regarding any given situation. That usually results in better intelligence.

Before we began the trip to Asia, the President told me that he wanted to quietly explore the possibility of a whirlwind cross-country political trip after his return to the United States and before the upcoming November elections. From Manila, I called Sherwin Markman and instructed him to begin initial but confidential planning for such a presidential trip. Midway through our Asian journey, the President became so pleased with how it was going that he told me that I could definitely schedule the political trip. He wanted to do it not only to assist Democratic candidates, but also to report to the nation concerning the unity he found among the SEATO alliance, the high morale of our troops, and his belief that we were winning the war in Vietnam.

Thus, I authorized Markman to assemble a team and immediately use a presidential airplane to tour the country for the purpose of recommending a precise itinerary for the President. Markman's team consisted of himself and Doug Nobles from my office, representatives from the office of the Military Aide, the White House Communications Agency, and the Secret Service.

On October 27, after the President's return to Manila from his visit to Vietnam, Markman sent me his team's recommendation for the presidential trip. They suggested that the trip should begin on Friday, November 4, and conclude on Monday, November 7, the day before the elections. During that period, the President would make twenty-five speeches in twenty-two cities in seventeen states. When I presented their recommendation to the President, I believed that he approved it.

I then authorized Markman to act. I told him that he had to move fast because time was short and he had only a few days to organize the vast array of security, communications, logistic, and advance people who were essential for the success of the President's trip. His team had to be quickly assembled and deployed at each of the suggested presidential stops in sufficient time to organize each event.

Markman located dozens of experienced advance men and, as rapidly as possible, dispatched them to each location, along with the other essential personnel. Of necessity, in each city Markman had to notify the political leaders and organize large teams of volunteers to support the presidential appearance, an undertaking that involved hundreds of people.

Although Markman followed the President's standard order regarding the proposed trip by informing everyone that there was nothing "definite" about the President's plans, no one believed him. The sheer number of people involved insured that the national and local media quickly learned about the breadth of the proposed trip. Naturally, they reported that the President was planning a massive political effort to retain control of Congress. And nobody truthfully could deny the accuracy of their stories.

While all of this authorized activity was taking place back in the United States, we arrived in South Korea following quick stops in Thailand and Malaysia. When we reached Seoul, the President was exhausted.

"Marvin," he began when we alone in his suite, "I am not going to make that trip when I return to the United States."

I was shocked. "Why?" I asked him.

"While I was in Manila, a call from my doctors at the Mayo Clinic advised me to have an operation to remove a growth on my throat and repair my hernia incision. They told me to have it done as soon as I get back."

I was very sensitive to his concern over his health, which I shared. But I wondered about his decision.

"Is it possible for your surgery to be postponed for a few days?" I asked.

"It should not. Therefore, I am not going to make the trip," he repeated.

"But, sir, you should be reminded that there are literally hundreds of people now working to make it a successful trip."

"Bring them home and let them know how much I appreciate each of them."

"Your proposed trip is in the press," I added, pressing him hard, trying to persuade him to reverse his decision. "It's public information that you have planned the trip."

"They had no business writing those stories," he said. "I have never given final approval to any such trip. It's always been just tentative. Nobody should have leaked anything else."

But I persisted. "By sending so many to twenty-plus states the local and national press could not help but determine our plans."

"Remember, I never finally said that I would do it. And now my doctors have told me that I need an operation."

I gave up the argument for the moment, but the following day, I again raised the issue with him. He was irritated with me, but I persisted. However, I could not budge him. Nonetheless, I delayed informing Markman or anyone else back in the United States. Instead, I told Bill Moyers, who I knew was already working on the planned campaign trip.

Moyers immediately saw that a cancellation would be an immense public relations mistake, and the two of us so advised the President one final time. We did our best. However, the President always thought that any trip by him was relatively simple to organize. More important, he believed that he had the right to retain all of his options until the last moment; that until he finally said "yes" to anything—whether it was a trip or a presidential appointment—he was not committed and was free to change his mind.

Thus it was that, reluctantly, I contacted Markman and told him that there would be no presidential trip. I instructed him to bring everyone home. Markman was shocked and raised the same arguments with me that I had already presented to the President. I told Markman that the decision was final and that it was his job to carry it out.

Markman did as he was told. Not surprisingly, the reaction from the people in each city was not only disappointment but anger. They felt they had been misled, and nothing Markman said to them, including reminding them that he had always told them that the President's trip was never definite, dispelled their fury.

When the President finally returned to Washington from Asia, the press asked him why he had cancelled the political trip. Instead of simply stating that it was at his doctor's orders, he denied that he had ever authorized or planned such a trip. That response resulted in a feeding frenzy by reporters all too ready to jump on the President. Once again, they excoriated him for his so-called credibility gap.

In retrospect, I feel that that I should have worked harder to change the President's decision. However, I am equally certain that no matter what I had said, he would not have made the trip. He was too tired and worried about his health to have done so, regardless of the political cost of cancellation. However, I understand that out of his exhaustion, and his conviction that he had never made a "final" decision, he believed that his public denial was the truth. His mantra always was, "I am not going until I say I am going, and none of you should ever forget that."

In my opinion, the so-called credibility gap was created by the press out of its own frustration with its inability to accurately predict the President's decisions.

Another cause of the "credibility gap" can be laid directly at the doorstep of Robert Kennedy. The Kennedy family, beginning with the patriarch father, Joseph Kennedy, always had a flair for seducing the press, and that ability had not diminished with the ascendancy of Robert Kennedy as the family's heir apparent. One part of his strategy involved developing and maintaining close relationships with key columnists and reporters. Another was his constant effort to undermine the credibility of Lyndon Johnson. I had learned about Kennedy's vaulting ambition when I discovered and successfully circumvented his attempt at a coup during the 1964 Democratic National Convention. From that time forward, the President and all of us who worked closely with him maintained a careful watch over everything Kennedy did.

Thus, as early as July, 1964, President Johnson, who by then knew all about Kennedy's machinations regarding the upcoming convention, was taped stating that, "We must watch them [the Kennedys] like hawks, every damn thing they do. He [Robert Kennedy] has been acting very ugly and mean. [After I told him he wouldn't be Vice President] he ran off and sulked."

Foiling of Robert Kennedy's 1964 convention plot did not stop him and his followers from continuing to work against the President. However, following the President's massive electoral victory in November, 1964, they were faced with the fact that Lyndon Johnson was both popular and had great public sympathy and trust. The Kennedy entourage was determined to chip away at these strengths, and their weapon of choice was their friends in the media. Their strategy was abetted by the fact that the President and his people were neither beloved nor admired by the eastern establishment, which of course included the most influential reporters and columnists.

Following the 1964 election, Robert Kennedy began hosting a series of weekly private meetings with five of the most influential newspaper columnists in Washington. These included such heavyweights as the columnist Joseph Alsop, a close social friend of the Kennedys, whose opinions were often respected not only in Washington but throughout the country.

Unknown to Kennedy, I possessed a reliable source of information regarding much of what that occurred in these weekly "secret" meetings of his. I learned that an important main subject discussed at the meetings between Kennedy and his friends in the press was the themes of stories they should highlight during the ensuing week. In every case, their stated purpose was to diminish and, if possible, destroy the credibility of Lyndon Johnson. Some of the President's mistakes were his own. Nonetheless, the Kennedy people deliberately planted destructive stories. An example was a column unfavorably comparing Lady Bird Johnson to Jacqueline Kennedy, a story that was so blatantly unfair that I had trouble containing my own anger.

Another source of Kennedy's anti-Johnson influence with the press was Ben Bradlee, the editor of the *Washington Post*, and a close personal friend of the Kennedys. Although the *Post* was owned by Katherine Graham, whose deceased husband, Phil Graham, had been one of Lyndon Johnson's closest friends and advisors, Mrs. Graham chose not to interfere with the pro-Kennedy bias of her editor. After Lyndon Johnson became President, Bradlee's Kennedy connection became apparent in the *Post's* increasingly slanted coverage against President Johnson. Mrs. Graham made no effort to control her newspaper's stories attacking the President. Lyndon Johnson was disappointed in the policies of the newspaper formerly run by his friend, but there was nothing he could do as the paper pecked away at him. As I learned to my sorrow, once a story appeared in such respected newspapers as the *Washington Post* or *The New York Times*, it was generally accepted as fact by most other reporters and columnists. Therefore, any number of subsequent writers often accepted a biased or mistaken article as gospel.

The November 1966 elections produced the unsurprising result of decreasing the overwhelming Democratic majority of the 89th Congress. In the House of Representatives, the Party counts changed from 295 Democrats and 140 Republicans to 248 Democrats and 187 Republicans, a loss of 47 Democratic seats. In the Senate, the numbers changed from 68 Democrats and 32 Republicans to 64 Democrats and 36 Republicans, a loss of 4 seats.

The President was disappointed, but not disheartened. He always expected some loss of strength in the midterm elections. Historically, it almost always happened with a sitting President. Still, the Democrats remained in firm control of both Houses of Congress. As the President told me, "What this means is that all of us—and that includes me—must simply work harder."

One factor diminished the adverse impact of the 1966 elections: the President had always sought to work with both political parties. As Senate Majority Leader and as President, his method had been to work with Republicans as well as Democrats. If he could manage to do it, he habitually reached out to as many Republicans as possible in the initiation as well as the passage of legislation. His relationship with the Senate and House Republican leadership vividly illustrates the bipartisanship he always sought. The President reasoned that his Party's diminished number in Congress was no reason for not continuing to move forward aggressively with his legislative program. As we will see, he was right, and his accomplishments continued to mount even in the 90th Congress, which took office in 1967.

TRAVELS AND TRAVAILS WITH THE PRESIDENT: A MISTAKE IN OHIO

The circumstances of the incident were these: during the late summer of 1966, the President embarked on a one-day flying tour with quick stops and speeches in several cities. They were, in large measure, speeches at airports where Air Force One would land and the President would disembark and make a short address to the gathered crowd. It was a hectic day, not only for the President, but for his staff, especially the speechwriters who had to prepare a different speech for each stop.

Toward the end of the day, we reached Columbus, Ohio, where a large and enthusiastic crowd had come to hear the President. The President bounded down the airplane steps and mounted the speaker's platform that had been assembled for him. "It is so good to be here in Dayton, Ohio," he began, then paused, totally puzzled, when the crowd began laughing. He turned around, and one of us standing behind him, shouted, "Columbus, Columbus. You are in Columbus, Ohio." The President corrected himself, but his audience continued to chuckle. He finished his speech as quickly as he could, and when he returned to his airplane, he was livid.

He waved his speech cards in the air. "It says 'Dayton, Ohio' right here," he stated, his piercing eyes looking at each of us standing around him. "I want to know which one of you is responsible for this mistake."

All of us silently shook our heads.

"Well, one of you did it, and I want to know who it was."

Still, there was only silence, and the President finally said, "All right, all of you get out except for Marvin."

"I want a full scale investigation," the President told me when we were alone. "Bob Kintner's supposed to be in charge of organizing my speeches, so put him in charge. Tell him to do whatever he has to do to find the person who did this to me."

Robert Kintner, who had been president of both ABC and NBC, had developed a severe drinking problem. He was a longtime friend of President Johnson. In an attempt to help Kintner, the President had brought him into the White House as one of his Special Assistants. However, Kintner was left with no real responsibilities, and never had enough work to keep himself occupied.

When we returned to the White House after the Columbus, Ohio, fiasco, I met with Kintner in my office and relayed the President's direction. I expected him to object to being cast into the role of detective, but I was wrong. He eagerly accepted the job and assured me that the President could count on him; that he would get to the bottom of the problem and quickly identify the culprit. I believed that his eagerness probably resulted from his thought that here, at last, was a specific project in which he could prove his mettle to the President.

One by one, Kintner summoned every member of the White House staff to his basement West Wing office. There, seated behind his big desk, the former president of two television networks did his best to adopt the fierce look and tone of a high-powered investigator. Kintner asked everyone, "What did you have to do with the President's speech? With his speech cards? What version did you see? Did you handle the cards? Did you notice the mistake? Who did you talk to about his speech? What has anyone told you?" Kintner was not helped by the nervous secretaries, none of whom claimed to remember the source of the incorrect speech or speech cards, and, of course, being fully aware of the President's anger, no one on the staff admitted culpability.

Kintner spent more than a week on his assignment. I imagine that a sense of futility gradually seeped into his consciousness, and I assume it was with a great sense of failure that he wrote his report to the President admitting that he was unable to uncover the person or persons guilty of the Columbus mistake.

Soon thereafter, it was my responsibility to—as diplomatically as possible— tell him that his talents were no longer needed at the White House, although, I added, the President would always be pleased to receive his thoughts and suggestions.

I thought that Kintner's departure from the White House went smoothly and without bitterness. However, in February, 1968, Kintner wrote a letter to the President that was as vitriolic as anything I had ever seen directed to the President, especially from someone the President considered to be a friend. What caused Kintner's uncontrolled anger at the President was the fact that Kintner's wife, Jean, had not been appointed to the Civil Rights Commission. In his letter, Kintner not only personally attacked the President, but went on to state that from then on he was going to support Robert Kennedy to replace Lyndon Johnson.

It is a measure of President Johnson's compassion for old friends that he reacted to this terrible letter with sadness and not with anger. He told me that he understood how frustrating Kintner's White House experience must have been, and admitted that, as President, he could have handled the entire matter much better. Kintner's bitterness, although hurtful, was understandable, the President said. "I tried so hard to help him, but I failed, didn't I?" the President continued. "I also imagine that he is still drinking."

"Yes, sir, I understand that he is," I said.

"Well, Marvin, there are always spats from time to time between friends. I understand that." The President surprised me by then saying, "Let's go ahead and appoint Jean to that job they want so badly. You write him a good letter telling him that he and I have known each too long to let something like this destroy our friendship."

I did as the President directed, and thus, two weeks after Kintner's uncontrolled diatribe against the President, his wife became a member of the Civil Rights Commission. I also wrote him a soothing letter. I assume that the President's action and my letter worked because thereafter their friendship was renewed, and once more Kintner's overlong memos began arriving, although, as before, the President did not often read them. For the rest of their lives, Kintner's anger was apparently forgotten.

Of course, the Ohio episode is only one example of the many problems our sorely beset speechwriters faced in mollifying our demanding President. Bob Hardesty, a senior writer on the staff, recalls one humorous incident. In Hardesty's article, "The LBJ the Nation Seldom Saw," he recalls a draft speech submitted to Johnson when he was a Senator:

> "That was the worst speech anyone ever wrote for me."
>
> The writer was mystified. "What was wrong with it, Senator?"
>
> "Matter? You filled that speech with words I can't pronounce."
>
> "Words like what, Senator?"
>
> "Like eons. You know I can't pronounce eons," he said, pronouncing it perfectly. "Besides, I don't even know what it means. Dammit, if you mean ages, say ages."

IOWA GOVERNOR HAROLD HUGHES: WHAT CONSTITUTES A LOYAL FRIEND?

Lyndon Johnson had a complex relationship with Harold Hughes. Hughes was a large man who was blatantly outspoken and painfully honest in whatever he had to say. He had been a combat infantryman during World War II who, because of his size, was responsible for carrying his platoon's heavy automatic rifle. He fought through North Africa and Italy from 1942 until the end of the war. He managed to survive with no physical wounds, but he paid a terrible price for his years of unremitting warfare. Although he had been a promising college football prospect before he entered the army, by the time of his discharge he was an alcoholic.

Hughes never returned to college. Instead, he became an itinerant truck driver intermittently working whenever he was sober enough to hold down a job. For over ten years, Hughes continued his besotted life, often going on binges that lasted for weeks. Then one day in the late 1950s, he awoke in a strange hotel and had no idea where he was, how he had gotten there, or anything else that had happened to him for over a week. He lay there, confused and very angry with himself. At that moment, as he often told his friends in later years, he decided to change his life.

He resolved never to have another drink, a resolution he never violated.

He told himself that he was an alcoholic and always would be an alcoholic; and that, as such, he could never take another drink. He also never denied his alcoholism, and his determination to overcome his addiction became his great strength.

By the late 1950s, Hughes had pulled his life together, and, amazingly, he was not only the owner of the trucking company for which he had formerly worked so haphazardly, but he had become a member of the Iowa commission that regulated that industry.

It was then that his friends began urging him to run for Governor of Iowa. He argued that he could not be elected. "I am an alcoholic and I always will be," he told them. "I will never hide that fact."

His supporters shrugged off his objections. They told him that he was a natural leader who inspired trust and admiration in everyone who knew him. "Moreover," they said, "you will be unique among politicians because, unlike the rest of them, you always say what you mean and what you tell us privately is exactly what you say in your public speeches."

Reluctantly, Hughes agreed, and in 1962 he ran for and was elected Governor of Iowa. It was then that he first met Lyndon Johnson, who took an immediate liking to this big, gruff, and frank man. The feeling was mutual. By 1964, when President Johnson was running for President and Hughes was running for reelection, the two of them had become close friends.

When the problem arose concerning the seating of the all-black Mississippi Freedom Democratic Party at the 1964 Convention. It was Hughes who gave the President the name of Sherwin Markman, his campaign manager, thus propelling Markman into the middle of the controversy I covered earlier in this book.

Following President Johnson's 1964 landslide victory—which was matched by Hughes's own overwhelming defeat of his Republican opponent—the President and the Governor became even closer friends. President Johnson especially trusted Hughes because Texas Governor John Connally, Lyndon Johnson's closest ally among the governors, also admired Harold Hughes.

In the next few years, Hughes's stature grew not only in his own state, but also with his fellow governors. In 1966, he was overwhelmingly reelected. Moreover, he was chosen as chairman of the national organization of

Democratic governors. Now Hughes had gained national prominence and became a man whose voice and opinions carried considerable weight around the country. Thus, his friendship and support was important to the President.

By the fall of 1966, I had installed Markman—who now had the title of Assistant to the President—in Richard Goodwin's old office on the second floor of the West Wing. By then, Markman's duties amounted to whatever the President or I assigned to him, and the President often referred to Markman as his "utility infielder," meaning that Markman was expected to perform competently whenever he was given a job to do. And of course the President was aware that Markman had been the political protégé of Harold Hughes.

One day that fall, Markman received a telephone call from Governor Hughes. Hughes asked for a meeting with the President to discuss the situation in Vietnam. "I am troubled by what we are doing there," Hughes told Markman. "I want to discuss my doubts with the President."

Markman said that he would do what he could, and he reported Hughes's request to me. I presented it to the President, who readily agreed to a private meeting with the Iowa Governor. Shortly thereafter, the two men spent more than an hour together in a private meeting in the White House living quarters.

A few weeks later, the Democratic governors gathered in West Virginia for their annual meeting. Governor Hughes was chairman and he opened the meeting with a speech. In it, he complained that he and his fellow governors were very unhappy with the President. "He never listens to us, especially regarding Vietnam," Hughes stated.

The press immediately picked up Hughes's remarks, and, within minutes, the story appeared on the Associated Press ticker tape.

The President had installed ticker tape machines in the Oval Office so that he could instantly know what each wire service was reporting. He habitually walked over to them every few minutes, bending over to carefully read the tapes. When he saw what Hughes had said, he immediately picked up the telephone and called Markman. "Go look at the AP story about what your former boss is saying about me," he ordered. "Read it and call me right back."

Markman did so, and instantly understood the President's anger. With some trepidation, he called the President. "I read it, sir," he said.

"You tell me what he thinks he is talking about," the President barked. "How can he claim that I don't listen to him when I just gave him more than an hour of my time. You arranged that meeting and he sure as hell knows that he was here."

"Yes, sir. He is wrong."

"You are damn right he is wrong, and he'd damn well better tell the public that he's wrong. I want you to get him on the phone right now and tell him that."

Markman was able to locate Governor Hughes quickly, who was still at the governors' conference. "The President is very upset with your speech," Markman began. "He wants to know how you can claim that he never listens to you when you just met with him."

"That's right, Sherwin," Hughes said. "We met all right."

"So how could you have made that speech of yours?"

"Because it's true. He did see me for an hour, and for that hour he talked and talked and talked. I couldn't get a word in. He never gave me a chance to tell him what's bothering me. So when I said that he doesn't listen to us, that's the absolute truth."

"You could have interrupted him at any time," Markman said.

"Well, I didn't."

"What do you want us to do now?" Markman asked.

"I've been talking to the other Democratic governors down here and they want a group of us to meet with the President regarding Vietnam so we can tell him our concerns."

"I'll see what I can do," Markman told him.

Markman reported his conversation to me. The President then asked me to call Hughes and talk to him myself. "I want to know whether he is for me or against me," the President said. "I'd also like to find out which of those governors are my friends."

The next morning, I reached Governor Hughes. As it happened, our conversation was recorded and transcribed.

After our opening pleasantries, Hughes said, "I suppose Sherwin has related the essence of what I told him last night."

"Yes, he said that I should call you because there was a feeling that the President should meet with a group of Democratic governors."

"Well, they asked me to request an audience with him, Marvin, so that they could relate their feelings."

I then pressed him for the names of the governors who were behind his request, and Hughes listed fourteen governors, including, to my surprise, Texas Governor John Connally. I then asked him whether there were any Democratic governors who opposed his request.

"Carl Sanders," Hughes said, referring to the Georgia Governor. "He didn't feel it was proper. He felt it was the wrong thing to do and wouldn't go to such a meeting."

Hughes then admitted that he was not speaking for a number of other Democratic governors. Nevertheless, the list he gave me was large enough to cause concern.

Hughes continued by saying, "The contact with the President has been frequent, though it has been all a one-way exchange. They felt they should have an opportunity to tell the President what was wrong. They wanted an opportunity to communicate their side of the story as well as listening. I am carrying a message, Marvin."

"Let me get back in touch with you. I don't know what his schedule would permit."

"I thank you," Governor Hughes concluded.

Ultimately, the President did meet with a representative group of Democratic governors, and, although he took the opportunity to brief them and argue hard explaining the reasoning behind our Vietnam policy, he made a special effort to listen to what they had to say. I do not know whether Governor Hughes was content that the President had granted his request, but he always claimed that his personal support for the President never wavered—a claim about which the President had his doubts.

Hughes not only spoke out against what we were doing in Vietnam, but, it seemed to us, he did so on every possible occasion. The President felt personally hurt, even betrayed, because he had always considered Hughes to be his loyal friend. The President could not comprehend why a friend would seek to hurt him deliberately. Hughes, on the other hand, claimed that he never attacked the President personally; that his disagreement was limited to only one policy issue; and that, looking at the total picture, he was a firm supporter of Lyndon Johnson. Although I had no reason to doubt Governor Hughes's sincerity, I could not fathom his distinction regarding the most divisive issue facing the President. It was the President's belief that, even if Hughes disagreed regarding Vietnam, he should demonstrate his loyalty by muting his public criticisms. Hughes never did and, as a consequence, President Johnson never fully trusted him again.

Jumping forward in time, in the winter of 1967–1968, at a time when the President had not yet withdrawn from the presidential race and Robert Kennedy was actively although not yet formally pursuing his own campaign for President, Governor Hughes decided to run for the Senate. For that purpose, he organized a large fund-raising dinner in Iowa. Despite Hughes's knowledge that the President's most formidable opponent for the Democratic nomination would likely be Kennedy, Hughes asked Kennedy to come to Iowa as the principal speaker at the Hughes dinner.

When I learned of Hughes's invitation to Kennedy, I called the Iowa Governor and asked him about the meaning of Kennedy's presence at the dinner.

"The only reason I am having Kennedy is because Kennedy can help me raise money I need for my campaign," Hughes responded.

"Does that mean that you are supporting him for President?" I asked.

"I support the President and I will lead the Iowa delegation which will also support the President," Hughes said.

"But what are we to make of all your public criticisms of the President regarding Vietnam?"

"I happen to disagree with him on that," Hughes said. "And I will continue saying so. That doesn't mean that as far as everything else is concerned, he is not a great President. I believe he is a great man."

"Well, that's wonderful," I said, permitting myself to express a touch of sarcasm. "I appreciate that and I know that he will."

In fact, the President could no longer count on the support and loyalty of the Iowa Governor, but Hughes was only one of a growing number of increasingly vocal dissenters to the war. Vietnam had became the issue that was consuming the presidency, and the President believed that anyone who claimed to support him should not be making speeches attacking his most intransigent problem.

In private, the President was concerned about the accuracy of the reports he was receiving that we were making "progress" in Vietnam. By the end of 1966, despite an increase in efforts by both our allies and the South Vietnamese, the actions of the North Vietnamese and the Viet Cong continued to expand. The President had been told by his most trusted advisors that we would break their will to resist. In that, it seemed that we had seriously underestimated their dictator leader, Ho Chi Minh, whose steely resolve was unfettered by a Congress or public opinion. Thus, as the year ended, the President reluctantly approved the plan urged upon him by McNamara, the Joint Chiefs, and General Westmoreland (who commanded our troops in Vietnam) to increase the total number of American forces there to about 383,500 by the end of 1966 and to 425,000 by the middle of 1967. The President's advisors told him that with that escalation they were confident we would not only meet the increased threat from North Vietnam but, at last, we would move to the offensive. Sadly, they were wrong. At the same time, the President's ability to convince the press and the American people was rapidly diminishing.

BILL MOYERS: A PRODIGAL SON LOST

Bill Moyers looked upon Lyndon Johnson as his surrogate father, and his affection was returned in kind by the President. In 1966, I sadly witnessed the unraveling of their special relationship.

Moyers was born in Hugo, Oklahoma, in 1934, but he grew up in Marshall, Texas. He attended North Texas State College, the University of Texas, and the University of Edinburgh. Finally, in the fall of 1957, he enrolled in the Southwestern Baptist Theological Seminary and received his bachelor of divinity degree in 1959. He had agreed to teach Christian ethics at Baylor University in Waco, Texas, when Senator Lyndon Johnson offered him a job in Washington as a personal assistant. Moyers had worked for Senator Johnson as a summer assistant in 1954. He later stated that he decided not to pursue the ministry. Instead, he chose to serve Lyndon Johnson.

Moyers and Senator Johnson immediately formed a close, almost filial relationship. As Moyers later put it, Lyndon Johnson became "a second daddy" to him. The feelings were mutual. Moyers's advancement as an important Johnson aide was mercurial. He soon became the Senator's executive assistant, second only to Walter Jenkins on the Johnson staff. When Senator Johnson ran for Vice President in 1960, Moyers was deeply involved in the campaign, especially in the preparation of speeches and coordination of the development of policy positions. As such, he and I worked closely together.

During that 1960 campaign, Moyers also functioned as Lyndon Johnson's liaison with the Kennedys. They saw him as a young man who in their eyes was that rare breed: a Texas intellectual. Thus, after the 1960 election, Moyers—with Vice President Johnson's enthusiastic concurrence—was selected as deputy to Sargent Shriver, President Kennedy's brother-in-law, to run the new President's cornerstone program, the Peace Corps.

On the day of President Kennedy's assassination, Moyers was a passenger in a small airplane flying toward Waco, Texas. Hearing of the shooting, he diverted the plane to Dallas and rushed to Love Field, where Lyndon Johnson was still waiting on Air Force One. Moyers boarded the plane in time to witness the swearing in of the new President. He returned to Washington with President Johnson, where he was immediately named to the White House staff as a Special Assistant to the President.

As the Johnson presidency began, Moyers, who was then twenty-seven years old, played a key role in organizing and supervising the 1964 Great Society task forces. During the 1964 presidential campaign, Moyers reprised his central role of speechwriter and coordinator of policy papers for the President.

Through the first half of 1965, George Reedy continued to be the President's Press Secretary. The President was fond of Reedy. Reedy was a good-natured man who loved to talk, and who endlessly told Lyndon Johnson anecdotes to anyone who would listen. That habit, although amusing to others, did not sit well with the President, who perceived Reedy's vociferous nature as a source of leaks, although he never believed that Reedy intended to hurt him. Nonetheless, by July 1965, President Johnson was determined to replace Reedy as his Press Secretary. In that regard, Reedy submitted a letter of resignation saying his hammertoes were too painful and he badly needed an operation that would keep him incapacitated for up to six months. The President accepted the resignation because the President was not comfortable with Reedy's performance as Press Secretary after learning that the

White House Press corps had lost confidence in Reedy's answers and speeches.

President Johnson surprised me by asking if I would take over Reedy's role. "You know how to keep your mouth shut," he told me.

"Oh, no, sir," I said. "I am absolutely the wrong person to deal with the press."

"Who do you suggest?" the President asked.

"How about Bill Moyers?"

"Don't you think he's pretty young for that job?"

"I think that you should try him and see how he does."

Thus, on July 8, 1965, a month after Moyers's thirty-first birthday, the President appointed him as Press Secretary.

Moyers was an instant success with the press. He was pleasant, smart, forthcoming, and accessible. In time, the reporters came to trust him more than they did his boss, and they began looking at him as their ally in dealing with the President. Moyers socialized with them and listened sympathetically to their complaints and ideas. In turn, Moyers became the focus of favorable stories. All the publicity seemed to allow Moyers to form an image of his own power and influence with the President.

At one point during his tenure as Press Secretary, Moyers sent me a handwritten note in which he candidly expressed his views of our respective roles. He described mine as one whose "fierce duty is to protect the President from others," and said that the President was "fortunate" to have me. Moyers also wrote that "no one loves the man more, or serves him more competently" than I. As for his own utility, Moyers wrote that he perceived it to be one of protecting the President "from himself."

Unfortunately, President Johnson did not always agree with Moyers's view of his own role. The President became increasingly disturbed by news stories he believed emanated from Moyers that anticipated decisions that the President had not yet made final. He also suspected that stories critical of him sometimes originated from loosely stated opinions that Moyers had voiced to his friends in the media. Still, the President withheld his hand because he genuinely cared for Moyers and refused to give credence to any thought that Moyers's loyalties were changing.

Everything came to a head in September 1966, when tragedy struck the

Moyers family. Bill's brother, James, was working in his Executive Office Building office as a writer for the President when one horrible day he committed suicide. His death was totally unexpected and came as a terrible shock to all of us. To Bill, his brother's self-destruction was devastating.

Moyers began engaging in actions that can only be described as bizarre. Without going into detail, it seemed to me that he became a lost young man who had misplaced himself, losing the way that had been his defining quality. It was all very disturbing to a President who retained such affection for Moyers. Throughout that fall of 1966, Moyers's distressing actions did not diminish, but now a dimension was added that angered the President even more: Moyers began overtly giving statements to the press concerning presidential opinions and plans that the President had never authorized.

In one instance, a well-known reporter took the trouble to telephone me to complain about Moyers, saying, "Bill Moyers is doing no good for the Johnson administration—the way he handles the press in there is just terrible every day. What we want to know is what the President knows, not what Bill Moyers wants us to know. Really, I think that he contributes a great deal to the credibility gap, as people say. I think something should be done about it."

The President asked me to speak to Moyers and make him aware of his distress. I did, but it did no good. Then the President personally called Moyers in and gave him the same lecture, but Moyers was unwilling or unable to change.

Everything continued to worsen until one day when Moyers publicly announced that the President would be flying to the LBJ Ranch that weekend. The President saw that report on the ticker tape and instantly called me, angrily instructing me to order Moyers to retract his announcement because the President definitely was not going to the Ranch.

When I got Moyers on the telephone, he said, "But he told me that he was going down there."

"Bill, you and I both know that what he meant was that he was *thinking* of going to the Ranch and that's not the same thing as authorizing you to publicly announce it. He always wants to keep his options open until the last possible moment."

"I don't care," Moyers said. "He said that he was going. As far as I'm concerned, he's going."

"Please don't do this," I pleaded, but Moyers adamantly refused to change his public statement.

We found another way to inform the press that there would be no presidential trip to the Ranch that weekend. However, our action led to some very disturbing behavior by Moyers.

On the day that the President was supposedly flying to the Ranch, Moyers— knowing full well that there would be no such trip—showed up at Andrews Air Force Base and boarded Air Force One. He sat on the airplane, all alone, until one of the guards, realizing that something was very wrong, phoned me at the White House.

"What should I do with him?" the guard asked.

"Tell him to get off the plane and come back to the White House," I said.

A few minutes later, the guard telephoned me again. "He refuses to leave," the guard reported.

I put the guard on hold and walked into the President's office to tell him what Moyers was doing. The President reacted with both anger and concern.

I asked the guard to get Moyers off of Air Force One. With some difficulty, the guard removed Moyers from the airplane. However, Moyers did not return to the White House. Instead, he went home. For several days, he remained there, even refusing to answer his telephone.

That incident proved to be the last straw. It was obvious that Moyers, for whatever reasons, had become unreliable and, however much residual affection the President had for him, he should no longer remain at the White House, especially as the President's Press Secretary.

President Johnson asked me to inform Moyers of his termination and tell him that he should find another job. However, in this instance—unlike others—I believed that the President personally had to speak to Moyers. Reluctantly, he agreed.

I was present when the president summoned Moyers into the Oval Office for that difficult conversation. In a soft voice filled with sadness, the President said to Moyers, "I don't believe you fit in here anymore."

To his credit, Moyers did not argue. In fact, he appeared to have expected the President's statement. Looking at both of them, it seemed that their deep hurt was equally shared.

On January 31, 1967, Moyers resigned as Press Secretary and departed the White House—and his service to Lyndon Johnson—forever. Moyers was replaced by George Christian, an older and highly experienced Texan who had been Press Secretary for Governor John Connally for three years and who had been working at the White House since the previous summer. Happily, Christian turned out to be an excellent choice, and he remained Press Secretary for the remainder of the President's term in office.

It is a measure of the depth of the schism between Lyndon Johnson and Bill Moyers that—as of this writing—after more than thirty years have passed since their parting, Moyers remains the only former intimate of Lyndon Johnson who has refused to furnish an oral history of his experiences with President Johnson to the Johnson Library.

The entire sad story is summed up by Moyers in a letter he sent to my office during the year (1967) that he worked at *Newsday*. In it, he said that he was depressed because he was no longer in the government and was "at odds" with President Johnson. He revealed that the private sector did not satisfy him because he could no longer serve "deeper purposes." He admitted that the breach between himself and the President occurred for "perfectly understandable reasons," and that after the death of his brother "I didn't handle my life very well." He said that his rupture from the President was "my own fault." He referred to the President as his "second daddy" who had done more for him than anyone else. Finally, Moyers asked for the chance to "repay my debt" to the President "as a friend who honors and loves him as he is."

As Moyers has since stated (see *The Shadow Presidents*, Michael Medved, Times Books, 1979), "I wish that I had known him later and worked for him at a more mature period of my life. There were mistakes I could have avoided, too much that was just young foolishness. . . . I worked for him when I was too young, too impetuous, too superficial. . . ."

Although Bill Moyers was not happy at *Newsday*—which he left after only one year—he later found his niche in television.

1967

★

A PRESIDENCY IN FULL STRIDE

By the beginning of 1967, Lyndon Johnson had been President for slightly more than three years, and I had been with him for two of those years. The 1966 election was behind us, but despite the smaller Democratic majorities in Congress, the president was determined to press forward with his full agenda. However, the war in Vietnam continued and pressed ever harder on the President's programs and his ability to lead the country. Yet his extraordinary energy never flagged.

Michael Beschloss, in appearances promoting his book of transcripts of Lyndon Johnson's taped telephone conversations, *Reaching for Glory,* has engaged in misdirected accusations of dishonesty regarding President Johnson's leadership concerning the Vietnam war. He unfairly transformed President Johnson's privately expressed uncertainties about the ultimate success of American policy in Vietnam into an alleged breach of faith with the American people. Beschloss states that Lyndon Johnson did not publicize his doubts, and he argues a President may not properly harbor personal doubts about a policy unless he reveals those doubts to the public. In my opinion, Beschloss misstates the historical record and misconceives the duties of a President.

Every military and civilian expert advising President Johnson unequivocally assured him that each action he authorized in Vietnam was not only correct but would lead to victory. President Kennedy had selected all of these men. Added to them was General Dwight Eisenhower, with whom President Johnson continuously consulted and who also supported our Vietnam policy. In addition, the President's actions regarding Vietnam were supported by Admiral Hyman Rickover, the man famously credited for leading the development of America's nuclear fleet of submarines.

The only dissenting voice in the upper echelons of government was that of George Ball, who it will be recalled had been directed by the President himself to be the devil's advocate. But his directed voice stood alone among those advisors.

Of course, the President had personal doubts. He would not be human if he did not. But not being certain of eventual victory and constantly questioning the advice he was receiving should not subject him to derision by a future historian who discovers his doubts but ignores the fact that as President he had to make decisions even when there were questions no one could answer. The simple fact is that like all other Presidents, Lyndon Johnson relied on the advice he was receiving, and in so doing he did his best to perform his duty as he saw it.

The fact that he did not share his questions with the public is an unfair criticism. I venture that all Presidents in all crises harbor some doubts about the wisdom of the course they choose. But having chosen, they know that they must rally the country behind that choice. In so doing, one never hears the President speak of his doubts. The reason is simple: if he does so, he inevitably dilutes the strength of his leadership in the course he has decided to take.

This function of leadership reminds me of the philosophy espoused by Supreme Court Justice Felix Frankfurter regarding the nature of the judicial process. He wrote that a judge often is presented with a case for decision where the arguments on either side are almost equally balanced. Nonetheless, he must rule one way or another, and in rendering his judgment he must not reveal the conflicts in his own mind. He must write his opinion in such a way that the winning argument is expressed as forcefully as possible, and in such a way as to give the appearance of inevitability. Only in that way, Justice Frankfurter argued, can there be strength and certainly in the judicial process and the law.

In my opinion, Lyndon Johnson saw his responsibility regarding American policy in Vietnam precisely that way. On balance, he believed that the course we must follow was the course set by treaty and advocated by the best minds he could find to advise him. Although he hated the war with all of his heart, he saw that his duty was to lead the country—and its people—toward the strongest possible support of that policy. In doing so, he was performing his responsibility as President. In no way was he attempting to mislead the American public.

In the White House, our work continued at its usual hectic pace, although some critical staff positions changed. George Christian had replaced Bill Moyers as Press Secretary. Jake Jacobsen, my colleague, and Milt Semer, our expert on housing and urban development, departed to form their own law firm. Jack Valenti, although always remaining responsive to any presidential request, was now happily ensconced as President of the Motion Picture Association of America. And of course almost all of the holdover staffers of President Kennedy, with the notable exception of Larry O'Brien, had either resigned, or like Dick Goodwin, had been asked to resign. By 1967, those of us now in the White House West Wing were both experienced and unquestionably loyal to Lyndon Johnson.

Later in 1967, two significant additions were made to the staff. Barefoot Sanders came over from the Department of Justice, where he had been an Assistant Attorney General. He replaced Henry Hall Wilson as Legislative Counsel to the President. Barefoot was an outstanding combination of affability, intelligence, and unfailing good judgment. The President also brought in John Roche, a delightfully articulate and zestful professor at Brandeis University, thus bringing an intellectual heavyweight to his senior staff.

To demonstrate the variety of work the President did each day, I have attached as Appendix 3 his daily diary for January 9, 1967. The diary illustrates how tightly packed with telephone calls, meetings, and presentations was the President's day, which did not end until 12:10 A.M. the following morning.

I also have attached as Appendix 4 a summary of some of my own activities during that same month. In January 1967, I wrote 306 memos to the President, 127 other memos, and 566 letters. My assistant, Jim Jones, also wrote 99 memos to the President, 320 others memos, and 386 letters. In addition, two of my secretaries produced 541 memos and letters, making a grand total of 2,345 memos and letters produced by my office during that single month. On top of all that, my office was called some 400 times every day. In all my duties, I was assisted not only by Jim Jones, but also by Markman and Bill Blackburn, as well as my secretaries, Mary Jo Cook (who was my associate), Lynn Reagan, Carol Currie, Ruby Moy, and Nell Yates. My staff was hardworking and loyal, willing to stay late into the night to finish whatever difficult task remained on my desk.

As I have written, the President did not permit the war or his diminished congressional majorities to deflect him from his efforts to construct The Great Society. He devoted unflagging energy leading the Congress as it continued to enact historically significant legislation. During 1967, under the President's leadership, the Congress, among other accomplishments, enacted and the President signed the following:

- An increase in Social Security benefits
- Treaties governing the exploration of outer space, including the prohibition of nuclear weapons
- An increase of 22 percent in health spending
- An increase of 10 percent in education spending
- Expanding the program for guaranteed student loans
- Funding $200 million for the Asian Development Bank
- Creating the Inter American Bank
- Creating a pilot program to train and find jobs for the disadvantaged
- The Public Broadcasting Act
- The National Commission on Product Safety
- The Air Quality Act
- The Meat Inspection Act
- Prohibiting age discrimination in employment
- Creating the food stamp program
- The Anti-Racketeering Act

Most of these enactments, which—like the revolutionary Medicare program created in 1965—are taken for granted today, were new, innovative, and significant at the time they were brought to life by Lyndon Johnson.

In achieving these legislative victories, full credit must be given to Sen. Everett Dirksen, the Senate Republican Leader. In this respect, the following memorandum concerning a recorded conversation between Senator Dirksen and me on June 14, 1967, illustrates how this worked:

WATSON: Senator, we have an ox in the ditch on the railroad legisla-
         tion in the House.
DIRKSEN: Yes.
WATSON: It looks as if we have bipartisan support and bipartisan op-
         position. Surprise and disappointed to some extent. [Then
         he reads to the Senator a news story regarding Congress-
         man John Anderson of Illinois.] We need all the support
         we can get, Senator.
DIRKSEN: I know you do.
WATSON: If there's anything you can do.
DIRKSEN: I'll get hold of him tomorrow.
WATSON: Thank you, sir.

An illustration of the successful working of the President's concept was
the close liaison that Sherwin Markman developed with Congresswoman Julia Butler Hansen. Congresswoman Hansen, a powerful political force from
the state of Washington, was a writer of children's poetry who had also served
as Democratic Leader of the Washington Senate. She was a strong personality
whose drive and intelligence resulted in her selection as the first woman chair
of an important subcommittee of the House Appropriations Committee, in
this case the subcommittee that controlled appropriations for the arts.

Markman's first encounter with her took place in 1965 when, as a member of the Appropriations Subcommittee that controlled foreign aid spending, she and a Republican colleague traveled to South America to study the
effectiveness of America's participation in the Alliance for Progress, a creation of President Kennedy to foster closer relationship between the United
States and Latin America. Markman was asked to escort and, if possible, influence these two Members of Congress, and he traveled with them to
Colombia, Peru, Chile, and Brazil.

It was a demanding assignment made no easier when Markman con-
tracted dysentery in Chile. Despite his illness, he soldiered on. Worse yet,
Congresswoman Hansen, a devout Christian Scientist, prevailed on Markman to avoid all medication. Beyond that, the Congresswoman insisted
every day on having—literally—three-martini lunches. Worse yet, she insisted that Markman always join her.

Markman survived the experience, which established a close relationship between him and the Congresswoman that lasted through the remainder of the Johnson administration. On her part, Congresswoman Hansen always referred to Markman as her "man in the White House." Time after time, she would call Markman or invite him to join her at one of her liquid lunches. There she would tell him her problems with the government (or problems of her constituents) that she expected Markman to solve for her.

Markman tried to help her every time she asked, and most importantly she knew and appreciated it. Her voting record was almost 100 percent favorable to the President's programs. On the rare occasion when her vote did not track the President's wishes, it was so trivial that Markman was not obliged to ask for it. Thus, through more than two years, Markman performed favors for her while not making any requests of her.

Then, one summer day, Markman's hard-won relationship with Congresswoman Hansen paid off superbly. It came in the form of funding for the construction of the Kennedy Center for Performing Arts in Washington. Roger Stevens, the well-known New York impresario, had been tasked with heading the development of the Kennedy Center, which in 1967 was still incomplete. More federal money was urgently needed, and although large and small private contributions had been sought and secured, additional appropriations were essential. Without them, the project could not be finished.

Whether or not those funds would be appropriated was under the control of Congresswoman Hansen as chair of the critical subcommittee with sole jurisdiction over that decision. To Stevens's dismay, she had reached the conclusion that far too much money already had been invested in the project, and she announced that not another penny would be approved by her committee, thus effectively killing any appropriation.

That was the state of affairs when Stevens came to me at the White House, begging for help with the Congresswoman. I conveyed his concern to the President, who authorized me to do what I could to help him. I was aware that the Congresswoman had been assigned to Markman, and I dispatched Stevens to talk to him and determine what could be done. Thus, Stevens met with Markman and explained his problem.

Markman immediately telephoned Congresswoman Hansen, who invited him to join her for lunch. Fortifying himself in advance as best he could—probably ineffectively—by drinking a lot of milk, Markman met her at the Democratic Club on Capitol Hill. As expected, Congresswoman

Hansen's lunch was preceded by several martinis, all of which Markman felt he was required to share with her. Markman has no idea whether he was drunk or sober when finally he broached the subject with her.

"Roger Stevens tells me you are holding up his Kennedy Center money," Markman began.

"I am indeed. We've already spent too much on that project."

"And I suppose he's right that without your support, that appropriation will never get out of your committee," Markman continued.

"That's true too."

Markman sighed. "I have never asked you for a thing, Julia. You know that, don't you?"

"Yes."

"Well, now I am asking. The President wants the Kennedy Center finished, and he needs your help. On his behalf, I'm asking you not to block it."

"Go on," she said, obviously unhappy.

"He needs you on this. He has always come through for you. I have always come through for you. Now we are asking you to swallow your objection and appropriate the money."

The Congresswoman stared at Markman for a long moment. Finally, she took a deep breath and nodded her head. "I don't like this at all," she said. "But I will go along with the President. I suppose I owe him that. Just make damn sure that you tell him how I feel, and while you are at it, you can say the same thing to your Mr. Stevens."

Thereafter, the money was duly appropriated and the Kennedy Center was completed. What is not generally known—or appreciated—is the willingness of Lyndon Johnson to expend his political capital not only to build what has become the cultural center of Washington, but simultaneously, to enhance the legacy of the slain President he replaced. Unhappily, the good things done by President Johnson often are ignored, not only by the contemporary press but by many historians.

By the fall of 1967, the Vietnam War had become increasingly grim. Robert McNamara, the Secretary of Defense for both Presidents Kennedy and Johnson, had begun showing signs of fatigue and wanted to resign. President Johnson, although realizing that McNamara had to be replaced, also knew that as President, he did not have the luxury of quitting. For him, there was nothing good about the war. The deaths and injuries of Americans in that country haunted him. Yet neither he nor anyone around him saw any way out of the war. To escalate too much was to risk a superpower confrontation—and a nuclear exchange—that must at almost all costs be avoided. However, not to escalate was to continue the stalemate. It was a dilemma for which none of his advisors had a solution.

GHETTOS AND RIOTS

The first major urban riot in an American inner city took place in the Watts section of Los Angeles for five days during August 1965 at a cost of thirty-four lives and $35 million. That disruption and devastation should have served as a wake-up call to the rest of the nation, but it did not.

President Johnson's first response, largely based upon his belief that proper legislation could solve almost any problem, was to push hard for laws equalizing the status of black Americans. The most dramatic example was the Voting Rights Act, which he signed on August 6, 1965, almost simultaneously with the outbreak of the rioting in Watts. That law was rapidly followed by the enactment and implementation of multiple antipoverty programs during the following months and years.

Despite these advancements, the black ghettos continued to seethe; the phrase "black power" appeared and became a rallying cry to inner city militancy; and a new generation of black leaders led by men such as Stokely Carmichael and Malcolm X began replacing the likes of Whitney Young and Roy Wilkins—and even Martin Luther King—as heroes of young urban blacks.

By the beginning of 1967, President Johnson saw an emerging—and very disturbing—picture of great trouble ahead in the inner cities of America. He knew that in order to prepare to address the inevitable problem, he must first understand its causes. To him, the obvious poverty and lack of economic opportunity were self-apparent, and he had no doubt that these must be addressed as quickly and thoroughly as possible. Yet he instinctively realized that something more was going on within the inner cities. Clearly, his antipoverty and civil rights legislation were neither solving the problem nor moderating an obviously worsening situation. Tensions continued to mount. He wanted to know why.

The President's approach to the problem was both traditional and unique. He consulted acknowledged experts in urban affairs, whose reports he received and carefully studied. He consulted with the two black men with whom he was most closely allied: Louis Martin at the Democratic National Committee, and Clifford Alexander, his Deputy Assistant Special Counsel in the White House. From these men, he received the traditional answers: inner city blacks were frustrated and their frustrations grew from lack of opportunities and from prejudice against them; and they were impatient with the slow and nonviolent pace of their conventional leaders. The experts' advice was to increase the pace of civil rights, education, and job opportunities. But the President was moving as rapidly as Congress and the budget would permit, and it was not working.

Lyndon Johnson was not content, and now he took a highly unusual step, which began when he summoned his staff to a meeting with him in the Cabinet Room.

"I am looking for volunteers," he began. "To start with, I want one of you to go live in a black ghetto and then report back to me about what is going on and why. Which of you wants to be the first to do that?"

There was a moment of hesitancy. Then Sherwin Markman raised his hand, and although several others quickly did the same, the President nodded toward Markman and told him to come into the Oval Office.

"I need for you to go out as soon as possible," the President said.

"How do you want me to arrange it?" Markman asked.

"That's up to you," the President said. "You are a smart lad and I'm sure you can figure it out. What I want is for you to pick a city where there is a large black ghetto. You go there and live in that ghetto for a week or two. Talk to as many people as possible. Look at everything and listen to as many people as you can. I don't want you living in some downtown hotel and commuting into the ghetto. That's not the same as living there, which is what you will do. And I don't want to read about you in the newspaper. Don't let anyone know that you work here, and don't you get into any trouble. Is that clear?"

"Yes, sir, but may I ask a question?"

"Go ahead."

"Why do you need someone like me to do this job? I mean, you have experts all over the government, and I definitely am not one of them. I am white, middle class, and came here from Iowa, which is hardly a hotbed of urban problems."

"Son, that is exactly why I want you to do this job for me. You are right that I have all the experts I will ever need, and I have listened to all of them. What I want is someone like you to go out and then tell me what you think about what you see and hear. Your lack of expertise means you have no pre-conceived notions, and the fact that you are from Iowa means your reactions and opinions will be far closer to those of the average American than any of those so-called experts of mine. So get yourself on your way as soon as you can arrange it."

Markman returned to his office and thought about his mission. He knew how strongly the President felt about leaks, and that meant not telling out-siders about this mission. But Markman realized that without help, as a middle-class white man there was no way he could live inside an urban ghetto and carry out the President's orders. He concluded that he needed a guide who both knew the ghetto and could be trusted. He had to locate a street smart, highly intelligent black man who would keep his mouth shut.

Markman did not know anyone fitting that description. That meant he had to tell someone else about the President's plan. The one friend he be-lieved had the necessary contacts was Nick Kotz. However, there was a prob-lem with asking Kotz for help: Kotz was a reporter. More than that, he was a Pulitzer Prize–winning investigative reporter who worked in the Washing-ton Bureau of Markman's hometown newspaper, the *Des Moines Register*. In crossing a line that often inhibits Washington insiders, Markman had re-tained his longstanding close friendship with Kotz. So Markman decided to share his need with Kotz and to ask for his help while also requesting Kotz not reveal the story. In return, Markman promised Kotz exclusive access if and when the President authorized public disclosure—something Markman was reasonably certain eventually would occur.

Kotz agreed to help and offered to introduce Markman to Ken Vallis. A short time later, Vallis, then a federal employee at the Department of Labor, came to Markman's White House office, and the two of them quickly be-came comfortable with one another.

Vallis had been born and raised in the ghettos of Chicago, but had suffi-cient innate intelligence and ambition to have worked his way out and up into a position of responsibility in the federal establishment. Like Markman, he was in his midthirties. Although upwardly mobile, Vallis had maintained his contacts in Chicago, and he remained intimately acquainted with who was doing what in its inner city. Thus, Chicago became the obvious choice for where Markman would go.

A White House Aide secretly living in the Chicago ghetto was more sensitive than it might be in any other city. That is because in those years, Chicago was under the firm control of Mayor Richard Daley, one of the last of the old-style political bosses. Daley's friendship and support were important to President Johnson. Markman knew that the mayor would be unhappy if he learned from the press that the President was sending in one of his assistants to gather intelligence regarding the ghettos of Daley's city. Knowledge of what was happening in Chicago was sufficiently important to take that risk. With the President's approval, I told Markman to go forward with his trip, although not before strongly repeating the President's direction that there must be no publicity.

In late January 1967, Markman, accompanied by Vallis, went into the Chicago ghettos. The cover story they concocted was that Markman worked for Sargent Shriver's Office of Economic Opportunity, and he had been dispatched to discover which programs were working, which were not, and what more the federal government could do in Chicago. Under that cover, Markman and Vallis lived first in Chicago's South Side ghetto, after which they moved into the far worse ghetto on the West Side of the city.

In both locations, the two of them worked through every day and long into each night, talking to as many people and observing the activities of as many programs as possible. While doing so, they slept in apartments within the ghettos. Their quarters were small, crowded, and infested with rats. It was hard work, but to Markman, living in this new world where he found himself to be the only white among a sea of black faces was a deeply moving and educational experience that filled him with reactions and ideas that he was eager to share with the President.

At the end of Markman's stay in Chicago, the city was struck by a powerful blizzard, the worst in many years. Not only were all forms of public transportation shut down, but the streets were so covered with deep drifts of blowing snow that even walking was difficult and dangerous.

Markman telephoned me at the White House and told me that he had completed his work in Chicago, but the blizzard had trapped him inside the city. He had no idea how long it would be before he could get out. I instructed him to call me back in half an hour. Then I informed the President of Markman's situation.

"It's pretty dangerous out there, isn't it?" the President asked.

"Yes, sir. He's still in the ghetto and I understand that he is now alone because his escort has left to go see his family."

"He's got to get himself out," the President said. "I'm worried about his safety. I don't want anything to happen to him."

"There is nothing moving in Chicago," I said.

"Then tell him to walk, if that's what he has to do. I'm sure that he can find some way to get himself safely back here as quickly as possible."

Markman called and I asked him to return to Washington immediately. As it happened, he had traveled light; what he had with him fit into one small suitcase. Carrying that suitcase, he said good-bye to his hosts and began the long walk toward Chicago's "Loop"—its downtown. There were no buses, no subways, no taxis, no vehicles of any kind on the streets. He was one of the very few pedestrians struggling through the snow.

His walk was both eerie and exhausting, but Markman trudged on for several hours until he reached the central railroad station. He thought that trains would be the first public transportation to move, and if he stayed there he should be able to get on board the first one headed toward Washington. He was right and was lucky enough to find a seat on an overnight train that left the station shortly after he arrived.

Back in the White House, Markman wasted no time preparing his report to the President. His mind was teeming and his biggest problem was limiting the length of his memorandum. He knew that the President strongly preferred memos no longer than a single typewritten page. As Markman wrote, he realized that his report would far exceed that limit. But he could not stop himself, and the final version that he handed to me for delivery to the President covered seven single-spaced pages. He was very apologetic when he handed me his report to the President because he was fearful that the President would never read it.

However, the President not only read the entire memorandum, but was so pleased with it that he often carried it with him, tucked into his inside jacket pocket. For months afterward, whenever he thought it might help him persuade reluctant congressmen to support a particular piece of legislation targeting the problems of inner cities, he would pull it out and read portions to them.

When the President used Markman's memo in that manner, he typically began by saying, "I want you to listen to what one of my young assistants saw and reported to me. You should know that this young man is no wild-eyed radical. He came here from Iowa. His background is about the same as most of your constituents, and this is what he told me."

The President's use of Markman's memo illustrates both the reasons why the President chose this novel way of studying the problems of inner cities, and how instinctively he found ways to successfully communicate with Members of Congress.

I will not repeat everything that was in Markman's long memorandum, but I want to quote from a few of his observations. They give some flavor of the value the President saw in his report. Much of the following remains relevant today, over thirty-five years later:

Without exception all of the people I spoke with are convinced that the riots of last summer will be repeated, expanded and intensified this year. . . .

Besides living in obvious poverty which I saw—the rat- and roach-infested atrociously high priced . . . apartment hovels, the loitering in the streets; garbage on the ground, the poor and torn clothing—the people of these ghettos also live with a deep-felt bitterness. It was expressed to me in many forms, but it always came out as a belief that the ghetto Negro lives in a world which is severed from ours . . .

The ghetto Negro feels that the building inspectors work for the landlords, the garbage collectors just don't care about their neighborhoods, the police are vicious, etc. . . .

I asked many people to describe to me the heroes of the youngsters in the neighborhood. I received amazingly similar responses: The heroes were the pimps and the crooks; those who dressed sharply and drive shiny cars; the only men they saw who apparently had it made in the world. These youngsters form the gangs of the ghettos—and the gangs are widespread and powerful. . . .

I met for two hours with one . . . man who encouraged the riots last summer and undoubtedly will do so again. . . . He says the Negro must control his own destiny. A man such as this is dangerous because he is highly educated, intelligent, energetic, and listened to. He is plowing the soil but the seeds are already there.

The feeling of alienation from the governmental structures leads directly to their major criticism of the U.S. poverty program. In almost all instances the response was that the poverty program does not reach the people and is controlled by the city government.... This is why they demand that they must have a voice in their own programs and that the money come to them without local government intervention.

Despite the bitterness, the probable violence, and those who would incite the situation, there is, nevertheless, some considerable sign of hope. . . .

Perhaps the most dramatic indicator to me was the great number of highly motivated and able Negroes who are giving intellectual as well as line leadership to fighting the problem. . . .

I have returned from my all too brief exposure with several conclusions:

(1) There are a lot of things which are working. These can be discovered and must be encouraged.

(2) The riots will continue to come and measures other than police action . . . must be employed. . . . If we do not stop the violence the backlash will destroy the political base which permits us to go on to the deeper solutions of the problem.

(3) We must fight through the dilemma of the political necessities of working through the local governmental organizations versus the negative reaction of the Negro to programs which do this and which they feel do not get to them. . . .

Word of the success of Markman's journey into Chicago's ghettos quickly spread among the President's staff, and it was not long before Markman and several others made similar trips into ten other cities and reported their findings to the President. In the end, the President himself leaked the story to the press, and many articles appeared, including one by Markman's friend, Nick Kotz.

Harry McPherson, in his book *A Political Education* (Little, Brown & Company, 1972), wrote: "A number of us went out from the White House in 1967 and 1968 to spend a few days in the Negro neighborhoods of New York, Chicago, Cleveland, Baltimore, and other northern cities. We knew we could not learn much about them in the course of a long weekend. What we hoped to gain was a sense of how the people who lived there felt about their future: specifically, whether they thought conditions might be improved through peaceful processes, or only through violence; or that nothing would help."

Markman also went into the ghetto of Washington, and later traveled to the inner cities of Oakland and Philadelphia. One year later, Markman returned to each of the cities he had visited in an attempt to measure the extent of progress, but as I will discuss, and as he had predicted, massive riots took place during the summer of 1967. Thus, his follow-up observations were not encouraging.

However, on his initial trip to Philadelphia, Markman found a reason for optimism. In Philadelphia, his old friend and classmate Federal Judge Leon Higginbotham escorted him. Judge Higginbotham, who was later elevated to the U.S. Court of Appeals, took a leave of absence from his judicial duties to lead Markman around the inner city. There he introduced Markman to Reverend Leon Sullivan.

Markman's first exposure to Sullivan was impressive. It was a cold, miserably rainy Sunday morning when Judge Higginbotham suggested that Markman join him at the church where Sullivan was preaching. The church was quite large and as Markman approached it, he expected that attendance would be sparse because of the terrible weather. He was wrong. Every seat was filled. And Reverend Sullivan did not disappoint anyone. His presence was electric and the crowd, including Markman, enthusiastically responded.

Sullivan, a tall, fit, intense, but friendly man, was as impressive in person as from a distance. At Judge Higgonbotham's urging, Sullivan invited Markman to meet with him the following morning at a job-training facility that Sullivan had started within the Philadelphia ghetto.

The next day, Sullivan escorted Markman through the school that he called "OIC," which stood for Opportunities Industrialization Center. Markman observed a tightly run educational program that had an enrollment of twelve hundred persons. "We have a waiting list of ten thousand," Sullivan explained. "And we are able to place 80 percent of our graduates in decent jobs."

"Is Philadelphia the only city with this program?" Markman asked.

"Absolutely not," Sullivan said. "We are working hard to duplicate what we have here in as many cities as possible."

"How are you doing with that project?" Markman asked.

"Fair, but we need a lot more financial help."

As Markman said good-bye to Sullivan and congratulated him on his good work, Sullivan said, "These days, everywhere you go you hear angry young blacks shouting, 'Burn, baby, burn!' What I want to do is change that slogan to 'Build, brother, build!'"

When Markman returned to the White House from Philadelphia, not only did he deliver another lengthy report to the President, but he also met with him. I listened as Markman enthusiastically told the President about Leon Sullivan and his job-training program. "I think that he is exactly the kind of Negro leader you are looking for," Markman concluded. "And his program hits the bull's-eye of what you want to encourage. What I recommend is that you go to Philadelphia to see the man and his operation for yourself. I think that will send out a much needed message."

The President said that he would consider Markman's suggestion. A short time later, he asked me to plan a trip for him into the Philadelphia ghetto.

The first thing I did was alert the Secret Service. I told them to arrange security for the presidential trip to Philadelphia. Their reaction was immediate—and very negative. The agent-in-charge emphatically said, "We are dead set against it. It's far too dangerous. You are talking about taking the President into one of the most dangerous ghettos in the country, a place where violence and rioting are highly likely. It's unsafe and we strongly advise him not to do it."

One must understand that whenever the Secret Service objects to presidential travel on grounds of security, their view must be taken seriously. This is still true, and was especially so in those years when the Kennedy assassination was fresh in our memories. Nonetheless, it is the President—and not the Secret Service—who must make the ultimate decision as to where he travels. There are times when the President's view of the national interest overrides the security concerns of his bodyguards. As President Johnson once said to me, "Ultimately, I have to decide what is more important to the country, my personal safely or what I believe should be done."

Regarding his proposed trip to Philadelphia, the President told me, "I appreciate the concerns of the Secret Service. I know that the ghettos can be dangerous, but it sounds to me like this Reverend Sullivan has developed a wonderful program. More than that, the fact that there has been so much trouble in the ghettos—and there is likely to be more—makes me believe that it is important that I personally go into a ghetto to demonstrate that I am their President too, and that I am no more afraid to visit them than any other group in America. Besides, I should encourage men like Sullivan, and what better way is there than to go visit him where he is doing such good work?"

The Secret Service objections to the president's decision to go inside the Philadelphia ghetto resonate in the contemporary world. It may be recalled that on September 11, 2001, in the hours immediately following the early morning terrorist attacks, President Bush, who was then in Florida, had Air Force One fly him first to a military base in Louisiana and then to another base in Nebraska, before finally returning to Washington late that day. I am certain that his peripatetic movements were the result of strong urgings from the Secret Service and others concerned with his safety.

I know that it is difficult to reject the strong recommendations of the Secret Service. However, they have only one interest: the security of the President. He, on the other hand, has the broader responsibility of representing the needs of all the people. To do that, he sometimes must take risks regarding his personal safety.

President Johnson's 1966 journey to the Far East was one of those occasions when he refused to follow the advice of the Secret Service. They opposed his trip to Vietnam as far too risky. They also opposed his visit to Thailand for the same reason. When the President decided to go despite their objections, he told me, "I just have to do what I think is right." He made the same decision later that year when—as a part of his December trip around the world, which I will describe later—he again visited Vietnam. At that time, the Secret Service repeated their protests. He went anyway, because he never doubted that in doing so he was leading the nation.

The constant presence of the Secret Service becomes a distasteful burden to any President. That was certainly the case with President Johnson. He felt that they inhibited his freedom of movement and his sense of privacy. He understood that they were needed, but he never fully accepted their constant presence. In our time, it took twenty-six agents to guard the President around the clock, and because the Secret Service is not immune to the bureaucratic virus, it always wanted more people assigned to it.

In one hilarious instance at the LBJ Ranch, his impatience boiled over. As usual, whenever he was at the ranch, the President drove his own car. On this day, I was riding with him. When we reached the entrance gate to the ranch, the President asked me to unlatch it. When I got back into the car, we drove through, but as the Secret Service vehicles stopped to close the gate behind us, the President suddenly sped away, leaving the Secret Service far behind and out of sight. As he did so, the gleeful President turned to me, and said, "I've always wanted to do that. I've finally gotten rid of them."

Then the President, who knew all the roads around his ranch very well, executed a number of turns and completely lost his Secret Service escorts. The radio in the President's car immediately crackled with the obviously upset voice of Rufus Youngblood, then the head of the presidential Secret Service detail and the man who had thrown himself on top of Lyndon Johnson in the moments after President Kennedy was shot in Dallas. Now, Agent Youngblood, who knew very well that the President could hear every word he said, ostensibly spoke to me, barking, "Wisdom [my code name with the Secret Service] do you copy?"

The President shook his head at me, indicating that I should not reply to Youngblood.

"Wisdom, answer me," Youngblood repeated. When I still said nothing, Youngblood stated, "Wisdom, you *must* answer me. Please tell the President that we are only doing our job. The law requires us to protect him. We have no choice. If anything happens to him, it will be our necks as well as his."

The President heaved a sigh and stopped his car. "All right, you can tell them where we are," he said, and, within moments, Youngblood and his men once more were following close behind the President.

Another failed attempt by President Johnson to shake off the constant burden of the Secret Service presence occurred when he decided he wanted to attend a party at the home of Governor and Mrs. Averill Harriman. He wanted to go there without being followed by his guards. There is a seldom-used tunnel between the East Wing of the White House and the Treasury Department building across the street. Telling only me, the President walked through the tunnel and out of the tunnel where he was met by a car driven by a friend of the Harrimans. That was necessary because in Washington, there is no automobile available for a President to drive himself—a fact that greatly contributed to President Johnson's sense of entrapment. In any event, the President's effort failed because a full contingent of Secret Service agents was waiting for him and followed along as he drove to the Harriman party.

Regarding his visit to the Philadelphia ghetto, his decision to go was firm and the Secret Service had to accept it. As it turned out, the trip was a resounding success. There was no trouble, the crowds were large and enthusiastic, and the President was greatly impressed by both Reverend Sullivan and his OIC job-training program.

On the President's return to the White House, he invited Sullivan to come visit so the President might listen to the Reverend's ideas at length and without interruption. It was a Saturday. Minutes after Sullivan departed, the President summoned Markman and Clifford Alexander, the black Deputy White House Counsel, into the Oval Office.

"I want to get more federal money for Sullivan's projects, and I want to do it as soon as possible," the President told them. "So you two boys go see Sargent Shriver and tell him to get his agency moving on that right away."

"We'll do it first thing Monday morning," Markman said.

"No! I don't want you to wait. See him today. Right now."

The two assistants immediately started making phone calls from my desk. Not surprisingly, they discovered that Shriver was not in his office at the Office of Economic Opportunity, which he headed. Instead, he and his wife, Eunice—the sister of President Kennedy—were hosting a large garden party at their suburban Maryland home. With some reluctance, Shriver agreed that he would see Alexander and Markman whenever they could get there.

The Shriver party was in full swing when they arrived. Shriver excused himself from his guests and for almost an hour met with them in his study while they brought him up to date regarding Sullivan, his program, and the President's wishes that immediate money be diverted to it from Shriver's agency. Shriver had no choice but to agree, although he pointed out that his budget was limited and other programs would receive fewer funds. Nonetheless, he saw to it that significant funds quickly found their way to Philadelphia and Reverend Sullivan.

Sullivan's OIC program prospered as a result of the President's support, and soon thereafter it expanded into many more inner cities around the United States. Sullivan went on to great personal achievements. He became the first black member of the board of directors of a major American company, Chrysler Corporation. More important, he developed what was known as "The Sullivan Principles"—a set of guidelines that came to govern the relationships between American business enterprises and then tightly segregated South Africa. The unrelenting pressures created by the application of these principles had a powerful influence on the ultimate demise of apartheid.

As predicted, despite everything President Johnson attempted, riots within American inner cities burst forth during the spring and summer of 1967. They began in April and did not end until September. Although the riots following the murder of Martin Luther King in 1968 were even worse, those that occurred during 1967 were terrible enough. They began in Nashville and soon engulfed cities such as: Houston, Texas; Rockford, Illinois; Tampa, Florida; Elizabeth, New Jersey; Cincinnati, Ohio; Grand Rapids, Michigan; Atlanta, Georgia; Tucson, Arizona; Milwaukee, Wisconsin; and New Haven, Connecticut.

They spread like uncontrolled forest fires, and the worst of them took place in Newark and Detroit during July and August. The Newark riots went on for six days and nights, and resulted in twenty-six deaths and one thousand five hundred injuries. Detroit's nine days of violence was even more severe, and cost 43 lost lives, 657 injuries, 7,231 arrests, and $150 million in property damage.

The President was hugely disappointed that his antipoverty and civil rights programs had not prevented the rioting. In the end, he had no choice but to restore law and order by giving all possible support to local and state law enforcement agencies, and when those proved inadequate—such as in Detroit—to make use of federal troops.

Nonetheless, although stopping lawlessness was his first priority, the President's deeper concern was to discover the root causes of the riots. In that regard, he did not require experts to tell him that they were the result, as he said, of "privations and indignities and . . . past oppression and neglect." The evidence of that was "all too plentiful" and he wanted to "dig below the surface." Thus, on July 27, 1967, the President created the National Advisory Committee on Civil Disorders headed by Gov. Otto Kerner of Illinois and Mayor John Lindsay of New York. That committee immediately commenced its work, and in February 1968, furnished a report that called for doubling and tripling of funding for the President's antipoverty programs. The Committee was silent regarding how the President was to pry the additional funds out of Congress, especially while the war continued to rage in Vietnam.

There was no shortage of other suggestions to the President—from both the left and the right sides of the political spectrum. From the left, the Chief of Staff to Vice President Humphrey, Bill Connell, sent us a memorandum urging us to "coordinate top governmental search-and-destroy operations aimed at neutralizing the black power–peacenik coalition" for which $90 million should be funded from either the government or the Democratic National Committee.

From the right, J. Edgar Hoover and the FBI urged "measures . . . to diminish opportunities of potential rioters and to bring public pressure to bear on them [by]: (a) full exposure of the 'sordid character and activities' of the individuals and organizations involved in the demonstrations; (b) rioters subject to the Selective Service Act should in no way be allowed to evade the draft; (c) prompt and forceful notification to agitators of the consequences of their acts; (d) vigorous prosecution of all arrested for violation of . . . laws in connection with these riots; (e) intensive studies of speeches and writings of Stokely Carmichael and others to determine whether there is a basis for prosecution; and (f) psychiatric observation and examination should be provided for some of these agitators after their arrest."

These suggestions and many others clearly illustrate that in the minds of many contemporary observers, there was a convergence of the inner city riots, the "black power" battle cry raised by a new crop of militant young African-American leaders, the marches and acts of civil disobedience organized by Martin Luther King and his followers, and the increasing militancy of those who opposed American policies in Vietnam. Such was the complicated national fabric with which the President had to deal during the final two years of his administration.

RIOTERS, DEMONSTRATIONS, AND MARTIN LUTHER KING, JR.

Of course, there is a clear distinction between riots and demonstrations. But either deliberately or through lack of proper control—by the participants or the authorities—the latter can become the former with every bit as much violence and destruction. During 1967, the demonstrations came from two initially separate sources—antiwar sentiment and the American blacks' struggle for civil rights. In time, the civil disobedience and marches led by Martin Luther King fused with the protests against the war so that seemingly the two movements almost appeared to be one. In the mind of Dr. King, fusing his fight with the antiwar movement was a difficult and troubling direction for him to take. But take it he did, and not necessarily to the ultimate advantage of his followers. Thus, the various causes became virtually indistinguishable in the minds of people like J. Edgar Hoover.

The President did not have the luxury of lumping all of them together. He was constantly required to separate the causes, the influences, and, accordingly, the manner with which each movement should be dealt. Yet he never shirked his responsibility. He opposed violence, upheld the law without violating the law, and never lost his focus on either the imperative American interests in Southeast Asia or the equally essential war on poverty in America.

Let me first deal with the antiwar protestors who organized, marched, and, to the extent they could manage it, attempted to disrupt the nation and its government. Although I have no problem acknowledging that large numbers of Americans—particularly students subject to the draft—genuinely abhorred the war in Vietnam, and were sincere in their advocacy of "peace and love," it must also be said that their protests were materially aided and abetted by foreign governments and their agents whose true objective was to weaken the United States.

The Soviet Union was considered a powerful threat to the United States, and its agent, the American Communist Party, was both active and well funded. In those days, their objective was undermining, wherever possible, America's influence in Southeast Asia. China too was an active participant in promoting subversion. Acting separately or in unison, they employed multiple means to achieve their goals, and our intelligence agencies furnished us with a constant stream of reports concerning their activities.

Both the Soviets and the Chinese distributed cash to some leaders of the antiwar protestors. Our intelligence agencies were well aware of those activities, but could never stop the flow of money. I do not know the grand total of cash deliveries that were made, and I doubt if any agency had that information. However, I recall that there was an interesting variation in the Chinese and Soviet methods regarding cash. The Chinese never distributed bills larger than twenty dollars on the theory that no one paid attention to persons using currency of that denomination or smaller. The Soviets, on the other hand, had no such compunctions, and their cash infusions could come in any size bills.

One of the most insidious operations of the Soviet Union was the "anti-war" school that they operated at a location just outside of Moscow. The "school" had many projects. Among them was the development of antiwar slogans. Those slogans, invented by Soviet experts in the American idiom, were first tried out in Norway. If they appeared to work there, they were introduced into the eastern United States where, if the slogans were good enough, they were deliberately spread throughout the country, especially onto university campuses. One of the most effective, still recalled by all who lived through those times, was, "LBJ, LBJ, how many kids did you kill today?" That was only one among many results of what was, without doubt, a highly effective propaganda operation.

The activities of this Soviet school were not limited to slogans. It also trained operatives, especially American Communists, who were sent back to the United States to infiltrate the peace movement in this country. Other functions of the school included development of editorial arguments and news stories that they then attempted—and often succeeded—in placing in the American press.

The concern over the activities of the Soviet Union cannot be overstated. An illustrative example is an intelligence report that came to the President from the CIA. Citing what the Agency described as "credible sources," it described a Soviet "contingency plan" to invade the United States. Specifically, the CIA report stated that the Soviet plan called for landing troops on the Atlantic coastlines of South Carolina or Georgia, where the Soviets expected the local black populations to rise up in support of the invasion. The CIA stated that the Soviet scheme was grounded in their belief that there was deep resentment and unrest among American blacks, especially in the South, and that they would eagerly embrace the Communists once given the opportunity to do so.

When he read the CIA report, the President reacted with total disbelief. "They may have such a contingency plan," he told me. "Although I doubt even that. Maybe this is something that goes back to the days of the Cuban missile crisis. In any event, I think that it's a ridiculous report. It will never happen. I know that the world is a dangerous place, but in this instance, whoever prepared this report should be put out to pasture."

"What do you want me to do about it?" I asked.

"I suppose that I can't complain about something as outlandish as this," the President said. "If I do, someone probably will leak that we don't take the Soviet threat seriously enough. So just file it away and forget about it, which is about what it is worth."

However, there were more realistic reasons for concern. One day the White House security people discovered that a listening device had been planted inside the Oval Office. It consisted of a sophisticated microphone hidden behind one of the President's couches. I was told that it had a broadcast range of one mile. Despite everyone's best efforts, the culprit was never found, nor did we ever learn how long the microphone had been in place. Back then, "sweeping" the Oval Office for listening devices was not an easy task. It took six to eight hours to complete. Because the process was so disruptive, it only was done when the President was out of town, which was not that often.

Later in 1967, the FBI furnished us with a detailed summary of Soviet intelligence activities in the United States, which they characterized as "extremely active." At that time, the FBI reported that they had identified 317 Soviet agents then engaged in espionage efforts throughout the country. This was serious subversive activity that could not be ignored.

As I have stated, there were great numbers of sincere Americans who opposed the Vietnam War. However, that truth does not diminish the equally accurate reality that our enemies infiltrated, financed, and encouraged the work of the protestors.

One problem with our constant struggle against these foreign influences was the number and variety of our own intelligence agencies. It was a never-ending struggle to harmonize their work, and it is as vexing a problem in contemporary times as it was in ours. In our administration, the President directed me to coordinate their activities. Thus, I convened regular White House meetings of high officials of such acronymed agencies as the FBI, CIA, Department of Defense, National Security Agency, and the National Security Council, among others. To further complicate the problem, each military service within the Department of Defense had its own—and separate—intelligence operation. I never ceased my efforts to bring them all together. However, ultimately their inherent and apparently implacable institutional jealousies seemingly trumped their ability to focus on a unified effort to protect the national interest.

I have previously pointed out that in the President's opinion—and my own—the FBI and its Director, J. Edgar Hoover, were the most reliable of these agencies and leaders. Joseph Califano, in his book *The Triumph and Tragedy of Lyndon Johnson* (Simon & Schuster, 1991), is mistaken when he writes that "LBJ disliked and mistrusted . . . Hoover. . . ." The fact is that the President and Hoover had known each other for decades, and their relationship was solidly grounded in mutual trust and respect. President Johnson never lost faith in either Hoover or the Bureau. He relied on their thoroughness and accuracy throughout his presidency. Thus, the President had no reluctance when he reappointed Hoover as Director of the FBI. In no way was the President pressured into this action. On the contrary, his belief that Hoover was the best man for that job never wavered.

In those days, we had no inkling of the scandalous rumors regarding Hoover's personal life that surfaced after his death in 1972. On the contrary, we knew him as a dedicated public servant who had taken an obscure division of the Department of Justice and built it into a great law enforcement agency. A Washington, D.C., native, Hoover held a Master of Laws degree from George Washington University. In 1924, at the age of twenty-nine, Harlan Fiske Stone (who later became a Supreme Court Justice) selected Hoover to head the Justice Department's Bureau of Investigation, which in 1929 was renamed the Federal Bureau of Investigation—the FBI. Hoover directed the FBI until his death. During that extraordinary tenure, he established professional qualifications for FBI agents, created a promotion system based on merit, established the National Crime Laboratory, which used the latest science and technology, and began the National FBI and Police Academy in Quantico, Virginia, which has been called the best postgrad course for law enforcement in the world. Without doubt, J. Edgar Hoover was a patriot. What isn't as well known is that he was also a man who held dear some of the most basic tenets of democracy. In a 1950 speech he gave in New York, he stated, "The virtue of tolerance and the ability to respect different opinions, beliefs, and ideas have enriched the life of America. Tolerance is the eternal virtue through which good conquers evil and truth vanquishes untruth."

The President's faith in the FBI and Hoover far exceeded his trust in any of his own Attorneys General. Robert Kennedy, who remained in the post to which he was appointed by his brother until mid-1964, was no friend of Lyndon Johnson. Kennedy had his own agenda, and despite his later attempts to align himself with Martin Luther King, he was the man who authorized the FBI to engage in close surveillance, including wiretaps that disclosed intimate details of King's activities and personal life. When Kennedy resigned to run for the Senate, he was replaced by Nicolas Katzenbach, Kennedy's chief deputy. Although to my knowledge Katzenbach never demonstrated any disloyalty to the President, his background as a creature of the Kennedys resulted in something less than our complete trust in him. Katzenbach ultimately resigned to replace George Ball as Undersecretary of State.

His successor as Attorney General was Ramsey Clark, who in turn had been Katzenbach's deputy. Clark's father, Supreme Court Justice Tom Clark, was an old and trusted friend of Lyndon Johnson, and a tough-minded Texan for whom the President had the highest admiration. In order to pave the way for his son's appointment, Justice Clark resigned his position on the Supreme Court so that no one could argue that there was even an appearance of a conflict of interest. Thus, the President assumed that the son was a reflection of his father. As it turned out, Ramsey Clark was neither as tough-minded nor as trustworthy a friend as Justice Clark. However, once appointed, Clark remained Attorney General until the end of Johnson's administration.

J. Edgar Hoover perceived the tensions between President Johnson and each of his Attorneys General, and being the consummate bureaucrat that he was, took full advantage of the fissure. He took two unusual steps, both of which were approved. The first was to assign a high-ranking deputy, Deke Deloach, as his liaison to the White House. In that capacity, Deloach was in daily contact, first with Walter Jenkins and later with me, on all matters relating to the FBI's activities. As such, I came to trust and rely on him as though he was a member of the White House staff. My relationship with Deloach resulted in far closer coordination between the President and the FBI than was enjoyed by any other agency of the government.

The second—and far more unusual—action taken by the FBI Director was to send some of his most sensitive reports directly through me to the President without furnishing any copies to the Attorney General. The fact that the FBI is a part of the Department of Justice did not stop Hoover from engaging in this practice. Hoover's position was that it was up to the President to decide with whom, if anyone, this information was to be shared. Because the President had his own doubts about his Attorneys General, he accepted Hoover's practice.

The peace demonstrations continued to grow in intensity throughout 1967. Within the West Wing of the White House, we could hear their chanting while they marched along Pennsylvania Avenue and camped in Lafayette Park across the street. Sometimes I watched them when I came to work or walked outside for some fresh air. To me, they sometimes looked cold and hungry. On one occasion, I took pity on them and suggested that we send them sandwiches and milk. The instant the Secret Service learned of my idea, they went ballistic. "Don't encourage them!" they told me. "If you make it any easier for them, they simply will multiply." Sadly, I complied with their objections, although I knew that those youngsters could include the children of any of us.

In October 1967, the antiwar demonstrations culminated with a plan to massively march on Washington. In anticipation of the event, the President convened a meeting with Secretary of Defense Robert McNamara, Attorney General Ramsey Clark, and Director of the General Services Administration Lawson Knott. McNamara reported that the demonstration sponsors would claim to have 200,000 persons. Clark responded that the FBI believed that 40,000 to 50,000 was a realistic number. The consensus was that they planned to move against the White House, the Capitol, and the Pentagon, among other government buildings. Clark reported that they were attempting to secure 1,000 buses in New York alone, but had only been able to locate 150. The advisors assured the President that they could control the crowd, and it was agreed that the Department of Justice would be in charge. In answer to the President's question, they told him that sufficient personnel was available to handle any problems that might arise. Finally, the President was urged to be out of the White House on the days of the demonstration.

President Johnson did not follow that advice. Just as was the case when he traveled into the Philadelphia ghetto earlier that year, he decided where he should perform his responsibilities. In this instance, he thought that it would be a mistake to abandon the White House and give the impression that he was running from the protestors.

On Sunday, October 22, the final day of the demonstration, the President, as he was approaching the White House after attending church with

Mrs. Johnson and his daughter Lynda, asked Mrs. Johnson and Lynda if they would like to drive around and observe what the demonstrators were doing. They agreed, and the presidential automobile turned and drove to the Lincoln Memorial. There were only about 150 people milling around the area, and Mrs. Johnson, always conscious of the inherent beauty of the nation's capital, was distressed at all the litter and refuse scattered everywhere.

The President was curious about what the "hippies" looked like, their dress, age, and the flags, bedrolls, blankets, flight bags, and flowers that they carried. He wanted to see more of them. So he ordered his car to cross the Potomac River and go toward the Pentagon where the demonstrators were then massed. There the car was blocked by police barricades, but the Secret Service Agent in charge identified only himself, and the President's car was passed through. They then drove up to the lines of soldiers guarding the Pentagon. The President did not attempt to pass through that line, but contented himself with slowly circling the building and quietly observing the confrontations between the soldiers and the demonstrators. Then, thoughtfully and without incident, he ordered his car to return to the White House.

The demonstration was nowhere near as successful as the planners had hoped. Law enforcement agencies estimated the crowd at between 15,000 and 30,000, below even the FBI's conservative prediction, although the demonstration leaders claimed that their number totaled between 150,000 and 210,000 people. In any event, those three days of demonstrations generated extraordinary publicity from a sympathetic press. In that sense, they achieved success in their objective of fomenting resistance against the President and our policies in Vietnam.

Summarizing that weekend's demonstrations, J. Edgar Hoover reported the following FBI conclusions to the President:

> The rally constituted a victory for the elements of subversion who had been seeking to instigate a clash between the demonstrators and the forces of law and order. . . . The crowd was emotionally conditioned . . . by skilled agitators who brought the mob to the brink of violence and then sought ways to trigger it. . . . The key agitators and lawbreakers were not students. . . . They were vicious rioters, hoodlums, and subversives who were willfully acting in clear violation of the law. This is how the press should have described the incident, so that the public would not have been grossly misled. . . . The entire

affair represented . . . that segment of society comprised by the subversive-criminal-hoodlum element of the "New Left" supported by the Communists. . . . It was the seedbed of traitorous action on the part of individuals who may be expected to be of increasing concern to this Nation's stability and security in the near future.

Through the year, the FBI constantly furnished us with reports on the demonstrations and the influence of Communists upon them. On October 24, I summarized many of these for the President. Among other things, I stated that the FBI had concluded that the demonstrations were backed by the Communist Party; that a rally in Los Angeles was headed by a former member of the Communist Party; that numerous Communist Party members had participated in picketing a federal office building in Seattle; and the Progressive Labor Party, a pro-Chinese Marxist group, had sponsored a demonstration in New York. I am attaching my memorandum as Appendix 5. Nowadays, many people might scoff at the FBI reports, but, from our perspective at the time, we were receiving formal intelligence from the nation's principal law enforcement agency. We were expected to—and did—accept its credibility and take its warnings seriously.

The October demonstration also marked one of the last instances where there was no melding of the antiwar and civil rights movements. On the same weekend that the antiwar demonstrators were marching, a separate "black caucus" rally was held at the Lincoln Memorial. Amazingly, as the FBI reported, the African American speakers urged their people not to go to the Pentagon because of fear that blacks would be "slaughtered." Instead, they separately marched to a playground where, according to the FBI, they held their own rally.

Soon thereafter, however, there was a convergence of the riots, the antiwar demonstrations, and the civil rights movement led by Martin Luther King.

King's organization, the Southern Christian Leadership Conference, began its existence rightly and justly espousing the need for full civil rights for African Americans, while promulgating its philosophy that the most effective method to achieve that goal was through massive demonstrations and nonviolent civil disobedience. In becoming a nationally recognized leader of his race, King was following in the footsteps of other great blacks who had preceded him. These men included Thurgood Marshall, Roy Wilkins,

Whitney Young, Phillip Randolph, and James Farmer, all of whom the President knew, respected, and trusted. From time to time, the President met with all of these men—including Dr. King—although to my knowledge he never had a private conversation with Dr. King and he never changed his view that Dr. King's methods were totally counterproductive to the President's primary objective: to have Congress pass new and meaningful civil rights legislation.

Dr. King, however, took the black movement farther than those who came before him. Although, as he often stated, he abhorred violence, that did not mean obedience to existing laws, even those that he might otherwise believe were just and fair. To him, it was appropriate to violate any law if that action served to advance their cause. Thus, he disregarded laws aimed at protecting the public against violence, even if the regulation of marches and demonstrations was reasonable. He also advocated sit-ins and boycotts, regardless of their legality, because it seems that King believed that the end of racial inequality justified any nonviolent means of achieving it.

The President totally disagreed with King's methods. Although the President admired Dr. King as a marvelous public speaker—and even adopted his theme of "We Shall Overcome" in his pivotal civil rights speech to Congress on March 15, 1965—the President's focus was on the enactment of legislation. He believed that every effort should be targeted on securing the votes of Members of Congress and that because illegal marches, demonstrations, sit-ins, and boycotts were anathema to so many Americans—and thus to their representatives in Congress—leaders like King only succeeded in making progress more difficult to achieve. The President knew that any lasting change (such as Dr. King and all African Americans wanted) had to become a part of the legislative framework of our nation. He knew that he could recommend such legislation, but that only Congress could enact it. Both he and the Congress must act in order to achieve the goal that both the President and Dr. King held so dearly. But the President believed that Dr. King's methods of civil disobedience were detrimental to convincing an already recalcitrant Congress. It was therefore strange that the nation's most committed civil rights President and the most cherished leader of African Americans found themselves at odds while working for the same objective.

Two other aspects of Dr. King's leadership and life were disturbing to the President. The first involved possible influence on King of known present and former members of the Communist Party, and the second concerned King's personal life.

As for the former, the FBI regularly sent us reports concerning King that included information that King's chief advisor was a New Yorker by the name of Stanley Levison who "was a secret member of the Communist Party in July 1963 ... [who] continues his ideological adherence to Communism." The FBI also stated that Levison had previously served as an active agent of the Soviet Union within the United States. According to the FBI, Levison was not the only close Communist advisor to King. The FBI identified several others in their numerous reports to the President.

I am attaching as Appendix 6 a formerly "secret" memorandum from FBI Director J. Edgar Hoover dated April 19, 1967. It is typical of many such reports that preceded it. In it, Hoover states, among other disturbing conclusions, that the FBI has facts revealing that King is a man whom the Communist Party considers to be a Marxist. As I have previously stated, Lyndon Johnson—as would any President—gave great credence to "facts" that the nation's chief law enforcement body officially stated it had uncovered.

When the FBI first reported Levison had become critically influential with King, it presented its evidence to then Attorney General Robert Kennedy, who authorized intensive, close, and continuing surveillance of King by the FBI. That included bugging his hotel rooms whenever he traveled around the country. The surveillance continued for years and revealed not only the depth of King's reliance on Communists such as Levison, but also details concerning King's personal life.

The FBI reports regarding King were sent to the White House. Each of them was routed to me to read or have read, summarized, and analyzed. Each included the legal justification for the FBI's actions, by beginning with the statement that "reliable sources" had informed the Bureau that Levison and other known Communists were principal advisors to King.

According to the FBI, at first King resisted the importunings of Levison and others to publicly oppose our involvement in Vietnam. In 1965, King had informed the U.S. ambassador to the United Nations, Arthur Goldberg, that "he is not strong enough to carry on two struggles at the same time: a civil rights battle and the Vietnam peace struggle."

However, King's ambivalence continued for only a short period of time. Ultimately, he bowed to the constant urgings of Levison and others. The

FBI reported to the President: "[regarding] King, Jr., and his position on your Vietnam policy he is now following the Communist lines and seems to have embraced their Communist lines, motives, and purposes in this country." In the April 19, 1967, attached Hoover memorandum he states that the FBI has concluded that King's antiwar speeches are a result of the influence of the subversive persons all around him; that King has become "a conscious instrument of the Communist Party"; and that "his closest advisors, speech writers, and supporters are active Communists and their status is known to King."

It is sad to reflect that Dr. King may have perceived that he had to get help from whomever he could, such as from the Communists, then the most dangerous enemy of the United States. Still, as I look back, I can understand that after almost two hundred years of neglect and broken promises to his people, he believed he had little choice but to accept help from wherever it came. I imagine that in his eyes he was dealing with a southern white President whose belief and total commitment to his cause was very difficult for Dr. King to accept. Thankfully, in this respect Dr. King was proven wrong.

By 1967, despite embracing the antiwar positions of the Communists and others, King found himself at odds with black radicals such as Stokely Carmichael and H. Rap Brown. In an August 1967 report to the President, the FBI stated that, "King feels it is now necessary for his organization to disassociate itself from the Student Nonviolent Coordinating Committee (SNCC). King says that SNCC is opposed to the principle of nonviolence . . . and the organization's basic aim is the destruction of the government of the United States. . . ." Thus, King attempted to distance himself from those blacks advocating riots and violence within the United States.

Nonetheless, Dr. King's followers began to march with the demonstrators opposed to the Vietnam War, and since these demonstrations often—and deliberately—were violent, King's fastidious distinctions did not appear to be of substantive importance. As I have previously noted, President Johnson believed that the law must be obeyed, and equally important, that disobedience of the law was not helpful in convincing Congress to enact the civil rights and antipoverty legislation that the President believed was more truly targeted at uprooting the causes of injustice in America.

The other aspect concerning Dr. King dealt with his personal conduct. As is apparent from the attached excerpts from the March 12, 1968, "Current

Analysis of Dr. Martin Luther King" prepared by the FBI (Appendix 7, which has now been declassified), those details of the report have been withheld from public scrutiny pursuant to a U.S. District Court order obtained by the King family.

However, I read all of those reports—and my assistant, Sherwin Markman, read many of them—when they were initially delivered to the White House. Thus we are familiar with the detailed FBI information concerning Dr. King. Although we are not enjoined from revealing those facts, in deference to the spirit of the court order I will not repeat those details here. It is sufficient to say that the substance of that personal information concerning Dr. King was distressing.

It is notable that although copies of the King FBI reports concerning his antiwar statements and the Communists' influence over him were sent to the Attorneys General and other interested law enforcement and intelligence agencies, the FBI reports that dealt with King's lifestyle were sent only to the President "for his eyes only" while specifically noting that no copies were being furnished to the Attorney General. However, at the President's direction, all such reports were read by me and those, such as Markman, to whom I gave the task of reading and summarizing.

Although shocking, those FBI reports concerning Dr. King's personal life showed nothing more than that he was as human as the rest of us.

TRAVELS AND TRAVAILS FOR
THE PRESIDENT: SURINAME

In April 1967, the President was scheduled to attend a summit conference of the Presidents of the American Republics to discuss the Alliance for Progress, the program first initiated by President Kennedy to strengthen the bonds among the nations of the Western Hemisphere. The meeting was to be held in the coastal resort town of Punta Del Este, Uruguay, where the Alliance for Progress was born six years earlier. The summit conference was to held between April 12 and April 14.

Two weeks before the summit began, Colonel James Cross, who functioned both as Military Aide and Chief Pilot of Air Force One, came to my office to tell me that although Air Force One could fly nonstop from Washington to Punta del Este, the runway there was too short to permit a full load of fuel for the return journey. Accordingly, it would be necessary for the President's plane to stop somewhere during the return trip in order to take on additional fuel.

My initial thought was that this was a nonproblem; that all Cross had to do was locate an airfield, land there, refuel, and we quickly would be on our way home. As I soon discovered, this was a naive assumption. As soon as the State Department learned that the President had to make a stop while returning from Uruguay, they informed me that the location of the refueling stop posed a diplomatic dilemma.

"What would that be?" I asked, surprised.

"We believe that if the President's airplane stopped in any country that attends the summit conference, then there is a substantial risk that the other attending countries will be offended," they told me.

"That's ridiculous," I replied.

"But nonetheless likely," they said.

"What do you suggest?" I asked.

"The President must refuel in some country that isn't attending the summit conference."

"And what countries are those?"

"Guyana or Suriname are two that we recommend."

I asked Colonel Cross to choose where he wanted to stop. He suggested Guyana, telling me, "They have an airport about a half hour's drive from their capital of Georgetown. That will work for us."

The State Department also informed me that even as simple an action as landing to refuel Air Force One would be considered an important presidential visit by any host country, especially one as small as Guyana. I summoned Sherwin Markman to my office and instructed him to assemble and lead a team to fly to Guyana to prepare for the President's short stop there. The various agencies involved—State Department, Secret Service, White House Communications, and Air Force One personnel—all indicated that they needed time to adequately do their job. Thus, with some reluctance, I dispatched all of them to Guyana several days before the day the President was scheduled to arrive.

There were enough people under Markman's direction on that trip to fill the large military transport plane that carried them to Guyana from Andrews Air Force Base outside of Washington. It was late afternoon when they landed. They were met by the American Ambassador, who told Markman that Guyana's Foreign Minister was on his way to the airport from George-town, but that it would be another half hour before he arrived.

Just as Markman was thanking the Ambassador, one of the Air Force pi-lots on his team indicated that he wanted to talk to him privately. The pilot led Markman on a walk down the main runway of the airport.

"Look at these potholes," the pilot said, pointing to several that looked big enough to hold a small Volkswagen. "We were damn lucky to have landed without wrecking ourselves."

"Can they be repaired before the President gets here?" Markman asked.

"I don't want to gamble on that," the pilot said.

"What do you suggest?"

"Air Force One can't land here," the pilot stated. "It's too dangerous. I'm recommending against it."

Markman did not argue, and he and the pilot returned to their airplane. He asked the radio operator to patch him in to me at the White House, and he reported the pilot's opinion.

I instructed Markman to take off now, telling him that we would decide where else we would land to refuel.

It was now nighttime in Guyana, and as the plane circled above that country, I had several rapid conversations with Colonel Cross and the peo-ple at the State Department. Their recommendation was that the Air Force One refueling should take place in Suriname, a small country immediately south of Guyana. At that time, it had not yet gained full independence from the Dutch and thus would not be present at Punta del Este. Suriname also had an about-to-be-abandoned—but still partially operational—American air base that was about an hour's drive from its capital of Paramaribo. When Markman radioed me again, I instructed him to take his group there.

"Do they know we are coming?" Markman asked me.

"Not yet," I said. "I expect you to get the necessary invitations after you land."

"But we are a military aircraft," Markman protested. "If we land without clearance, won't they consider that a breach of their sovereignty?"

I laughed and said, "Just do it, Markman. And while you're at it, don't get us into any trouble."

It was almost midnight when the big air force jet approached the Suriname airfield. No one responded to the pilot's radioed requests for permission to land. Then, just as he was considering aborting, the runway lights came on, although there was still no contact with the control tower.

They landed without further incident. Markman and the pilot walked to a lighted shack that served as a makeshift control tower. Inside, they found two young and sleepily confused U.S. Air Force enlisted men.

"Who in the hell are you?" one of them demanded. "We didn't give you any clearance to land here. We don't have any authority from the government here to do that."

"Please relax," Markman said. "We're an advance party for the President. Air Force One will be stopping here to refuel if we can arrange it."

The young airmen were shocked, but quickly recovered. "What do you want us to do?" one of them asked.

"Do you have a telephone?" Markman asked.

"Yes, but it doesn't always work."

Turning to the pilot, Markman asked, "How does the runway look to you?"

"Fine. Air Force One can easily land here. All we have to do is arrange for the refueling."

Markman nodded and handed the airman a note on which Markman had copied a telephone number I had given him. It was the home phone of the American Chargé d'Affaires in Paramaribo. "Since we don't have an Ambassador, the Chargé is the highest ranking American in this country," Markman explained. "Do you think you can get him on the telephone for me?"

"It's awfully late, sir," the airman said.

"It can't be helped," Markman said. "I'll take any heat from him."

It took a while before a connection could be made and the Chargé brought to the telephone. Markman explained who he was and his mission. "We need you to get the Suriname government to issue an invitation to the President, who will be landing here to refuel on his way home from Punte del Este. While you are at it, I would appreciate some kind of after-the-fact permission for us to have landed here tonight. Can you do all that as quickly as possible?"

"I think so," the Chargé responded, obviously shocked. "But I had better drive out there and see you first. I can't do anything until morning anyway."

"We'll be right here," Markman said. "By the way, there are several dozen of us who need to be housed for over a week. Do you think you can help us?"

"I will work it out."

The Chargé arrived at the airfield in less than an hour. During the wait, despite the lateness of the hour, Markman radioed me again and told me he was confident that everything would fall into place.

Markman's prediction turned out to be accurate. Before noon the next day, the Chargé had accomplished his mission with the Suriname government. They happily extended their invitation to the President, approved the presence of Markman's team, and arranged rooms for all of them at Paramaribo's most luxurious hotel.

The government of Suriname eagerly began organizing preparations to welcome the American President during the one hour it would take to refuel Air Force One. They assembled a large contingent of singers and dancers and cleaned and decorated the airfield until it looked like a colorful fair. In the meantime, Markman's team completed their preparations and did what they could to assist in planning the welcoming ceremonies. Still, they found that they had plenty of time to lounge around the swimming pool at the hotel. While there, as they happily discovered, they were treated as honored guests of the country. Sheepishly, Markman reported all of this to me, and I told him he had better enjoy it all, because once he met up with us again, I would see to it that his workload would make up for lost time.

The Punte del Este Summit was an exhausting experience for President Johnson. As he later wrote in his book *The Vantage Point,* they "were days of work as intensive as any I had experienced, except during a major crisis." As we approached our stop in Suriname, he was very tired and in no mood for more festivities, although he begrudgingly agreed to leave his airplane and participate in the program that had been prepared for him.

As it turned out, a heavy thunderstorm struck the airport just as we arrived. There was enough visibility for Air Force One to land, but the waiting decorations were ruined, and the performers and crowd were soaked and miserably cold. To the President's relief, there was no possibility of any outdoor ceremony, although he greeted the Suriname officials on Air Force One. That meeting was friendly but blessedly short.

When Sherwin Markman boarded Air Force One with the Suriname officials, he intended to stay behind to express the President's appreciation for their efforts and his regret that the storm had forced cancellation of their plans. However, he was asked to remain on the airplane because he would be flying back to Washington immediately. There was no time to thank and say good-bye to the people who had worked so hard to greet the President.

ISRAEL: THE SIX-DAY WAR AND THE U.S. RELATIONSHIP

Most Americans believe that the Cuban Missile Crisis of October 1962 was the closest we ever came to nuclear war with the Soviet Union. They may be wrong.

On June 5, 1967, the Six-Day War began between Israel and the Arab states of Egypt, Syria, and Jordan. In total disregard of President Johnson's views to the contrary, the State Department initially declared that the United States would be "neutral in thought, word, and deed." The fact is that when that war began, the President was greatly concerned that Israel might not survive, which he was determined never to allow. Thus, he followed developments very closely. Johnson believed—just as he did regarding Vietnam—that American treaty commitments obligated us to ensure the continued existence of the Jewish state.

The President and American military leaders were amazed by the success of the Israeli armed forces. However, they also knew that the one threat that the Israelis could not withstand would be the intervention of the Soviet Union, and in particular its formidable Mediterranean fleet. If that occurred, there was a substantial risk that Israel would be overrun.

Several days into the war, when it appeared that Israel was headed toward total victory, the Soviet fleet suddenly turned from its position that was a safe distance from the hostilities and began steaming directly toward Israel. On receiving this ominous news, the President joined his principal military and civilian advisors in the Situation Room located in the basement of the White House West Wing.

The question before them was what, if anything, should the United States do about the imminent Soviet threat, which all agreed was real, dangerous, and potentially decisive. More specifically, the issue soon became: Should the American Sixth Fleet, which was then positioned three hundred miles west of the Syrian coast, be ordered to move to block the Soviets? There was no doubt that if this was done it would raise the stakes to very high levels because it could lead to a direct military confrontation between the two superpowers. If America acted now, and if the Soviets did not yield, there might be no turning back. The President knew that this was no game of "chicken." If he gave the order to head them off, it meant that the two fleets would meet, and if the Soviets did not turn away that could mean war, and any war between the United States and the Soviet Union could all too easily lead to a nuclear exchange.

President Johnson did not hesitate, and ordered the American fleet to move forward. The two fleets were now steaming, as one of the military men put it, "nose to nose," heading directly toward one another. It was a situation as dangerous—perhaps more dangerous—than the Cuban missile crisis, and everyone present knew it.

At that moment, Aleksey Kosygin, the Soviet premier, activated the "hot line" between Moscow and Washington. He signaled that he wanted to communicate directly with President Johnson. The premier's demand was short and simple: "You must turn back your fleet."

The President's reply was an equally blunt, "No, you turn your fleet!" The dialogue ended on that note, and the American and Soviet fleets continued their intersecting approach.

Those of us in the Situation Room tensely waited. Finally, the news was flashed to us: the Soviet fleet had turned; they were not going to confront the United States. A possible war between us had been averted, and Israel was no longer threatened with loss of its military victory. The Israeli nation was saved, and the relief in the Situation Room was palpable.

It was terribly frustrating to President Johnson that many American Jews believed that Israel's marvelous victory was achieved without American assistance. Even putting aside the fact that American military aid was the backbone of Israeli armed strength, that mistaken thinking ignored the fact that the President's courageous decision to face down the Soviet naval threat was a decisive component of Israel's ultimate success.

Afterward, the Israeli government was effusively grateful to the President and had no hesitancy in saying so both privately and publicly. Still, the American Jewish community, whose intellectual leaders often were in the forefront of the antiwar protests, refused to acknowledge the critical importance of

President Johnson's decision to risk war in order to checkmate the Soviet intervention on behalf of the Arab nations.

Thereafter, as the President often told me, he could never understand how those Jewish leaders could oppose our policies in Vietnam while simultaneously urging us to actively support Israel's war. To him, their views were inconsistent and logically unsupportable.

The President did what he could to persuade the American Jewish leaders that protecting the viability of our allies and honoring our treaty commitments was the same whether it involved Israel or Vietnam. He dispatched several Jewish members of his White House staff to meet with those leaders and explain his position. It was his hope that, at a minimum, he could diffuse their public criticism of his Vietnam policies and stop such actions as their recent full-page advertisement opposing the Vietnam War. Sadly, neither he nor his staff succeeded in muting their dissent.

Nonetheless, and despite such hurtful provocations by American Jewish leaders, the President's support of Israel never faltered. To President Johnson, Israel's viability was grounded in his belief in the Bible. In that belief, he received the unstinting support of his most trusted religious advisor, Reverend Billy Graham. For example, during the height of the Six-Day War, Reverend Graham told the President that regarding the viability of Israel, "Reading the Old Testament is like reading tomorrow's newspaper."

Before—and especially after—the Six-Day War, the Israelis had little trust in the American State Department. Their distrust was only heightened by the unauthorized State Department announcement that the United States would be "neutral" in that war. Thus, Israel asked if President Johnson would agree to set up a direct channel of communication, one that would bypass the State Department and could be activated whenever they chose. The President agreed, and he sent word to them that anytime they wanted to communicate directly with him they should do so through me. In turn, the Israelis designated Abraham Feinberg, then Chairman of the American Bank and Trust Company in New York, as the man who would speak for them.

The Israelis activated the Feinberg-Watson channel on several occasions when they wanted specific information conveyed directly to the President, and when they thought that officials at the State Department might be blocking or delaying Israeli requests for assistance.

One instance occurred when the Israelis had a critical need for oil-drilling equipment that they believed was being unnecessarily delayed by State Department red tape. Feinberg called, requested a meeting, and I invited him to the White House where we met in my office. He explained how badly Israel needed oil and how frustrating it was that this need was not recognized by the people at the State Department.

I knew something about oil drilling from my years working for Lone Star Steel, so I asked Feinberg, "Do the Israelis know the approximate location for their drilling from seismic or some other kind of scientific tests?"

"No," Feinberg replied. "They know where the oil is from their study of ancient parchments and scrolls."

I was astonished, but I accepted Feinberg's explanation and immediately passed his request to the President, who approved it. I then called Walter Rostow, the National Security Advisor, and instructed him to see to it that the State Department acted rapidly and positively on Israel's request. A day or two later, he reported that the necessary permits had been approved and the equipment was being shipped to Israel. I informed Feinberg, who was grateful to the President. I never learned the reason that the people at State were being difficult, but it was enough to know that the President's order had been promptly fulfilled.

TRAVELS AND TRAVAILS FOR
THE PRESIDENT: GLASSBORO

Ten days after the successful conclusion of the Six-Day War, Soviet Premier Aleksey Kosygin traveled to New York City to attend a session of the United Nations. President Johnson saw this as an opportunity to meet with the Soviet leader and lessen the extraordinary tensions that had developed between the two countries because of both the Six-Day War and the conflict in Vietnam. The President issued an invitation to Premier Kosygin, stating that inasmuch as Kosygin was visiting in the United States, he would be most welcome at the White House.

Kosygin replied that he would be delighted to see the President, but he did not consider his appearance at the United Nations to be a visit to the United States. He sent word that it was not appropriate for him to come to the White House, but he would be happy to see the President at the United Nations in New York City.

President Johnson did not accept Kosygin's reasoning, and for a time it appeared that the two leaders had reached an impasse and that there would be no meeting between them. However, both sides felt that such a result would be ridiculous, and an effort was made to find a compromise. What was finally done was to take a map and a ruler, lay one end of the ruler on the White House and the other on the United Nations headquarters, and then note a location that was precisely halfway between the two points. That place was Glassboro, New Jersey, the home of what was then called Glassboro State Teachers College.

The agreement was reached at five o'clock in the afternoon. It called for the two leaders to meet at Glassboro at eleven o'clock the following morning. One hour later, a public announcement was made, and an hour after that I summoned Sherwin Markman to my office.

I told him that once more he had been selected to lead a team for the President, only this time it would be a full-fledged summit conference between President Johnson and the Soviet Premier. Markman's responsibility would be to make certain that everything was made ready in Glassboro. "This time you won't have ten days to get ready," I told him. "The summit conference is going to start about sixteen hours from now."

I called New Jersey Governor Richard Hughes and informed him of our plans. He responded by pledging his total cooperation and said that he would make available every possible state facility.

I then repeated to Markman the President's requirements regarding what he expected at the site of the summit meeting. He wanted a place at the Glassboro college that was large enough to accommodate a meeting of several dozen representatives of the Soviet Union and the United States, but that at the same time was not forbidding and uncomfortable. He wanted rugs on the floor wherever meetings were held so that aides would make minimal noise when walking around. He wanted a small, informal room where intimate and private meetings between the President and the Premier could take place. He also wanted preparations made for a luncheon of the senior members of both delegations, which meant facilities for cooking a fine meal as well as a dining area. Finally, the President wanted separate facilities where each delegation, if they wished, could meet privately.

I emphasized to Markman that although I realized that he had very little time to prepare and that the pressure would be great, I expected him to accomplish his task diplomatically and without upsetting the people in Glassboro who would be our hosts.

I instructed him to assemble his team within the next hour and I told him that they would be taking off immediately on a presidential jet that was standing by at Andrews Air Force Base. The team consisted of Richard Moose from the National Security Council staff, Secret Service agents, persons from the White House press office, representatives from the White House Communications Agency, and the Navy Commander and his men who ran the dining room in the West Wing of the White House. The entire group was organized in time to board the presidential airplane and land at the Philadelphia airport—the closest one to Glassboro—shortly after ten o'clock that night.

The White House team was met by a motorcade of New Jersey State Police, who convoyed them the hour's drive to Glassboro. It was close to eleven when they arrived at the front entrance of the large Victorian residence of Dr. Thomas Robinson, President of the college. Markman, accompanied by the Chief of the State Police, walked up to the door of the mansion, which was named "Hollybush." They had to push their way through a throng of reporters who had already assembled and were waiting for them.

Markman knocked on the door and introduced himself to Dr. Robinson and his wife. The Robinsons had already learned from the press that the White House team was there to prepare a place where the summit conference could be held, now less than twelve hours away.

Dr. Robinson was cordial and helpful, and Mrs. Robinson was nervous and apprehensive. Dr. Robinson told Markman that he had been thinking of where on the small campus the meetings should take place. He recommended the auditorium in the college Administration Building. He asked the White House group to follow him there.

As soon as he stepped inside the Administration Building, Markman knew that the facility would not work. It was far too sterile. As politely as possible, he told Dr. Robinson that they must find another location. Actually, as Markman later told me, he had already decided that the only place that came close to meeting the President's requirements was the spacious residence of Dr. and Mrs. Robinson.

Markman expressed his opinion to Dr. Robinson as soon as they returned to Hollybush. Then, with Mrs. Robinson's grudging consent, the entire group carefully explored the old house. It had a large living room (for meetings of the full delegations from both nations), Dr. Robinson's small study (for any private session between the President and Kosygin), a big kitchen, and a lovely formal dining room. It would do.

However, there were a few problems, all of which had to be solved that night. The first obstacle was a total lack of air-conditioning. It was a warm June night and the forecast for the next day called for hot and humid weather. Hollybush was over one hundred years old. Not only did it not have air-conditioning, but its wiring would not support the power necessary to operate even minimal window units. Worse yet, the power coming into the house was inadequate unless the electrical company furnished a new outside transformer.

These problems were attacked with vigor and determination through the rest of the night. The power company delivered and installed the transformer, electricians rewired the house, fourteen window air-conditioning units were located and installed, and before dawn the old house was comfortably cool.

There was a plethora of other difficulties. Among them was the necessity of obtaining a large conference table and chairs, finding and installing heavy-duty kitchen equipment to prepare the luncheon, constructing and installing doors between the meeting rooms, placing heavy drapes over the windows to ensure privacy, installing private telephones for the Soviet and American delegations, and constructing a security fence that would keep the press and public a safe distance from the conferees. Finally, much of the Robinsons' furniture had to be removed to make room for the meeting. To accomplish all this, almost fifty men representing many skills were located, came, and voluntarily worked through the night. Miraculously, they got it all done in time.

As the night wore on, Mrs. Robinson became increasingly distraught about what was being done to her home. From time to time, Markman had to stop everything while he tried to calm her. At 3 A.M., he finally persuaded her to try to get some sleep, but a few hours later she was back, more nervous than ever.

At around 7 A.M., Markman reported to me that all would be ready. He described everything that had been done, and he dictated a suggested scenario for the day's meetings and luncheon, which was now only four hours away. Basically, it called for the President to arrive in Glassboro by helicopter at 11 A.M., five minutes before Kosygin's motorcade would get there from New York City. The president would greet Kosygin at the front entrance of Hollybush. The two delegations would then meet for two hours, break for a joint lunch, and conclude their day with more meetings until their adjournment, which was scheduled for 3 P.M. Kosygin then would drive back to New York and the President would helicopter to the Philadelphia airport where Air Force One would be waiting to fly him to Los Angeles to attend a large fund-raising dinner.

I relayed the President's approval to Markman, and later that morning the President's party, which included Secretary Rusk, Secretary McNamara, and me—along with the Secret Service agents—boarded the presidential helicopter and flew to Glassboro.

While we were airborne—and thus out of reach of Markman—one of the FBI agents who had been delegated by the Bureau to be present at the Summit Conference approached Markman and asked to be shown the room that had been set aside for private meetings of the Soviet delegation. It was located on the second floor of Hollybush, and Markman watched as the Agent carefully examined it.

"If it's all right with you, we would like to secretly plant some microphones around this room," the agent stated

Startled, Markman thought a moment, and then shook his head. "I don't think that you should do that," he said.

"Why not?" the agent asked. "This is a golden opportunity to gather intelligence. I don't think we should waste it."

"The risk is too great," Markman said. "If they find out that we tried bugging them here, it might blow everything apart."

"I guarantee they won't discover a thing," the agent said.

"I won't argue that, but I don't want to take a chance."

The agent did not press Markman and appeared to acquiesce. When Markman told me about it later, I said, "What the FBI probably did was install the listening devices with or without your consent. If they really thought it was an important intelligence opportunity, you can bet they didn't waste it just because you didn't like it."

When the presidential helicopter landed on the college baseball field, I followed closely as the President strode toward the waiting Markman. "All right, tell me what you have planned for me," he barked at Markman.

Markman began explaining the schedule that the President had approved earlier that morning, which was to begin almost immediately because Kosygin's motorcade from New York was due in just a few minutes. However, the President interrupted Markman's recitation, growling, "I don't like it. I want to spend more time alone with Kosygin."

As Markman began stuttering his reply that there was no time left, I stepped between him and the President. "Mr. President," I said, "Markman has worked all night on this. I am certain that he has done a good job and I am sure that you will have as much time with Kosygin as you need."

The President hesitated a moment, then shrugged and said, "Let's get going."

Markman later told me that he would be forever grateful for that moment of intervention because by then there was no time to make a single change in the plans. Quite literally, Kosygin and his people were entering Glassboro.

The President greeted the Soviet Premier as his car drove up to Hollybush. After some preliminary photographs, the meetings between the two delegations began. After only a few minutes, the President asked Kosygin if he would like to meet privately. Kosygin agreed, and the two leaders, accompanied only by the translators and me, went into Dr. Robinson's adjoining study. After shutting the door behind them, they sat facing each other across a small table.

The meeting started out slowly because each leader was accompanied by his own translator. Unfortunately, the translator furnished by our State Department turned out to be so tentative that after a few minutes, the President waved him aside. From then on, Johnson and Kosygin both relied on the quick responses of the Russian expert.

Kosygin began their conversation by caustically observing that it was naive of the United States to support the three million Jews of Israel against the one hundred million Arabs who surrounded them. The President's reply was unambiguous.

"America believes that Israel's right to exist is established by the Bible," he said. "Israel is also legally recognized by the United Nations. We will never abandon Israel's cause."

"Does that include risking possible unlimited nuclear war, which is what you just did?" Kosygin responded.

"Yes, even that," the President said.

They then moved on to the subject uppermost on President Johnson's mind—the Vietnam War. Although it was true that in the spring of 1967, most of the President's advisors were assuring him that the tide of war was moving strongly in favor of the South Vietnamese and their allies against the Communists, the President was determined to bring North Vietnam to the peace table. In that, the President was eager to enlist the help of the Soviet Union, and Kosygin seemed to be receptive. He told the President that he was in close contact with Hanoi and that they had assured him that if the bombing of North Vietnam was stopped they would meet with the Americans. The President responded positively, and Kosygin promised him that he would actively pursue the possibilities of peace.

The two leaders then spoke about the specter of nuclear conflict. Both of them stated that they were aware of the dangers and the importance of doing everything possible to avoid such a catastrophe. In that conversation, the President said, "My younger daughter, Luci, is just giving birth to my first grandchild, a son. I know that you too are a grandfather, and I have been thinking that you and I are only two of millions of grandfathers around the world, but that there is immense difference between all the others and us. We can actually accomplish something that will make the world a safer place for our grandchildren. That is our great blessing and even greater responsibility."

Listening to the President speak those words to the Soviet Premier in that small room in Glassboro, I was aware of the depth of his sincerity. The President had always loved children and now he just had been blessed with the birth of a grandchild of his own for whom he fervently hoped he could help make a better world.

"I agree with you on that, Mr. President," Kosygin said.

A short time later, when the President saw Luci and his new grandson, Lyndon, for the first time, he told her how he had used the fact of Lyndon's birth to emphasize the opportunities for peace that he and the Soviet Premier shared. Luci has since said that she has never forgotten how touched she was by her father's use of her son's birth in the cause of peace.

At the luncheon for the senior members of both delegations, Defense Secretary McNamara, seated two chairs away from Premier Kosygin, leaned past the President, who was between them, and with far more emotion than I had ever heard from McNamara, expressed his vision of the tragedy that would follow a nuclear holocaust. McNamara emphasized how the entire world would suffer immense destruction and loss of life, and that such a horror must at all costs be avoided. Kosygin listened impassively to McNamara's plea except to dryly remark that most assuredly he shared McNamara's concern.

While the leaders of the two superpowers were enjoying their sumptuous lunch at Hollybush, Markman and Richard Moose led the small group of Kosygin's Kremlin aides to the college cafeteria for a quick bite to eat. The menu there was hot dogs and baked beans. Markman was embarrassed and apologetic when the Russians furnished tins of caviar that they shared with the Americans. They also produced a bottle of vodka, which, Markman later assured me, was politely refused. It was a relaxed, pleasant lunch, and two groups of young assistants exchanged anecdotes concerning their similar problems while working for powerful bosses. However, when the issue of Vietnam was broached, the conversation became tense and the subject was dropped.

At the main luncheon and the full delegation meetings that followed, the discussion also turned to Vietnam. Each side forcibly stated its position. President Johnson carefully explained the necessity for America to honor its treaty obligations. The Soviet Premier argued that the United States was only carrying out the imperialistic policies that the French had followed for so long but had been forced to abandon.

At midafternoon, the President and Premier Kosygin once again excused themselves and, with only myself and the Soviet translator present (because the President had dismissed the American translator), adjourned to Dr. Robinson's study to resume their private discussions. They continued to argue the question of Vietnam, with the President prodding Kosygin to actively seek ways to bring the North Vietnamese to a peace conference. Kosygin did not reject the President's idea, and as their conversation continued, the President became increasingly relaxed and informal, even to the point of using his marvelous storytelling ability to amuse Kosygin while making a point.

In the midst of their private meeting, there was a knock on the door, and the chief of Kosygin's security detail walked in with nothing more on his mind than seeking autographs from the President and the Premier on some Glassboro postcards. I was shocked, and the President, although obviously unhappy, said nothing. Kosygin, on the other hand, signed the postcards with a flourish, and the President reluctantly did the same. Later, the Soviet security chief bragged to Lem Johns, the head of the President's Secret Service detail, about the courage the Russian had just demonstrated by breaking in on his boss. He chided Johns on whether Johns would be equally bold with the President. Johns laughingly responded, "No way would I ever do that. Not if I wanted to keep my job."

As the two leaders concluded their private meeting, they discussed whether it made sense for them to meet again before Kosygin returned to Moscow. They agreed that their meeting had gone reasonably well and should be continued. However, the Soviets had to return to New York City and the President was scheduled to fly to Los Angeles that evening. They decided to return to Glassboro on Sunday, two days later.

On our flight to Los Angeles, President Johnson told me that he would like to obtain the two chairs and small table in Dr. Robinson's study that he and Kosygin had used for their private meetings. He said that the furniture would make an interesting display at the presidential library he already was considering.

I called Markman and instructed him to arrange to purchase that furniture from Dr. and Mrs. Robinson. When Markman returned to Glassboro on Saturday morning to prepare for the Sunday summit meeting, he called the Robinsons aside and relayed the President's wishes to them. He explained that their furniture would become a historical artifact for which the State Department would pay them a fair price.

"You can have the little table and one of the chairs," Mrs. Robinson responded. "But the rocking chair has been a family heirloom for generations and I don't want to part with it."

"What if we have the best craftsman we can find make an exact duplicate of that chair and give it to you?" Markman asked.

"Then you use the duplicate at the President's library," Mrs. Robinson snapped.

It was apparent to Markman that Mrs. Robinson was quite upset, and

Markman dropped the subject for the time being. He called me and passed on Mrs. Robinson's suggestion that the duplicate be used at the president's library. As I expected, the President rejected that idea.

Markman then contacted New Jersey Governor Hughes and asked him if he would help persuade the Robinsons to part with their rocking chair. He did, and a short while later, when Markman next saw the Robinsons, they told him that they had changed their minds after listening to the Governor, and that they now agreed that their furniture could be displayed at the Johnson Library. That is where the two chairs and little table can now be seen, enshrined within a glass case honoring the Glassboro summit conference.

As planned, on Sunday both delegations returned to Glassboro to resume their meetings. This time, however, Premier Kosygin brought his daughter with him. When we learned that she planned to attend, we hastily arranged for both Mrs. Johnson and the Johnsons' daughter Lynda to also come to Glassboro. The President's helicopter took the ladies on a leisurely flight over the more scenic parts of New Jersey while the afternoon conference was taking place. Mrs. Johnson as always was a gracious hostess during their excursion, but she later told me that Kosygin's daughter was nervous and kept asking when they would return because her father did not want her to be late.

The Sunday meeting between the Soviets and the Americans was far less tense than it had been on Friday. Once more, as on Friday, the President and Premier Kosygin spent a great part of their time alone (except for the interpreters and me) in the study. The President, who was always at his finest in face-to-face meetings with people, believed that the private meetings were his best opportunity to persuade the Soviet leader to help him find peace in Vietnam. In the end, although Kosygin professed to commit himself to that goal, the Soviet Union never was much help. Perhaps they had only minimal influence over the North Vietnamese. Perhaps their efforts were countered by the influence of the Chinese. Perhaps Kosygin did not have sufficient authority to deliver on his promises, or perhaps Kosygin wanted to continue the conflict to test America's staying power. After all, from the start North Vietnam enjoyed material and political support from both the Soviet Union and China. In any event, the Glassboro summit did not succeed in achieving that primary objective.

Nonetheless, I do not consider our two days of meetings to have been a failure. After all, the two leaders spent considerable time in close personal contact with one another. If nothing more, each learned that his adversary was a human being, not a demon. Even in that short time, we discovered something about the personalities, the strengths, and the weaknesses of our opponents on the far side of the globe. In a universe where the participants in a meeting have the power to make decisions that could save or destroy civilization, the importance of intimate dialogue can never be discounted.

The conference adjourned in late afternoon. As we were saying our good-byes, we learned that Premier Kosygin had scheduled an 8 P.M. televised press conference to be held at the United Nations. President Johnson immediately decided that he also should appear on television to report on the summit conference, but he wanted to make his report before Kosygin's. By that time, we were on the helicopter bound for Philadelphia where Air Force One awaited us. Once on board, the pilot, Colonel Cross, told the President that if Air Force One were to land, as it normally did, at Andrews Air Force Base, there was no way that the President could be transported to the White House before the 8 P.M. Kosygin press conference.

The President asked Colonel Cross if there was anything that could be done to speed things up.

"Well, sir, we could land Air Force One at National Airport," he suggested. "That would save just enough time to get you to the White House and on television before Kosygin."

"Good," the President said.

"There is just one problem, sir," Colonel Cross continued. "Landing this big airplane at National would violate one or two FAA regulations. Planes our size are not permitted in and out of that airport. The runway is considered too short."

"But can you land us safely?" the President asked.

"Yes, sir, I can."

"Then do it," the President ordered.

Because Colonel Cross was piloting Air Force One, the control tower at National gave him clearance to land there. We touched down smoothly and all of us scurried to the helicopter waiting to whisk us to the White House. On my way to the waiting helicopter, I noticed that the front wheels of Air Force One had come to rest only a few feet short of the end of the runway. I was happy not to have known that in advance. The President, on the other hand, simply was pleased that he was able to get on television before Kosygin.

TRAVELS AND TRAVAILS FOR THE PRESIDENT: WILLIAMSBURG

In early November 1967, President Johnson decided that he would take a weekend off and travel with his family to historic Williamsburg, Virginia, for two days of worry-free relaxation away from the pressures of the war, the screaming antiwar protestors, and his vacillating feelings regarding whether or not he should seek reelection. He wanted to attend the annual dinner of the Gridiron Club (an always enjoyable evening of political songs and satire hosted by an elite group of Washington journalists), then attend church on Sunday, followed by a round of golf with his daughter's fiancé, Marine Captain Charles "Chuck" Robb. It was a fine idea, and Sherwin Markman was asked to travel to Williamsburg to prepare the way for him.

"Just make certain that whatever church you choose doesn't have some publicity-hungry minister who will take advantage of my presence," the President instructed. "I don't want him sermonizing me on any political matters."

"I will be careful," Markman said.

On Friday, November 10, Markman drove to Williamsburg with several Secret Service agents.

Finding a lovely home for the First Family proved to be no problem. The Rockefeller family, whose representative was Arkansas Gov. Winthrop Rockefeller, owned historic Williamsburg. When Markman spoke to Governor Rockefeller, the Governor immediately made Bassett House available, explaining that it was a large colonial mansion with floorboards dating from before the Revolutionary War, and that it was beautifully sited within spacious, tree-lined grounds. The Governor also made arrangements for the President and his guests to play golf on Sunday at the Williamsburg golf course.

Markman then broached the subject of church for the President. The Governor's response was immediate. "The President should attend the most historic church in Williamsburg, Bruton Parish Episcopal."

"Who is the minister there?" Markman asked.

"Cotesworth Lewis," the Governor stated. "I've known him for years. He's a good man."

"Is there any chance he would embarrass the President?" Markman asked.

"Absolutely none," he said. "He thinks highly of President Johnson. I'm certain of that."

"Would you talk to him anyway?" Markman asked. "We need to be sure."

"Happy to do it," the Governor said. "If there's any problem, I'll let you know immediately. If you don't hear from me, everything is fine."

Markman never heard from the Governor and assumed that he had had a satisfactory conversation with Reverend Lewis. Nonetheless, knowing how strongly the President felt on the subject of being trapped in the congregation of a haranguing minister, Markman decided to personally visit with Reverend Lewis.

He was concerned about the possibility that he might be accused of attempting to "censor" the minister, if the man decided to play that game. Thus, Markman spoke with the Secret Service Agent in charge of ensuring security for the President in Williamsburg.

Markman asked the Agent, "If the President is planning to attend the Bruton Parish church, isn't it appropriate for you to check out the minister to make sure that neither he nor anyone else there will be a threat while the President attends his church?"

"Of course," the Agent agreed.

The two of them called on Reverend Lewis that afternoon. Lewis, a courtly and impressively earnest man, was relaxed and friendly when Markman and the Agent sat with him in the small study of the church.

"I hope that you understand the reason for my questions," Markman began. "The President is considering attending your church tomorrow morning. If that causes you difficulty, just tell us now and we will have him go elsewhere."

"No, not at all," he replied. "I will be honored to have him seated as our guest."

Markman probed further. "What about your sermon, sir? We need to be certain that you won't take advantage of the President's presence to embarrass him."

"I would never do anything like that," Lewis stated. Then, without being asked, Lewis handed Markman and the Secret Service Agent several typed pages. "This is the sermon I will give tomorrow," he said. "You can see there's nothing in it that will bother the President."

Markman and the Agent read the Lewis sermon. It contained nothing political. A relieved and satisfied Markman returned it to Lewis. "All of us appreciate your willingness to cooperate," Markman said.

"It will be a proud moment for me, and an historic occasion for our church," Lewis said.

A short while later, Markman reported to me regarding what he had done. Markman told me that he, the Secret Service, and Governor Rockefeller were all satisfied that the President had no cause for concern at the church. Markman added that the President could look forward to a carefree weekend.

On Saturday evening, Sherwin Markman spent the most relaxing moments he ever experienced with the President. Following the Gridiron dinner and after everyone else in his family had gone to bed, the President, sitting alone and sipping a scotch in the living room of the loaned Rockefeller house in Williamsburg, motioned to Markman to join him. The President was all smiles as he pointed toward the bar and asked Markman to fix himself whatever he wanted. The President seemed contented and happy as he regaled Markman with anecdotes and hilariously repeated some of the Gridiron skits that had so amused him at the dinner. Finally, the President, his arm draped around Markman, walked him to the door and bade him good night. "You are a fine young man," the President said. "I am proud that you are serving on my staff." Markman felt like he was floating on a cloud.

Sunday began innocently enough, with Markman joining the President and his family as their motorcade drove the short distance to the Bruton Parish church. Markman did not enter the church because there were a few remaining details that needed to be handled. However, several Secret Service Agents and a small pool of reporters followed the First Family inside, totally unprepared for what was about to occur.

Let me quote from Lady Bird Johnson's book *A White House Diary* (Henry Holt & Company, 1970) concerning what happened next:

The Reverend Cotesworth Pinckney Lewis gave short shrift to any biblical text and launched into a general discussion of the State of the Union and of the world. . . . And then I froze in my seat as I heard him say, "And then there is the question of Vietnam. But there is a rather general consensus that something is wrong in Vietnam—a conviction voiced by leaders of nations traditionally our friends, leading military experts and the rank and file of American citizens—we wonder if some logical, straight-forward explanation might be given?" . . . and on and on. . . . I turned to stone on the outside and boiled on the inside. . . . Later Lyndon looked at me with a wry smile and said, "Greater love hath no man than that he goes to the Episcopal Church with his wife!" . . . The minister was ready with plenty of mimeographed copies which he distributed to the press afterward.

Markman was milling with the crowd outside the church, which included the larger group of reporters who normally accompanied the President. All of them were waiting for the President to emerge from the church service when suddenly the door to the church burst open and the pool reporters ran out, shouting to their colleagues, "You'll never believed what just happened in there!"

For an instant, Markman and the others had visions of a shooting or a heart attack, but an instant later, Markman overheard one of the pool reporters breathlessly state, "That Reverend just gave the President holy hell!"

Markman did not need to hear another word. Feeling nauseated, he quietly walked to the end of the waiting presidential motorcade and stood behind the last car, trying to be as inconspicuous as possible and wishing that he could disappear.

At that moment, the President and Mrs. Johnson came out of the church, displaying tight smiles. The President stood on the top stoop and slowly turned his head, his eyes sweeping over the waiting crowd. Markman had no doubt what the President was doing, and his fear was confirmed an instant later when his gaze finally located him. His eyes glaring, the President motioned to Markman to come join the President's group. Taking a deep breath, Markman walked toward the President, wishing that he could be anywhere else in the world but right there.

"Go sit in one of the cars," the President snapped at Markman. "I want to talk to you back at the house."

Markman did as he was told, dreading what he knew was coming.

When the President arrived back at the Rockefeller house, all of his pent-up anger and frustration exploded, and since he could do nothing to Reverend Lewis, his full wrath was directed at Markman.

"How in the hell could you have let that happen?" the President shouted at Markman. "Didn't I warn you? Weren't you listening to me?"

"I tried, Mr. President. I talked to him—and so did the Secret Service."

"Then you were all damn fools," the President said.

"But, sir, he even gave us a copy of his sermon."

"And you simply swallowed what he told you."

"But how could I have known?"

"Because you are supposed to be smart and anyone with any sense should have seen through him."

"I did my best, sir," Markman lamely replied.

When Mrs. Johnson slipped into the room and gently reminded the President that he was scheduled to play golf with Chuck Robb, the President nodded and started following Mrs. Johnson out of the room. Markman's brief hope that the President's harangue was over was dashed when the President turned and stated, "I'm not finished with you. Stay right here until I get back."

Markman did as he was told. For several hours, he sat alone in the Rockefeller living room, skipping lunch as he anxiously waited. Above all else, he wanted out. He knew that there was nothing he could have done to avoid the scheme of a determined preacher willing to lie in order to achieve his goal. But the President believed otherwise, so much so that Markman was convinced that he was about to be fired or forced to resign. If Markman could have done as he wished at that moment, he would have quit and run away.

Markman's faint hope that the round of golf somehow would calm the President disappeared the moment the scowling President strode back into the room. Then, as if he had never stopped, the President continued to berate his hapless assistant.

Markman assumed that his ordeal would end when the President departed to board the helicopter for the short flight back to the White House while Markman returned in one of the Secret Service automobiles. When that time came, however, Markman's hope was shattered because the President ordered Markman to get on the helicopter with him.

Throughout that noisy journey from Williamsburg to Washington, Johnson, with no let-up, continued his attack on Markman. Mrs. Johnson and the rest of the group on the helicopter were embarrassed and distressed, but the President's anger was incendiary, and no one tried to interfere. By now,

Markman had ceased all efforts to defend himself and, doing his best to meet the President's angry gaze, he sat and absorbed every shouted word hurled at him.

Even after landing on the South Lawn of the White House, Markman's ordeal continued. Instead of releasing him to go home, the President directed Markman to accompany him into the Mansion. There, in the Yellow Sitting Room on the second floor, Markman was forced to bear another half-hour of the President's wrath. Finally, when the President told Markman that he was free to leave, Markman spoke again.

"I will resign in the morning, Mr. President," Markman said.

"Like hell you will!" President Johnson shot back. "You're not quitting until I say you can!"

A puzzled Markman did not argue; he only nodded his head and quietly departed.

The following morning a thoroughly defeated Markman was waiting in my office when I returned from my bedroom meeting with the President, who was still angry about his experience on Sunday. I attempted to calm him—and defend Markman—but it was hopeless. He would not listen to me and I dropped the subject.

Now, alone with me in my office, Markman repeated everything he had done trying to forestall any attack on the President at the Williamsburg church. I was convinced that he could have done nothing more, and I told him so.

"But the President won't listen to me," Markman said. "If he feels that way, then I should resign."

"Don't!" I said. "The President will calm down. I'm sure of it. I know he likes you. Just give him a little time."

"I can't take much more, Marvin."

"Just suck it up," I said. "It's going to pass."

Markman sadly shook his head.

"I have a suggestion," I said. "Since he won't listen to you—or me either, for that matter—why don't you write him a memo detailing everything you did. I'll make sure he reads it. Maybe it will make a difference."

A couple of hours later, Markman handed me his report. That evening I put it among the President's night reading. The next morning, when the

President handed me the stack of papers, I saw that he had initialed Markman's memo without comment and he said nothing more to me about it.

President Johnson never again mentioned the subject to Markman, and Markman was neither fired nor did he resign because of it.

Several weeks later, Markman was invited to attend a formal White House dinner honoring a foreign dignitary. When he walked through the receiving line, the President gripped his elbow, squeezing it gently. Then, turning to the guest of honor, the President said, "I want you to meet one of my most trusted assistants and one of the brightest young men I know." Markman, at last knowing that the President's anger had passed, basked in the glow of what he knew was typical presidential overpraise intended to make up for the hell through which Markman had suffered.

Roger Wilkins (the nephew of the great American black leader of the NAACP), who was an Assistant Attorney General from 1966 until 1999, tells a story that also illustrates the manner by which President Johnson would clearly indicate—without ever saying so directly—that he was apologizing. As Wilkins has recalled the incident, the President, while attending a meeting in the Cabinet Room, told an anecdote in which he used the word *Nigra*. According to Wilkins, the President immediately realized his mistake but said nothing more about it at the meeting. However, when it adjourned, the President asked Wilkins to come into the Oval Office. There, the President said nothing about his slipup. Instead, in a soft and caring voice, he spent considerable time asking Wilkins about his work and family. The President never apologized directly, but Wilkins clearly understood that this was the President's way of saying that he was sorry for what he had said.

These experiences of Markman and Wilkins reflect my own observations of Lyndon Johnson. As long as I knew him, he could never bring himself to apologize directly for anything he did or said. However, when he realized that he had wronged someone, he always found a way to let that person know that he was sorry—just as he did with Markman and Wilkins.

SEEKING REELECTION WITHOUT A CANDIDATE

As the summer of 1967 wore on, the 1968 presidential election drew ever closer. Under the Constitution, despite the two-term limitation imposed by the Twenty-second Amendment, adopted in 1951 as an "antidote" to Pres. Franklin Roosevelt's four elected terms, Lyndon Johnson was eligible for re-election because he had served less than two years of President Kennedy's term of office.

Although almost everyone believed that President Johnson would seek reelection in 1968, he had never committed himself. In fact, he was torn in both directions, and his thinking constantly vacillated.

On the one hand, he believed that he had accomplished remarkable results during his time in office, particularly his historic legislative achievements in civil rights and the war on poverty, including Medicare, Medicaid, Head Start, and so many other historic and innovative laws, including those involving conservation, education, and job training. He also knew that there was so much more to be done, and he believed that there was no better man who could work effectively with the Congress.

There was also the unfinished and frustrating war in Vietnam that was causing such increasing divisiveness within the United States and was so destructive of his dream of creating a Great Society. Furthermore, his two principal foreign policy advisors, Secretary of State Rusk and Secretary of Defense McNamara, had been in office since January 1961—a very long time for cabinet officials. Secretary McNamara, in particular, was becoming increasingly exhausted and frustrated with the never-ending conflict.

The President, however, could not permit himself the luxury of exhaustion. With all his heart, he felt his heavy responsibility to continue leading the country. Otherwise, he believed, his presidency would end inconclusively and unfinished.

On the other hand, the President was deeply concerned about his health. He was haunted by the specter of another massive heart attack like the one he suffered in 1955, or a stroke that—like President Woodrow Wilson—would leave him incapacitated while he was still in office. He often spoke of the fate of the men of the Johnson family, so many of whom had died relatively young—in their fifties for the most part. On August 27, 1967, President Johnson reached his fifty-ninth birthday, and he spoke to me about his fear that he had only a limited time to live, which, he was convinced, would be even less if he tried to serve another term as President.

In addition, the domestic turmoil regarding Vietnam continued to escalate. It seemed that almost everywhere the President traveled he was met by protestors. Of course, he still could travel wherever he wished. Even in out-door rallies, the Secret Service and local law enforcement agencies were able to ensure his personal security. Or, alternatively, he could—and did—schedule his speeches at indoor events or at military bases where he could be assured of a friendly reception. Still, the protests and demonstrations were unpleas-ant to a man who needed public approval, and in time they became a heavy burden on him.

Nonetheless, those of us who knew the President best believed that his personal doubts would disappear as his reelection campaign developed and the election drew closer. Perhaps we refused to see the obvious, but I hoped and thought that the President might be like a prizefighter who, once the bell rang, would be in the center of the ring giving everything he had to achieve the best for his country.

The President knew all about our programs to organize for his reelection, and he made no move to stop our efforts on his behalf. I concluded that he was retaining all his options, and with his tacit approval, we continued mov-ing forward. I felt strongly that the President should seek reelection and I was determined not to cease working on his behalf unless he specifically told me to stop.

From the beginning, I was the person the President charged with the principal responsibility for all things political. I quite naturally assumed the mantle of organizing his putative reelection campaign. This task consumed increasing amounts of my time. By October, I had commandeered and staffed additional office space in the West Wing that I used exclusively for my activities relating to the President's reelection. As I have stated, the Pres-ident's private statements that he was not going to run did not slow down my political efforts, and of course he knew it.

By that fall, the President had agreed to add other key people to work at the apex of his developing campaign organization. They were:

• *Larry O'Brien.* In 1967, O'Brien was President Johnson's Postmaster General. In 1960, he had been campaign manager for President Kennedy. O'Brien was still loyal to the Kennedys, although many of them had never forgiven him for continuing to serve Lyndon Johnson after the assassina-tion, something O'Brien had done not so much out of loyalty to President Johnson as his sense of duty to the country. O'Brien had a talent for working with the Congress, and of course this impressed the President. However, although O'Brien had never demonstrated any disloyalty, the President believed that O'Brien remained faithful to the Kennedys. Still, we always sought and listened to O'Brien's counsel, and the President looked upon him as a talented political advisor.

• *Abe Fortas.* Fortas was a sitting Justice on the Supreme Court. Nonetheless, in the President's eyes, Fortas remained his most trusted lawyer. The President never hesitated to involve Fortas whenever and however he wished. Fortas, in turn, never objected, and that included his willing involvement in the strategy meetings preparing for the President's reelection campaign. In fairness, it should be pointed out that Justice Fortas was not the first Supreme Court Justice to continue to advise the President who appointed him to the Supreme Court. He was only following in the footsteps of such Supreme Court giants as Felix Frankfurter and William Douglas, among many others.

• *Arthur Krim.* Arthur and his wife, Dr. Mathilde Krim (who later gained well-deserved fame as a national leader in the struggle against AIDs), had become close personal friends of the Johnsons. Krim was CEO of United Artists, and thus a powerful figure in the motion picture industry. He was also a New York lawyer, a partner of the famous trial lawyer Louis Nizer. By the 1960s, he was a wealthy and highly respected man who had easy access to other men of wealth. He was a soft-spoken, sincere man who had the total trust of the President as well as all of us on his staff. He was a natural choice to lead the effort to raise what I considered an immense amount of money needed for the upcoming presidential campaign.

• *James Rowe.* Rowe was an experienced and well-connected lawyer who had worked in and for various administrations. After graduation from Harvard Law School, Rowe had been one of the final law clerks for Oliver Wendell Holmes. After that, he had served as an administrative assistant to President Roosevelt. By 1967, Rowe had become the prototypical Washington "insider," a somewhat younger version of Tommy Corcoran, another Washington power lawyer (I thought Corcoran was somewhat disrespectful because when he spoke to the President, he continued to call him Lyndon). Nevertheless, because Corcoran had been a prominent member of President Roosevelt's "brain trust," he did have periodic access to President Johnson. However, unlike Rowe, who was an easy fit, Corcoran was not placed within our small group.

• *Clark Clifford.* Clifford was another Washington "inside" lawyer. A native of Missouri, he had served in President Truman's White House, first as Naval Aide and later as Special Counsel. He had remained in Washington and built a powerful list of clients. In 1964, Clifford—along with Abe Fortas—was charged by the President with dealing with the Walter Jenkins tragedy. By 1967, Clifford's contacts within government and his knowledge of how to manipulate the process had become legendary. Unlike most lawyers, he never kept track of the time he spent on a case. One story—perhaps apocryphal—was that he once solved a critical problem for a client with one telephone call. When he presented the client with his bill for $100,000, the outraged client protested that it was obscene to be charged such an amount for a simple call. Clifford responded, "But, sir, it took me a lifetime to learn precisely whom to call and what to say when we spoke." In 1967, Clifford held no official position in the Johnson administration, but the President admired his wisdom and, as one of the "wise men," he was privy to the most sensitive information concerning Vietnam, about which President Johnson constantly consulted with him. The President also respected Clifford's political acumen, and thus he was also included among the leaders of the developing campaign.

• *John Criswell.* Criswell, a young man from Oklahoma, had served as Administrative Assistant to Oklahoma Senator J. Howard Edmundson. In 1965, although Cliff Carter had served as the President's liaison within the Democratic National Committee, we believed it was good to add people who were younger and more vigorous but equally loyal. This was considered crucial in the run-up to the 1968 campaign. A number of people, including my assistant Jim Jones (who also was an Oklahoman), recommended Criswell. Thus, with the President's blessing, we placed Criswell at the DNC. As I have stated, John Bailey remained in place as Chairman, and Criswell's formal titles were unassuming. At first he was listed as Deputy Director of News Information. Later, he became Director of Congressional Support. Those titles had no relationship to the reality of his actual authority, which was to coordinate the DNC as directed by the White House and reelection committee. Although there was a difference of opinion among our small group of top political advisors as to the proper role of the DNC in the reelection campaign, there was no dispute that Criswell should be one of us.

During the last several months of 1967, our presidential politics divided into two primary activities, both of which continued despite any doubts among us concerning whether the President would seek reelection. The first was to develop a plan and political structure for the upcoming nationwide campaign. The second was our constant watch over every act and word of Senator Robert Kennedy—including whatever inside intelligence we were fortunate enough to gather—all for the purpose of gauging his intentions and plans for 1968, and specifically whether he intended to oppose President Johnson either indirectly or by announcing his own candidacy for the office.

One of the first and most thorough analyses of the President's upcoming campaign was a White Paper prepared by Larry O'Brien and submitted by him to the President—with copies to the rest of us—in October 1967. O'Brien had worked on his paper for months. In that process, I sent him many memos containing the thoughts of others I trusted, including several papers from Bill Connell, then the Chief of Staff for Vice President Humphrey. In his White Paper, O'Brien stated that his sole purpose was to secure Lyndon Johnson's reelection. He said that achieving that goal would not be easy, and the election would not be won at all unless there was a massive effort on behalf of the President.

The O'Brien paper called for radical changes in polling as well as learning to take full advantage of the rapidly developing field of computer technology. O'Brien also recommended that the entire campaign organization be headed by a full-time, knowledgeable campaign director who answered to a task force of political experts who also would work full time on the President's reelection. O'Brien visualized the task force as an essential tool separated from the Democratic National Committee, with only the campaign director standing between it and the President. Such a structure, O'Brien believed, would attract far more competent people than are usually involved in political campaigns. He thought that they would need to function for at least a year before the election itself.

O'Brien also dealt at length with the issues that must be faced by the President and his campaign organization. These started with the primary question: "Why should I vote for four more years of LBJ?" The White Paper then gave a number of suggested answers and arguments that should be expressed by the President and his supporters.

O'Brien spent considerable space analyzing the difficulties that the

President must surmount during his campaign. He wrote that these started with the fact that unlike 1964 when the President was always on the offensive against Barry Goldwater, now he would be forced to constantly defend his policies, an innately more difficult and politically dangerous posture.

In addition, O'Brien believed that the fabric of the Democratic Party had been seriously weakened during the past few years. It now faced severe organizational problems, and it was neither "staffed nor equipped to conduct a successful presidential campaign." O'Brien stated that the state Party organizations "are flabby and wedded to techniques that are conventional and outmoded"; the Party had "lost contact with the voters"; the traditional large-city power base of the Party was "fractured in last year's elections"; Democrats had moved to the suburbs but the Party organization had not followed them there; the blacks, always so supportive of the Party, were showing signs of unrest; and the probable candidacy of Alabama Governor George Wallace could be dangerous to the President's chances of victory.

O'Brien concluded that the President risked losing the South, splintering groups representing the liberal left, and alienating women as well as young people who were increasingly hostile to the Vietnam War. In addition, O'Brien observed, many blacks were unhappy with the slow pace of reform, and whites in significant numbers—and not only in the South—believed that the President had done too much for blacks and not enough for whites.

Finally, O'Brien predicted how the Republicans would exploit each of these weaknesses during the campaign. Reading O'Brien's White Paper was a sobering experience that caused me considerable concern. Nonetheless, O'Brien's ultimate conclusion was that the President's reelection "is attainable and it will be accomplished." But, he added, doing so would require "a full year—starting in November 1967—to implement" O'Brien's detailed recommendations.

There was considerable discussion and disagreement among us concerning many of O'Brien's recommendations. Nonetheless, we quickly formed the small "task force" that he suggested. I should add that although the President placed me in the position of untitled chairman of this group, he was insistent that my role be kept as confidential as possible. This led to some uncomfortable moments for me. For example, at the insistence of George Christian, our Press Secretary, I reluctantly granted an interview to *The New York Times*. In answer to a direct question, I felt I had no choice but to tell them that I had "no official role" with the DNC, which I stated was run by John Bailey and John Criswell. To compound my dissembling, I also told the *Times* that I had nothing to do with arranging political patronage. In a perfect world, I would have answered more accurately, but in this instance, as in so many others, my public utterances (of which, thankfully, there were very few) necessarily reflected what the President did not want me to say.

An example of the President's intense desire for secrecy, especially regarding sensitive political matters, occurred in December 1967 when I sent him a memorandum by John Criswell. In it, Criswell wrote about a conversation he had with Arkansas Governor Orville Faubus, a notorious opponent of civil rights. Criswell noted that either Faubus or another candidate that Faubus considered strong likely would oppose Senator Fulbright's bid for re-election in 1968. Fulbright was then the Chairman of the Senate Foreign Relations Committee, and although he formerly had been a close personal friend of the President, their relationship had long since soured because of Fulbright's highly visible opposition to the Vietnam War. Criswell wrote that it is "encouraging" that Faubus is "enthusiastically" against Fulbright. Criswell probably thought that the President would be pleased with his report. However, that was not the President's reaction. Instead, he was concerned about public disclosure of highly sensitive matters such as were contained in Criswell's memo. What the President said was, "Let's watch these memos . . . and when a Senator or Congressman is mentioned, be sure to file them in your personal file, so they can be taken with us and not be left over for others to see."

In December 1967, the President also questioned the wisdom of O'Brien's suggestion that the DNC should be strengthened. Looking for support, he asked Jim Rowe to study and react to the O'Brien paper. Rowe's written response to the President was surprising and typically direct: "Frankly, I must disagree most strongly with your view that the Committee is not important . . . I think it is most important that you enthusiastically revive it publicly, in one way or another . . . Frankly, [the Party leaders] feel you don't care about the Party. They also feel, unfairly or not, that you and Marvin Watson do not care about their problems, and never have, because 'Texas is a one-party state'. . . . Even if they are wrong, the fact remains that almost 100 percent of the Party leaders believe what I have said above is true." Rowe went on to make specific recommendations, including firing Chairman Bailey and replacing him with someone strong, such as Larry O'Brien, and creating a Party substructure of powerful regional groups.

Criswell endorsed the idea of a greater role for the DNC. However, he took issue with O'Brien regarding the senior "task force" that would act as a board of directors overseeing the campaign. Criswell had no problem with the idea of a task force, but he disagreed with the suggestion that its members should be the "elder political statesmen" envisioned by O'Brien and Rowe. He believed that those people would be too important, too successful, and too busy to effectively lead the President's campaign. As Criswell put it, "They are in business and they are trying to make a buck. They are caught in a conflict for themselves. On the one hand they want to be in the middle of it all and be involved. On the other, they have tremendous commitments of their time to their clients. When you balance the one against the other, you find a very small amount of time actively to go and do."

The President did not change his view of the relative unimportance of the DNC. Nor did I. Neither of us took personally the criticisms contained in the O'Brien, Rowe, and Criswell memos. We respected each of these men, and we honored their right to express their opinions to the President. As I have written, the President's rule was that although any of us were free to disagree with him, there were two caveats: our difference of opinion must remain private, and once the President reached a final decision, it was our obligation to support it and him—or resign.

President Johnson knew, regardless of what the local Party leaders believed, that he—and I acting on his behalf—spent an inordinate amount of time every day dealing with them and their problems. Any look at my daily logs and the transcripts of my calls demonstrates the breadth of my contacts with these leaders. Of course, it is obvious that the President and his staff bore a primary obligation to deal with the unending array of problems facing our country. Inevitably, time spent working on the concerns of Party leaders was time lost to the nation.

The President also thought that the DNC's function in any campaign for his reelection should be limited to its traditional role of registering potential Democratic voters and doing everything possible to ensure that they voted. In any reelection campaign, the President believed that he should have his own organization, one that was dedicated and loyal only to him, and one that operated separately from the formal machinery of the Party. That had been the case in 1964 when the President's landslide victory was achieved without substantial assistance from the Party. He felt that should be the case in 1968—should he choose to run.

The other reason for the President's lack of confidence in the DNC was that in late 1967—over four years after the assassination of President Kennedy—the Party machinery, in large measure, remained under the control of politicians whose primary loyalty was to the Kennedys. These people were not Johnson people, but in the President's opinion, they were actual or potential supporters of Robert Kennedy.

There also was sharp disagreement among the President's senior advisors on the subject of Robert Kennedy's intentions for 1968. Some, such as Jim Rowe, believed that Kennedy would never run against a sitting President because by doing so, Kennedy would so fracture the Party that he would destroy himself along with the President.

To me, Kennedy's vaulting ambition once again had been vividly illustrated when in June 1967 he tried unsuccessfully to arrange a secret meeting with Soviet Premier Kosygin before the Glassboro summit. Kosygin refused the request, but the President had learned of it anyway. That attempt served to reinforce our belief that Robert Kennedy was actively considering running for President.

Kennedy was steadily escalating his verbal barrage against Johnson's policies in Vietnam, although thus far he refrained from personally attacking the President while continuing to repeat his mantra that he supported the reelection of President Johnson. Nonetheless, the President was mindful of how strongly Robert Kennedy had publicly backed our Vietnam policy when his brother had been President. President Johnson came to the conclusion that Robert Kennedy had deliberately changed his stance in order to create an opportunity to replace Lyndon Johnson as President.

The President's opinion was supported by information we received concerning the thinking of Robert Kennedy's chief advisors. For example, during the summer of 1967, we learned that the Kennedy plan was to steadily increase the antiwar pressure on the President until he was forced into a corner where his only alternative was to seek an honorable settlement of the Vietnam war during 1968 and then decline to run for reelection for reasons of health. Of course, as I have made clear, the President was already doing everything he could to bring North Vietnam to the peace table, but they refused to respond to every overture. Nonetheless, the Kennedy people were saying that the President wanted war, and therefore, "The time to get on the Kennedy bandwagon is now."

One other fact should be noted regarding Robert Kennedy's developing strategy to oppose Lyndon Johnson for the Democratic presidential nomination, and that was Kennedy's public posture regarding Martin Luther King. It was, after all, Kennedy who as Attorney General authorized the FBI to engage in close personal surveillance of King. Thus, Kennedy was responsible for—and was the original recipient of—the detailed FBI reports regarding King's personal escapades and the influence that several known Communists had over him. Of course, Kennedy never publicly acknowledged these facts, but to President Johnson, the sight of Kennedy's late-blooming public embrace of King was the height of political opportunism.

As 1967 drew to a close, Robert Kennedy continued to withhold any overt announcement of his intentions, although his public endorsements of the reelection of President Johnson became less frequent until by year-end they ceased entirely.

In December, Minnesota Senator Eugene McCarthy became an active candidate by entering the New Hampshire Democratic primary. The McCarthy candidacy was enthusiastically supported by great numbers of young antiwar activists who might otherwise be important Kennedy allies. Thus, the McCarthy move caused more problems for Kennedy than for President Johnson, who felt he had little to fear from the Minnesota senator.

One side note to the tense relationship between the President and Robert Kennedy is that their antagonism did not disturb the comfortable friendship between Johnson and Ted Kennedy, who was then the Junior Senator from Massachusetts. Of course, the President always expected the younger Kennedy to support his brother if he decided to run for President. But that aside, the President and Ted Kennedy liked and trusted one another.

Our campaign for Lyndon Johnson continued functioning through the end of 1967. Initial money was raised; a Johnson organization was quietly put in place; political leaders were contacted and committed to the President; thorough regional and state-by-state political analyses were made; and constant polling was begun. All looked good for the President. It was clear to us that his renomination was assured and his reelection was most probable.

Meanwhile, the President refused to actively campaign. Neither did he publicly acknowledge or endorse the efforts being made on his behalf. In fact, President Johnson privately ruminated that he would not run for re-election. In December, he specifically considered issuing a statement withdrawing as a candidate. He instructed me to have it prepared for him to deliver before the end of the year. However, he reconsidered once again, and he did not make that statement. Moreover, he did not instruct us to stop our work on his behalf.

FALSELY MALIGNING A DECEASED PRESIDENT

The historian Michael Beschloss, in his appearance on the television program *60 Minutes* while promoting his book on the Lyndon Johnson tapes, *Reaching for Glory* (Simon & Schuster, 2001), leveled the accusation that President Johnson was mentally ill during the time of his presidency. In his book, the Beschloss charge is "attributed" to two persons, Richard Goodwin and Bill Moyers.

There are a number of things that must be noted about this contention. First, through all the years that I knew and worked with Lyndon Johnson, I never observed him act in any way other than with total normalcy, or, to put it another way, consistent with the power of his personality and the force of his intellect. Second, both persons cited as sources by Beschloss involuntarily left the White House, and in both instances, in my view they are expressing opinions that they are not qualified to make.

Beschloss quotes from Lady Bird Johnson's tape-recorded diary as supposed support of his skewed conclusion that the President was not stable. But Mrs. Johnson, whom no one has ever accused of being anything other than sensible, caring, and totally normal—and, of course, knew her husband better than anyone else—confided to her private diary that she did not "want" her husband to react to the Vietnam War in any other way than he did. Her full statement, from *A White House Diary*, is as follows: "We talked about the short nights Lyndon has been having for several months. He asked to be waked up whenever there was an operation going out. He won't leave it alone. He said, 'I want to be called every time somebody dies.' He can't separate himself from it. Actually, I don't want him to, no matter how painful.

In Washington, he seldom gets to sleep until about two." To any fair observer, these are the reactions one would expect from a man who cares deeply about the consequences of his unavoidable decisions.

Regarding Richard Goodwin, it must be noted that the man is a biased witness. He neither liked nor supported Lyndon Johnson. He made no secret of his disloyalty to President Johnson, even while he continued on at the White House following the assassination of President Kennedy. He has confirmed his anti-Johnson feelings many times through the ensuing years. I allowed Goodwin to resign because of his undisguised disloyalty. He did not want to depart, but he had no choice. I think it is fair to conclude that Goodwin's prejudices against Lyndon Johnson have never subsided.

Furthermore, Goodwin's quoted statements about President Johnson are not properly supported by the cited footnotes in the Beschloss book. Goodwin is said to have claimed that a psychiatrist told him that the President was suffering from "disintegration." However, the Beschloss footnote to that Goodwin quotation reveals that the psychiatrist actually stated that it would be "an ethical violation" to give an opinion regarding President Johnson in the absence of "a full clinical evaluation." Thus, Goodwin's claim of psychiatric underpinning to his own prejudiced opinion is mistaken because, as the footnote demonstrates, no reputable psychiatrist would reach a conclusion regarding the mental stability of the President based upon the amateurish statements of an untrained observer.

As for Goodwin's quoted claim that Bill Moyers told him that he consulted a psychiatrist concerning President Johnson, in a statement made to Pulitzer Prize–winning reporter Nick Kotz, which Kotz revealed to Sherwin Markman, Moyers denied the truth of the Goodwin statement.

In addition, Beschloss's quotations from Goodwin about Moyers do not appear to support the conclusions that Beschloss wants to reach. Beschloss writes that Moyers was "worried about . . . the President's psychological and emotional destruction." However, the actual quotations from Moyers that he cites are these: that the President's "depression came from the realization . . . that this was a road from which there is no turning back"; that his depression came from his knowledge that he was sending "large numbers of troops to Vietnam [which] would likely mean the end of his presidency"; that he sometimes became "morose, self-pitying, angry"; and that he was "tormented." To me, these are nothing more than the reactions that one would expect from a leader whose never-ending responsibilities included conducting a tragically inclusive war.

It also must be noted that during Bill Moyers's final months in the White House, he was suffering through quite a bit of emotional stress. As Moyers later wrote, the breakdown of his relationship with the President was "tragically unnecessary, and my own fault."

After permanently leaving the White House, Moyers mounted an unsuccessful effort to return, something he very much wanted to do. I have previously quoted from his letter, in which he wrote that his "affection" for the President was undiminished, and that Moyers continued to love Lyndon Johnson "as he is."

The enduring love of Bill Moyers for Lyndon Johnson "as he is," and his desire to be permitted to return to the Johnson fold, is inconsistent with the conclusion—as wrongly asserted by Beschloss—that Moyers believed that Lyndon Johnson was mentally ill.

How does one prove the stability and sanity of a friend and mentor with whom one has worked for long hours every day for years? It is something like the famous definition of pornography given by Supreme Court Justice Potter Stewart: "I know it when I see it." Just think about anyone one knows well. If the person is not delusional, can view a real problem with reason and insight, deals effectively with other people, reacts with laughter, anger, sadness, joy, impatience, concern—you name it—appropriate to the occasion, then one judges the friend as balanced and sane. The opposite is also true. If one's friend claims to see and hear things that are not there, cannot use his or her mind to properly deal with a real problem, reacts strangely to others, meets a happy event with anger or a tragedy with joy—again, you name it— then one knows that the friend has emotional problems.

With Lyndon Johnson, he was never other than normal in dealing with any problem or person. Certainly, he got angry when he had reason to be angry (such as Williamsburg). He also got over it. Can any of us claim that we never acted that way? Regarding the President's reactions to the Vietnam War (cited as the so-called "reason" for the accusation that the President acted inappropriately), there is no doubt that the President often was very distressed and concerned about that entirely real dilemma in which we were embroiled. But who would not have been? Lyndon Johnson was, after all, the Commander in Chief who issued or approved the orders that placed so many Americans in harm's way. Now these young Americans were being killed or wounded by the thousands. Of course the President was affected. Not to have cared about those casualties would have been inhuman and heartless, and Lyndon Johnson's heart was large enough to embrace them all.

In other words, to be affected by something that is truly painful is the very definition of normalcy. If the President had no reaction or exhibited signs of happiness because of that war, then indeed he could be fairly judged as mentally unsound. But President Johnson was not unstable—ever. To charge him now, so many years after he is gone, is egregiously wrong.

Lyndon Johnson was the most human of men, and more than most felt and showed the total range of emotions. Yet, he never lost sight of the awesome burden of his responsibilities. His conclusions always reflected his best, most rational judgment, and the judgments of the most competent people he could summon to advise him. Not once in the hundreds of times that he ordered me to carry out a decision did I feel any need to delay or somehow to "protect him from himself" as others have claimed. Although there were times when he reacted emotionally to a problem or an individual, he always recovered quickly, and by the time I left his presence his directions to me were appropriate and never had to be delayed or diluted by me or anyone else.

SOME VINTAGE MOMENTS

The year 1967 was not entirely a stressful one for the President. There were times of joy and a sense of high achievement during the course of the year, three of which stand out in my memory.

On June 13, he appointed Thurgood Marshall as the first African American justice of the U.S. Supreme Court, an act for which he always will be remembered and of which he was surpassingly proud.

The President and Marshall had known and admired each other for many years. When Lyndon Johnson became President, he began looking for an opportunity to make a historic appointment to the court. Although his friend Abe Fortas was President Johnson's first appointment to the Supreme Court, he did not forget about Thurgood Marshall. In 1961, President Kennedy had appointed Marshall to the Second Circuit Court of Appeals. In

1965, President Johnson, already thinking about improving Marshall's chances for confirmation by the Senate, asked Marshall to resign from his lifetime appointment and become Solicitor General in the Justice Department. The President believed that as Solicitor General, Marshall would appear constantly before the Supreme Court as the principal advocate for the United States, and thus would add another qualification to his already outstanding reputation as a judge and lawyer.

Typically, President Johnson promised nothing to Marshall while persuading him to take the new job, although the President's intentions may have been clear. In any event, Marshall accepted the offer. He did a superb job as Solicitor General. Then, on July 13, 1967, the President summoned Marshall to the Oval Office and told him that he was about to become the President's nominee to the Supreme Court.

Marshall, of course, was overjoyed, but the President, knowing that he was making history, was equally pleased that he was breaking through another unjust racial barrier.

The President and Marshall continued their close friendship even after the Senate confirmed the new Justice later that summer. An example of their relationship is contained in messages they exchanged while Marshall was on the Court. For example, when the President asked Justice Marshall "to come over here sometime and take your shoes off" whenever the two of them might find the time to be alone, the Justice replied that he would do just that whenever the President wished.

Another marvelous high point of the year occurred on December 9, when the President's older daughter, Lynda, married Charles Robb in a beautiful ceremony in the East Room of the White House. The wedding, which followed a week of festivities around Washington, was one of the capital's finest social events. I have seldom seen the President happier—or prouder—than when he gave his daughter's hand in marriage. It was a sublimely contented moment for him. He loved his daughter's outgoing personality, which strongly resembled his own, and he greatly admired the Marine captain she married, a man who shortly would be shipped to Vietnam to fight as an infantry officer

The year 1967 ended with a dramatic flourish when, on December 19, the President flew to Australia to attend the funeral for his friend Prime Minister Harold Holt. Holt had drowned while scuba diving among the coral reefs off the Australian coast. His body was never found. He was a great friend of Lyndon Johnson and had made certain that Australia, a member of SEATO, honored its treaty obligations by fully supporting South Vietnam—including furnishing troops who fought alongside those from the United States, South Korea, New Zealand, and the Philippines

As it turned out, that flight was the opening leg of a round-the-world journey of 28,210 miles. We completed the entire trip in 112 hours and 20 minutes, of which we spent 59 hours and 15 minutes in the air before we returned to Washington late on Christmas Eve. Making matters even less comfortable, we were required to fly in a backup Boeing 707, which did not have sleeping quarters for the President. The primary Boeing 707 that usually served as Air Force One was undergoing repairs and a checkup. During this arduous trip, the President asked the Military to make him a bed on the plane. Then—as always showing his special thoughtfulness about me—he also had them make a bed for me. Sergeant Major Gulley later told me that the men who built those beds were impressed with a President who took care of his people and not just himself. However, in accordance with longstanding practice, the substitute aircraft became Air Force One because the President was flying on it.

Before the unexpected death of Prime Minister Holt, the President had planned to spend Christmas with the American troops in Vietnam and he wanted the option of visiting with the Pope on his way home. Because Vietnam is more than halfway around the world from Washington, to continue flying west was as easy as returning across the Pacific. Without making any definite commitment, the President asked Jack Valenti to arrange for an invitation to visit the Vatican, but only if the President found that it was feasible. The Pope agreed, but no decision had been made by the time we left Washington for Australia.

The timing of the Holt funeral, which required the President to leave Washington on December 19, disrupted his plan to spend Christmas in Vietnam. Nonetheless, he was determined to go to Vietnam even if the trip occurred a few days before the holiday. Our schedule looked like this: December 19, departed Andrews Air Force Base; December 20, departed Pago Pago, Samoa; and December 22, departed Melbourne, Australia. On December 23, we left Korat, Thailand, for Cam Ranh Bay, Vietnam, on what was to become the longest day of my life.

On our flight to Cam Ranh Bay, the large American base in Vietnam, President Johnson told me that he would make his final decision regarding visiting the Pope after we departed from Vietnam. Until that time, nobody else was to be informed of the possibility of flying to the Vatican, especially the press corps accompanying us. Thus the normal advance planning for a presidential trip was not permitted.

We landed in Vietnam just before 9 A.M. on December 23. Before and after our flights in and out of Cam Ranh Bay, we were escorted by a squadron of American fighter planes flying so close to us that we could see the expressions on the pilots' faces. At the American base, the President spent an hour and a half with the American troops. He shared a meal with them, made a speech, and privately met with as many individuals as possible. He was very pleased that he had the opportunity to do all that.

We were airborne at 10:25 A.M. on December 23. As we headed north, the President asked that I call our Ambassador in Pakistan and request the Prime Minister to meet us at the airport near Karachi. The Ambassador and the Prime Minister agreed to the meeting. When I reported that the Prime Minister would be "so pleased to welcome his friend President Lyndon Johnson once again to his country," the President agreed that we would fly west, and after our stop in Pakistan, we should arrange for his visit with Pope Paul VI.

While Colonel Cross made the necessary radio calls to secure landing rights and refueling in Pakistan, I telephoned the American Ambassador there to inform him of our plans. I told him we would be arriving in about three hours, and that if possible the President would like to meet with Pakistan's Prime Minister while we were on the ground. The two leaders previously had met. One time was when, as Vice President, Lyndon Johnson went to Pakistan and with much fanfare invited a Pakistani camel driver to come to the LBJ Ranch in Texas, where he was greeted warmly. Later the Vice President gave him a pickup truck that was shipped to him in Pakistan.

We landed at 2:05 P.M. Karachi time. The Pakistanis had literally rolled out a red carpet for the President. The two leaders met in the terminal building. Relations between the two men—and between our two nations—were quite strong in those days, and their meeting, although short, was relaxed and friendly.

At 3:25 P.M., we took off for Italy. It was decided that because of threatened demonstrations, the best place for us to land was Ciampino Airport, a partially abandoned American air base close to Rome. Fortunately (once again, like Suriname), it still had a functioning control tower and landing lights that worked.

The airfield was some distance from Rome and the Vatican. Thus, before leaving Washington, Cross had made arrangements (unavoidably breaking the President's order for total secrecy) for two presidential helicopters to be shipped to Europe for the purpose of transporting the President and his party from the base to the Vatican.

However, on the flight from Pakistan, Cross told me that the helicopters would not be ready for the President when we arrived at Ciampino Airport. Apparently they had been dismantled for shipment to Spain, where they were now located. However, there would not be sufficient time to reassemble, test, and fly them to Italy before we landed. While Air Force One flew toward Rome, Cross and I spent hours trying to locate a helicopter that could be used to transport the President to the Vatican. Unfortunately, there was no serviceable American helicopter at Ciampino Airport. However, Sargeant Major Bill Gulley discovered that there was a single usable helicopter located at the American Sixth Fleet headquarters in Naples that was assigned to the commanding admiral. It was immediately flown to Ciampino so it would be ready for the President the moment he arrived.

Air Force One landed at Ciampino at close to 8 P.M. It was still December 23 local time. As I stepped off the airplane, I did not see a helicopter. I hesitated for a moment, knowing that if the President had no transportation, there would be a serious problem. Just then, I heard the sound of rotors, and a few minutes later the military helicopter settled down next to the Air Force One.

I walked up to the helicopter pilot the moment he shut down his engine. "Do you know Rome?" I shouted up to him. "Can you find the Vatican?"

"No, I am not from around here," the pilot yelled back.

"All right, just you stay right there," I shouted as I hurried to the control tower.

"Do any of you have a street map of Rome?" I asked the men inside.

"Yes, sir," one of them said.

I grabbed the map, circled the airport and the Vatican with my pen, and trotted back to the helicopter "Can you use this?" I asked, shoving the map into the pilot's hands.

"I think so," he said, sounding none too confident. "I'll do my best."

"Well, I'll pray for you," I said.

There was no more time, because the President and every Catholic who was with us on Air Force One were now boarding the helicopter.

In the spirit of Christmas, I did not join them because to have done so would have deprived one of our Catholic passengers the opportunity of seeing the Pope. I stayed behind at Ciampino, worrying every minute that they were gone. I was thinking that if the world only knew what chances we now were taking with the President of the United States and his friends and staff as they flew at night to a destination about which their pilot had no experience, we would be strung from the highest lamppost.

But it all worked out. In the nighttime darkness, the helicopter lifted off from Ciampino only ten minutes after our arrival. The pilot found the Vatican, and with skill and luck, landed in its garden. The President spent an hour and a half with the Pope before returning to Air Force One, very satisfied and jubilant.

At 11:05 P.M.—still on December 23—Air Force One took off from Ciampino.

Once again, we were required to refuel on our flight back to Washington. This time, our stop would be Lajes Field, an American base in the Portuguese Azores Islands. It was now December 24, Christmas Eve. About an hour before we landed there, the President asked me if there was an American post exchange at the Lajes base. I walked into the cockpit where Colonel Cross was piloting the plane. After hearing the President's question, Cross radioed ahead and found out that there was an exchange but that because it was close to 2 A.M.—and Christmas Eve at that—the exchange quite naturally was closed. However, for the President and his party they reported that they would open so that everyone on our airplane had an opportunity to do his Christmas shopping, something that was impossible during our hectic circumnavigation.

By the time we landed at Lajes, the post exchange was open, lighted, and staffed by friendly if somewhat sleep deprived military personnel. It was quite a sight when all of us—including the President of the United States—rushed around the exchange, choosing and buying whatever we saw and liked before scurrying back to Air Force One in time to take off the moment the refueling was completed.

We finally landed at Andrews Air Force Base at 4:30 A.M. on December 24, 1967. All of us were totally exhausted from our four-and-a-half-day journey around the world. The President immediately helicoptered back to the White House where Lady Bird, Lynda, and Luci and her family were up and waiting to lovingly greet him.

A small jet was made available to take me and Ted Connell (who had been our advance man in Australia and stayed with us for the remainder of the trip) back to Texas to be with our own families for Christmas. I was exhausted but thankful and happy to be reunited with those I loved in time to celebrate the joyous holiday.

1968

★

"CAMPAIGNING" FOR REELECTION

When I returned to Washington after the euphoria of the President's trip around the world and the joys of the 1967 holiday season, there was no avoiding the realities of the issues with which the President must deal during 1968. Although we could not foresee the monstrous tragedies of the assassinations of Martin Luther King and Robert Kennedy, and the explosive riots that thereafter consumed the nation, there were nevertheless immense problems that we knew must be faced. They began with the continuing and seemingly endless escalation of the war in Vietnam, and they embraced everything associated with the presidential election that would take place in November.

As January began, I continued my role as President Johnson's political agent. As such, I did my best to deal with the problems created by the mixed signals resulting from his desire to retain all of his options.

In the first place, I was aware that he had never deviated from his privately stated intention not to run for reelection. As of January, his thinking remained grounded in his conviction that his health would not permit him to survive another four years as President, and his fear that—like President Woodrow Wilson—he would be incapacitated while still in office. Now he told me he intended to include his withdrawal as part of his State of the Union address scheduled for January 17.

Nonetheless, at no time did he relieve me from my political responsibility to "organize" a reelection campaign on his behalf. He required me to function as best I could, but without any public encouragement from him. Thus, he expected me to continue preparing for his campaign while at the same time he prohibited me from forming any "official" Johnson for President organizations or actively seeking or appointing persons who would function as Johnson campaign leaders around the country. Even in Washington, the small group of Rowe, O'Brien, Fortas, and Criswell (coordinated by me) was neither formally proclaimed nor permitted to operate for Johnson in any but the most informal manner.

On the other hand, I was not stopped from forming "spontaneous" Johnson groups. I was allowed to privately give them encouragement, but I could not publicly assist them. I never slowed my ceaseless telephone calls to political leaders throughout the nation whereby I sought support for the President. I spent a great deal of time seeking all possible political intelligence, which I would deliver to him. In my reports to him, I emphasized those facts demonstrating his strength, the certainly of his renomination, and the high probability of his reelection, especially against Richard Nixon, the man we assumed would be the Republican nominee.

The President never told me to curtail my efforts on his behalf. At the same time, he never said anything I could interpret as a personal commitment that he intended to run for reelection. To me, he was a man who, although he may have privately decided not to run, was not so certain that he was willing to close out his other options. In other words, as always, his actions were consistent with his belief that until he formally and publicly announced his intentions, his thinking was only "preliminary" and was not binding on him. All of this resulted in a strange campaign effort, one that was both incomplete and frustrating to me (who knew the reason behind his behavior) and to his other supporters who were not privy to his thinking. I labored with as much energy as I could muster because I knew that he always could change his mind—and I fervently hoped that he would.

On the evening of January 17, as he and I stood in his bedroom preparing to depart for the Capitol where he was to deliver his State of the Union address, I thought that he had made his choice.

The President had the text of the main speech in his hand, and on the table beside his bed lay the paper containing the paragraph whereby he withdrew from the presidential campaign. The inclusion of that paragraph at the end of his address was so secret that it had not been disclosed to his regular speechwriters, and it had not been typed as part of the body of the speech. Instead, the President's trusted writer and friend Horace Busby had separately drafted and typed the paragraph, which the President intended to read at the conclusion of his address to Congress.

As the President and I left his bedroom, I saw that the Busby draft was still on the nightstand. I had no idea whether this was deliberate or merely forgetfulness. Under normal circumstances, I would have brought this to his attention. But I did not say a word because I fervently hoped that he was purposefully leaving it behind. So I said nothing.

At the Capitol, the President as always was greeted warmly and his speech was enthusiastically received. When he completed delivering the body of his prepared text, he reached into the inside pocket of his suit coat, obviously intending to pull out the Busby paragraph. I saw him fumble with the pocket, then reach into his other inside coat pocket. Nothing was there, and for a moment he appeared puzzled and distressed. I saw him give a slight shrug and smile as the applause washed over him.

As we were riding back to the White House, he turned to me and asked, "What happened to that withdrawal paragraph?"

"You left it in the bedroom," I said, fully expecting him to ask me why I had permitted that to happen.

Instead he said, "I suppose it's just as well." However, he did not add that he had changed his mind about not running for reelection.

Thus, our so-called campaign continued with neither encouragement nor disavowal from the President.

Despite the President's public silence regarding his intentions, our efforts on his behalf did not flag during those first three months of 1968. Yet, despite how hard I worked attempting to increase his political strength and convince him to go forward, other factors finally determined and reinforced his decision.

He continued to be concerned about his health, a worry that was only exacerbated by the crescendo of events all around him.

The worst of these, of course, was the war in Vietnam and the constant press reports concerning the vanishing public support of American policy there. The President despised the war. It was killing Americans. It was destroying his dreams for a Great Society by sucking up immense amounts of money. Simultaneously, as he realized more than anyone else, it was causing the disintegration of his public approval and thus his ability to lead the nation. Nevertheless, it was his conviction—and that of his senior advisors— that the well-being and safety of America from the worldwide ambitions of hostile Communist governments required the United States to continue the Vietnam struggle. Thus, despite the costs to the country and to him, he saw no way by which we could simply quit and run away. Still, the President never ceased his search for an honorable solution, a search that ultimately became decisive in his decision not to seek reelection.

Two developments regarding Vietnam became critical. First, Secretary of Defense McNamara, exhausted and discouraged, told the President that he wanted to resign. The President accepted McNamara's decision, although he asked him to remain in office until March 1. The President often said, "It sometimes takes me months to hire or appoint someone, but it takes only seconds to accept a resignation."

On January 19, the President nominated Clark Clifford to succeed Mc-Namara. Six days later, on January 25, North Korea, in international waters, seized the American navy ship the USS *Pueblo* and captured its crew.

Then, on January 30 and 31, the North Vietnamese launched their so-called Tet offensive. The attack was not a surprise, and General William Westmoreland, the U.S. commander in Vietnam in whom the President had great confidence, had positioned his forces in anticipation of the enemy's initiative. When it came, the attack was simultaneously directed against most of Vietnam's largest cities and district capitals, including an unsuccessful attempt to occupy the American Embassy in Saigon. Our military leaders considered the Tet offensive a military disaster for North Vietnam because they sent eighty-four thousand men into battle and lost forty-five thousand of them, numbers that far exceeded all the casualties suffered by the United States during its previous years in Vietnam. Furthermore, the offensive did not succeed in permanently capturing a single targeted city.

However, Clark Clifford strongly disagreed with the assessment by our own military. In his opinion, the Tet offensive demonstrated a failure in our own intelligence; clearly showed the failure of our "pacification" policy, which by 1968 had issued so many optimistic predictions; and, in sum, constituted a public relations victory for the Communists and their supporters because of the serious erosion of support by both the public and the Congress.

The President agreed with Clifford that the Tet offensive proved to be a masterstroke of political propaganda. Perhaps it was the audacity and breadth of the attack, or the fact that the American public (although not our military) was shocked by the ability of the North Vietnamese to mount and coordinate such a massive action, but whatever the reason, the vast majority of American media treated the entire affair as a North Vietnamese triumph. A few lonely voices attempted to point out the truth of the debacle, but they were drowned out—ignored is perhaps a better word—by the loud chorus of stories that slavishly echoed the false Communist party line that North Vietnam had achieved a remarkable military victory.

The "emotional and exaggerated reporting of the Tet offensive" (as President Johnson described it) was red meat for the well-disciplined—and Communist-influenced and -financed—leaders of the protest movement within the United States. They were in full battle cry, and the intensity and violence of their opposition continued to escalate with the constant drumbeat of their claim that America was being militarily defeated in Vietnam.

Protests and demonstrations were not the only matters that escalated as a result of the Tet offensive. Unfortunately, it was precisely at this moment that General Westmoreland and the Joint Chiefs requested an additional 205,000 American troops in Vietnam, an increase that would bring the number of Americans there to above 725,000.

The President ordered Clifford to conduct a full-scale study and reassessment of American policy in Vietnam, and in particular the military's unexpected demand for additional American troops, which would require a substantial call-up of reserves. Clifford's conclusions came quickly. He recommended that the military request should be denied. Clifford was joined in his conclusion by McNamara, who on his last day on the job stated that adding more American forces would achieve nothing because the Communists would match us man for man.

The President immediately presented the issue to the "wise men" with whom he long had consulted regarding Vietnam. In all that time, these senior advisors had urged him to stay the course in Vietnam because it would ultimately bring victory. Now, however, they suddenly reversed their advice. Led by President Truman's always hawkish Secretary of State, Dean

Acheson, they told the President that the Vietnam War was "unwinnable." Shocked and disheartened by this abrupt change by McNamara, Clifford, and the "wise men," the President made his historic decision that finally ended American escalation in Vietnam. Of course, that decision created myriad other problems associated with possible American extrication from that war.

This was the backdrop to the political decision that President Johnson had to make, a decision that could not be indefinitely delayed. Its timing was unavoidably controlled by the dates of the upcoming primary elections, some of which required him to formally announce his candidacy, and all of which necessitated some kind of effort—whether authorized or not—on his behalf in order to avoid potentially disastrous defeats.

As I have written, Senator Eugene McCarthy had announced his own candidacy for President in December. By January, he had become the lightning rod for those people—especially young people—who opposed the war in Vietnam. In the White House, we had no great concern regarding the threat posed by McCarthy. On the other hand, we continued to focus on Robert Kennedy and his intentions. We considered Kennedy to be the most dangerous potential opponent, and although the consensus was that he could not wrest the nomination from the President, his potential for disruption was enormous. In particular, we worried about the effect of the McCarthy candidacy upon Kennedy's decision. The McCarthy campaign already was costing Kennedy the loss of many young supporters who otherwise might have constituted the core of his followers. Even such lifelong Kennedy acolytes as Richard Goodwin, the former Johnson staffer, had joined the McCarthy campaign. In our view, Kennedy was being pushed on one side by those who disliked the President, and on the other by the enthusiasm of those who supported McCarthy.

As the President's principal political operative, I used my best efforts to deal with his ambivalence and the McCarthy and Kennedy challenges, while at the same time doing all that I could to build a campaign structure that would be effective if the President finally decided to seek reelection.

The New Hampshire primary, scheduled for March 12, would be the first election we had to face. The President prohibited me from forming an "official" Johnson organization there, and of course he also refused to announce his candidacy. Nonetheless, I did what I could within the limitations he imposed and I kept him fully informed. For example, on January 8, I wrote him that our informal organization in New Hampshire was "proceeding very rapidly" and was moving toward developing two thousand neighborhood coordinators in "every single section of the state." I reported that "enthusiasm all over the state is excellent." I went on to tell him that the "McCarthy people seem to be at a standstill," and that "we have already been able to enlist the support of a good number of professors as well as students at both Dartmouth and the University of New Hampshire," along with some of the smaller colleges. Finally, I reported that the "pro-Kennedy camp . . . seem to be losing the few supporters that he had." My conclusion was that "we are in a good position to give McCarthy a very sound trouncing."

On the same January day that I sent that memorandum to the President, Kennedy once again publicly announced that he was prepared to support the reelection of President Johnson. A week later, Jim Rowe sent the President a lengthy report stating his opinion that "Kennedy has made a political judgment that he cannot take the nomination away from you in 1968; or, if he could, it would inevitably result in a shattered Democratic Party which would go down to defeat . . . and destroy Bobby forever." Rowe also wrote that Kennedy "is under constant and public attacks from his own supporters. . . . The young are calling him a 'fink.' They are angered because he will not run against you himself and because he will not support McCarthy." Rowe concluded with the recommendation that the President open a dialogue with Kennedy with the objective of persuading Kennedy to support the President in 1968 and thus help himself in 1972, which Rowe believed was Kennedy's true objective. Rowe suggested himself as the intermediary between the President and Kennedy. Otherwise, Rowe believed, "there is a very good chance . . . [Kennedy's] followers will push him over the brink."

The President asked Larry Temple, a trusted senior White House Special Assistant who had formally served under Texas Governor John Connally, to comment on Rowe's suggestions. Temple's opinion was that there was little chance that Kennedy could be persuaded to openly support the President because Kennedy would not "think that it is in his best interest to have the Johnson-Humphrey ticket reelected by a large majority" (thus strengthening Humphrey's position for the 1972 election). Temple nonetheless concluded that he saw nothing wrong with an attempt to open a dialogue with

Kennedy, although he believed that it should be done by someone other than Rowe, who Kennedy perceived as too close to Humphrey. Temple suggested that the President find someone who Kennedy believed would support him in any "heads-up race" against Humphrey, although Temple knew of no one who might fit that description.

The Kennedy issue continued to percolate in the White House through the remainder of January. The day after the President received the Temple memo, John Roche, the New England intellectual who was serving him as a White House Special Consultant, weighed in with additional intelligence regarding Kennedy's dilemma. Roche reported that there "has been great agitation in the Kennedy compound" fueled by such leading columnists (and Kennedy supporters) as Mary McGrory and Charles Bartlett, although "the two Teds [Kennedy and Sorensen]" were "telling everybody to cool it." The cause of the "agitation" was that Robert Kennedy had received what he "considered 'hard' evidence that [the President] was not going to run." Roche cited as sources for Kennedy's conclusion an alleged statement by Pat Nugent, then the President's son-in-law, that the President planned to "be back home in 1969"; a statement by Mrs. Johnson about "how nice it will be to escape Washington"; and a report from a Senator close to the President quoting the President as saying that "if the Republicans put up Rockefeller [the President] could relax about the future of the Republic and let Hubert carry the mail." Thus, Roche reported, Kennedy had put his troops on "red alert." Roche concluded by urging the President to organize for battle, "announced by indirection in Massachusetts," and then "flatly declare in time for the later primaries."

A week later, I had a long (and secretly recorded) conversation with Larry O'Brien concerning the Kennedys. Despite remaining on board with President Johnson, O'Brien had retained his close ties with both Kennedy brothers. O'Brien had separately met with both Ted and Robert Kennedy. In considerable detail, he reported to me on what had been said at these meetings. My impression was that O'Brien was more forthcoming regarding his conversation with Ted Kennedy than with his brother, Robert. In any event, I furnished the President with my summary of O'Brien's meetings.

Regarding Ted Kennedy, then the Senator from Massachusetts, O'Brien reported that the younger Kennedy had said that "the President had always been wonderful to him"; that "the relationship had been just wonderful";

and that "he wanted to keep it that way." Ted Kennedy was afraid, however, that the President would put him on the spot in Massachusetts. O'Brien reported that Ted Kennedy, although he "is not an independent guy in all of this," and who had "his problems" that "he would prefer not to have," had reacted "very warmly and significantly" to O'Brien's suggestion that the President and Robert Kennedy should reach an accommodation whereby the two Kennedys would support the President for one more term.

O'Brien's report on his talk with Robert Kennedy was not as satisfying to us. Apparently Robert Kennedy had invited O'Brien to lunch to express his concern about White House actions "kicking me around." Kennedy went on to tell O'Brien that he had done "the right thing in 'staying on.'" O'Brien pointed out that he "still . . . [has] a pretty good relationship with" Kennedy and that Kennedy was "anxious to sit down and talk concretely." However, O'Brien said nothing to me about Kennedy's future plans.

A few days later, the columnists Rowland Evans and Robert Novak—who had a long history of opposition to the President, and who had conducted a long-running personal campaign against me—published an article inaccurately "reporting" that the President had finally decided to permit O'Brien to take "full charge" of his campaign by ordering me "to defer to O'Brien" in all "campaign planning." The column went on to state that in assuming his new authority, O'Brien would also displace Jim Rowe, John Criswell, Abe Fortas, Cliff Carter, Arthur Krim, and Clark Clifford.

Obviously, someone had leaked the false story to the columnists. At the President's direction, I embarked on an investigation regarding the source of the leaks. In my report to the President, I concluded that O'Brien or his agent was the person who had spoken with either Evans or Novak. The President agreed with me, which of course did nothing to increase his trust of Larry O'Brien.

In early February, Ted Sorensen, who had been President Kennedy's chief speechwriter and now served as an intimate advisor to Robert Kennedy, had lunch with John Criswell and DeVier Pierson, a presidential aide on our White House staff. Obviously, Sorensen had been dispatched by Kennedy to deliver a message, but the question was whether the intention was to honestly communicate with us or to dissemble.

Both Criswell and Pierson furnished the President with written summaries of their lunch with Sorensen. They reported that Sorensen stated that

"Bobby meant what he said" when he publicly announced that he was supporting the President; that "he didn't intend to oppose" the President; that he had "no plan for involvement in any primaries"; that he could not "control" a slate of "dissident" delegates filed on his behalf; and that he intended to "disown this group." Thus, Sorensen assured Criswell and Pierson that Kennedy would not run for President. Finally, Sorensen "volunteered to be a point of contact with Bobby."

Criswell concluded his memo by observing that, "In all the previous contacted [sic] I have had with Ted I have considered him about the coldest fish I have ever met. Today I thought his attitude, conversation and general demeanor was close to warm." Pierson's conclusion was that, "It is hard to say how sincere he is."

My own opinion—and that of the President—was that nothing Sorensen said changed our minds that Robert Kennedy, while spreading as much disinformation as possible, was forging ahead with his plan to run for President in 1968. The President's response was to ask them to keep "plenty" of continuing contact with Sorensen.

On the day following Sorensen's lunch with Criswell and Pierson, Johnson received a long memorandum from Jim Rowe that shook our budding campaign organization to its core. In it, Rowe informed him that "this is where I get off the train." The cause for Rowe's sudden and unexpected withdrawal from the President's team was that Rowe believed that the President was ignoring the necessity of setting up a viable campaign organization. Of course, I too was acutely aware of that problem, but the crucial difference between Rowe and me was that I knew that the reason lay in the President's ambivalence about running for reelection, a critical fact I was not permitted to share with anyone. Thus, I labored on despite the President's lack of active direction. But now Rowe refused to continue, and his refusal came as a brutal shock to the President.

In his lengthy memo to the President, Rowe laid out his reasoning. His primary complaint was that the President had failed to set up a campaign organization despite months of urging by Rowe. More specifically, Rowe wanted Larry O'Brien, rather than a Texan, to lead the President's campaign. Rowe, born in Montana and educated at Harvard, thought that the country— fairly or unfairly—lacked confidence in Texans. When the President had resisted Rowe's suggestion, Rowe had offered to lead the campaign jointly with O'Brien. What triggered Rowe's extreme reaction now was his belief that the President had approved Rowe's compromise idea, but for reasons undisclosed to Rowe, had changed his mind without telling Rowe. Rowe mistakenly believed that—as had happened before—the President's refusal to go forward was based upon his reaction to the "leaked" Evans-Novak story that O'Brien was going to head the President's campaign.

Despite stating that he was resigning, Rowe's memo continued to urge the President to accept O'Brien, whom Rowe described as a "pro" whose "political judgment is excellent." In short, Rowe argued, "the President needs" O'Brien.

Rowe detailed other reasons behind what he described as his "sudden explosion." They were: (1) his belief that despite the President's approval of jointly naming O'Brien and Rowe to head his campaign, O'Brien was now being frozen out of crucial political strategy meetings; (2) Rowe's opinion that the people selected to lead the Johnson effort in various states were "ridiculous" choices; and (3) his conclusion that, although the President had agreed to the suggestions in the O'Brien White Paper of the previous fall, those ideas never had been implemented. Rowe also thought that secret amounts of money were being raised and spent. In fact, only some initial money had been raised for the President, so there was very little spent except for those funds under the control of the Democratic National Committee.

In short, Rowe complained to the President that "the signals are being called by Watson and Criswell . . . not me or O'Brien." Rowe wrote, "I do *not want,* and I will *not accept,* responsibility for the primaries [emphasis in the original]."

Jim Rowe had not pulled any punches in his memorandum to the President. Although he described his statement as "polite and friendly," it was in fact a hard-hitting and quite personal attack on both the President (for allegedly going back on his word) and me (for "secretly" controlling political matters without having any public responsibility for running the campaign). Nonetheless, the President typically ignored those aspects of the Rowe memo and focused on the great value Rowe would bring to any campaign. Thus, the President, with me present, immediately met with Rowe. At that meeting, Rowe was the focus of the President's impressive ability to persuade. By the end of the meeting, Rowe had returned to the fold. His return was accomplished despite the fact that none of his complaints were satisfied.

The President remained uncommitted, and our organization—such as it was—continued to reflect his uncertainty and his lack of full confidence in O'Brien.

With Rowe pacified, we continued as best we could constructing an organization that could be instantly activated once President Johnson decided to run. I received constant reports regarding the political situation in every state. I refamiliarized myself with the methods by which national convention delegates would be chosen from each state, and I maintained close contact with the persons controlling those processes, whether they were via primaries or political conventions. I ordered continuous polling both nationally and in critical states, and syndicated pollsters, such as Elmo Roper, furnished me with advance copies of their findings. The results were invariably positive. There was no doubt in my mind—despite the active campaign of Eugene McCarthy and the incipient threat of Robert Kennedy—that the President would be renominated and very probably reelected. And of course I made certain that the President was made fully aware of these facts.

Naturally, there were problem areas. One of the most vexing was California, where the Democratic Party leadership was divided among such people as its Governor (Pat Brown), its Los Angeles Mayor (Sam Yorty), and its legislative leader (Jesse Unruh), who we learned was secretly urging Kennedy to announce his candidacy. We were attempting to field a slate of Johnson delegates to run in California's June primary, a list of people we hoped would be reasonably acceptable to all the political factions in that state. Preparing that list was akin to being a juggler. I assigned principal responsibility to Irv Sprague, the man on our staff most intimately familiar with the troubles of California politics. Although Sprague worked hard to achieve a consensus, he never succeeded.

As March began, Kennedy continued to watch from the sidelines while McCarthy and his zealous backers increased their efforts. John Roche, carefully monitoring his left-leaning friends, told the President that he should be concerned about McCarthy because of our own "inertia"; the "crusading zeal of the antiwar young"; and the "organizational talent of the Communists and the hemi-demi-semi Communists who have been out of circulation [and making money] since Henry Wallace." Roche was particularly concerned about their activities in New York, Michigan, Washington, and Minnesota (McCarthy's home state). Roche wrote the President that "I cannot overemphasize the urgency of this kind of focus." Upon reading Roche's memo, the President noted, "I agree with this—talk to Jim Rowe and get it done." In response, we did our best, but without an announced candidate, it was like swimming through molasses.

On March 12, voters went to the polls in the New Hampshire primary. Lyndon Johnson was not on the ballot and had neither campaigned nor authorized anyone to campaign on his behalf. Nevertheless, Eugene McCarthy, the only person on the Democratic ballot, did not manage to win a majority of the votes. The final tally in the Democratic primary (with the President being only a write-in candidate) was 49.5 percent for the President and 42.4 percent for McCarthy. In the White House, although we felt both pleased with the victory and relieved that we had dodged a bullet, this was a clear warning that if the President was to go forward, he must announce his candidacy and formally organize, especially in those states where primary elections soon would be held. The date of the next primary was April 2 and the state would be Wisconsin.

On March 16, four days after the New Hampshire primary, Kennedy finally made his decision and announced his candidacy for President. By doing so, he ignored the rationale (and thus aborted the predictions) of experienced politicians such as Jim Rowe. Apparently he also refused to follow the advice of his brother, Ted Kennedy, as well as experienced Massachusetts leaders like Congressman (later Speaker) Tip O'Neill. In addition, Kennedy's decision incensed large numbers of people, including politicians, who had gone on record supporting Eugene McCarthy. Regarding McCarthy, I learned that it was Kennedy's plan to take care of him by offering the position of Secretary of State—an offer, I was told, that McCarthy summarily refused.

I learned about Kennedy's announcement the night before it was made. When I informed the President, he directed me to immediately call leading politicians around the country to assess whether or not they would support him in a direct confrontation with Kennedy. Simultaneously, the President asked Texas Governor John Connally to telephone his fellow Democratic Governors. Bill Connell, Vice President Humphrey's energetic and competent Chief of Staff, also did a state-by-state analysis of how the Kennedy candidacy would affect the selection of convention delegates. Our resulting reports to the President were positive: by taking on the President directly,

Kennedy's audacious move only strengthened the President's support, and the President remained supremely strong. It was clear that Kennedy could not defeat Lyndon Johnson as the presidential nominee of the Democratic Party.

It did not take long for us to learn of a surprisingly large number of negative reactions to the Kennedy candidacy. The most amazing came from Richard Cardinal Cushing, Boston's premier Catholic prelate. Cushing had presided over the funeral mass for President Kennedy and long had been closely associated with the Kennedy family. Thus, we assumed that the Cardinal would be one of Robert Kennedy's most vigorous supporters. We were shocked when we learned that the truth was precisely the opposite.

What happened was this: Eugene Rostow, who had been dean of the Yale Law School and was now serving as Under Secretary of State for Political Affairs (and was the brother of Walter Rostow, the President's National Security Advisor), was visiting Boston. While there, he and an assistant paid a courtesy call on Cardinal Cushing. Rostow reported to the President that at that meeting, the Cardinal expressed "high admiration for the President and the Secretary of State." The Cardinal then told Rostow that "he thought it best for the country if the President is reelected." The Cardinal also warned that we should "look out for the Kennedys—they always grab what they go after." The Cardinal described "Bobby as 'ruthless.'" He told Rostow that "the family is divided; Ted Kennedy is not entirely behind this campaign." Finally, Rostow reported that Cardinal Cushing "spoke of serious damage to the Democratic Party if the [Bobby Kennedy] movement continues.... Bobby...made many enemies for President Kennedy and the Cardinal didn't think these enemies had forgotten."

Robert Kennedy's brother-in-law, Sargent Shriver, also expressed his restlessness when he told John Criswell that he would rather be known as a Shriver than as a Kennedy.

Massachusetts Congressman Tip O'Neill revealed his private opinions when he spoke to Charles Roche, a Larry O'Brien protégé who had remained on the White House congressional liaison staff. O'Neill told Charles Roche that Ted Kennedy had called O'Neill and said to him that "Bobby was crazy to think about running and that he was the most unpopular man on the Hill." O'Neill had advised Ted Kennedy to tell his brother not to run and "Teddy indicated he agreed that it would be a bad idea to make the race." Roche further reported that "Tip later talked to Kenny O'Donnell [President

Kennedy's chief of staff] . . . and Kenny told him [O'Neill] that he also advised against Bobby making the race. Tip said that he didn't know anyone who favored the campaign, certainly none of the people he considered competent."

Nevertheless, ignoring all this advice—and that of a great number of political leaders throughout the country— Robert Kennedy was now formally in the race for President. In doing so, Kennedy seemed to be following the drumbeat urgings of his many friends in the media. Among them, we later learned to our sorrow, was Walter Cronkite, the "dean" of American broadcasters and a man the President had always regarded as his friend.

Looking back on it now, I would agree with the observation then made to us by New York Congressman Lester Wolff: "Bobby is more his father's son than his brother's brother."

Toward the end of March, the President learned that Charles Roche (our staffer supposedly closest to Robert Kennedy) had located a member of the Kennedy entourage "who is willing to provide whatever information he can to help with your reelection." One of these reports stated that the Kennedy people "think former Secretary McNamara will come out against the President"; that they "are not worried about Larry O'Brien [who] . . . will lend all the support he can"; that they are concerned "that the president will make a deal with McCarthy"; and that "Bobby's goal was second spot in '68 so that he would be out front in '72."

Whether that intelligence was accurate, and whether we ultimately would use the informant, soon became moot because his services were offered to us only a few days before March 31, 1968.

During the final week of March, I received both positive and negative reports concerning the President's strength in the country.

On the one hand, I learned about the total disarray the Kennedy candidacy had caused among the so-called antiwar groups. There was great bitterness toward Kennedy by McCarthy and his followers. Even such longtime Kennedy acolytes as our discharged former staffer, Richard Goodwin, was quoted by New York's future Governor, Hugh Carey, as saying that "the Kennedys double-crossed McCarthy and there is a very deep and bitter personal feeling."

Problems also arose for us. Stanley Steingut, the powerful Democratic boss of Brooklyn, suddenly became evasive with me. He told me that the

Democratic Party in New York "had degenerated" and that there "is nothing you can do about that now." Steingut stated that he was "being flexible and fluid"—which was not good news for me to hear.

In addition, the President's good friend Washington Senator Warren Magnuson told me that the delegate nominating conventions in his state had become "a pretty rough thing. . . . I have never seen anything like it." Magnuson said that the Kennedy people were "all committed and it's the damndest thing you ever saw. . . . It's bad. I've never seen anything like this. . . . I never even thought they could do this in King County, in the caucuses, I thought that around the universities it might happen, but it was every one."

On March 26, I received more bad news from California. Ed Pauley, one of our key political backers there, telephoned the President to tell him about three recent political polls. One showed Kennedy with 42 percent, Johnson with 32 percent, and McCarthy with 17 percent. Another, which Pauley described as "more accurate," showed Kennedy with 34 percent, Johnson with 33 percent, and McCarthy with 16 percent. Finally, Pauley quoted from a poll he said most accurately predicted actual ballot results. That poll had Kennedy at 38 percent, Johnson at 30 percent, and McCarthy at 17 percent. These were very disturbing numbers. Pauley's conclusion—which echoed what the President had been hearing for months—was that the President was losing ground in California because there was a "lack of authority in a small steering committee or individual to make decisions and things that need to be done."

I continued my surveys of likely delegates to the Democratic National Convention. The numbers never significantly changed. As March 31 approached, I reported to the President that he had no reason to doubt the certainty of his renomination.

Nonetheless, the President refused to act, and I continued working on his phantom campaign with all the energy that I could muster.

MARCH 31, 1968

At 9 P.M. on Sunday, March 31, President Johnson was scheduled to address the nation. The announced subject was Vietnam. However, to the surprise of most of the world, he concluded his speech with these fateful words: "I shall not seek, nor will I accept, the nomination of my party for another term as your President."

In choosing March 31, the President was well aware of the fact that President Truman had chosen March 31, 1952, as the date he announced his withdrawal as a candidate for reelection.

The President had summoned his favorite speechwriter, Horace Busby, to draft the words he would utter at the conclusion of his speech. Although no longer a member of the President's staff, Busby spent much that Sunday honing the fateful paragraph that was a rework of the language prepared (but not delivered) as the ending to his State of the Union speech in January.

Also at the White House that day were the President's dear friends Arthur and Mathilde Krim. Arthur never stopped trying to convince the President not to withdraw. His daughters, Lynda and Luci, and Mathilde Krim agreed with Krim's arguments. Lady Bird Johnson did not say much, but the President already knew that she supported his decision.

As for myself, I continued my political work on his behalf throughout that weekend. I held meetings in my White House office all day on Saturday. My diary shows that, among others, I spoke with Cliff Carter, our senior agent at the DNC, about the delegate selection situation throughout the country; I discussed "advancing" the President's campaign trips with Jack Valenti and Marty Underwood, our most seasoned advance man; and I analyzed the New York situation with the President's trusted friend Jake Jacobsen. None of these people knew about what was then happening in the Mansion, and I did not tell them.

Amazingly, earlier that week the President had agreed with our recommendation that the man in charge of his campaign would be Terry Sanford, then the Governor of North Carolina. Larry O'Brien had been rejected, and the President had instructed me to meet with Sanford as quickly as possible. Thus, at 3 P.M. on March 31—just a few hours before the President's speech—I, along with Jim Rowe, sat down with Governor Sanford in my White House office. We discussed the details of the President's campaign for reelection.

Again, I was the only person at that meeting who was aware of the struggle going on in the Mansion. I withheld that information from Governor Sanford and Rowe. Our conversation took place in the context of an active and willing candidacy by Lyndon Johnson. I did this with a clear conscience because I knew that until he actually uttered the words, the President believed that he had made no decision and was perfectly free to go in any direction he chose. Beyond that, I believed—and vehemently hoped—that the President would change his mind.

At 6:30 P.M. I telephoned Governor Sanford to tell him to stand by because I might need to talk to him later that night. At seven, I walked over to the Mansion where the argument was still going on. When I returned to my office forty-five minutes later, I told my secretary, Mary Jo Cook, that the President still "had not made up his mind. . . . [regarding] saying he won't run."

Finally, at 8:30 P.M., my wife, Marion, and my daughter, Kim (and a friend of hers), joined me to listen to the President's speech. I still was not certain about what he would say. A few minutes before he went on the air, the President summoned me to his side. He told me that he had made his decision; that he was going to announce his withdrawal at the end of his speech; and that as soon as he began his speech I should begin making telephone calls to those who should be personally notified before he publicly made his announcement.

I had less than thirty minutes to speak to as many people as possible before they heard the President on television. Before my first call, I told Mary Jo Cook to summon as many members of the President's staff as possible, telling them that he wanted them at the White House while he was making his speech, but without informing them what he was about to say. Of course, most of them probably knew by the time they arrived.

Even Vice President Humphrey had not been told in advance, and now he was in Mexico. I asked the White House operators to quickly locate him. Demonstrating much about the order of things that year, my daily log shows my first half-dozen calls that evening were as follows: 9:12 P.M., former Defense Secretary Robert McNamara; 9:14 P.M., Jim Rowe; 9:21 P.M., Chicago Mayor Richard Daley; 9:22 P.M., Vice President Hubert Humphrey; and 9:26 P.M., AFL-CIO President George Meany. The President personally had notified Secretary of State Dean Rusk and Secretary of Defense Clark Clifford before he began his speech.

When I did reach the Vice President, his reaction was a long moment of silence before he finally said, in an uncharacteristically soft voice, that he would come back to Washington as soon as possible.

I continued making my telephone calls to Cabinet Officers, key Senators and Congressmen, close friends of the President, and longtime supporters, until almost 1 A.M. when I finally left for home, a sad and deeply disappointed man.

I am attaching as Appendix 8 my secretary's diary of my activities on March 31, 1968. It shows better than any words I write now the heated pace of that historic day.

The full reasons behind the President's decision not to seek reelection are multiple and can be clearly understood from the events I have recited of the days and months leading up to March 31. From the time when he almost resigned, it was apparent that the President was concerned about his health, a concern that was shared by Mrs. Johnson. Also heavily on his mind was the worsening situation in Vietnam and most especially the loss of public support for the war. Making matters worse, our military picked this time to demand even further increases in the number of American troops in Vietnam. Finally, Clark Clifford, the new Secretary of Defense, also chose this time to inform the President that he rejected the judgment of the uniformed services under his command, and that he strongly recommended that American policy now should concentrate on seeking a negotiated settlement of the war.

Thus, as the President so clearly stated in this speech of withdrawal, his total focus was now on negotiating a peaceful settlement regarding Vietnam, one that had to begin with an agreement by all sides to attend a peace conference. To achieve that, the President said he must no longer be seen as a politician, but solely as the American head of state. He believed that he must rise above all domestic politics, which he was doing by removing himself from the contest for the American presidency.

One other fact is equally clear: He did not withdraw because he feared that he would not be renominated or reelected. Without exception, every poll of delegates and every survey of voters clearly demonstrated that he would defeat both Kennedy and McCarthy for the Democratic nomination; and that Richard Nixon, the probable Republican nominee, would not unseat him in the general election. The most that can be said regarding the effect of Robert Kennedy's candidacy—as so many of his own people predicted—was that more than anything else it would prove to be destructive to Kennedy himself, not only in 1968, but also his prospects for 1972. Although it is true that Kennedy's candidacy would cause difficulties for Lyndon Johnson, none of them were insurmountable. If there was any correlation between the Kennedy campaign and the President's decision, it was that it added pressure on him, which he neither needed nor wanted in addition to all the other concerns he bore as President. It was another weight added to his fear that he would not survive another campaign and another four years in office.

Of course, the President's withdrawal did not end the political season, but it most certainly changed it. The decision caught Hubert Humphrey flat-footed and required him to instantly form a campaign that could compete with his fellow Minnesotan, Eugene McCarthy, who had been in the race since December, and Robert Kennedy, who was now openly seeking the office.

The first test would be the Wisconsin primary election, scheduled for the Tuesday following the President's Sunday night withdrawal. There, although Lyndon Johnson's name remained on the ballot (without his consent), McCarthy was the only active candidate, and the world knew that the President was not running for reelection. The people of Wisconsin could vote for neither Kennedy nor Humphrey, and they were wasting any vote for Lyndon Johnson. Under those circumstances, it was expected that McCarthy would win an overwhelming victory. As it happened, McCarthy garnered only 56 percent of the vote. As it is said in political parlance, McCarthy did not meet expectations. The press played that "fact" heavily, to the advantage of both Humphrey and Kennedy.

Other than weakening the public perception of McCarthy's strength, the most tangible result of the Wisconsin primary was that some of those closest to him no longer felt he was a winner. One of those was Richard Goodwin, who up until then was high in the McCarthy hierarchy. Following the Wisconsin primary, Goodwin jumped ship and in a blink of an eye was out working for Robert Kennedy.

Another—and not unexpected—result of the President's withdrawal was that Larry O'Brien resigned as Postmaster General to assume the role of

Campaign Manager for Robert Kennedy, a post he retained for the remainder of Kennedy's short-lived candidacy.

THE NATION MARCHES ON:
HORROR, HOPE, AND HORROR AGAIN

Although Lyndon Johnson was no longer a candidate for elective office, he remained President of the United States. As such, he was responsible for the welfare of the nation required to deal with any and all crises that might occur. There would be no respite for him during the ten months that he remained in office.

On Thursday, April 4, 1968, Martin Luther King was assassinated in Memphis, Tennessee. The President—and the rest of us in the White House—were shocked and horrified. As much as President Johnson disagreed with Reverend King's methods, he knew that the two of them shared the same goal, and the President always respected Dr. King as a powerful and effective leader of vast numbers of Americans.

In the White House, we had no doubt that the King assassination would cause great trauma, especially in the inner cities of America, although when it came—which was almost instantly—we were amazed at its breadth and ferocity. Within minutes of the killing, the President cancelled a political speech he was about to give at the Washington Hilton Hotel. The President also signed a decree designating April 7 as a national day of mourning.

However, nothing President Johnson did or could do stopped or even diminished the wave of violence that erupted that same night. By then, Washington, Baltimore, and Chicago were in flames. That was soon followed by burning and looting in virtually every major city in the country. Disruption was everywhere. Local police were overwhelmed. National Guards were mobilized in an effort to regain control of the cities. In Washington, federal troops were ordered out in force, and for the first time since the Civil War, the nation's capital was governed by military force. But nothing seemed to work, and the cities continued to burn.

In the midst of this tragedy, the President was faced with the question of whether he should attend Dr. King's funeral in Atlanta. He received conflicting opinions from a number of sources. Some political advisors suggested that it would be better if he did so. However, the Secret Service in particular told him that to go to Atlanta in the midst of all the violence would be extraordinarily dangerous. In the end, the President followed their advice.

We read that the Vice President was going to the King funeral and I called and verified his plans.

"Have you read the FBI reports on Dr. King?" I asked him.

The Vice President answered, "It no longer matters. From now on, regardless of the information we received from the FBI, Dr. King will be thought of as a martyred saint. There is nothing we will ever be able to do or say that will change that perception."

Humphrey's prediction has proved to be totally accurate.

Very quickly following Dr. King's murder, the President summoned to the White House the most knowledgeable people he could find, including the most respected leaders of the African American community. He asked them for their wisdom and guidance as he struggled to contain what had become a national tragedy.

By the weekend following Dr. King's murder, the President was receiving a steady stream of advice from these experts. Yet nothing seemed to slow the accelerating pace of destruction. Washington was but one of innumerable cities that were aflame. Whole neighborhoods were under the control of violent, angry mobs. Fourteenth Street—only blocks from the White House—was being destroyed. Travel within the nation's capital was difficult at best, and very dangerous at worst. Some of the black experts who were working with the President could not travel alone to and from the White House and their hotels. One of these men, Judge Leon Higginbotham, the federal judge who had escorted Sherwin Markman (and, later, the President) through the ghetto of Philadelphia, worked at the White House so late one night that the police recommended that he sleep in the West Wing. Judge Higginbotham refused their advice. He wanted to go back to his hotel. So, accompanied by Markman and in a White House car with a military driver, the Judge returned to his rooms, and Markman did not leave until he was sure his friend was safely in bed.

The damage to Washington was enormous, and what happened in the capital was duplicated in black ghettos everywhere. In the end, there was nothing the President could do but dispatch an ever-greater number of troops to the cities with instructions to maintain law and order. They did their best, but only the passage of time ultimately distilled the black anger and restored peace in our cities.

On April 10, in the midst of the riots, there was a change of the guard in Vietnam. General William Westmoreland, who had been the American commander there, was replaced by General Creighton Abrams, a good man who was destined to preside over the American deescalation and ultimate withdrawal from that country.

In the middle of the afternoon of that same day, Johnson asked me to come into the Oval Office. Without preliminary, he told me that the following morning he intended to send my name to the Senate as his nominee to replace Larry O'Brien as Postmaster General. I was stunned, totally surprised, but proud and pleased the President had such confidence in me. I happily accepted his offer and thanked him profusely.

"I'll hate to lose you," the President continued. "But you've more than earned this appointment. I only wish that I had appointed you and Clark Clifford to my cabinet years ago."

My confirmation hearings went quickly and smoothly, and my own Congressman and longtime friend, Wright Patman, accompanied me throughout the process, as did Texas Senators Ralph Yarborough and John Tower (which was a pleasant surprise since he was a Republican whom I had opposed politically for many years).

On April 25, I was confirmed by the Senate and sworn into office in a lovely White House ceremony on the steps leading from the Oval Office to the Rose Garden. An unexpected moment came while I was at the podium giving my acceptance speech. My four-year-old son, William, sat at the feet of the President Johnson. While the President listened to me, William carefully and deftly untied the president's shoelaces. Just as William completed his task, the President looked down and saw what had been done to him. In a photograph taken at that instant—and included in this book—one can see the startled, unhappy glare of the President of the United States as he stared down into the innocent eyes of my youngest child. Later, the photo was given to William, lovingly inscribed to him "from his friend Lyndon Johnson."

On that occasion, Johnson honored me with the following words: "I have indicated . . . in the past something about the respect that I have for Marvin Watson . . . I do not think he needs any assurances of how I feel about him—and I don't need any about how he feels about me. . . . He has served here in the White House for more than three years . . . I have found him always cool in crisis, and we have had enough of them for me to test him. He has been constant in his service and his devotion and he has always been wise and frank in his counsel."

Joining me at the Post Office Department as a part of my key staff—most of them leaving the White House to do so—were Peter Rosenblatt, Doug Nobles, Dr. Lloyd Taylor, William "Bill" McSweeny, Mary Jo Cook, and Lynn Reagan. My staff had researched my new position and informed me that I was now the seventy-fourth Postmaster General of the United States, that Benjamin Franklin had been the nation's first Postmaster General, and that I was eighth in line of succession to the presidency.

From that final week of April 1968 until the end of the Johnson administration, I was no longer intimately involved in the daily affairs of the President and the workings of the White House. Instead, I was charged with administrating the Post Office Department and its 752,000 employees, which was to say the least a full-time occupation. The Department is a vital commercial link (and remains so even in this age of the Internet). Without it, all segments of the economy would grind to a halt. In President Nixon's administration the Post Office Department, with the passage of the Postal Reorganization Act, became the United States Postal Service, changed its logo from a post horse in speed with saddlebags and rider to a bald eagle posed for flight and moved from the Post Office Department Building to L'Enfant Plaza. The Postmaster General would no longer serve in the President's cabinet, nor is he in line to succeed the President.

I enjoyed my nine months of service as Postmaster General. It was challenging and rewarding. President Franklin Roosevelt had transformed the postal service from a haven for political patronage to a body of dedicated professional civil servants. I was proud to be given the opportunity to lead them, and I did my best to do so. I was also happy being in the President's cabinet and—sort of—my own boss.

Also, in early January 1969, the President visited me in my Postmaster General office when we had a reception for him. He was the first President to come to the Post Office Department, and all of us were proud to be his hosts. Later, during the first few months of his presidency, President Nixon did the same and the Postal Service personnel were equally thrilled by such presidential recognition.

Although I had been relieved of my duties as the President's Chief of Staff, he did not hesitate to call upon me whenever he thought I could be useful to him. In the remaining months of his term, he asked me to manage the 1968 Democratic National Convention on his behalf. Later, after Hubert Humphrey was defeated by Richard Nixon, he appointed me as his "Transition Officer" to coordinate the transfer of the government to his successor. This latter job was new to American government. However, before describing these tasks, I want to discuss the events of the remainder of the first half of 1968.

Amid the tragedy of the murder of Martin Luther King and the ensuing riots, the President received one piece of good news. On May 3, the North Vietnamese and the Viet Cong sent word that they agreed to sit down with us and the South Vietnamese at a peace conference to be held in Paris. This was a significant breakthrough after years of frustrating intransigence on their part, and the President believed that it was a direct result of his decision not to seek reelection. Of course, he knew as well as anyone that merely agreeing to meet was only the first step of what undoubtedly would be a long and arduous process. But it was a start.

In the meantime, the war in Vietnam went on as ferociously and costly— in both human and financial terms—as ever. However, the President's personal connection with the war, always close, had become far more intimate because both his sons-in-law, Chuck Robb and Pat Nugent, were now serving in Vietnam.

Robb, in particular, was providing the President with vivid personal letters of the vicious fighting on the ground. He was a Marine infantry captain in a front-line combat unit, an extraordinarily dangerous assignment. In his few quiet moments, he would sit down and write to the President, describing the conditions and dangers that he and his men faced every day and night. These letters deeply affected the President. Often, late in the evenings, he would ask those of his staff still working in the West Wing to gather in the Cabinet Room. With his feet up on the table, the President read them lengthy passages from Robb's letters. The President told his assistants that he was sharing Captain Robb's letters because he wanted them to learn—as he too was learning—what it was like for American boys to constantly risk their lives in that far-off land.

Despite the North Vietnamese agreement to meet in Paris, opposition to the war continued to build in the United States. By now, the President had fully adjusted to the dissent. He could live with it because he knew that he hated the war as much as any protestor, and that he was every bit as ready to end it. The difference was that he also knew that he had to do so in a manner that would not weaken American credibility and national security. To him, the bedrock fact remained as it had been at the beginning: we should not be seen as abrogating our solemn treaty obligations, including those in that part of the world.

Although President Johnson always encouraged free and open discussion among members of his Cabinet, including disagreement about any proposed policy or action, he expected them to support whatever decision he ultimately made. Thus he reacted when Secretary of Labor Willard Wirtz, at a meeting of the Cabinet, announced that his wife did not understand why we were fighting in Vietnam, and a moment later, Secretary of the Interior Stewart Udall made the same observation.

"Do the two of you want me to go to your homes and explain our policies to your wives?" he asked.

"No, sir," they both replied, abashed.

"I suppose you expect me to personally brief them," the President continued.

They shook their heads.

"Haven't the two of you been sitting here for years? Haven't you been listening to all the briefings and discussions we've had about Vietnam? Have you ever uttered a single word dissenting to what we are doing there?"

Wirtz and Udall did not argue, and when they were given the chance to speak, they quickly assured the President that they would make certain that their wives understood American policy.

After the Cabinet meeting adjourned, the President asked me to stay behind. When we were alone in the Oval Office, he told me, "What Wirtz and Udall said in there broke my heart. I'm absolutely certain that those two have been saying a lot more to hurt us than they will ever admit to me. If they didn't agree with what we are doing in Vietnam they should have said so at the time, and if they still don't agree they should resign. Their wives should understand that as well. Instead, they probably feel free to hurt me behind my back. It makes me sick!"

President Johnson was right, but of course as we later learned, Secretary Udall was never fully loyal to Lyndon Johnson, a fact he conclusively proved when two days before the President left office and without informing him, he secretly renamed the stadium in Washington after Robert Kennedy.

Finally, in January 1969, just before he left office, the President proudly announced, as author Robert Dallek writes in *Flawed Giant* (Oxford University Press, 1998), that "for the first time since the 1950s, the country could expect to have a budget surplus."

The amazing part of these achievements is that he did it while he was a "lame duck" President on his way out of office. That is quite a commentary on Lyndon Johnson's unsurpassed talent to move the Congress.

On June 5, the nation was struck once more with horrifying tragedy when Robert Kennedy was assassinated in Los Angeles on the night he won the California primary. When the news was conveyed to the President, his immediate reaction was horror and incredulity that it could happen to two brothers within one powerful family. The President instantly reached out to Kennedy's wife and children, offering them whatever assistance was within his power to give. He grieved for them and with them. Despite all of their differences, he and Robert Kennedy always would be joined within the same short years of American history.

One further thought kept recurring to me after I learned that Robert Kennedy had been shot: I was conscious of how much more hideous the national reaction would have been if Lyndon Johnson had been seeking re-election and Kennedy had been assassinated immediately after the California primary. My nightmarish belief was that if it had happened that way, there would have been a tidal wave of accusations that somehow the President had conspired to kill his young Kennedy opponent. The conspiracy theories—then and now—have never disappeared concerning the death of President Kennedy. I had no doubt that they would have exploded if in any way President Johnson was seen to benefit from the death of Robert Kennedy.

Despite the war and the riots and the President's withdrawal from the political arena, he never ceased pushing for the enactment of the greatest possible number of legislative bills in pursuit of his dream for a Great Society. Amazingly, even during 1968, he was able to achieve some notable successes with the Congress. In 1968, the President was responsible for the enacting of the following legislation:

- Guaranteeing fair housing
- Creating a bill of rights for Native Americans
- Advancing safety on city streets
- Guaranteeing breakfasts for schoolchildren
- Regulating corporate takeovers
- Creating truth-in-lending practices
- Addressing safety standards in gas pipelines
- Diminishing fire hazards
- Promoting international monetary reform
- Creating Redwoods Park and Biscayne Park
- Expanding programs for the investigation of diseases such as heart disease, cancer, and stroke
- Advancing the beautification of America through the protection of scenic rivers and trails
- Controlling dangerous drugs
- Creating a code of military justice.

THE 1968 DEMOCRATIC CONVENTION AND NIXON'S ELECTION AS PRESIDENT

It is, of course, impossible to predict the course of events if Robert Kennedy had lived. No one can say with certainty whether, after his victory in California, Kennedy would have gone on to capture the Democratic nomination for President at the Party's August convention in Chicago. However, it is my belief that Kennedy would not have won the prize he sought. In 1968, delegates to the National Convention were selected in a radically different manner than in later years. Then, most delegates were chosen in state Party conventions. Primary elections were very much the exception. Except for states like California and a few others, delegations mostly consisted of dedicated Party workers and officials. As such, the majority of the delegates were named and controlled by the regular Party leaders. Those persons, in turn, were heavily influenced by the Party's sitting President, Lyndon Johnson.

Accordingly, it was clear to me that no one could be the Party's nominee without the acquiescence of Lyndon Johnson.

After Robert Kennedy's assassination, the active candidates were Vice President Humphrey and Senator Eugene McCarthy. In addition, an attempt was made to replace Robert Kennedy with his brother, Massachusetts Senator Ted Kennedy. At the same time, President Johnson, while holding firmly to his announced decision not to run for reelection, nevertheless retained firm control of the Party leadership and machinery. In that way, the President controlled more than enough delegates to deny the nomination to anyone he opposed. As August approached and the national trauma resulting from the multiple causes of the Vietnam War and assassinations of King and Kennedy did not abate, the President withheld his endorsement—and the release of delegates under his control—until it was clear that (a) the nominee would support his policies, especially regarding Vietnam; (b) the Party platform adopted at the convention did likewise; and (c) the nominee selected a running mate compatible with the President's program.

The President had no illusions regarding what would happen on the streets of Chicago when the convention convened. As early as January 1968, the FBI began furnishing reports predicting violent demonstrations aimed at disrupting the August convention. The FBI warned that antiwar protestors already had been furnished "sacks full of money" by the Communists to foment violence in Chicago. We were well aware that the protestors had many other supporters, but the concern of our principal law enforcement agency could not be ignored.

The FBI had concluded that the Communists and their sympathizers had dual purposes: creating violent riots resisting the Vietnam War and encouraging riots among African Americans. The FBI also believed that the ultimate objective of these and other disruptive tactics—including a predicted attempt to poison Chicago's water supply—would be to force the convention to nominate Eugene McCarthy, Ted Kennedy, or Senator William Fulbright (the antiwar Chairman of the Senate Foreign Relations Committee who had been—but was no longer—a close friend of the President). Whether or not the FBI was totally correct, its prediction of major riots in Chicago was all too accurate.

We shared the FBI intelligence with Richard Daley, Chicago's Mayor. Daley, in turn, did his best to prepare his city for the onslaught, although as he often told us, the press never ceased demonizing him for his efforts to bring peace to Chicago.

Matters were not helped by our Attorney General, Ramsey Clark. Clark was unbending in his reluctance to act in support of Mayor Daley. Clark's opinion was that the demonstrators had a right to express themselves under the First Amendment, and that the federal government should not interfere with them. When others such as myself countered by pointing out that convention delegates also had their rights of assembly, including the right to unimpeded passage to wherever they needed to go in Chicago, Clark was unmoved. Even in the face of the FBI's prediction that between 50,000 and 100,000 demonstrators initially would be transported to Chicago, and that their number would swell to 500,000 on key days of the convention, Clark still refused to act. Finally, realizing that his position was infuriating the President, I called Clark from Chicago. I explained the horrible situation that was consuming the city and interfering with the rights and obligations of the duly elected delegates. Following strong disagreements between us, Clark offered his resignation. I refused, telling him that I could not accept it; only the President could make that decision. Apparently, Clark never raised the matter with the President, but neither did he take any action to help control the riots in Chicago.

In the two and a half months between the assassination of Robert Kennedy and the opening of the convention on August 16, every indication was that matters would become even worse than the FBI had predicted. And, of course, our worst nightmares came true—all duly televised live for the entire world to see.

As he had done in 1964, the President once again asked me to act as his eyes and ears at the convention, reporting directly to him while he remained at his ranch in Texas. My task was made easier because I had been elected as a delegate from Texas. As I have previously explained, the delegates to the 1964 Democratic Convention (unlike delegates to the conventions of today) were in large part experienced party officials who had been selected at their state conventions rather than through primaries. Thus, their votes were far easier for the political leaders to know and influence.

By early August, Hubert Humphrey was not yet assured of the nomination, nor would he be without the endorsement of the President. Eugene McCarthy remained an active candidate, and on August 9 he received the endorsement of Texas Senator Ralph Yarborough. That was more a psychological than a political blow to Humphrey, because the Texas delegation already had been selected and it was pledged to Governor John Connally as a "favorite son." Governor Connally assured us that he intended to do the President's bidding. Because the Texas delegation was governed by the "unit rule" (meaning that the state's entire vote would be cast as directed by a majority of its delegates), the vote of Texas was under the firm control of Connally.

On August 22, two days before I arrived in Chicago, I spoke with Mayor Daley in a conversation I recorded. He wanted troops sent into his city as a show of force to stop the riots from developing, but he did not want to publicly ask for them. I told him that the President and the Secretary of Defense "are strong to do it for you," but when I did not continue and promise him the troops, he knew precisely where the problem lay.

"What we need is a good Attorney General," he said. "We need a new Attorney General. Half the trouble brought upon the President has been brought on him by the Attorney General. After all, he has no guts and never had any guts."

I did not argue with the Mayor. Instead, I urged him to have the Illinois Governor send a telegram to the President requesting federal troops. To that suggestion, the Mayor demurred. Instead, he told me that "the problem is the Democrats don't have any guts anymore [and] I don't think they [federal troops] will be necessary." The Mayor then emphasized his point by stating: "We never requested . . . we never intended to bring them into the city." In other words—apparently for the record—the Mayor was telling me that his Chicago police force was capable of handling anything that developed.

In that same telephone conversation, I raised the subject of the possible nomination of Lyndon Johnson at the convention. What I told Daley was that "several delegates have asked, written, and wired me saying they wanted to nominate the President for reelection." The Mayor responded that he had heard the same thing, and two weeks earlier, he had asked the President to run again. Then I told Daley to forget about our conversation, and I asked him to say to the television people "that those you have talked to have said they are going to put [President Johnson's] . . . name in nomination."

My purpose in making this request of Mayor Daley was, as I told him, to "scare some of these McCarthy people to death"; that is, to stop whatever momentum they thought they were developing as the convention was about to open. Daley's answer to me was, "I'll do it."

Despite endless speculation to the contrary, then and since, Lyndon Johnson never wavered from his March 31 decision not to seek reelection. As I have indicated, his name was used as a threat and a tactical tool to influence the convention's outcome. He was human, of course, and he was legally entitled to seek another term. I believe that the talk of placing his name in nomination, or of the convention coming to him with a request that he reconsider his decision, was both gratifying and flattering to him. But he never would have acceded to the temptation to run again. All of the reasons that led him to withdraw on March 31 remained equally true on August 26, the day the convention opened in Chicago.

I arrived in Chicago on August 24, two days before the convention was scheduled to begin. I was immediately struck by the massive numbers of protestors already present in the city, and the rapidly escalating violence of their demonstrations. I found it extraordinarily difficult to leave my hotel to go anywhere. The Chicago police were doing their best to protect the rights of the delegates, but they were clearly overwhelmed by the sheer mass of people who were out on the streets. Most distressing of all was the fact that the demonstrations had become the major story of the media covering the convention.

Yet the business of the convention had to be conducted. It must adopt a platform and nominate candidates for President and Vice President. All of us associated with the convention were determined to do our jobs. As I have written, Lyndon Johnson was not a candidate, although if he had wished it, he could have been the Party's nominee in a heartbeat. Thus, the mere possibility of his being selected gave him great influence over the convention. It was my purpose to use the President's authority to achieve tangible results; namely, an acceptable platform and candidates committed to carry out his programs, particularly regarding Vietnam.

When I arrived, Senator Ted Kennedy was emerging as a possible replacement candidate for his slain brother. The effort was led by his brother-in-law Stephen Smith. However, it was now far too late for them to mount a successful effort. The vast majority of the antiwar delegates had coalesced around Eugene McCarthy and, unless the President changed his mind about running, it was obvious that the party would nominate either McCarthy or Humphrey.

I received precise intelligence regarding the probable votes in each state delegation. In New York, for example, I was informed that any effort by the President to seek the nomination would most probably "blow the Party apart." That was interesting but irrelevant information since the President was not about to change his mind. On the other hand, I concluded that Hubert Humphrey could not be nominated unless the President released the delegates under his direct or indirect control, and then intervened on Humphrey's behalf.

I reported the developing situation in Chicago to the President, including the fact that Humphrey appeared to be wavering in his support of the President regarding Vietnam. That was distressing information to the President, but more important, he saw his Vice President's vacillation as a blow to his ongoing efforts to organize a Paris peace conference. It was apparent to him that if our enemies saw that his administration was in disarray, his bargaining position would be materially weakened. Thus, the President asked me to meet with Humphrey as soon as possible, which I did.

As firmly as possible, I told Humphrey: "You must stay the course on Vietnam if you expect to be nominated." The Vice President knew without me telling him that my statement to him was made with the full knowledge and authority of the President. Nonetheless, I left the meeting unconvinced that my message had been effective with Humphrey. I said as much to the President, who immediately called Humphrey himself.

As President Johnson later described their conversation to me, he spoke to Humphrey "more in sadness than in anger" when he told his Vice President: "How can you change your position now? You have been with me regarding Vietnam for more than four years. You have agreed with every decision we have made, every step we have taken. Our policy is as much yours as mine. How can you not know that?" The President told me that Humphrey's response was unequivocal; he would not abandon the President. The President then said that he would permit Humphrey to be nominated if the remaining issues concerning the platform and the Vice President were satisfactorily resolved.

Regarding the platform, there was a massive effort from the antiwar wing of the party to adopt a statement condemning the President's policy in Vietnam. However, we controlled the platform committee and the floor of the convention. When it came to a showdown, we had the votes to win, and we did. In the end, following a protracted debate, the President's platform, now endorsed by Humphrey, was adopted by 60 percent of the delegates.

As for the selection of the Party's candidate for Vice President, I made it clear to Humphrey that although it was his choice to make, the person had to be acceptable to the President. I outlined to Humphrey the names of the President's suggestions for Vice President: Governors John Connally, Robert McNair, and Buford Ellington. However, Humphrey did not choose any of these three, and the President did not insist. I countered with a description of the qualities the President believed that the nominee for Vice President must possess. I told Humphrey that "the Vice President must add strength and commitment to the campaign." However, what the President actually wanted was a Humphrey running mate who would shore up Humphrey and prevent him from wandering from his commitment to support the programs of the President, including especially Vietnam.

Humphrey's eventual choice for Vice President was Edmund Muskie, the thoughtful, decent, and respected Senator from Maine. The President was pleased with Muskie's selection. Then, with the platform and the Vice President in place to the satisfaction of the President, he allowed the release of the delegates he controlled and influenced. Hubert Humphrey became the Democratic nominee for President of the United States.

One matter remained for me to handle for the President. His sixtieth birthday would fall on August 27, the second day of the convention. There was great pressure to permit the convention to honor him on that occasion. The issue thus became: should he come to Chicago? He asked me to consider all aspects of the question, organize whatever contingency plans that might be necessary, and make a recommendation to him, which he said he would follow.

It did not take me very long to understand that the worst possible thing for the President was to personally attend the convention. The demonstrators and the rioters controlled the streets. Despite their best efforts, the Chicago police had lost their city. They could not assure free movement and safe access by the convention delegates. Even Cabinet Officers such as myself could leave our hotels only with the greatest difficulty. Clearly, if the President were to appear, it would be like red meat to the demonstrators, giving them a focus that would only intensify their violence. At the same time, I saw no benefit to the President, to Hubert Humphrey, or to the city of Chicago if the President accepted the invitation to attend the convention. I had no doubts when I made my recommendation that the President should remain at his ranch. He did follow the convention on television. After constant briefings by me and others, including John Connally, whose judgments he valued and trusted, he agreed not to attend the convention.

Although the President had wanted to come to the convention and was disappointed that he did not, he was satisfied with the outcome. He believed that he had shored up the Party and its nominee whose support he could count on through the upcoming campaign. He believed that now he could give his undivided attention to convening the Paris peace conference without worrying about disaffection from his designated successor. He also felt that he had provided Humphrey with a clean financial slate because he had handed Humphrey a Democratic Party that began the convention free of debt and with a $3 million surplus.

Of course, the President realized that the television coverage of the convention—with all its violence and anger—had been a disaster for the Democratic Party. Instead of giving the Party and Humphrey a lift, as Party conventions normally do, the net effect was the creation of a mountain of adversity that had to be overcome if victory was to be achieved. Still, the President was confident that if Humphrey stayed the course, he would prevail over Richard Nixon.

Around Labor Day 1968, Richard Nixon contacted Reverend Billy Graham, a friend of Nixon as well as the President. To Graham, Nixon spelled out a proposal that he asked Graham to deliver to the President. Although nothing was in writing, I vividly remember Nixon's message. It went as follows:

1. After the election, should Nixon win, he would never embarrass President Johnson.
2. Nixon wanted to establish an ongoing confidential relationship with President Johnson through which Nixon, as often as possible, would seek the advice of the ex-President.
3. After he became President, Nixon would give Lyndon Johnson special assignments in matters concerning foreign policy.
4. Although Nixon would be obliged to point out what he considered to be failures of President Johnson's policies, he would never attack Johnson personally.

5. When the Vietnam war was finally settled, Nixon would give Johnson major credit for having ended the war.
6. Nixon would do everything possible to see to it that historians saw
Lyndon Johnson as a great American President.

Of course, the President was pleased to receive Nixon's message, although
he expressed some cynicism to me regarding Nixon's motives. The President
suspected that Nixon's true intent was to lull him into an implied obligation
not to vigorously campaign on behalf of Hubert Humphrey. In any event,
except for Nixon's forbearance from personal attacks on the President during the campaign, and very occasional consultations, Nixon never followed
through on his volunteered commitments to the President. Several years
later, however, when Nixon attended the opening of the Johnson Library on
the University of Texas campus, Nixon made a gracious speech recognizing
the accomplishments of his predecessor.

The President's campaigning for Hubert Humphrey was initially muted,
but that was not a result of the Nixon gambit. Instead, the President limited
his political activity because he was extraordinarily focused on getting the
Paris Peace Conference started. He believed that to the maximum extent feasible, he should remain above the political fray.

President Johnson had great personal affection for Hubert Humphrey, as
did all of us who knew him. Humphrey was that rare man who effortlessly
could light up a room with his happiness and optimism. The President was
equally charmed by Humphrey. That never changed, despite the President's
constant frustration with his Vice President's seemingly unquenchable thirst
to talk to anyone who might listen, thus becoming one of the premier leakers in the administration.

As the presidential campaign began in earnest, we started receiving indi-
cations that Humphrey regretted his commitment to the President that he
would stay the course regarding Vietnam, and that he yearned to break free.
The President and others in the administration were disappointed, even angry, with Humphrey, believing that any break with the President would disrupt the chances for peace. President Johnson asked me to maintain close
relations with the candidate and to do whatever I could to influence his
campaign. When I spoke to Humphrey, I constantly reminded him of his
obligations to the President, and the necessity that he not break his promises.

I also tried to convince him that if he broke with the President, he would lose the election. Ultimately, I did not succeed because on September 30, in a critical speech in Salt Lake City, Humphrey did break with the President by proposing an unconditional bombing halt in Vietnam.

Although Humphrey had the courtesy of informing the President in advance, he ignored the President's opinion that his speech would ensure his own defeat. As the President later told me, by placating the doves, who would have voted for him anyway, Humphrey had driven far greater numbers of hawks into the arms of Richard Nixon, and that was decisive in the close election that followed.

I campaigned hard on behalf of Humphrey. In the final days, so did the President. He did so because he believed that despite their differences regarding the war, Humphrey and the Democrats were better for the country than the Republicans. Throughout his life, the President had been a proudly partisan Democrat, although he never expressed his beliefs with bitterness, but often with humor. Typical of Lyndon Johnson's method was this anecdote that he sometimes told:

> We are, I think, the party with a heart. I heard a story the other day down in Houston about a fellow who was at death's door and rushed down to see one of the Houston transplant doctors. The doctor said, "Well, you are in luck. We have three hearts in perfect condition that you can choose from. One belonged to a twenty-five-year-old ski champion who was killed in an avalanche. One belonged to a twenty-year-old Hollywood dancer who was killed in an automobile accident. And the other belonged to a mean, spiteful, tightfisted seventy-eight-year-old Republican banker who died on the operating table just a few minutes ago. Now you can take your choice." Well, the man without a moment's hesitancy chose the banker's heart. The operation was successful. The doctor sent the man home and said that he believed he could live a normal life. But just before he left, he said, "I don't understand why, when you had the choice of an active, healthy young person's heart, why did you choose that mean old Republican banker's heart?" The man without quivering said, "Because I wanted to be sure that I was getting a heart that had never been used."

President Johnson's approach to and love of political battle did not change in the 1968 election. Nonetheless, he placed certain restrictions on the Vice

President's ability to make use of the perquisites of office that the President controlled. For example, despite the fact that the Humphrey organization was willing to pay for the privilege, the President often forbade any extensive use for political purposes of the presidential fleet of aircraft (including, in addition to Air Force One, a second Boeing 707 and two Jet Stars). That denial, plus what the Vice President and his staff perceived as uncompromising pressure on Humphrey from the President never to deviate from Lyndon Johnson's policies, caused a great deal of bitterness among Humphrey and his people. They knew that they needed the active support of the President—which, in the end, they received—but their dependence led to frustration and anger. When Humphrey ultimately lost the very close election, they blamed the President rather than their own campaign. Their negative feelings toward Lyndon Johnson persisted and were emotionally repeated to Sherwin Markman long after the fact at a 1998 White House reunion sponsored by the LBJ Library.

The most painful event of that campaign—and an action by Nixon that foretold the eventual duplicity of his Watergate scandal—occurred when Nixon authorized his agents, before the election, to secretly interfere with the President's agonizingly difficult efforts to convene the Paris peace conference regarding Vietnam.

It happened this way: As the 1968 election drew near, it appeared that all was in place for the peace conference to begin. Fearful that the opening of the conference would help Humphrey, Nixon authorized a secret operation designed to sabotage the American efforts to convene the meeting. To achieve his objective, Nixon authorized Anna Chenault, the widow of the famous World War II American general, to contact her friends at the highest level of the South Vietnam government and inform them that she was speaking on behalf of Richard Nixon. She proceeded to "authoritatively" assure South Vietnam's leaders that South Vietnam would receive a "better deal" in a peace settlement brokered under a Nixon administration than they ever could under either Johnson or Humphrey. Nixon's price, she told them, was that they must stall and not permit the Paris conference to convene before the date of the American election. They agreed. As a direct consequence, the representatives of South Vietnam suddenly and inexplicably began raising objections to various details regarding the proposed conference. It was enough. Their foot dragging prevented the conference from opening until after the election.

It did not take our intelligence services long to uncover the precise details concerning Anna Chenault's mission and the fact that she was acting for Richard Nixon and his campaign organization. The President was hurt, angry, and deeply disappointed when he learned these facts. He was outraged that the Republican candidate, for political purposes, had actively interfered with the most sensitive American foreign policy objective. The President believed that Nixon's acts went far beyond the pale of acceptable behavior.

President Johnson decided not to say anything because he believed that by doing so he would be perceived as using intelligence information for his own political purposes, and that would be counterproductive to his continuing efforts to start the Paris conference. However, he authorized all that information to be delivered to Hubert Humphrey, and Humphrey was informed that he was free to use it in any manner he deemed appropriate. Humphrey did not use the information, and nobody will ever know whether the public release of Nixon's actions regarding Vietnam would have changed the outcome of the fast-approaching election. But whatever might have happened, it is indisputable that Nixon acted against the interests of his own country—probably illegally—and got away with it.

The 1968 presidential election was surprisingly close, so close that with only some minor changes it could have been thrown into the House of Representatives for decision—something that has not happened since 1824. The final results for 1968 had Nixon winning with 43.4 percent of the popular vote and 301 electors; Humphrey with 42.7 percent of the popular vote and 191 electors; and Alabama Governor George Wallace with 13.5 percent of the popular vote and 46 electors.

Still, Nixon was the victor and Lyndon Johnson graciously accepted that fact. As a final act of grace toward his successor, President Johnson predicted that for the first time since the 1950s, the country could expect to have a budget surplus. Thus, as Robert Dallek points out in his book *Flawed Giant*, "he would now be able to leave town on January 20 'a happy man and a thankful man.'"

TRANSITION

The transfer of power from one administration to another—especially when it involves different political parties—had always been done in the most haphazard of manners. There had never been any structure to the massive job of changing governments. There was none between Truman and Eisenhower, nor between Eisenhower and Kennedy. The fact that transition had happened peacefully and with no undue disruption throughout our history was a matter of the nation's good fortune, not of planning. President Johnson resolved to do better.

Before the election, the President started planning for a better transition than in the past. A few days after Nixon defeated Humphrey, the President summoned me to the White House.

"I want the transition to Nixon to go smoothly and with no problems," he began. "And I want you to be the coordinator from our side."

At a meeting of the Cabinet, the President outlined his transition proposal. "This is the way I want it to work," he said. "Every department and agency of the government will prepare complete information in written form as to all programs, all budgets for which they are responsible. I want you to report the good and the bad. Hold back nothing. In other words, all of you are to fully cooperate with the Nixon appointees. If Nixon doesn't like what you are dong, so be it. But at least this will give him a running start, and I think that the country will be better off because of it."

Some time later, Nixon, accompanied by his wife, met with the President and Mrs. Johnson and me. The meeting took place in the family sitting area on the second floor of the White House Mansion. The Nixons were affable and friendly, and so were the Johnsons

When Nixon walked in, his first remark was, "You know, this is the first time I have been up here in the White House living quarters."

There was an awkward silence. I was shocked. I was thinking how telling an observation Nixon had just made. He was saying that in the eight years he served as Dwight Eisenhower's Vice President, he had never been invited into the President's house. That statement said volumes about the relationship between those two men, and it revealed how far President Eisenhower and his wife had distanced themselves from Richard Nixon. President Johnson must have had a similar reaction, but Nixon appeared totally oblivious to what he had just disclosed.

President Johnson congratulated Nixon on his victory, wished him well, and promised his complete cooperation. Then he said, "I intend for this transition to go as smoothly as possible. To achieve that, I have asked all

Cabinet members and Agency heads to prepare complete reports of their operations and plans. Everyone in the government will work as closely as they can with you and your people."

Nixon nodded, clearly pleased.

"Watson will be coordinator of the transition. I have given him the authority he needs to see to it that every department gives you and your people all information they require."

"This is excellent," Nixon said. "I'll name John Mitchell as our coordinator regarding the transition. I'm sure that he and Marvin will get along just fine."

And that is how it worked in the final weeks of the Johnson presidency. I found it easy to work with Mitchell. He was a serious man, fully committed to his job and to Nixon. Yet he always had an unmistakable twinkle in his eye, almost as if he were saying (although, of course, he never did), "Isn't this all such fun, sitting here playing these roles that have been given to us?"

Every department of the government had or was preparing whatever documents were necessary to fully brief the incoming administration. Also, every high officer of the government was available to meet with his Nixon counterpart for as many hours as it took to give them whatever they needed. The President was determined to disclose everything because he wanted the transition to be as seamless as possible.

I believe it worked just that way. In the Post Office Department alone, we prepared twelve thick briefing books describing all our operations, problems, and plans. I made certain that they were thorough before I handed them to my successor, Winton "Red" Blount. Later, he told me that he was surprised, pleased, and thankful for all that we did to assist him and all the other Nixon appointees.

Problems arose from time to time. Whenever they did, it was my job to solve them. On several occasions, I flew to New York City to meet with the President-elect and John Mitchell at their headquarters in the Pierre Hotel. They were always friendly, but they never hesitated to frankly voice any complaints. The most serious offender was our Attorney General, Ramsey Clark, and the Department of Justice, which was accused of not making information available on a timely basis. I had no doubt that Clark had a strong negative reaction to both Nixon and Mitchell, and that was why his cooperation was reluctant at best. However, I immediately called Clark, emphasizing the President's directive. Ultimately, Clark gave Nixon and Mitchell what they requested.

An additional problem arose with the military at the Pentagon. They were reluctant to transmit classified information to Nixon's people who had not yet received their security clearances. At first, I offered Mitchell the use of Deke DeLoach, the FBI's liaison with the White House, and Mildred Stegall, the woman on the White House staff in charge of security information, either as intermediaries or as expediters of security clearances. Mitchell refused my offer. Rather than argue about it, I decided to short-circuit the problem by having the military simply bring the classified information to me. Because I was the representative of the Commander in Chief, they agreed to do it. I then delivered the material to whomever Nixon wished to receive it.

As a result of my work on the transition, I developed a close relationship with the incoming President. A few days before January 20, 1969, when Nixon would be sworn into office, Reverend Billy Graham contacted me with a message from Nixon. What he told me came as a total shock: "Mr. Nixon would like to nominate you as the U.S. Ambassador to Australia and wants to know if you will accept the job."

"Why does he want to do that?" I asked Reverend Graham. "He knows that I've always been a Democrat and that I campaigned as hard as I could for Hubert Humphrey."

"He believes that our relationship with Australia is critical to achieving peace in Vietnam," Billy Graham replied. "He also thinks that Australia is very much like Texas and that having a Texan as our spokesman there is a smart move for him to make."

"I'm honored, but I don't think I can do it," I said. "I promised my family I would leave the government."

"Think about it, Marvin. Mr. Nixon seems to like and trust you. He says that your campaigning against him was only politics. Now, he wants you to serve your country again. I don't think you should turn him down. Please consider it some more and get back to me as soon as possible."

"I'll talk to Marion and the children," I agreed.

I had a long conversation with Marion that night. She said—as she always had—that she would adjust to whatever I decided to do. But, she added, she felt strongly that four years was enough; that I had done my duty to my country; and that she and our three children had seen precious little of me and needed me now.

I also spoke to President Johnson about Nixon's offer. He was pleased that Nixon had offered me an important post in his administration. But the President advised me that Marion was right and that it was better if I did as she suggested. "It's really up to you, Marvin," he said. "But in my opinion, you've done more than enough. I'll never forget what you've done for me after you didn't want to come here in the first place. I think that's enough."

So I called Dr. Graham and declined Richard Nixon's offer. At noon on January 20, 1969, I resigned as Postmaster General of the United States and, almost four years to the day after I first joined the federal payroll, I again became a private citizen.

AFTERWORD

As a matter of principle, I had not permitted anyone to offer me a job while I remained in the government. Fortunately, very soon after I resigned on January 20, I received several attractive opportunities. However, before I could respond, I had to once again resist the importuning of Lyndon Johnson. His previous advice that I should decline Richard Nixon's offer did not deflect him from asking me to return to Texas with him in order to supervise his activities as ex-President, including the development of the Johnson Library at the University of Texas in Austin. As always, he was persistent as he explained the historical importance of what he was asking me to do for him. However, I successfully resisted his efforts to recruit me. Reluctantly, he accepted my decision, which, happily for me, did not damage our close friendship.

The job opportunity that I finally accepted came from Armand Hammer, the chairman of Occidental Petroleum Corporation. In April 1969, I became president of Occidental International with responsibility for organizing its overseas activities. Initially, my family and I continued to live in the Virginia suburbs of Washington, but in 1971, we moved to Pacific Palisades, California. I was installed as one of two executive vice presidents serving in the Office of the President of Occidental Petroleum, the parent company of some 276 subsidiaries. During my years with Occidental, it grew from the thirty-seventh to the ninth largest American coorporation.

Throughout the next few years I maintained close contact with Lyndon

Johnson and his family. We spoke on the telephone and from time to time I saw him. Our relationship remained warm and trusting.

As for the other persons with whom I served on the White House staff, here is a brief sampling (by no means complete) of what some of them subsequently achieved:

- Bess Abeil become Executive Assistant to Joan Mondale, the wife of President Carter's Vice President.
- Cliff Alexander became Secretary of the Army under President Carter.
- Peter Benchley became a noted author, whose work includes the best-selling novel *Jaws*.
- Horace Busby became the publisher and editor of *The Busby Papers*, a widely read and respected political newsletter in Washington, D.C.
- Joe Califano became Secretary of the Department of Health, Education, and Welfare under President Carter, and later President of the Center on Addiction and Substance Abuse at Columbia University.
- Liz Carpenter later won the *Ladies' Home Journal* Woman of the Year Award in politics and public affairs.
- Douglass Cater founded the Aspen Institute and thereafter became President of Washington College in Chestertown, Maryland.
- George Christian became a widely respected political consultant in Austin, Texas.
- Ervin Duggan became President and CEO of PBS.
- Tom Johnson became publisher of the *Los Angeles Times* and thereafter President of CNN.
- Jim Jones became a Congressman from Oklahoma and thereafter was President of the Board of Governors of the American Stock Exchange followed by becoming Ambassador to Mexico.
- Bob Hardesty became President of Southwest Texas State University.
- Larry Levinson became a respected Washington lawyer.
- Harry McPherson became an author and an excellent attorney and a senior partner in a distinguished Washington law firm.
- Harry Middleton became Director of the LBJ Library and Museum.
- Dick Moose became Assistant Secretary of State for African Affairs.

- Bill Moyers became a highly regarded television commentator and producer of documentaries.
- Larry O'Brien became Commissioner of the National Basketball Association.
- DeVier Pierson became a distinguished Washington lawyer.
- Lynn Reagan went on to found her own successful CPA firm.
- George Reedy became dean and professor at Marquette University's College of Journalism.
- John Roche became an esteemed professor at multiple universities, including Brandeis, Columbia, the University of Chicago, and the University of Massachusetts.
- Peter Rosenblatt became a distinguished Washington lawyer and foreign policy advisor.
- Barefoot Sanders became a Judge of the U.S. District Court in Dallas, Texas.
- Larry Temple formed his own highly successful law firm in Austin, Texas.
- Jack Valenti became President and CEO of the Motion Picture Association of America.
- Henry Hall Wilson became President and CEO of the Chicago Board of Trade.

As 1972 drew to a close, it became apparent to me that Lyndon Johnson's health and strength was deteriorating. Then, on January 23, 1973, I was heartsick when Tom Johnson called from the LBJ Ranch to tell me that Lyndon Johnson had died. With deep grief, I recalled how often Lyndon Johnson had predicted that he would not survive another term as President. As it turned out, he was wrong, but by only two days. As I was making plans to attend his funeral, Mrs. Johnson called and told me that she and her daughters, Lynda and Luci, would like me to give the President's eulogy at his funeral service in Washington.

"You know how much Lyndon loved you," Mrs. Johnson said. "He wanted you to speak the final words for him. So do we."

I told Mrs. Johnson that I was honored and humbled, and that I would do my best.

On January 25, 1973, the National City Christian Church in Washington was filled with Lyndon Johnson's loved ones, friends, and admirers. Also present were President and Mrs. Nixon, Vice President Agnew, most of the Cabinet and the Supreme Court, as well as members of Congress and the diplomatic corps. My eulogy, which I have attached as Appendix 9, summarizes what I believed—then and now—about the greatness of Lyndon Johnson. I began the eulogy with these words that came from the deepest recesses of my heart:

> *"He was ours,*
> *and we loved him*
> *beyond any telling of it."*

I can best summarize my views on this giant of a man by repeating some of what I spoke at the commemoration of what would have been his seventy-fifth birthday on August 27, 1983:

"This dedicated young teacher of the children of migrant farm workers became the champion of the poor, the sick, the aged, and the disenfranchised. Always his emotional strength was the companionship and love of his wife, his daughters, and his family.

"He was a leader who believed in the American people, knowing that they would call upon their God-given inner strength to face the situation and deal with it in the proper way.

"He believed the American people were willing to sacrifice and that there was no limit to what the people of this nation would accomplish.

"Each of his programs were put into place to enhance the quality of life. To him, that anyone would go to bed hungry or in need of an education in this great land was unforgivable.

"His signature legalized more legislation than any other President. His programs were never offered to placate but to lift each person to a new and higher degree of personal dignity and life.

"Back in the days when streets were lit by gas lamps, a little girl walked with her dad as he went from lamp to lamp, lighting them.

"She asked her dad what he was doing, and he replied, 'I'm punching holes in the darkness.'

"Lyndon Baines Johnson was like that—he punched holes in the darkness by his dream of The Great Society."

APPENDICES

APPENDIX 1

Watson Daily Diary

Wednesday, January 17, 1968

8:20 A.M.	Nell in—said WMW to Mansion at 8:00
10:15	Returned to office.
	—Chet Carter in—Thinks he is going to resign 00 and out
10:25	T Geo Christian—go over Kintner memo
10:25	T Gov Daniels—re meeting in Califano's office—State of Union—12:00
10:27	T Califano—re above call—Daniels
10:45	F Robert Strauss—think he wants Presidential message—will write letter
10:46	F John Singleton—in city—want to see Prez
10:47	Seems entire White House staff is milling around
10:55	To Cabinet Room for meeting (Cabinet meeting)
11:05	Returned
11:15	Went over n/r
11:20	T Criswell—re last night's meeting (WMW went to Criswell's office, then both to Chairman Bailey's apartment for dinner meeting)
11:25	T Frank Ikard
11:30	T Bill Connell—re VP schedule & Gov. Shriver's call—Okay for VP to miss Cabinet meeting
11:40	Back to Cabinet meeting
12:12 P.M.	Returned
	—Placed call to Ambasador Clark—
12:15	F Sen Charles Herring
12:20	F Criswell—re meeting last night
12:30	T Amb Clark—re Sir Robert Menzies lecturing at University of Texas
12:40	T Amb Keith Waller—same as above

12:43 P.M.	T Bill Driver
	Nell out/ mjc in
	Dictation / mjc
12:47	To Cabinet Room
1:07	Returned
1:07	T Christian re briefing today
1:33	Hardesty, Manatos and Sanders in President's office
1:37	T Hopkins. You have Jones' Commission. Get more money for Duggan. Wants Mary Rather to have more $ than we were talking about too. See what you can come up with.
1:41	T Secy Udall
1:45	F President—twice!—re meeting in Fish Room today at 5:30—Told WMW who to invite to meeting
1:47	F Judge Moursund
1:49	F J Ed Connally—call after Feb 6 and let's talk about that
1:51	Mildred Stegall in/our—get report on Somebody—don't know who.
1:54	Sanders et al out of President's office
1:56	To Califano's office—re meeting at 5:30
2:02	T Tom Hughes re REA loans in Texas
	—Leonard Marks in, desperate for copy of State of Union speech. Must be translated into 37 languages—Sorry bout that!
1:10*	F President. Temple in.
	Set up 5:30 meeting
	—Goldstein in and out
1:22	T Col Cross re promotion for Chief Mills and others. Give me plain memo
1:22	T Ken—re make up man
1:24	T Sally—send a make up man to Mansion at 7
1:24	F Speaker McCormack—will send messenger after it
1:25	F Col Cross
	lunch—
2:26	T DeVier Pierson—you see former Gov Frank Clement for Prez re Tenessee politics and a pardon?
2:27	F Arthur Krim
2:29	F T Howard Samuels
2:31	F Al Barkan
	F President—
	—back to Barkan—Cudahy in Wisc, AG Lynch in Calif
2:39	F Prez
2:39	T Bill Driver
2:48	To Califano's office
2:50	Rtnd
2:52	T Betty Furness—you're to sit in Speakers Box tonite
2:53	T Gover Daniel—can you take later plane and make more calls?

*Diary had discontinuity.

3:37 P.M.	T Charlie Schultze—to cab room at 4:30—
	—on phone and talking to JRJ while mjc retyping page from State of Union message
3:56	To Barefoot's office
4:15	To Fleming re seat and camera on Betty Furness
4:12–	
4:17	Jimmy Phillips & Dr. Beutel in
4:20	T A Krim
4:23	F Prez
	—back to Krim
4:24	F Prez
	—back to Krim
4:26	F Ashton re seat for Betty Furness
4:30	Price Daniel—call Rockefeller & Rhodes. Listen tonight. Only 2 Rep. Governors to be called
4:40	To Mansion to *try* to get Prez up for a 4:30 meeting.
4:50–	
4:55	Back—and out via hall door
5:18	F Col ~~Rubley~~ Reilly of Mayor Daley's office
	—in/out Fish Room where Prez meeting with 49 (sic) people. I have no list and did not hear names given.
6:02	Gov Daniel and JRJ in
6:10–	
6:20	In Prez office
	—Prez to barber shop. Immediately called for WMW. Joined. Returned—over night reading for tonight—and signing/reading accumulation
7:10–	
7:15	Prez in—
7:17	F President re teleprompters
7:22	Fleming in re his part in speech tonight
	—Frantic search for Criswell, Fleming and Levinson
7:24	T Criswell—re people making good and bad comments. Senators and Congressmen—staff call to Sen ad Congressmen ~~for fa~~ for favorable comments in home states after message
7:30	T JJ Pickle "Yes, Marvin . . ." (re hand claps!)
7:35	T Levinson
7:38	F Criswell
8:06	F Turner Robertson, Chief Page—re distribution of speeches to Congressmen and Senators
8:35	To Diplomatic Rec Room to go w/Prez to Capitol for SOU message
10:25	Returned. Marion here.
10:30	T Criswell re tapings
10:45ish	All out

APPENDIX 2

Landmark Laws of the Lyndon B. Johnson Administration

1963

College Facilities
Clean Air
Vocational Education
Indian Vocational Training
Manpower Training

1964

Inter-American Development Bank
Kennedy Cultural Center
Tax Reduction
Presidential Transition
Federal Airport Aid
Farm Program
Chamizal Convention
Pesticide Controls
International Development Association
Civil Rights Act of 1964
Campobello International Park
Urban Mass Transit
Water Resources Research
Federal Highway
Civil Service Pay Raise
War on Poverty
Criminal Justice
Truth in Securities

Medicine Bowl National Forest
Ozark Scenic Riverway
Administrative Conference
Fort Bowie Historic Site
Food Stamp
Housing Act
Interest Equalization
Wilderness Areas
Nurse Training
Revenues for Recreation
Fire Island National Seashore
Library Services
Federal Employee Health Benefits

1965

Medicare
Aid to Education
Four Year Farm Program
Department of Housing and Urban
    Development
Housing Act
Social Security Increase
Voting Rights
Fair Immigration Law
Older Americans
Heart, Cancer, Stroke Program
Law Enforcement Assistance

National Crime Commission
Drug Controls
Mental Health Facilities
Health Professions
Medical Libraries
Vocational Rehabilitation
Anti-Poverty Program
Arts and Humanities Foundation
Aid to Application
Highway Beauty
Clean Air
Water Pollution Control
High Speed Transit
Manpower Training
Presidential Disability
Child Health
Regional Development
Aid to Small Businesses
Weather-Predicting Services
Military Pay Increase
G.I. Life Insurance
Community Health Services
Water Resources Council
Water Desalting
Assateague National Seashore
Whiskeytown National Recreation Area
Delaware Water Gap Recreation Area
Juvenile Delinquency Control
Arms Control
Strengthening U.N. Charter
International Coffee Agreement
Retirement for Public Servants

Food for Freedom
Child Safety
Narcotics Rehabilitation
Traffic Safety
Highway Safety
Mine Safety
International Education
Bail Reform
Tire Safety
New GI Bill
Minimum Wage Increase
Urban Mass Transit
Civil Procedure Reform
Federal Highway Aid
Military Medicare
Public Health Reorganization
Cape Lookout Seashore
Water Research
Guadalupe National Park
Revolutionary War Bicentennial
Fish-Wildlife Preservation
Water for Peace
Anti-Inflation Program
Scientific Knowledge Exchange
Cultural Materials Exchange
Foreign Investors Tax
Parcel Post Reform
Civil Service Pay Raise
Stockpile Sales
Participation Certificates
Protection for Savings
Flexible Interest Rates
Freedom of Information

1966

Food for India
Child Nutrition
Department of Transportation
Truth in Packaging
Model Cities
River Supplements
Teachers Corps
Asian Development Bank
Clean Rivers

1967

Education Professions Education Act
Air Pollution Control
Partership for Health
Social Security Increases
Age Discrimination
Wholesome Meat
Flammable Fabrics
Urban Research

Public Broadcasting
Outer Space Treaty
Modern DC Government
Vietnam Veterans Benefits
Federal Judicial Center
Civilian Postal Workers Pay
Deaf-Blind Center
College Work Study
Summer Youth Programs
Food Stamps
Rail Strike Settlement
Selective Service
Urban Fellowships
Consular Treaty
Safety at Sea Treaty
Narcotics Treaty
Anti-Racketeering
Product Safety Commission
Small Business Aid
Inter-American Bank

1968

Fair Housing
Indian Bill of Rights
Safe Streets
Wholesome Poultry
Food for Peace
Commodity Exchange Rules
U.S. Grain Standards
School Breakfasts
Bank Protection
Defense Production
Corporate Takeovers
Export Program
Gold Cover Removal
Truth-in-Lending
Aircraft Noise Abatement
Auto Insurance Study
New Narcotics Bureau

Gas Pipeline Safety
Fire Safety
Sea Grant Colleges
D.C. School Board
Tax Surcharge
Better Housing
International Monetary Reform
International Grains Treaty
Oil Revenues for Recreation
Virgin Island Elections
San Rafael Wilderness
San Gabriel Wilderness
Fair Federal Juries
Candidate Protection
Juvenile Delinquency Protection
Guaranteed Student Loans
D.C. Visitors Center
FHA-VA Interest Rate Program
Health Manpower
Eisenhower College
Gun Controls
Aid to Handicapped Children
Redwoods Park
Flaming Gorge Recreation Area
Biscayne Park
Heart, Cancer, and Stroke Programs
Hazardous Radiation Protection
Colorado River Reclamation
Scenic Rivers
Scenic Trails
National Water Commission
Federal Magistrates
Vocational Education
Veterans Pension Increase
North Cascades Park
International Coffee Agreement
Intergovernmental Manpower
Dangerous Drugs Control
Military Justice Code

APPENDIX 3

PRESIDENT JOHNSON DAILY DIARY:
JANUARY 9, 1967

THE WHITE HOUSE				Date __January 9, 1967__	
PRESIDENT LYNDON B. JOHNSON					
DAILY DIARY					
The President began his day at (Place)			The White House	Day ___Monday___	

Entry No.	Time		Telephone f or t		Activity (include visited by)	Expenditure Code
	In	Out	Lo	LD		
	8:22a				The President asked the operator to get Jack Valenti -- he was in New York "never mind"	
	8:44a				The President asked for Justice Fortas -- he was en route to Memphis, Tenn. -"never mind"	
	8:54a		t		Secretary McNamara	
	9:08a		t		Joe Califano	
	9:35a		f		Robert Komer	
	9:40a		f		Bill Moyers	
	10:35a		f		Courtenay Valenti	
	10:37a		f		Marvin Watson	
	11:30a				To Oval Office - w/ Tom Johnson	
	11:40a				To Marvin Watson's office briefly, to visit w/ him, then down the hall to Joe Califano's office. In Joe Califano's ofc was Secy Fowler. The Secy was going over the State of the Union message--in particular, the part concerned w/ Treasury. Also in the room was Robert Kintner. Secy Fowler left at approx12;10p and the President talked w/ Califano and Kintner	
	12:45p				Bill Moyers joined the group in Califano's office	
	12:50p				Clark Clifford " " "	

SEE TRAVEL RECORD
FOR TRAVEL ACTIVITIES

U.S. GOVERNMENT PRINTING OFFICE 1966 OF - 744-751

THE WHITE HOUSE
PRESIDENT LYNDON B. JOHNSON
DAILY DIARY   Date January 9, 1967
The President began his day at (Place)   The White House   Day Monday

Entry No.	Time In	Time Out	Telephone f or t Lo	LD	Activity (include visited by)	Expenditure Code
	1:00p				Back to the oval office	
	1:05p		t		Walt Rostow (pl)	
	1:12p	1:19p			The President to mjdr's office working the papers on her desk. Marvin Watson sent the President a note via mary s saying that Congwm Hansen called Sherwin Markman to report that the Committee named Cong. Perkins to replace Cong. Powell. The President upon reading the note, said to be sure to thank her for the information, that we wanted some lines in there.	
	1:19p		t		General Maxwell Taylor (b-1)	
	1:32p		f		Cong. Adam Clayton Powell - when yb reported this call the President said "tell him I'm not in the office, that I've gone to lunch .. you do not know when I'll be back, that I'll probably take a nap.. and tell him you'll put Bill Moyers on.	
	1:34p		t		Bill Moyers (pl)	
	1:34p		t		Harry McPherson (pl)	
	1:35p		t		yb "what did tell Cong. Powell? " --yb reported entire conv. w/the Cong. (b.2)	

SEE TRAVEL RECORD
FOR TRAVEL ACTIVITY   U   GOVERNMENT PRINTING OFFICE 1964 OF—766-731

THE WHITE HOUSE
PRESIDENT LYNDON B. JOHNSON
DAILY DIARY   Date January 9, 1967
The President began his day at (Place)   The White House   Day Monday

Entry No.	Time In	Time Out	Telephone f or t Lo	LD	Activity (include visited by)	Expenditure Code
	1:38p		t		Henry Wilson (pl)	
	1:43p	1:48p			To the Navy Mess --where he said hello to the Vice President and to Pierre Salinger. Mr. Salinger was the Vice President's guest at lunch.	
	1:48p				In Joe Califano's office -- to join those working on State of the Union: Acting Attorney General Ramsey Clark and Secretary Connor (who were working on their part of the State of the Union)	
	2:02p				The President returned to the oval office w/ Harry McPherson	
		2:25p			Bill Moyers	
	2:08p		f		Marvin Watson (pl)	
	2:10p		f		Marvin Watson (pl)	
	2:30p				The President into mjdr's office--looking at pics on mary s' desk. The President said that he wanted to send all pics where he looked good and none where he had on glasses or lokked fat.	
	The President said he wanted all pictures handled immediately--for mary s and yb to give them top priority.				The President called Henry Wilson from mary s' desk and asked him to come over to the mansion with him for lunch.	
	2:37p				To the mansion	

SEE TRAVEL RECORD
FOR TRAVEL ACTIVITY   U S GOVERNMENT PRINTING OFFICE 1964 OF—766-731

THE WHITE HOUSE
PRESIDENT LYNDON B. JOHNSON
DAILY DIARY

Date _January 9, 1967_

The President began his day at (Place) _____   Day _____ Monday

Entry No.	Time In	Time Out	Telephone f or t Lo	Telephone f or t LD	Activity (include visited by)	Expenditure Code
	3:30p		t		Joe Califano (pl)	
					All day today meetings were scheduled in Joe Califano's office w/ heads of various Cabinet Departments and various agencies to allow the particular individual in charge to review the part of the State of the Union message which pertains to his particular area.	
	4:05p		t		Tom Johnson	
	4:15p		+		BM (pl)	
	4:20p		t		Marvin Watson (pl)	
	4:25p		t		Henry Wilson (pl)	
	4:30p		t		Jake Jacobsen (pl)	
	4:32p		f		Bill Moyers	

SEE TRAVEL RECORD
FOR TRAVEL ACTIVITY

THE WHITE HOUSE
PRESIDENT LYNDON B. JOHNSON
DAILY DIARY

Date _January 9, 1967_

The President began his day at (Place) _____   Day _____ Monday

Entry No.	Time In	Time Out	Telephone f or t Lo	Telephone f or t LD	Activity (include visited by)	Expenditure Code
	4:40p		t		Joe Califano (pl)	
	4:55p		t		Bill Moyers (pl)	
	458p		t		Walt Rostow (pl)	
	5:05p		t		Marvin Watson (pl)	
	5:27p		t		Marvin Watson (pl)	
	5:30p				The President into mjdr's office-- The President kidded all four in the office and received a report from Juanita that Henry Wilson and Marvin Watson were talking to Cong. Adam Clayton Powell in MW's office. The President again said to make Oke not take pictures with his glasses on.	
	5:32p				The President to the oval office w/ Mike Manatos	
	5:33p		t		Joe Califano (pl)	
	5:38		t		Tom Johnson (on BM pl)	

SEE TRAVEL RECORD
FOR TRAVEL ACTIVITY

THE WHITE HOUSE
PRESIDENT LYNDON B. JOHNSON
DAILY DIARY

Date __January 9, 1967__

The White House

Day __Monday__

The President began his day at (Place)

Entry No.	Time		Telephone f or t		Activity (include visited by)	Expenditure Code
	In	Out	Lo	LD		
	5:40p	7:30 p			The President to the Cabinet Room for Meeting with the Senate Democratic Policy	
	OFF RECORD				Committee and Senate Committee Chairmen	
					w/	
					Senator Clinton P. Anderson, New Mexico	
					Senator Alan Bible, Nevada	
					Senator Daniel B. Brewster, Maryland	
					Senator Allen J. Ellender, Louisiana	
					Senator J. William Fulbright, Arkansas	
					Senator Philip A. Hart, Michigan	
					Senator Carl Hayden, Arizona	
					Senator Lister Hill, Alabama	
					senator Daniel K. Inouye, Hawaii	
					Senator B. Everett Jordan, N. Car.	
					Senator Russell B. Long, Louisiana	
					Senator Warren G. Magnuson, Washington	
					Senator John L. McClellan, Arkansas	
					Senator A. S. Mike Monroney, Oklahoma	
					Senator Edmund S. Muskie, Maine	
					Senator John O. Pastore, Rhode Island	
					Senator Jennings Randolph, W. Va.	
					Senator Richard B. Russell, Ga.	
					Senator George A. Smathers, Fla.	
					Senator John J. Sparkman, Alabama	
					Senator Stuart Symington, Mo.	
					The Vice Prsident	
					Mike Manatos	
					PMG Lawrence O'Brien	
					Henry Wilson	

Xerox copy of minutes of this mtg. to 27.

SEE TRAVEL RECORD
FOR TRAVEL ACTIVITY

U.S. GOVERNMENT PRINTING OFFICE 1966 OF—744-731

THE WHITE HOUSE
PRESIDENT LYNDON B. JOHNSON
DAILY DIARY

Date __January 9, 1967__

The White House

Day __Monday__

The President began his day at (Place)

Entry No.	Time		Telephone f or t		Activity (include visited by)	Expenditure Code
	In	Out	Lo	LD		
	7:30p				to oval office working desk w/ mary s	
	7:34p		t		William Mc C Martin, Chairman Fed Reserve Board (b-3) (in a memo this date,	
					Califano recommended Pres call Martin who is having a mtg of open market committee	
					tomorrow; also Pres to inform him of his tax program before mtg)	
					After reading the afternoon press briefing, the President read the tickers at the machines	
	7:47p		t		Joe Califano (l)--he wasn't there	
	7:48p		t		Bill Moyers (pl)	
	7:50p		t		Harry McPherson (pl)	
	7:54p		t		Mike Manatos (pl)	
					Working desk with mary s----	
	7:55p		t		Bill Moyers (pl)	
	7:56p		t		Bill MOyers (pl)--Ask Joe Califano to come in	

SEE TRAVEL RECORD
FOR TRAVEL ACTIVITY

U.S. GOVERNMENT PRINTING OFFICE 1966 OF—744-731

The White House
President Lyndon B. Johnson
DAILY DIARY
The President began his day at (Place)   The White House

Date January 9, 1967

Day   Monday

Entry No.	Time In	Time Out	Lo	LD	Activity (include visited by)	Expenditure Code
	7:58p				Joe Califano --re briefings on the State of the Union Message--The President also autographed a picture of himself with JC's sons and gave it to Joe Califano. "To Mark and Joseph Califano, from their friend --Lyndon B. Johnson" #A-3508-12A	
	8:12p		t		Marvin Watson (pl)	
	8:13p				Jack Valenti / Marvin Watson / joined Joe Califano and the President / working on the State of the Union Message	
	8:13p		f		Harry McPherson--returning the President's call	
	8:55p				The President, accompanied by the above three, went downstairs to the barbershop / haircut by Steve Martini y mrs. Martini	
	10:12p			f	Mrs. Patrick J. Nugent (the President still in the barbershop)	
	10:17p				The President returned to the office (small one) w/ / Tom Johnson / Jack Valenti	
	10:17p		t		Bill Moyers--immediately joined the above	
	10:18p		f		Mrs. Johnson	

The White House
President Lyndon B. Johnson
DAILY DIARY
The President began his day at (Place)   The White House

Date January 9, 1967

Day   Monday

Entry No.	Time In	Time Out	Lo	LD	Activity (include visited by)	Expenditure Code
	10:27p				Mrs. Johnson joined	
	11:27p				The President and group reading the tickers--Tom Johnson handed the President from the Sit Room Briefing Officer reporting that the rally which had begun at 7:00p in Panama had disbanded.	
	11:31p				The President went to the mansion with / Mrs. Johnson / Joe Califano / Jack Valenti / Tom Johnson / Mary Slater	
	11:35p		a		DINNER w/ Mrs. Johnson / Jack Valenti / Tom Johnson / Joe Califano / mary s Discussing the State of the Union Message, dogs and stories about Rover and Beagle and Joe Califano's puppy, PM Menzies, and the press.	
					At the end of the meal, Mrs. Johnson brought in a relic from the Punic Wars, 200BC that Ambassador and Mrs. Averell Harriman had given her and the President for Christmas. She then showed the salt shaker that Phyllis Diller had given the President, that now is in front of the President at White House meals.	
	12:10a				The President told Mrs. Johnson and mary s good night and went into his bedroom w/ / Jack Valenti, Tom Johnson, and Joe Califano	

THE WHITE HOUSE
PRESIDENT LYNDON B. JOHNSON
DAILY DIARY

Date _____

The President began his day at (Place) _____ Day _____

Entry No.	Time		Telephone f or t		Activity (include visited by)	Expenditure Code
	In	Out	Lo	LD		
					Today announced the four appointees to the Commission on Political Activity of Government Employees created by the 89th Congress to review and recommend changes in the Hatch Act and its amendments--Arthur S. Flemming, Frank Pace, Jr., Frank Wozencraft, Roger Jones.	
					Today announced his intention to nominate Rear Admiral James C. Tison, Jr., as a member of the Mississippi River Commission.	
					Today announced his intention to nominate General John P. McConnell for reappointment as Chief of State, U.S. Air Force, for a period of two years beginning February 1, 1967	
					Today announced the appointment of the Commission on Marine Science, Engineering and Resources. Named Julius Adams Stratton, Chairman of the Board, Ford Foundation, as Commission Chairman, and Richard A. Geyer, Head of the Department of Oceanography, Texas A&M University, as Vice Chairman.	

SEE TRAVEL RECORD
FOR TRAVEL ACTIVITY

GOV'T PRINTING OFFICE 1966 OF - 761-101

APPENDIX 4

WATSON CORRESPONDENCE COUNT

FEBRUARY 3, 1967

MEMORANDUM FOR MR. WATSON:

Re: Correspondence Count, January

	WMW	JRJ	Helen and Mary
Letters	566	386	341
Memos	127	320	200
Memos to President	306	99	-0-
TOTALS	999	805	541
GRAND TOTAL		2,345	

Carol

~~WMW~~: cc

APPENDIX 5

WATSON MEMORANDUM TO THE PRESIDENT

October 24, 1967
6:30 P.M.

Mr. President:

The attached is an FBI summary of demonstrations protesting U.S. intervention in Vietnam backed by the Communist Party.

On October 20, 60 individuals picketed the Induction Station in Los Angeles, led by the Students for a Democratic Society, which Gus Hall has described as going for the Communist Party.

On October 20 an anti-draft rally was held ~~in~~ at Southern California University.

The office of the Selective Service Board was picketed in Long Beach, California on October 25 by 55 people.

On October 22, 400 people held a rally in Los Angeles, headed by Irving Sarnoff, a former member of the Communist Party.

Five thousand individuals held a demonstration at the Induction Center in Oakland, California on October 20. There was some violence.

Sixty individuals picketed the entrance to the Armed Forces Induction Center at Fort Holabird, Maryland, on October 20.

A small group picketed the Induction Center at Salt Lake City on October 20. There were eight arrests.

Approximately 1,000 demonstrators picketed the Federal Office Building in Seattle on October 21. Numerous Communists Party members participated.

Other demonstrations on October 20 were in Chicago, Eugene and Portland, Oregon, Bethlehem, Pennsylvania, and on October 21 in Moscow, Idaho and Davenport, Iowa.

On October 22, there was a demonstration in Honolulu. About 250 participated.

The Progressive Labor Party, a pro-Chinese Marxist group, sponsored a demonstration at Brooklyn College on October 19. On October 20 they sponsored a demonstration at New York City. Approximately 40 demonstrators participated.

Marvin

SM:meg

APPENDIX 6

FBI MEMORANDUM TO THE WHITE HOUSE: APRIL 19, 1967

~~TOP SECRET~~

UNITED STATES DEPARTMENT OF JUSTICE

FEDERAL BUREAU OF INVESTIGATION

WASHINGTON, D.C. 20535

April 19, 1967

BY LIAISON

Mrs. Mildred Stegall
The White House
Washington, D. C.

Dear Mrs. Stegall:

As you know, Martin Luther King, Jr., President, Southern Christian Leadership Conference, was the principal speaker at the mass anti-war demonstration which took place in New York City on April 15, 1967.

I thought the President and Mr. Watson would be interested in the fact that certain portions of the speech which King made on that occasion were verbatim with portions furnished him by his close advisor, Stanley Levison, and constitute an attack on the United States' present foreign policy in Vietnam in a way which clearly duplicates the communist line on this issue. This is not surprising because Levison is a concealed communist and King knows it.

Based on King's recent activities and public utterances, it is clear that he is an instrument in the hands of subversive forces seeking to undermine our Nation.

By letter dated April 10, 1967, I furnished you with a comprehensive document entitled "Communist Influence in Racial Matters - A Current Analysis," which set forth in specific detail the manner in which these subversive elements, including Stanley Levison, have channeled King's activities into support of communist objectives.

The document sets forth facts revealing King to be a man considered and described within the Communist Party, USA, as a Marxist. It shows how in his opportunistic rise to prominence in the civil rights movement since 1956 he has been closely allied with communists. It demonstrates

~~TOP SECRET~~

GROUP 1
Excluded from automatic
downgrading and
declassification

Mrs. Mildred Stegall

that he has not only been willing but even eager to accept
communist aid, to support communist causes, to associate
and confer with prominent communist leaders, and to work
closely with and rely upon the advice and guidance of
dedicated communists with concealed affiliations, despite
the fact that they have been identified to him as such.
Finally, the document establishes that since 1956 communists
close to Martin Luther King, Jr., have blended their actions
skillfully into his organization, the Southern Christian
Leadership Conference, and have done so with his approval.

A rereading of the document makes it possible to
understand more readily why Martin Luther King, Jr., in a
previous speech condemned the United States as "the greatest
purveyor of violence in the world today," and why he willingly
played a key role in the anti-war rally on April 15, 1967,
where such Government leaders as the President, Secretary of
State Dean Rusk, and Secretary of Defense Robert S. McNamara
were viciously attacked as "buffoons," "fools," and "racists."

A copy of the speech made by King at the peace
demonstration on April 15, 1967, is attached for your
information.

You will recall that we sent the Attorney General
a copy of the same document mentioned above; however, he
is not being furnished a copy of this communication.

Sincerely yours,

J. Edgar Hoover

Enclosure

APPENDIX 7

Excerpts from March 12, 1968, FBI Analysis Regarding Martin Luther King Jr.

—————— FEDERAL BUREAU OF INVESTIGATION

SUBJECT: MARTIN LUTHER KING, JR., -
A CURRENT ANALYSIS

DATE: March 12, 1968

TABLE OF CONTENTS

i

SECRET

SECRET

Strong Communist Influence

Another complicating factor in the picture is the degree of communist influence on King. One of King's principal advisors is Stanley David Levison. Ostensibly only a New York City attorney and businessman, Levison is, in fact, a shrewd, dedicated communist. Levison has spent the major part of his life advancing communist interests.

Levison gravitated to Martin Luther King, Jr., in 1956. He has been as dedicated in his support of King as he has been in advancing communist goals. He has actively involved himself in fund-raising drives for King, served as his legal counsel in certain matters, suggested speech material for him, discussed with King demonstrations in which King was involved, guided him in regard to acceptance or rejection of various public appearances and speaking commitments, and helped him with matters related to articles and books King has prepared.

Levison edited most of the chapters of King's new book entitled "Where Do We Go From Here; Chaos Or Community?" Levison wrote one chapter of this book and the publisher's representative complained to King and Levison that it was obvious certain sections of the book were written by different individuals.

Stanley Levison has told Clarence Jones, another advisor to King, that under no circumstances should King be permitted to say anything without their approving it. Levison also informed Jones that King is such a slow thinker he is usually not prepared to make statements without help from someone. Levison is actively participating in the planning for King's "Washington Spring Project."

Explosive Situation

The combined forces of the communist influence and the black nationalists advocating violence give the "Washington Spring Project" a potential for an extremely explosive situation.

SECRET

PAGES 19 AND 20 ARE WITHHELD PER U.S. DISTRICT COURT, WASHINGTON, D.C.
CIVIL ACTION NUMBERS 76-1185 AND 76-1186

APPENDIX 8

WATSON DAILY DIARY: MARCH 31, 1968

★

Sunday, March 31

2:35ish -- mjc in -- clearing out office and cleaning up for Mr. Watson's 3 pm meeting with Gov Terry Sanford, PMG, Jim aRowe -- and man with SandersSxxx --- *Jim Cannon*

coffee -- cookies -- flowers -- music -- Gad! What kind of meeting must I be planning for? , POLITICS! That's what!

2:50ish -- Watson in --

3:10ish joined by Sanford and *Jim Cannon*.

3:20 -- PM G in

3:30 Jim Rowe in

TRaffic is so gosh awful today that nobody can get to the White House!

Watson talked to Spencer Oliver on phone x re Steve Reed appearing on TV show in California --18 years old. Good.

To Eddie Adams -- tell Maurice we're ready for all he's got.

coffee--and meeting in progress at 3:31 p.m.

3⁵⁵ Juanita in, looking for statement
Truman had prepared in not missing.
Top secret. Won't even ask over phone.
6⁵⁰ Meany *Watson thinks Buzz may have gotten it.*
joined at
some point
4⁵⁵ O'Brien out --

6¹⁰ T Cec Burney - See Terry
Sanford ? yes
6¹⁵ T Cannon - you + Gov here
at 7:30 yes
6¹⁸ F Marvella Bayh --

2

6 28 F Terry/Sanford
Let me have Hugh over here at
8 15. I won't say anything 'til
it's over + I'll just hold him
back.

6 30 Cec Burney — we won't get
together tonite. I'll have
Hugh Cannon here tomorrow.
Also Scooter says John Ben
says Harper are ready for
calling. Postpone that a
day or two.

6 32 T To Mansion to see President.
via JFK office —

7 To Rtnd — + back down hall to see JFK
(Prez has not made up
his mind re saying
won't run.)

7 45 — Rtnd — Chatting w/ MJE.

8 00 — F Prez + back to Mansion.

3

8³⁰⁻ Marion, Kim + Kim's friend in

Watson in/out

called Barefoot Sanders,
answered in —

4   re announ———— ———— for re-election

9:12   T   Secy McNamara
9:13   T   Justice Fortas
9:14   T   Jim Rowe
9:21   T   Mayor Daley — Chicago
9:22   T   Vice President Humphrey —
                    (in Mexico)
9:26   T   George Meany
9:30   T   Tom Lynch — Calif.
9:34   T   Cec Burney
9:36   T   Mayor Tate — Philadelphia
        — announcement made —

9:42   T   Bob Burkhardt —
9:43   T   Allan Shivers
9:44   F   Bill Connell (V.P.)
9:45   F   Buford Ellington / Mayor Daley
9:48

9:52   F   Kenneth Hahn — LA

9:56   Cong Zablocki
        — zillions calls —
        fanning them out
        to everybody — no time to read

12ᵈ Midnite —
Turned into a
Pumpkin — +
Went home

APPENDIX 9

WATSON EULOGY TO PRESIDENT JOHNSON: JANUARY 25, 1973

PRESIDENT LYNDON B. JOHNSON
A Eulogy

* * * * * * * * * * * *

by W. Marvin Watson
National City Christian Church
Washington, D.C.
January 25, 1973—10:00 A.M.

He was ours, and we loved him beyond any telling of it. We shared his victories and his defeats.

In victory he taught us to be magnanimous . . . in defeat he taught us to be without hate . . . to learn . . . to rally . . . to accept the challenge and to try again.

He believed that good men together could accomplish anything, even the most impossible of dreams. No matter who his opponent, he constantly sought to find that touchstone within the soul of every man which, if discovered, would release the impulse for honest and fair solution. Hate was never in this man's heart.

Each of you has your own memories of this man who served for 37 years in this city. I had the honor of being with him through the final four years of his Presidency . . . in those great moments of triumph when the American people endorsed him so strongly . . . in those magnificent hours when he stood before the Congress of the United States and led the way to the passage of laws long overdue that would lead to justice long denied . . . and in that darkening twilight when, as a man seeking peace, he was forced to continue a bitter war to honor our country's commitment to a small, far-off ally.

I watched the gray come into his hair.

I saw each deep line etch itself into his face as he gave all at his command to lead our country through the turmoil which surged around us.

I watched him as he used his great gift of persuasion to convince a Southern Senator that the time had come for the Civil Rights Act . . . I watched him formulate, secure passage and sign into law the most comprehensive legislative program in education, housing, conservation and health of any President in history . . . I watched him in the Situation Room at the time of crisis during the Six Day War when only his ability, his knowledge, and his sheer courage helped to keep that conflict from erupting into a wider confrontation.

I sat with him through those long nights as he endured the agony of Vietnam, as he sought the key to peace, and as he waited for word of men whom he had ordered into battle. Each was a human being to him, not a statistic; each was a name linked with wives and parents and children—he cared for people, not for numbers.

So desperately did he want a just and lasting peace . . . so much did he want us to reason together . . . so much did he yearn that man's goodness would triumph over man's evil . . . so often as friend turned to political foe, did he nod with sad understanding and pray that in the years to come, the sacrifices he was making would be worthy of the American people and serve ultimately as a firm platform on which to build a better world.

And through it all, I saw him earnestly seek God's wisdom for his decisions, for this was a man with a strong belief in the Almighty.

President Nixon, as you so eloquently stated in your message informing Congress of President Johnson's death, it was his "noble and difficult destiny to lead America through a long, dark night of necessity at home and abroad." If he could have chosen other circumstances in which to be President, perhaps he would have. But, America has a capacity to call forth the leadership it must have in those hours of its greatest need. We had Abraham Lincoln when he was needed. We had Franklin Roosevelt when he was needed. History will record that in the seventh decade of the 20th century, America had Lyndon Johnson when he was needed.

When you remember him, remember him please for two things—his devotion to his country . . . and his restraint.

So often in his Presidency, dissension escalated into violence. Yet always, no matter how critical the situation, his inner faith in the people came to the fore and his restraint in the uses of power permitted the people to confront each situation and overcome it utilizing the inherent rights of free men.

Those of us who loved him take comfort in the knowledge that before he died, he could see the dawn of domestic tranquility and of foreign peace with he gave so much of his great heart to bring about. The structure of peace which President Nixon, with great distinction and determination, is building in the world today will rest upon a foundation laid in loneliness and stubborn courage by Lyndon Johnson.

This man's restless, searching heart began to give out long before January 22nd. He gave so much of himself to so many that it is wondrous that God, in His grace, granted him four years to enjoy his retirement in the hill country he so deeply treasured.

Not for him the easy way.

Not for him any halfway measures.

He was a tall man of giant character, and when he committed himself, he committed himself totally. And he asked his countrymen to do the same.

He asked those who had much to be concerned for those who had least.

He asked us to live up to our national promise.

He asked us to be worthy of our heritage.

He asked us to be true to ourselves.

But, he never asked more than he was willing to give . . . and what he gave was good enough to confirm and advance the progress of the nation he served.

Lyndon Johnson loved a woman, and she was his greatest joy and his greatest comfort. He loved his children and his grandchildren and to see them together was a heartwarming experience, for it transcended normal family devotion.

And coupled with that he loved each of us, sometimes with wry amusement at our failures, often with sharp words at our imperfections, but always with a sweeping and generous understanding of our frailties. The dimensions of this man were vast.

He is gone from us now . . . and this afternoon we shall take him home and he will be forever a part of the hill country.

Last September, I had the opportunity to be with him when he spoke of America and of the future.

He knew then that he might not see another autumn, but this was not a man who welcomed or needed sympathy.

Years from now, when historians appraise him, his speech that day could serve as the cornerstone of their research for it reflected the true Lyndon Johnson. He gave much of himself to it, and it might well be his epitaph. He said:

"With the coming of September, each year, we are reminded as the song says, that the days are dwindling down to a precious few . . . the green leaves of summer will begin to brown . . . the chill winds of winter will begin to blow . . . and before we are ready for the end to come, the year will be gone.

"As it is with the calendar, so it sometimes seems to be with our country and our system. For there are those among us who would have us believe that America has come to its own September . . . and that our nation's span as mankind's last best hope will be done."

President Johnson continued:

"But I live by the faith that with each passing day we are always approaching nearer to the beginning of a new springtime and it is by that perspective that I see our country now.

"No nation can be more than the visions of its people. America cannot be more than we believe ourselves capable of becoming.

"I want to open the soul of America to the warm sunlight of faith in itself . . . faith in the principles and precepts of its birth . . . and faith in the promise and potential of its people."

That was Lyndon Baines Johnson, the 36th President of the United States of America.

The years will be lonely without him.

INDEX